SEXUALLY RELATED OFFENCES

BARRY HILL
LL.B. (Hons), Solicitor

AND

KAREN FLETCHER-ROGERS
Barrister, Gray's Inn

London
Sweet & Maxwell
1997

Published in 1997 by
Sweet and Maxwell Ltd of
100 Avenue Road, Swiss Cottage,
London NW3 3PF
Computerset by York House Typographic Ltd,
London W13 8NT
Printed and bound in Great Britain by
Butler and Tanner Ltd, Frome and London

No natural forests were destroyed to make this product;
only farmed timber was used and replanted

A CIP catalogue record for this book is available from the British Library

ISBN 0 421 583703

SEXUALLY RELATED OFFENCES

AUSTRALIA
LBC Information Services-Sydney

CANADA and USA
Carswell-Toronto

NEW ZEALAND
Brooker's-Auckland

SINGAPORE and MALAYSIA
Thompson Information (S.E. Asia)-Singapore

INTRODUCTION

"We recognise beauty only by comparing it with what we consider ugly,
We recognise goodness only by comparing it with what we consider bad,
Therefore to be or not to be balance each other,
Difficult and easy complement each other,
Long and short contrast each other,
High and low support each other,
Bass and treble harmonise each other,
Front and back follow each other." (*Tao Te Ching* of Lao Tzu, Chap. II)

The *Tao Te Ching*, the oldest book in the world, teaches that our appreciation of one quality depends upon our contrasting it with its opposite. Our concept of moral good arises from our appreciation of acts which are generally considered to be immoral, or bad. If one moves, so inevitably does the other.

The criminal law relating to sexual offences attempts to address questions concerning good and bad which are exceedingly complex. Indeed this particular area of the criminal law may be considered unique in that it affects both a person's interaction with others and intrudes into his private sexual life, attempting to regulate his desires and perceptions of what is right and proper.

The dilemma faced by the courts and legislature is in deciding not only whether certain behaviour should be considered criminal but also in striking a balance between upholding a person's basic freedom to enjoy their sexual life as they wish, protecting a person from himself and protecting others from harm.

While there are certain acts which are obviously unacceptable just as there are acts which are obviously permissible, there is, especially in this area of the law, a grey area where an act may be considered borderline depending on the constantly shifting moral code of society. Until recently, homosexual relationships between men were considered an evil, an affront to nature and a serious threat to society. Anal intercourse was a crime. A blind eye was turned to sex tourism.

It is vital therefore that built into any legislation in this area of the criminal law is a flexibility which keeps justice in step with society, or alternatively, that the legislature is quick to recognise a shift and legislate accordingly. Nevertheless, this needs to be tempered with a recognition that immoral conduct is not necessarily criminal and the courts must be careful not to impose establishment ideals on public morals. There are times, such as in the case of *R v. Wilson* (*The Times*, March 5, 1996) concerning the consensual branding of a wife's buttock by her husband, when the courts have properly decided that it is inappropriate to interfere in the private relationship between individuals.

STOP PRESS

The following amendments to procedure were made too late for inclusion in the main body of the work.

The Criminal Procedure and Investigation Act 1996, s. 47 and Sched. 1 remove the facility for witnesses to give oral evidence before examining justices—in future all evidence shall be tendered. The provisions apply to offences where the police investigation commenced on or after April 1, 1997.

As far as the Magistrates' Court Act 1980 is concerned, Schedule 1, para. 10 substitutes a new section 103(1): "In any proceedings before a magistrates' court inquiring as examining justices into an offence to which this section applies, a statement made in writing by or taken in writing from a child shall be admissible in evidence of any matter."

Subsections (3) and (4) are repealed.

The new section 103(1) requires a child's statement to be in writing to be admissible, thus precluding a video recording of the child's evidence. However, the Criminal Justice Act 1988, s. 32A(10) still applies and the video recording can be admitted as a document under section 5E of the Magistrates' Court Act 1980 (as inserted by Sched. 1, para. 3 of the 1996 Act).

The Criminal Procedure and Investigations Act 1996 repeals the provisions empowering magistrates to make witness orders at the committal of a defendant to the crown court for trial. The procedure for offences where the police investigation commences after April 1, 1997 is that a prosecution witness statement is to be read at trial unless the defence indicate within 14 days of committal that they object.

In consequence of the abolition of witness orders, amendments have been made by virtue of the Criminal Justice Act 1991 (Notice of Transfer) (Amendment) Regulations 1997 (S.I. 1997 No. 738) to the form of notice of transfer (Form 1) and the form of notice to the defendant (Form 2), used when a case is transferred to the crown court under section 53 of the Criminal Justice Act 1991 (see para. 3–02, ff.).

Form 1 is amended in so far as paragraph 8 and the heading "Schedule of Proposed Witness" is omitted.

Form 2 is amended by substituting a new paragraph 5:

"I enclose a list of witnesses—
   (a) indicating those whom the Crown proposes to call to give oral evidence at your trial; and
   (b) indicating those whose attendance at your trial the Crown considers unnecessary on the ground that their evidence is unlikely to be disputed;

together with copies of those statements or other documents outlining the evidence of those witnesses."

Barry Hill
Karen Fletcher-Rogers

August 1997

CONTENTS

PART II: ASSAULTS

CHAPTER 4. RAPE

CHAPTER 5. SERIOUS ASSAULTS

TABLE OF CASES

All references are to paragraph numbers.

TABLE OF STATUTES

All references are to paragraph numbers.

TABLE OF STATUTORY INSTRUMENTS

All references are to paragraph numbers.

Part I
EVIDENCE AND PROCEDURE

Chapter 1
Obtaining Evidence

Evidence in sexual cases normally consists both of statement evidence and medical evidence. However in appropriate circumstances a case may be based on either of these elements alone, for example when a child is of tender years. However a child's evidence cannot be excluded on the grounds of age alone. The Divisional Court stated on December 12, 1996 in an unreported case that a Recorder was wrong to exclude the evidence of a five year old girl on the grounds of her age alone.

1–01

A. EVIDENCE BY WAY OF INTERVIEW

I. THE CLEVELAND INQUIRY

The *Report of the Inquiry into Child Abuse in Cleveland* (1987, Cm. 412) endorsed that the following points should be observed in conducting interviews with children suspected to be victims of sexual abuse (para. 12.34):

1–02

- (a) the undesirability of calling them "disclosure" interviews, which precluded the notion that sexual abuse might not have occurred;
- (b) all interviews should be undertaken only by those with some training, experience and aptitude for talking with children;
- (c) the need to approach each interview with an open mind;
- (d) the style of the interview should be open-ended questions to support and encourage the child in free recall;
- (e) there should be, where possible, only one and not more than two interviewers for the purpose of evaluation, and the interview should not be too long;
- (f) the interview should go at the pace of the child and not the adult;
- (g) the setting for the interview should be suitable and sympathetic;
- (h) it must be accepted that at the end of the interview the child may have given no information to support the suspicion of sexual abuse and the position will remain unclear;

(i) there must be careful recording of the interview and what the child says, whether or not there is a video recording;

(j) it must be recognised that the use of facilitative techniques may create difficulties in subsequent court proceedings;

(k) the great importance of adequate training for all those engaged in this work; and

(l) in certain circumstances it may be appropriate to use the special skills of a "facilitated" interview. That type of interview should be treated as a second stage. The interviewer must be conscious of the limitations and strengths of the techniques employed. In such cases the interview should only be conducted by those with special skills and specific training.

1–03   The report also stated (para. 2.35) that it was unsuitable to have a parent present at an interview because of the suspicion of sexual abuse. However, the presence of a person familiar to the child (other than a parent) may be helpful to the child. That person must not take part in the interview, and should not be in direct eye contact with the child.

The consent of the parent must be obtained as must the child's where the child is old enough to give consent.

II. The Status Of The Report

1–04   The status of all the recommendations contained in the Report of the Inquiry into Child Abuse in Cleveland was discussed by the Court of Appeal in *R v. Dunphy* (1994) 98 Cr.App.R. 393. The report does not have the authority of statute.

1–05   The aim was to set out for the benefit of social workers and others what is considered to be the best practice when children are interviewed in connection with sexual abuse. But, the court doubted whether they were intended to be immovable so as to exclude all flexibility which might be required by the circumstances of a particular case.

1–06   It should however be regarded as expert advice as to what would normally be the best practices to adopt in seeking to ensure that a child's evidence was reliable. If they are not observed there are grounds for a judge or jury to consider with particular care whether the child is reliable. D was convicted on two counts of indecent assault. The victim, a child of eight was interviewed by a police officer in a way which the defence submitted was oppressive and in breach of the Cleveland guidelines. The courts however, having both read a transcript and viewed the video held that although there was pressure on the child, it was not pressure to give a particular answer. If there has been material in the video to show that the child's evidence at the trial had become tainted by the conduct of the interview, it would have been open to defence counsel to ask that the jury should see the recording.

III. Further Recommendations

1–07   The child must be aware that the interview is being recorded.

1–08   Expert evidence may be admitted in relation to the guidelines, and to the affects of over-interviewing children in cases. Where the reliability or truth-fulness of a child witness is in issue, only because the witness is a child, this is a matter within the experience of the jury. The judge is right to allow the evidence to be tested before the jury and therefore not exclude the evidence under section 78 of the Police and Criminal Evidence Act 1984 even where the same evidence may have been rejected by a Family Division judge in care proceedings (*R.v.D and others*, unreported, November 3, 1995, C.A.).

It is Crown Prosecution Service policy that the videotape may be shown to   **1–09** the child prior to the trial except where the tape has been ruled inadmissible. However, most children only see the tape when it is shown to the jury. Rulings on the admissibility of the videotape must be made in sufficient time to allow this to happen. The videotape may be the subject of the Sexual Offences (Protected Material) Act 1997.

A "Child Witness Pack" was published by the NSPCC and Childline in   **1–10** 1993 and the Home Office, Department of Health and the Lord Chancellor's Department all recommended its use with the assistance of an "independent adult". The pack was evaluated in 1996 ("The Child Witness Pack—and Evaluation", Home Office Research and Statistics Department—*Research Findings*, No. 29). It was concluded that the Pack was very useful, but was inadequately used, nor were the aspects of procedure it covered understood by barristers.

B. PHYSICAL EVIDENCE

Sexual assaults and sexual abuse of children are both likely to cause damage   **1–11** and leave behind marks. However, particularly with sexual abuse even the most gross examples may occur leaving no physical damage.

The consent of the parent or guardian should normally be obtained for the   **1–12** physical examination of a person under 16. However where the young person clearly has an understanding of what is about to happen, no assault will be committed by her doctor against the young person by the examina-tion. (See *Gillick v. West Norfolk AMA* [1986] A.C. 112 at 169/170, *per* Lord Fraser.) The doctor should ascertain that the patient has sufficient maturity and intelligence to understand the nature and implications of the examination.

In the *Armstrong Abduction Case* (1885) 49 J.P. 745, it was held that a   **1–13** midwife did not commit an indecent assault on a young girl if carrying out an examination for a proper purpose at the request of the girl's father or parents. A young girl could not consent alone.

Physical examination should take place as soon as possible and certainly   **1–14** before the victim has bathed. He or she will be asked to undress whilst standing on a clean sheet of paper. Clothing may be required for forensic examination and he or she will be examined for injuries, bruises, scratches, bite marks, etc.

I. Vaginal Examination

1–15   The vagina of a female victim will be examined since the presence of semen or alien material such as blood or hair is strong evidence of sexual penetration.

1–16   The absence of the hymen does not necessarily indicate penetration but new damage may be supportive evidence.

1–17   The woman's internal digital examination may be undertaken but this is unadvisable in pre-pubertal girls. Sometimes glass rods (Glaister rods) may be used, and medical instruments providing both light and magnification (an auroscope or a colposcope) may be employed.

1–18   Many adhesions and irregularities in the hymen which may initially seem suspicious may in fact be entirely innocent and natural.

II. Anal Examination

1–19   Anal assault and anal abuse may cause tearing and resultant injury and scarring in that area, and associated bruising.

1–20   Anal examination is normally in the left lateral position with the examination of the anus being limited to about 30 seconds. The knee-chest position is usually now avoided. Very young children are examined on the mother's knee, supine with the legs vertical.

1–21   Injuries are indicated on an imaginary twelve hour clock. The anus is viewed with the patient lying on her back with the 12 o'clock position towards the pubis and the six o'clock position towards the back or spine.

1–22   Abuse may also cause alterations in the skin condition and colour including thickening and cracking of the skin itself (lichenifaction or keralinisation). Finally abuse may also cause loss of muscle tone and the presence of certain muscle reflex actions. On the other hand abuse may leave no physical evidence at all, and lack of physical damage does not indicate abuse has not occurred. The absence of any physical damage may only show that an abuser was gentle and employed lubricants.

1–23   The finding of semen or other alien material in the rectum is strong evidence of abuse. Swabs may reveal semen or lubricants. Indeed semen in the anus is the only conclusive evidence of buggery.

1–24   The finding of sexually transmitted infections such as gonorrhoea or anal warts may be evidence of sexual abuse.

(a) Injuries

1–25   Tears, fissures and bruising, or tags or healed scars may be supportive evidence but is not necessarily conclusive proof of assault. Expert evidence would need to be examined very carefully. The difference between injuries caused by assault or abuse and other non-criminal causes such as chronic constipation sometimes leading to rectum distention (mega-rectum or mega-colon), or over enthusiastic examination by a parent of a child repeatedly infested with worms, is very difficult to distinguish and opinions may vary.

1–26   A fissure describes an open lesion which may bleed. There may be a number of causes. Upon healing they may scar, sometimes leaving a mound of skin known as a skin tag. Crevices in the anal verge known as an anal verge defect which may be suspicious must be distinguished from anal canal folds which are normal. Anal fissures are not uncommon in infancy. Associated with constipation they may be multiple and superficial. They are uncommon in children of school age.

Normal depressions at the six and 12 o'clock positions and other skin changes in those positions including skin tags may be misidentified as signs of abuse. Tears in other positions especially where they extend to the perianal skin may indicate anal abuse. Lacerations heal quickly and may or may not leave scars. Lacerations will be very painful for some children and may be associated with bleeding during the next bowel movement after buggery.   1-27

(b) Other indications

Abuse may give rise to anal muscles which are lax and weak. After buttock separations the external sphincter normally closes for some seconds and then relaxes. At this time anal dilation may occur (also known as reflex anal dilation or reflex relaxation). In some cases a funnel effect may be observed. Again however care must be undertaken to distinguish this from other, perfectly normal, muscular activity,   1-28

Anal tone should be recovered quickly and lack of tone may indicate continuing or long standing abuse. Reflex anal dilation is not considered usual. In such cases, the external and internal sphincter both open. Whilst the effect is not normal, and may be considered suspicious both the Police Surgeons Association and the Cleveland Inquiry considered that it is not of itself evidence of anal abuse (*Butler-Sloss* (1988) p.247). Approximately half a number of children examined with no history of sexual abuse show reflex anal dilation.

Dilated veins may indicate anal abuse. They may be seen immediately upon examination, or after prolonged (over 30 seconds) examination in non-abused children. Dilated veins will eventually disappear after anal abuse. Haemorrhoids are easily distinguished and are most uncommon in children prior to puberty. Reduction of anal folds may be associated with chronically repeated buggery although the Royal College of Physicians does not list reduced anal folds as a perianal indication of buggery.   1-29

Physical evidence is to be taken in context. Multiple indications especially if associated with a history of abuse revealed in interview by the child will be strong corroboration. A single tear in a young child (often at the six o'clock position) extending to the perianal area may also be a sign of abuse. Other, perhaps single signs, may be of much less significance.   1-30

III. SAMPLES

Swabs may be taken to find semen or other fluids and substances. High and low vaginal swabs may reveal semen which may remain in the cervical canal for up to a week but in the vagina for up to 72 hours. Such retention however   1-31 seems to be the exception rather than the rule and deterioration and vaginal drainage may remove evidence within hours. Internal and external anal swabs will be taken where buggery is suspected.

1–32   Oral swabs will be taken if oral intercourse is suspected as semen may remain under the tongue and between the teeth. No drink should be consumed prior to the supply of saliva.

1–33   Hair specimens will be taken especially any matted hair. They will be both cut and plucked. DNA testing is possible from the hair follicle. A sufficient number must be taken. If appropriate pubic hair will also be cut and plucked. Pubic hair is not consistent in colour or curl, head hair may vary in colour according to location and therefore representative samples must be obtained. Anal hair may be taken in cases of suspected anal intercourse.

1–34   Fingernail cuttings or scrapings may reveal tissue from the assailant. Specimens from each hand must be retained separately.

1–35   Finally, blood and saliva samples may be taken. Blood is needed to ascertain groupings and for DNA analysis, whilst saliva gives secretor status.

IV. Taking Of Intimate And Non-intimate Samples And DNA

1–36   The Royal Commission on Criminal Justice recommended that the power to take samples for DNA analysis should be "essentially on the same basis as applies now to the power to take fingerprints". Accordingly, sections 54 to 59 of the Criminal Justice and Public Order Act 1994 introduced changes to Annex D of the Codes of Practice issued under the Police and Criminal Evidence Act 1984 (PACE). Part 5 of Annex D to the Codes of Practice is set out in full in Appendix 1. Charts progressing the taking of non-intimate or intimate samples and DNA are set out in Appendices 2, 3, and 4.

1–37   Section 63 of the 1984 Act states that a non-intimate sample can be taken without consent from a person in police detention or a person being held in custody on the authority of a court. An officer of at least the rank of superintendent authorises the taking of the sample when he has reasonable grounds for suspecting the involvement of that person in a recordable offence and believes that the sample will tend to confirm or disprove that suspect's involvement.

1–38   A non-intimate sample may be taken without consent from a person whether or not they fall within the previous category if they have been charged or informed that they will be reported or cautioned for a recordable offence and either a non-intimate sample has not been taken from the person in the course of the investigation of the offence by the police, or a non-intimate sample has been taken but it was not suitable for or was insufficient for analysis.

1–39   A non-intimate sample may be taken from a person who has been convicted of a recordable offence after April 10, 1995. A person may be required to attend a police station so that a sample can be taken within one month of the date of the charge or conviction, or in either case the date the investigating officer was informed that the sample was not suitable or was insufficient (ss. 63A(4) and (5)).

The person must be given seven days notice of the requirement and must 1–40 be directed as to the time of day or between which specified times he must attend. He may be arrested by any constable if he fails to attend (s. 63A(7)).

(a) Non-intimate samples

Section 58 of the Criminal Justice and Public Order Act 1994 defines a non- 1–41 intimate sample as:

(i) a sample of hair with roots (other than pubic hair). This was discussed in *R v. Cooke (Stephen)* [1995] Crim.L.R. 497. It was argued that the sample comprising the hair plucked from the head including the hair roots and sheath, was an intimate sample. The plucking of the hair was the means by which the hair sheath was obtained. The sheath was required for DNA sampling. The Court of Appeal upheld the defendant's conviction of kidnapping and rape. The hair was a non-intimate sample, and even if it was an intimate sample and its obtaining had constituted a technical assault upon the defendant the evidence was so strong against him that it should nonetheless be admitted in evidence under section 78 of PACE 1984. Its taking did not cast doubt upon the accuracy or strength of the evidence, as would be the case in, for example, a disputed confession. The rule is confirmed by section 63A(2) of PACE;

(ii) a sample taken from a nail or from under a nail;

(iii) a swab taken from any other part of a person's body including the mouth but not any other body orifice;

(iv) saliva; and

(v) a footprint or a similar impression of any part of a person's body other than a part of his hand.

Before a non-intimate sample is taken without consent the suspect must be 1–42 told that authorisation for taking the sample has been given (PACE 1984, s.63(6)(i)) and the grounds for giving authorisation including the nature of the offence in which it is suspected the person from whom the sample is to be taken has been involved (PACE, s.63(6)(ii) and (7)).

In all cases in which a non-intimate sample is taken, whether with or 1–43 without consent, the suspected person must be told also that the sample, or information derived from the sample may be the subject of a speculative search and may be checked against the profiles of named convicted persons contained in the searchable database, against any recorded crime stain and against other samples or profiles which may have been taken from a suspect in connection with the investigation of an offence.

In relation to speculative searches, section 64 of the Criminal Procedure and Investigations Act 1996 amends section 63A of the Police and Criminal Evidence Act 1984 in that it gives the police the power to search fingerprints and DNA databases speculatively in respect of samples taken from persons suspected of involvement in a recorded offence, but who have not been arrested, cautioned or convicted. This brings England, Wales and Northern Ireland into line with Scotland, which already had the power. People who were not covered before amendment include those dealt with by way of summons and those who have been informed that they will be reported for a recordable offence for example, avoiding a decision on disposal. This came into force on July 4, 1996.

(b) Recordable offences

1–44   A recordable offence is one listed in the National Police Records (Recordable Offences) Regulations 1985 and are:

> (i)   any offences which carry a sentence of imprisonment on conviction;
>
> (ii)   loitering or soliciting for the purposes of prostitution (Street Offences Act 1959, s.1);
>
> (iii)   improper use of the public telecommunications system (Telecommunications Act 1984);
>
> (iv)   tampering with a motor vehicle (Road Traffic Act 1985, s.25);
>
> (v)   sending letters, etc., with intent to cause distress or anxiety (Malicious Communications Act 1988, s.1); and
>
> (vi)   having an article with a blade or point in a public place (Criminal Justice Act 1988, s.139).

(c) Intimate samples

1–45   By section 62, an intimate sample can be taken from a person in police detention when an officer of at least the rank of superintendent authorises the taking of the sample when he has reasonable grounds for suspecting the involvement of that person in a recordable offence, and for believing that the sample will tend to confirm or disprove the suspect's involvement and the person gives his or her written consent to the taking of the sample.

1–46   Section 62 further provides that an intimate sample can be taken from a person not in police detention when the person is one from whom at least *two* non-intimate samples have been taken in the course of the investigation of an offence which have proved unsuitable or insufficient for the purposes for which they were taken; and an officer of at least the rank of superintendent authorises the taking of the sample if he has reasonable grounds for suspecting the involvement of that person in a recordable offence, and he believes that the sample will tend to confirm or disprove the suspect's involvement, and further that the person gives his or her consent in writing.

1–47   Where a person who is not in police detention consents to the taking of an intimate sample for elimination purposes, authorisation is not required.

1–48   Before the sample is taken the suspect must be told:

> (i)   that authorisation for the taking of the sample has been given;
>
> (ii)   the grounds for giving authorisation including the nature of the

offence in which it is suspected the person from whom the sample is to be taken has been involved;

(iii) that the sample or information derived from the sample may be the subject of a speculative search and may be checked:
   (a) against the profiles of named convicted persons contained in the searchable database; and
   (b) against any recorded crime stain; and
   (c) against other samples or profiles which may have been taken from a suspect in connection with the investigation of an offence; and

(iv) if consent is refused without good cause adverse inferences may be drawn by a court.

A person who is not legally represented at the time a request for an intimate sample is made must be reminded of their entitlement to free legal advice.   1–49

An intimate sample is defined by section 65 of the Police and Criminal Evidence Act 1984 as: 1–50

"(a) a sample of blood, semen or any other tissue fluid, urine or pubic hair;

(b) a dental impression—dental impressions may only be taken by a registered dentist;

(c) a swab taken from a person's body orifice other than the mouth."

Saliva is no longer classified as an intimate sample.

(d) Other definitions

- An *evidential sample* is a sample given by a suspect or a defendant which is an exhibit in a case.   1–51
- An *elimination sample* is a sample taken from a victim or a witness for the sole purpose of excluding them from the police investigation.
- A *crime stain* is a sample left at the scene of a crime.
- A *profile* is the information obtained from a sample or a crime stain.
- A *searchable database* contains information from samples obtained from convicted persons.
- A *statistical database* refers to information from profiles retained anonymously and intended to be used for frequency analysis.

By section 64 a sample must be destroyed as soon as practical after: 1–52

(i) the conclusion of the proceedings; or
(ii) a decision has been made that he or she shall not be prosecuted; or
(iii) the person has been eliminated from enquiries.

A sample may only be retained if it was taken for the purpose of the same investigation of an offence where another person has been convicted of the offence, in which case the sample is retained as an exhibit. In these circum-   1–53 stances, the sample is retained in case it is needed for further comparative analysis in the event of subsequent miscarriage of justice proceedings.

1-54   The profile derived from a sample whether or not it is an excepted sample may be retained but shall not be used in evidence against the person entitled to its destruction or for the purpose of any investigation of an offence (Criminal Justice and Public Order Act 1994, s.64(3A), (3B) and s. 57). For technical reasons information obtained from a DNA sample cannot easily be erased.

1-55   A sample or a profile can be entered on the searchable database only after a defendant has been convicted. It cannot form part of the searchable database prior to the outcome of the proceedings. A search can only be made against data already held.

1-56   Where a sample should have been destroyed it can only be used to build up the statistical information for DNA frequency database and not in prosecutions. Its inclusion in the statistical database however does not affect the reliability of that database (see para. 1.83 below).

C. DNA

1-57   DNA is deoxyribonucleic acid. It is the basic genetic material contained in almost all living cells in the body. It is the material from which chromosomes are made and is therefore unique to every individual.

The sole exception is the case of genetically identical twins or monozygote twins where DNA will be the same.

1-58   DNA is found in blood, but only in the white blood cells. It is not present in either red blood cells or plasma. DNA is found in semen in the sperm heads. A DNA sample is not obtained from the semen of a man who has undergone a vasectomy. DNA is found in hair but only in the live cells in the hair root. The hair shaft is dead and contains no DNA material. Samples must therefore be plucked or pulled out intact. Normally about 10 hair roots will be required although analysis of a single hair root is possible.

DNA is found in the mouth. It is not considered to be found in saliva but a mouth swab may pick up sufficient epitheleal skin cells from the inside of the mouth to make DNA profiling possible.

I. DNA Profiling

1-59   DNA profiling is a method of identifying individuals from their genetic material. It is based upon a discovery made by Professor Jeffreys, a Lister Research Fellow at Leicester University. He discovered that a particular sequence of the DNA molecule greatly varies in unrelated individuals. This sequence is highly repetitive but varies in length, the number of repeats and their location. The possible identification of individuals by analysis of this sequence was discovered by Professor Jeffreys in 1984 and is subject to world wide patent obtained by the Lister Institute of Preventive Medicine and exclusive world wide rights are now held by Cellmark Diagnostics, part of ICI. The United Kingdom patent was granted in 1987 and the same year the technique was successfully used by the Leicestershire police to identify the murderer of two 15 year old girls and to eliminate from their enquiries a 17 year old youth who had confessed to and been charged with the second murder, but who was in fact innocent (*R v. Pitchfork and Kelly* [1990] Crim.L.R. 473).

The DNA extracted from a sample or a stain is cut into small lengths by   1–60
specific restriction enzymes. These fragments are placed in a gel and are sorted by size by a process of electrophoresis, which involves drawing them by electromagnetic force along a track in the gel. The fragments with a smaller molecular weight travel further than heavier ones. A pattern of bands is transferred from the gel to a membrane. A DNA probe which is radio-active is added and excess DNA washed off. The bands that are revealed are then recorded as X-ray film. The auto-radiograph produced can then be photographed and compared with other profiles.

The radio-active probe may be a multi-locus probe (MLP) which is used in   1–61
parentage cases. In cases where the DNA is very small (*i.e.* microscopic) or is broken down, or degraded due to age or poor storage, a single locus probe (SLP) may be used. This will examine just one location and reveal two bands – one inherited from the father and one inherited from the mother. This method is extremely sensitive and may be used where the sample is very limited, such as a single hair root. A SLP is normally now used in criminal cases.

The identification of individuals relies upon the probabilities of two   1–62
sample profiles matching. The original approach is that DNA distinguishes two unrelated persons. Related persons will share a significant proportion of their DNA profiles. Two brothers will have over half their profiles share bands. It is said however that the probability of two unrelated persons sharing a number of bands by pure chance is increasingly remote with more bands. This is known as the *match probability*. This should not be confused with a likelihood ratio.

The two were discussed in *R v. Dean*, *The Times*, January 10,1994. There   1–63
are two questions which are quite distinct:

(i)   What was the probability that an individual would match the DNA profile from the crime sample, given that he was innocent?

(ii) What was the probability that an individual was innocent, given that he matched the DNA sample?

It was described in *Dean* as the "prosecutions fallacy" to give the answer to the first question as being the answer to the second. This fallacy had led the judge to speak of probability approximating "pretty well to certainty" and as a result the conviction was unsafe.

The Crown will present the DNA evidence as a likelihood based upon a   1–64
Bayesian analysis. Bayes' Theorem concerns statistically the probability of particular events taking place to the probability that events conditional upon them have occurred. This is based on the investigations of the mathematician Thomas Bayes 1702–1761. This is a ratio of:

> Probability of the evidence given defendant at crime scene
> ──
> Probability of evidence given defendant not at crime scene

II. THE CORRECT APPROACH IN COURT

1–65   The fallacy is to assume that the top figure is equal to one. Because the evidence is not 100 per cent certain, the top figure should be less that one, thus decreasing the likelihood. (A fuller description of the mathematical argument is to be found at [1995] Crim.L.R. 465). It was held in *R v. Adams* [1996] Crim.L.R 898, that the Bayes Theorem may be a useful tool for statisticians but it is not appropriate for juries themselves to attempt to use it to reach their decisions in DNA cases for two reasons: first, the theorem requires that items of evidence be assessed separately according to their bearing on the guilt of the accused before being combined in the overall formula. This is too rigid an approach; secondly, and more importantly, the attempt to determine guilt or innocence on the basis of a mathematical formula, applied to every piece of evidence is inappropriate to the jury's task. They should apply common sense and knowledge of the world. Statistical methods of analysis lead to unnecessary complexity for juries.

The fallacy was again discussed in the case of *R v. Doheny and Adams* (unreported, 1996). It was pointed out that if the DNA specimen shows that one in one million people share that profile it is shared between 26 men in the United Kingdom. There is not a one in a million chance the defendant committed the offence, the chances are one in 26. The importance of the DNA evidence depends upon its supporting other evidence that the defendant was the guilty person.

The scientist should adduce the evidence of the DNA comparisons together with his calculations of the random occurance rates. The Crown should serve upon the Defence details of the calculations and the Forensic Science Service should make available to a defence expert, if requested, the databases upon which the calculations were based. The scientist should not be asked his opinion nor use terms which may give the impression that he is expressing an opinion on the likelihood that it was the Defendant who left the crime stain. The scientist will properly explain to the jury the match between the DNA in the crime stain and the DNA in the defendant's blood sample, and on the basis of empirical evidence give evidence of the random occurance ratio. If he has the necessary data and expertise he may say how many people are likely to be found with matching characteristics. He should not attempt to give any statistical evidence that it was the defendant who left the stain at the crime scene. The judge should explain to the jury the relevance of the random occurance ratio and the extraneous evidence which supports the case. The judge should use words to fit the facts of the case but the following was given as an appropriate example:

> "Members of the Jury, if you accept the scientific evidence called by the Crown, this indicates that there are probably only four or five white males in the United Kingdom from whom that semen stain could have come. The

decision you have to reach, on all the evidence, is whether you are sure that it was the Defendant who left that stain or whether it is possible that it was one of that other small group of men who share the same DNA characteristics."

The Court of Appeal, when ordering a retrial in the case of *R v. Gordon*   1–66
(Michael) [1995] 1 Cr.App.R. 290, has subsequently reaffirmed the validity and value of DNA evidence but expressed concern over the presentation of match possibilities and statistical probabilities.

There are three reservations often made to DNA profile evidence: 1–67

(i) Random match

The system is based upon the extreme unlikelihood of a random match between unrelated persons. Fear has been expressed that random matches may be more common than was originally believed. Original research in the USA undertaken on behalf of the FBI is feared to have been corrupted by the assumption that matches were caused by duplicate sampling without necessary corroboration of that fact.

The Home Office information place random matches as high as one in 40   1–68
million, but a national data base may show hundreds of matches, although the possibility of these occurring in a similar geographical location is still said to be rare.

Comparisons of DNA profiles obtained from members of remote Amazon tribes not surprisingly show similarities. Random matching may vary according to racial or ethnic groups. The random breeding required to produce purely random matching may not in fact occur. For purely random breeding the Hardy-Weenberg equilibrium is required. This necessitates:

(a)   a large population. This must be on a national scale. In *People v. Castro* 545 NYS (2d) 985, the population of New York was considered to be too small. The defendant was Hispanic. The possibility of random matches may vary between various minority races within a population;

(b)   there must be no selective breeding and therefore no tendency for smaller groups to breed together. Humans do not breed at random. The choice of partner will be affected by geographical, linguistic, racial and religious factors;

(c)   there must be no mutation of genes;

(d)   there must be no migration or immigration with other groups; and

(e)   there must be no natural selection with regard to one genetic type.

Within a small group who have a tendency to interbreed, *e.g.* an ethnic minority, the chance of a random match may be high.

(ii) Contamination   1–69

Contamination is a problem recognised by the laboratories who take measures to guard against it. Contamination by other DNA may have occurred at the scene from which the crime stain was taken. Bacterial contamination may cause fake bands.

1–70   It has been suggested that other problems may occur during the testing. The restriction enzyme may not totally separate the required strands which being heavier will not travel to the correct location. The reverse, a "partial restriction" can occur if the enzyme cuts the DNA in too many places, producing extra bands.

1–71   Alternatively, the labelled radio-active probe may combine with a similar but not identical DNA strand to the desired one. Spill-over has been feared in some cases where samples may spread to adjacent tracks.

1–72   Contamination problems may be increased with the use of polymerase chain reaction (PCR) which allows very small quantities of DNA to be increased. Because of its very ability to use dust like samples of DNA it is feared it may amplify contaminants.

1–73   *(iii) Misreading*

Due to early examples of misreading in America where mistakes as high as one in 50 were recorded, great care is taken in confirming readings which can now be confirmed by computer, although rulers are still used.

However, bands may naturally vary slightly in location and be misaligned. This is referred to as "band-shift". Even tests repeated on the same sample can give slightly different results. Reading of bands therefore must include an element of interpretation and are subjective.

1–74   In *R v. Dean The Times*, January 10, 1994, the Crown and defence argued over discrepant bands. One was due to stringency—relating to the stage of the procedure when excess DNA is washed away. The other differing band remained unexplained and was, the defence submitted a mis-match.

1–75   In *R v. Gordon* [1995] 1 Cr.App.R. 290, it was stated that "any scientific analysis or measurement would produce some variation between samples from an identical source, allowance had to be made for some acceptable range of variation in assessing whether there was a match". The defence submitted that a variance of plus or minus one millimetre was insufficiently precise or secure to justify the use of the statistical database to calculate the match probability.

Gordon was alleged to have raped two women. It was accepted that both rapes were committed by the same man. The defendant's DNA sample overlapped with the sample from rape one and rape one overlapped rape two. However, the defendant's sample did not overlap the sample from rape two. It was therefore submitted by the defence that Gordon could not have committed either rape. Other problems arose from the control tracks. The centre one did not accord with the control sample. This was explained as being probably due to a temperature variation. However, it was subsequently discovered that the side tracks had not been measured, nor were they consistent with the control either. The samples had been tested at different laboratories. There were sufficient reservations to throw doubt on the second stage of the exercise, the statistical evaluation.

1–76   In *Dean*, the older method of MLPs was used, in *Gordon* the newer method using an SLP was used.

Errors will occur if samples are mislabelled. 1–77

III. DNA Searchable Database

The searchable database contains information concerning the DNA profiles 1–78
of persons convicted of, or cautioned for recordable offences. The Forensic
Science Service compile the information on computer. If a search against the
database indicates that a suspect may have been involved in another offence,
he or she must be asked to supply an evidential sample for comparison for the
purposes of the subsequent investigation.

Section 64 of the Criminal Procedure and Investigations Act 1966 amended section 63A of the Police and Criminal Evidence Act 1984 by allowing
the police to search the DNA (and fingerprint) data bases speculatively in
respect of samples obtained from people suspected of involvement in but not
yet arrested, cautioned or convicted of, a recordable offence.

IV. Use Of Samples And Profiles

Section 64(3B) of PACE 1984 states that "where samples are required to be 1–79
destroyed . . . information derived from the sample of any person entitled to
its destruction shall not be used in evidence against the person so entitled."

The situation in *R v. Kelt* [1994] 2 All E.R. 980, must therefore now be 1–80
interpreted in the light of PACE 1984 as it is now enacted. In that case a
blood sample obtained in the course of a murder enquiry in 1988 was
compared with blood found from a previous robbery. The defendant was
still a murder suspect at the time the comparison was made. It was held that
provided the police had acted in good faith the public interest would not be
served if a sample lawfully obtained in connection with one investigation
could not be compared with blood left at the scene of another serious
crime.

In *R v. Cooke* [1995] 1 Cr.App.R. 318; [1995] Crim.L.R. 497, C had been 1–81
a suspect in an enquiry the police were investigating into the rape of a
woman, K, in 1990. Subsequently, he was arrested for a serious assault upon
another woman, S, in 1991. He agreed to provide a sample of hair in the
second enquiry upon an assurance that it would only be used in that later
investigation. It was however compared with semen recovered from the rape
of K and discovered to match. The police had misgivings about its admissibility and took a further sample of plucked hair from C in circumstances
which may have constituted an assault (see above). The trial judge ruled that
the sample obtained specifically in the investigation of the assault upon S was
not admissible in the trial relating to the rape of K but did admit the further
specimen. The Court of Appeal described this as a sensible conclusion.

In *R v. Nathaniel* (1995) 159 J.P. 419; *The Times*, April 4, 1995, a sample 1–82
of DNA was obtained from N in 1991 during an investigation into the rape
of two Danish girls. N gave the sample upon the undertaking that it would be
used in that investigation and would be destroyed if he was prosecuted and
cleared. He was also warned that if he refused to provide the sample without

17

good cause the jury in the case involving the Danish girls could draw inferences from his refusal. He was acquitted. However, before the profiles and information was destroyed, a match was discovered with samples from a rape and robbery in 1989. The DNA evidence should have been excluded under section 78 of PACE 1994. The court was particularly concerned that the sample had been provided as the result of a sanction—the inference which could be drawn by the jury. Section 78 was invoked despite the fact that the police had not acted at all in bad faith. The delay in destroying the information has been due to a back-log, not a deliberate action.

1-83　　In *Nathaniel* it had been conceded that the inclusion of the sample in the statistical database had been in breach of section 64(1) of the Police and Criminal Evidence Act 1994. The case predated the inclusion of section 57 of the Criminal Justice and Public Order Act 1995 of the new sections 3A and 3B which provides that the information derived from the samples shall not be used (a) against the person so entitled to its destruction or (b) for the purpose of any investigation of an offence. It was argued by the defence in the case of *R v. Willoughby*, unreported, November 12, 1996, that this prevented its inclusion in the statistical database. The Common Sergeant dismissed this arguement questioning the concession made in *Nathaniel*. He stated that there had been a confusion between "investigation", which is the gathering of evidence, and the interpretation to be put upon that evidence once it had been gathered by an expert. This statistic exercise is outside the investigatory process. The Court of Appeal then heard on application for leave to appeal on this point but, endorsing the decision of the Common Sergeant, refused leave to appeal. Further appeals where the statistical database has been used to provide the frequency analysis will not be allowed.

V. Privilege In The Defendant's DNA Sample

1-84　　In *R v. R The Times*, February 2, 1994, R took his own sample for a private DNA test. Application was made by the Crown Prosecution Service to interview the scientist who had carried out the DNA test on the defendant's blood sample. There is no property in a witness. The question however was whether the material was subject to legal professional privilege under sections 9 and 10 of PACE 1984.

　　The Court of Appeal held that the sample was given in circumstances of confidence and was an item brought into existence and therefore made for the purpose of legal proceedings under section 10(1)(c) of the Act and was therefore subject to legal privilege.

Chapter 2
Evidence in Court

All the basic rules of evidence apply to sexual offences as they do to any other criminal allegation. In addition there are specific provisions intended to protect the victims of sexual offences, to prevent publication of information which may lead to their identification, and to limit, to what is reasonable and necessary their cross-examination in court. This latter protection is not always provided by the court in a way which achieves this aim and it remains a matter of public concern that often victims are left with the feeling that it is they who have been put on trial.

A. COMPETENCE AND COMPELLABILITY

Although in general all persons are considered able (competent) to testify and can be forced to do so (compellable) there are special rules in respect of the competence and compellability of certain categories of witness and whether their testimony is for the prosecution or defence.

2–01

I. OF A SPOUSE

Police and Criminal Evidence Act 1984, s. 80:

2–02

"(1) In any proceedings the wife or husband of the accused shall be competent to give evidence—
    (a) subject to subsection (4) below, for the prosecution; and
    (b) on behalf of the accused or any person jointly charged with the accused.
(2) In any proceedings the wife or husband of the accused shall, subject to subsection (4) below, be compellable to give evidence on behalf of the accused.
(3) In any proceedings the wife or husband of the accused shall, subject to subsection (4) below, be compellable to give evidence for the

prosecution or on behalf of any person jointly charged with the accused if and only if—

(a) the offence charged involves an assault on, or injury or a threat of injury to, the wife or husband of the accused or a person who was at the material time under the age of sixteen; or

(b) the offence charged is a sexual offence alleged to have been committed in respect of a person who was at the material time under that age; or

(c) the offence charged consists of attempting or conspiring to commit, or of aiding, abetting, counselling, procuring or inciting the commission of, an offence falling within paragraph (a) or (b) above.

(4) Where a husband and wife are jointly charged with an offence neither spouse shall at the trial be competent or compellable by virtue of subsection (1)(a), (2) or (3) above to give evidence in respect of that offence unless that spouse is not, or is no longer, liable to be convicted of that offence at the trial as a result of pleading guilty or for any other reason.

(5) In any proceedings a person who has been but is no longer married to the accused shall be competent and compellable to give evidence as if that person and the accused had never been married.

2–03 (6) Where in any proceedings the age of any person at any time is material for the purposes of subsection (3) above, his age at the material time shall for the purposes of that provision be deemed to be or to have been that which appears to the court to be or to have been his age at that time.

Definition of 'sexual offence'

2–04 (7) In subsection (3)(b) above, 'sexual offence' means an offence under the Sexual Offences Act 1956, the Indecency with Children Act 1960, the Sexual Offences Act 1967, section 54 of the Criminal Law Act 1977 or the Protection of Children Act 1978.

2–05 (8) The failure of the wife or husband of the accused to give evidence shall not be made the subject of any comment by the prosecution.

(9) Section 1(d) of the Criminal Evidence Act 1898 (communications between husband and wife) and section 43(1) of the Matrimonial Causes Act 1965 (evidence as to marital intercourse) shall cease to have effect."

"Wife" and "husband" refer to persons whose marriage is recognised under English law. In *Khan* ((1987) 84 Cr.App.R. 44, but decided on the law before the 1984 Act came into force) a woman had gone through a Moslem ceremony of marriage with the accused who was already married under English law to another woman. It was held that the woman who underwent the Moslem ceremony was competent and compellable for the prosecution since her position was the same as that of a mistress, or a woman who had not gone through a ceremony of marriage at all, or a woman who had gone through a ceremony of marriage which was void because it was bigamous.

2–06 Where a spouse is competent but not compellable, and is called as a witness for the prosecution, it should be explained to her, in the absence of the jury and before she takes the oath that she has a right to refuse to give evidence but that if she chooses to give evidence, she may be treated like any other witness (*R v. Pitt (I.B.)* (1982) 75 Cr.App.R. 254). Failure to give such a warning will necessarily justify interfering with a guilty verdict (*R v. Nelson* [1992] Crim.L.R. 653).

"For the prosecution" in section 80(1) means that the spouse is competent   2–07
irrespective of whether her evidence is against the accused spouse or his co-accused.

Following the case of *R v. Woolgar* [1991] Crim.L.R. 545, "jointly   2–08
charged with an offence" means what it says and not "jointly indicted", therefore it appears that where under section 80(4) a spouse is neither competent nor compellable to testify in respect of an offence with which both husband and wife are jointly charged, it does not apply if husband and wife are charged with separate offences on the same indictment.

(a) Failure to testify

By virtue of section 80(8), the failure of a spouse to testify shall not be made   2–09
the subject of any comment by the prosecution. This is mandatory, and breach of the prohibition would amount to a material irregularity in the course of the trial (*R v. Brown* [1983] Crim.L.R. 38). It does not follow however that such a breach would result in a conviction being quashed—it would depend on all the circumstances. In *R v. Dickman* (1910) 5 Cr.App.R. 135, counsel inadvertently commented upon the failure of the spouse of the accused to give evidence but the jury were told to dismiss the comment from their minds and the appeal against conviction was dismissed. In *R v. Hunter* [1969] Crim.L.R. 262, where the judge warned the jury to ignore the comment, the conviction was upheld. However, in *R v. Naudeer* [1984] 3 All E.R. 1036, the defendant, a man of good character was convicted of theft. During the trial, prosecuting counsel had suggested that the failure of N's wife to give evidence had deprived the jury of what would probably have been material evidence. The judge failed in his summing-up to give any direction to the jury in this regard. On appeal, the court quashed the conviction on the grounds that the breach was central to the overall justice of the case, particularly since the accused was a man of good character and the question of his *bona fides* was central to the offence itself. It was the duty of the judge, depending upon the circumstances of each case, to remedy such a breach in his summing-up.

(b) Ex-spouses

Under section 80(5) a person who has been, but is no longer married to the   2–10
accused is competent and compellable to testify in any proceedings which take place after January 1, 1986, about any matter, whether it occurred before or after that date (*R v. Cruttenden* [1991] 2 Q.B. 66). No longer married means where the parties are divorced and where a voidable marriage has been annulled. It does not cover the situation where the parties have been judicially separated or are just not co-habiting.

2-11   II. OF CHILDREN

The competence of children to give evidence in criminal proceedings is governed by the Criminal Justice Act 1988, s.33A, as by amended by the Criminal Justice and Public Order Act 1994, Sched. 9, para.33:

"(1) A child's evidence in criminal proceedings shall be given unsworn.

(2) A deposition of a child's unsworn evidence may be taken for the purposes of criminal proceedings as if that evidence had been given on oath.

(2A) A child's evidence shall be received unless it appears to the court that the child is incapable of giving intelligible testimony.

(3) In this section 'child' means a person under fourteen years of age."

2-12   As far as the competency of children aged 14 or over is concerned, they should be treated in the same way as adults. It was intended by the Minister when introducing the amendment which became subsection (2A) that the words "unless it appears" refers to unintelligibility appearing in the course of the child's evidence and that it was not the government's intention that the courts should hold a preliminary investigation or question the child in advance to determine whether the child is capable of giving intelligible evidence (*Hansard*, H.C., col.1026, February 24, 1994). Therefore, the procedure should be that the child should commence testifying and only if it then appears that the child is incapable of giving intelligible evidence, should the court determine whether its testimony should be halted or allowed to continue.

2-13   In *R v. D and others*, *The Times*, November 15, 1995, it was held by the Court of Appeal that in deciding the competency of a child witness, the court should ask if he could understand questions and respond coherently and intelligibly, although it remained relevant to inquire as to his ability to distinguish between truth and fiction and between fact and fantasy as part of that test. Moreover, where a child or young person gave evidence before a jury and then retracted it and it was possible for the jury to believe the first version of his testimony, the jury could be allowed to consider all that he had said to them although the judge should give the jury a strong warning as to the dangers of relying on such evidence.

B. CORROBORATION

2-14   Until recently, corroboration was required as a matter of law in respect of the evidence of accomplices, complainants in sexual offences (sections 2, 3, 4, 22 and 23 of the Sexual Offences Act 1956) and the unsworn evidence of children. As far as the unsworn evidence of children is concerned, the need for corroboration was removed by section 34 of the Criminal Justice Act 1988 (CJA). The Criminal Justice and Public Order Act 1994 (CJPOA) abolished the need for corroboration in the other cases.

2-15   Section 32 of the CJPOA 1994 states:

"(1) Any requirement whereby at a trial on indictment it is obligatory for the court to give the jury a warning about convicting the accused on the uncorroborated evidence of a person merely because that person is—
    (a) an alleged accomplice of the accused, or
    (b) where the offence charged is a sexual offence, the person in it is alleged to have been committed, is hereby abrogated."

Section 34 of the CJA 1988, as amended by section 32(2) of the CJPOA 1994, states:

    2–16

"(2) Any requirement whereby at a trial on indictment it is obligatory for the court to give the jury a warning about convicting the accused on the uncorroborated evidence of a child is abrogated."

Section 32(3) of the CJPOA 1994 states:

    2–17

"Any requirement that—
(a) is applicable at the summary trial of a person for an offence, and
(b) corresponds to the requirement mentioned in subsection (1) above or that mentioned in section 43(2) of the Criminal Justice Act 1988, is hereby abrogated."

Section 32(4) of the CJPOA 1994, states:

    2–18

"Nothing in this section applies in relation to—
(a) any trial, or
(b) any proceedings before a magistrates' court as examining justices, which began before the commencement of this section."

Section 33 of the states CJOPA 1994:

    2–19

"(1) The following provisions of the Sexual Offences Act 1956 (which provide that a person shall not be convicted of the offence concerned on the evidence of one witness only unless the witness is corroborated) are hereby repealed—
    (a) section 2(2) (procurement of woman by threats)
    (b) section 3(2) (procurement of woman by false pretences),
    (c) section 4(2) (administering drugs to obtain or facilitate intercourse),
    (d) section 22(2) (causing prostitution of women), and
    (e) section 23(2) (procuration of girl under twenty-one).
(2) Nothing in this section applies in relation to—
    (a) any trial, or
    (b) any proceedings before a magistrates' court as examining justices, which began before the commencement of this section."

I. THE EFFECT OF THE CHANGES

The effect of the changes brought about by the Criminal Justice and Public Order Act 1994 was considered by the Court of Appeal in *R v. Makanjuola*;

    2–20

R v. Easton [1995] 2 Cr.App.R 469. The two applicants applied (unsuccessfully) for leave to appeal, following the conviction in each case of an indecent assault on a young girl. It was argued that the trial judge should, in his discretion, have given the jury a full corroboration direction notwithstanding section 32 of the Criminal Justice and Public Order Act 1994. Lord Taylor L.C.J. said that "if that were right, Parliament would have enacted section 32(1) in vain. It is clear that the judge does have a discretion to warn the jury if he thinks it necessary, but the use of the word 'merely' in the sub-section shows that Parliament does not envisage such a warning being given just because a witness complains of a sexual offence or is an alleged accomplice". The Court also considered whether, if the exercise of the judge's discretion is appropriate, the full old-style warning should be given, *i.e.* using the phrase "dangerous to convict on the uncorroborated evidence", explaining the meaning of corroboration, identifying what evidence under the old rules is capable of being corroboration, what evidence is not so capable, and the respective roles of judge and jury. Lord Taylor said: "It was, in our judgment, partly to escape from this tortuous exercise … that Parliament enacted section 32."

II. GUIDANCE

2–21   The Court was invited to give guidance as to the circumstances in which, as a matter of discretion, a judge ought in summing-up to a jury urge caution in regard to a particular witness and the terms in which that should be done. Lord Taylor said:

> "The circumstances and evidence in criminal cases are infinitely variable and it is impossible to categorise how a judge should deal with them. But it is clear that to carry on giving 'discretionary' warnings generally and in the same terms as were previously obligatory would be contrary to the policy and purpose of the Act. Whether, as a matter of discretion, a judge should give any warning and if so its strength and terms must depend upon the content and manner of the witness's evidence, the circumstances of the case and the issues raised. The judge will often consider that no special warning is required at all. Where, however the witness has been shown to be unreliable, he or she may consider it necessary to urge caution. In a more extreme case, if the witness is shown to have lied, to have made previous false complaints, or to bear the defendant some grudge, a stronger warning may be thought appropriate and the judge may suggest it would be wise to look for some supporting material before acting on the impugned witness's evidence. We stress that these observations are merely illustrative of some, not all, of the factors which judges may take into account in measuring where in the scale of reliability and what response they should make at that level in their directions to the jury. We also stress that judges are not required to conform to any formula and this Court would be slow to interfere with the exercise of discretion by a trial judge who has the advantage of assessing the manner of a witness's evidence as well as its content."

In summarising the judgment, it was again stressed that where it was 2–22 appropriate for the trial judge to give some sort of warning to the jury this should not be done simply because the witness is a complainant in a sexual case or an accomplice. Further that there will need to be an evidential basis for suggesting that the evidence of the witness is unreliable, more than mere suggestion by cross-examining counsel.

If any question arises as to whether the judge should give a special 2–23 warning, the question should be resolved by discussion with counsel in the absence of the jury before closing speeches. Moreover, where the judge does decide to give some warning, it will be appropriate for him to do so as part of the judge's review of the evidence and his comments as to how the jury should evaluate it rather than as a set-piece legal direction.

The Court also emphasised that it would only interfere with a trial judge's 2–24 exercise of his discretion if the exercise was unreasonable in the *Wednesbury* sense.

C. EVIDENCE OF OTHER ACTIVITIES OF THE DEFENDANT

Questions of admissibility of evidence of other activities often occur in sexual 2–25 cases. Such evidence may be of other actions usually criminal, committed by the defendant, and evidence of objects such as photographs or magazines possessed by the defendant which tend to show a propensity towards the criminal activities alleged. It is clear from the leading case of *DPP v. Boardman* [1975] A.C. 421, that there are no special rules applying to cases alleging sexual offences. The normal rules of admissibility generally apply. Secondly there is no rule that the fact that the other activity which is sought to be introduced, is or is not itself criminal should be considered as relevant to the decision. The admissibility is a matter for the judge after he has had regard to all the facts and the other evidence available.

The general rule is that the prosecution may not adduce evidence of the 2–26 defendant's commission of other offences or like behaviour since it does not directly implicate the defendant in the offence charged. It is therefore not relevant and in any event, its prejudice to the defendant outweighs its probative value.

To this rule however, there is the exception where the evidence falls into 2–27 the category of that known as similar fact (see *Makin v. Att.-Gen. for N.S.W.* [1894] AC. 57; *DPPP v. Boardman* [1975] A.C. 421; *DPP v. P* [1991] 3 All E.R 337; *R. v. Ananthanarayanan* (1994) 98 Cr.App.R. 1).

A detailed analysis of the law relating to similar fact evidence can be found 2–28 in works on the law of evidence. Here it is proposed to mention only those cases where similar fact evidence has been adduced in the context of sexual offences. Most of the cases consider similar fact evidence with regard to its relevance to corroboration. Obviously, since the passing of the Criminal Justice and Public Order Act 1994, the importance of this evidence as corroboration has diminished. However, the case law is still pertinent in so far as it deals with the admissibility of similar fact evidence in support of the prosecution case.

2–29 It has been held (*R v. Montgomery Simpson* (1994) 99 Cr.App.R. 48) that where the prosecution allege persistent sexual abuse of young girls over a long period, the evidence of one victim will be admitted as similar fact evidence in relation to other counts in the indictment where the similarity is sufficiently strong, or there is some other sufficient relationship in time or circumstances or otherwise between that evidence and the abuse charged that it is fair to admit it because of its positive probative value despite its prejudicial effect.

2–30 Indeed, independent evidence of misconduct on a different occasion is admissible as similar fact, irrespective of whether that misconduct is the subject of a count on the indictment.

I. A Problem

2–31 The danger to this approach is where there may be innocent collusion or concoction between the prosecution witnesses. How the court should tackle the problem has been addressed by case law.

2–32 In *R v. Ryder* (1994) 98 Cr.App.R 242, it was held that there are four possible situations:

(i) where a real possibility of collusion is apparent to the judge on the face of the documents, he should not allow the similar fact evidence to be led;

(ii) if a submission is made raising the suggestion of collusion, the judge may find it necessary to hold a *voire dire*;

(iii) the evidence is admitted but at the end of the case the judge takes the view that there is a real possibility of collusion he should tell the jury in summing up not to use the evidence as corroboration; and

(iv) even if the judge himself is of the view that there is no real possibility of collusion, but the matter has been argued, he should leave it to the jury.

(i) R v. W

2–33 In *R v. W(C)* (1994) 99 Cr.App.R. 185, the appellant was charged with various offences (which occurred 10 to 20 years previously) of sexual abuse against children to all of whom he was related or *in loco parentis*. At the trial an application was made, unsuccessfully, to sever the counts on the indictment on the ground that there was a real possibility of concoction between the complainants. During cross-examination of the prosecution witnesses, there arose the possibility of collusion or contamination (although the complainants and their parents denied it): they strongly disliked the appellant; some of them hated him because he was too strict a disciplinarian; he was violent towards his second wife; and the witnesses had discussed the offences which had taken place between 1979 and 1980 between themselves and as a family in 1987. In summing up, the judge directed the jury that the complainants could be mutually corroborative if they had first ruled out any possibility of an untruthful concoction between witness B and witness A. He made no reference to the possibility of innocent contamination. The appellant appealed on the ground that the judge should have held a *voire dire* and that in the circumstances of the case, the conviction was unsafe and unsatisfactory.

Held:

(i) that a bare assertion by the defence that there might be collusion or contamination did not warrant the holding of a *voire dire*—the judge should only hold a *voire dire* if something contained in the committal papers, or something put before him by way of credible evidence on behalf of the defence, raises an issue for him to consider and he believes it necessary to hear evidence to enable him to properly consider it;

(ii) the cross-examination of the prosecution witnesses had elicited facts bearing on the possibility of collusion or at least contamination of the witnesses' evidence. Thus the case had reached the situation where the judge should have directed the jury not to use the complainant's evidence as corroboration and the resultant conviction was unsafe and unsatisfactory.

(ii) R v. H

In *R v. H(A)* [1995] 2 Cr.App.R. 437, the appellant was charged with sexual 2–34 offences against his adopted daughter and step-daughter aged nine and 14 years at the relevant time. The offences were alleged to have been committed between 1987 and 1989, and on separate occasions. The girls confided in the appellant's wife in 1992 when complaints were made on the same day. There were similarities between each girl's account of the nature of the offences, but each denied that they had collaborated or concocted a false story. The trial judge directed the jury that there were similarities in the complainant's accounts and that if they, the jury, were sure that the two girls had not collaborated to concoct a false story against the appellant, then the jury could consider the evidence of one of the complainants as corroborating that of the other. The appellant, following conviction appealed first to the Court of Appeal and then to the House of Lords.

Held, dismissing the appeal that where on an application to exclude evidence on the ground that it does not qualify as similar fact evidence, the submission raises a question of collusion (deliberate or unconscious), the judge should approach the question of admissibility on the basis that the similar facts alleged are true and determine whether the probative force of the evidence made it fair to admit it, notwithstanding its prejudicial effect. Generally, collusion was not relevant at this stage. If a submission was made which raised collusion in such a way as to cause the judge difficulty in applying this test he might be compelled to hold a *voire dire*. If in the course of the trial it became apparent that no reasonable jury could accept the evidence as free from collusion, then the jury should be directed that it could not be relied upon as corroboration or for any other purpose adverse to the defence. Where this was not so, but the question of collusion had been raised, the judge should draw the attention of the jury to the importance of collusion and tell them that if they were not satisfied that the evidence could be relied upon as free from collusion, it could not be used as corroboration or for any other purpose adverse to the defence. Applying the above principles, as the judge had correctly allowed the complainants' evidence to be used as similar fact evidence and had correctly left the question of its reliability to the jury, the convictions should stand.

2–35　　In *R v. Boardman* (above), the headmaster of a boy's school was accused of the attempted buggery of S, and inciting H to commit buggery. The defence was a total denial of the facts. The evidence of each boy was admitted on the count involving the other boy. The court held there was the necessary striking similarity between the allegations: "The similarity would have to be so unique or striking that common sense makes it inexplicable on the basis of co-incidence" (*per* Lord Salmon at 462).

It would appear that the striking similarity must point to the defendant and constitute "the stock-in-trade of the seducer of small boys" such as inviting the victim to the defendant's room to watch television—*R v. Inder* (1977) 67 Cr.App.R. 143.

The similarity depends very much on the details of the facts. Approaching, young boys in an amusement arcade and offering them a meal or money was held to be admissible in *R v. Johansen* (1977) 65 Cr.App.R.101, but was held not to in *R v. Novac* (1976) 65 Cr.App.R. 107. In *Novac* the facts were held to be inadmissible because they related to the surrounding circumstances and not to the commission of the crime itself. This appears now to be a false argument and evidence of facts relating to the surrounding circumstances can be "strikingly similar" (see *R v. Scarrott* [1978] Q.B. 1016 and *R v. Butler* (1987) 84 Cr.App.R. 12).

2–36　　In some circumstances even a previous offence may be admitted. In *R v. Ball* [1911] A.C. 47 H.L., a brother and sister were indicted for incest in 1910. Evidence showed that they were cohabiting but to show that this was evidence of a sexual relationship as opposed to an innocent one, evidence was adduced that they had a guilty passion towards each other resulting in the birth of a child prior to incest becoming a crime in 1908.

II. Sexual Propensity

2–37　　Despite the assertion above, that as a general rule, sexual offence cases are subject to the same considerations as other criminal cases, and that no distinction should be made between criminal and non-criminal activities, there is one area where specific rules do apply. This occurs where the prosecution wish to adduce evidence to show the defendant's proclivity to certain sexual activity. The situation occurs often when, but it is not limited to, occasions when, upon searching an accused' residence the police find pornographic magazines or photographs. Such evidence is admissible against the defendant when identity is in issue, or when the facts are admitted but some innocent explanation is put forward. The evidence is not admissible where the issue is whether the act alleged by the complainant ever took place.

Such objects will always be admissible where they were used to commit the offence itself, of course.

(i) R v. Thompson

In *R v. Thompson* [1918] A.C. 221 H.L., a man approached two boys on a   2-38
Friday and committed an act of gross indecency. He made an appointment to meet the boys again the following Monday. The police were informed and on Monday arrested a man identified to them by the boys, as being the man who committed the offence on the Friday. On the Monday the man performed acts described as equivocal. The prosecution introduced evidence that upon his arrest he had with him powder puffs, and from his home were recovered photographs of naked boys. There appear to be two lines of reasoning for its admission. The incriminating evidence confirmed the identity of the defendant as being the man involved on Friday. The evidence also rebutted any suggestion that the equivocal actions on Monday were innocent.

(ii) Innocent explanation

Evidence of the defendant's sexual inclinations has been admitted to rebut   2-39
innocent association on a number of occasions. In *R v. King* [1967] 2 Q.B.338, questions concerning the defendant's homosexuality were admitted to rebut a defence that the defendant invited young boys back to his flat and shared a bed with one purely as an act of charity.

In *R v. Lewis* (1983) 76 Cr.App.R.33, evidence of the defendant's possession of material indicating his interest in paedophilia was admissible on three out of four counts of indecency with children where the defence was one of innocent association, but not on the fourth count where the facts were completely denied.

III. ITEMS USED IN THE OFFENCE

Clearly where the items are, or perhaps may be, used in the commission of   2-40
the offence they are admissible. So, in a case of gross indecency pictures (postcards) found in the defendant's possession may be admitted in evidence as things which a man intending to commit such an offence may have about him, and might use as an adjunct to assist him in the commission of the offence by using them to inflame his victims' on his own passions. They are not admissible merely to prove he has a "dirty mind"—*R v. Gillingham* [1939] 4 All E.R. 122 (see also the approval of Thompson in *R v. Twiss* [1918] 2 K.B. 853 and *R v. Mackenzie and Higginson* (1910) 6 Cr.App.R. 64 C.C.A. concerning apparatus and paraphernalia used for procuring unlawful sexual intercourse).

IV. DENIAL OF THE FACTS

In *R v. Cole* [1941] 105 J.P. 279, the defendant was charged with gross   2-41
indecency and indecent assault. There was no issue as to identity, nor any

defence of mistake to admitted facts. The defence was one of complete denial of the acts charged. It was held that indecent letters found in the possession of the defendant should not have been admitted in evidence.

In *R v. Wright* (1990) 90 Cr.App.R.325, the defendant, a headmaster was charged with sexual offences against boys. The prosecution sought to introduce evidence of a booklet recovered from his study which, if his, would indicate homosexual inclinations. It was held that evidence such as the possession of incriminating articles or other evidence showing the defendant to have a leaning towards such acts has never been admissible in the English criminal courts.

In *R v. B, The Times*, February 19, 1997, this view was confirmed. Evidence of the possession of homosexual pornographic magazines against a grandfather charged with indecent assaults against two of his grandsons, the acts being denied should not have been admitted.

D. PROTECTION OF WITNESSES

I. PROTECTION OF IDENTITY

2–42   The general principle of law is that justice should be in open, public and that the media should have the right to publicise fairly all facts given in court. Section 121(4) of the Magistrates' Court Act 1980 for example states that "subject to the provisions of any enactment to the contrary, where a magistrates' court is required by this section to sit in a petty-sessional or occasional court-house, it shall sit in open court". There has however, been recently a discernible change of attitude which may well affect the approach taken by the Courts in future and all the cases referred to below must now be viewed in the light of this more modern, decent and reasonable approach.

The Trials Issues Group in its *Statement of National Standards of Witness Care in the Criminal Justice System* states, in paragraph 17.1, with regard to any case: "unless it is necessary for evidential purposes, defence and prosecution witnesses should not be required to disclose their address in open court. Exceptionally, it will be appropriate for the defence and prosecution to make applications for the non-disclosure, in open court of the names of the witnesses". This extends protection from publication to information given in open court.

2–43   There are occasions when a court may decide to sit in camera. This is based upon a common-law power of the court. One exception may be if a witness would refuse to testify in public. The exception is outlined by Viscount Haldane L.C. in *Scott v. Scott* [1913] A.C. 417. The evidence must be of such a character that it would be impractical to force an unwilling witness to give evidence in public.

2–44   There are however, other procedures now available to the court (see para. 2–81). They include the use of screens and the allowing of the witness to write down their name and address and hand these details to the court. If the witness is reluctant to give evidence through fear, section 23 of the Criminal

Justice Act 1988 may be considered so that the witness' statement may be read to the court (see for example *R v. Holt, R v. Bird, The Times,* October 31, 1996).

However, the mere fact that a witness may find his or her evidence embarrassing has in part been held to be not a sufficient reason to hold the court *in camera* (*R v. Malvern Justices, ex p. Evans* [1988] Q.B. 540). In that case, a defendant had to give details of her personal life which were "embarrassing and intimate". It was held by the Divisional Court to be inappropriate to hold the court *in camera,* although the proceedings were still lawful. The question arose in *R v. Malvern Justices, ex p. Evans; R v. Evesham Justices, ex p. McDonagh* (above) in what circumstances a Magistrates' court could sit in private or prohibit publication of a *defendant's* address. The Court has inherent jurisdiction to sit *in camera* if the administration of justice so requires, but there has to be compelling reasons for the Court to adopt such a course. Similarly, Magistrates have jurisdiction to protect the identity of a witness or even a defendant, but only if revealing that person's identity would frustrate or render impracticable the administration of justice. Sympathy for the defendant's well-being or risk of economic damage are not reasons for witholding. 2–45

The protection of public decency is not a sufficient reason to hold the court in camera (*Scott v. Scott* (above)).

The procedure to be adopted for an application for evidence to be heard *in camera* is set out in the Crown Court Rules 1982, r.24A. The person making the application must give notice of the application seven days prior to the start of the trial both to the Court and the other side. A copy of the notice will be displayed within the precincts of the court. The application is itself heard *in camera* after arraignment but prior to the swearing in of a jury. The trial is then adjourned for 24 hours or until the application is decided. A judge may not generally set aside the procedure and hear evidence *in camera* unless some emergency occurs which justifies the lack of compliance (*Re Goodwin* [1991] Crim.L.R. 302). 2–46

In *R v. Tower Bridge Magistrates' Court, ex p. Osborne* (1987) 88 Cr.App.R.28 it was held that if a solicitor wishes the Magistrates to make an order to withold, it is generally necessary for the Justices to hear the reasons *in camera.* If the Court finds substance in the application it may then continue *in camera* to determine the application itself. The Court must then, in open court, announce its determination.

The publication of details of hearings held in camera is an offence— Administration of Justice Act 1960, s. 12. 2–47

(a) Young children

Young children are protected by the Children and Young Persons Act 1933, ss. 37 and 39. 2–48

Section 37 states:

"(1) Where, in any proceedings in relation to an offence against, or any conduct contrary to, decency or morality, a person who, in the opinion of the court, is a child or young person, is called as a witness, the court may direct that all or any persons, not being members or officers of the court or parties to the case, their counsel or solicitors, or persons otherwise directly concerned in the case, be excluded from the court during the taking of the evidence of that witness: Provided that nothing in this section shall authorise the exclusion of bona fide representatives of a newspaper or news agency.

(2) The powers conferred on a court by this section shall be in addition and without prejudice to any other powers of the court to hear proceedings *in camera*."

2–49   Section 39 states:

"(1) In relation to any proceedings in any court ... the court may direct that—(a) no newspaper report of the proceedings shall reveal the name, address, or school, or include any particulars calculated to lead to the identification of any child or young person concerned in the proceedings, either as being the person by or against or in respect of whom the proceedings are taken, or as being a witness therein; (b) no picture shall be published in any newspaper as being or including a picture of any child or young person so concerned in the proceedings as aforesaid; except in so far (if at all) as may be permitted by the direction of the court.

(2) Any person who publishes any matter in contravention of any such direction shall on summary conviction be liable in respect of each offence to a fine not exceeding level 5 on the standard scale."

(b) Contempt of court

2–50   The correct procedure to protect witnesses from publicity is to make an order under section 11 of the Contempt of Court Act 1981 which states:

"In any case where a court (having power to do so) allows a name or other matter to be withheld from the public in proceedings before the court, the court may give such directions prohibiting the publication of that name, or matter in connection with the proceedings as appear to the court to be necessary for the purpose for which it was so withheld."

In *R v. Arundel Justices, ex p. Westminster Press Ltd* [1985] 2 All E.R. 390 it was held that a court can only excercise a power under section 11 if the court has first allowed that name to be witheld from the public in the court proceedings. Where, therefore, a magistrates' court allows a defendant's name to be mentioned in public proceedings against him the court no longer has jurisdiction to give direction under section 11 of the Act prohibiting publication of the name.

2–51   Complainants in rape cases are separately protected (see below), but witnesses in other sexual cases may be provided for by the use of this section. It is not used to protect defendants from unwanted publicity to benefit their comfort or feeling (*Evesham Justices, ex p. McDonagh* [1988] Q.B. 553), nor to protect the privacy of a defendant to save embarrassment or other inhibitions arising out of medical conditions, such as his status as being HIV positive (*R v. Westminster City Council, ex p. Castelli; R v. Same, ex p. Tristran-Garcia*, Times Law Reports, August 14, 1995).

II. COMPLAINANTS IN RAPE CASES

The Sexual Offences (Amendment) Act 1976, s. 4 protects the identity of   2–52
complainants in rape cases:

"(1) Except as authorised by a direction given in pursuance of this section—
   (a) after an allegation that a woman or man has been the victim of a rape offence has been made by the woman or man or by any other person, neither the woman's or man's name nor her address nor a still or moving picture of her or him shall during that person's lifetime—
      (i)   be published in England and Wales in a written publication available to the public; or
      (ii) be included in a relevant programme for reception in England and Wales,
      if that is likely to lead members of the public to identify that person as an alleged victim of such an offence; and
   (b) after a person is accused of a rape offence, no matter likely to lead members of the public to identify a woman or man as the complainant in relation to that accusation shall during her lifetime—
      (i)   be published in England and Wales in a written publication available to the public; or
      (ii) be included in a relevant programme for reception in England and Wales;
      but nothing in this subsection prohibits the publication or inclusion in a relevant programme of matter consisting only of a report of criminal proceedings other than proceedings at, or intended to lead to, or on an appeal arising out of, a trial at which the accused is charged with the offence.
(1A) In subsection (1) above "picture" includes a likeness however produced.
(2) If, before the commencement of a trial at which a person is charged   2–53
   with a rape offence, he or another person against whom the complainant may be expected to give evidence at the trial applies to a judge of the Crown Court for a direction in pursuance of this subsection and satisfies the judge—
   (a) that the direction is required for the purpose of inducing persons to come forward who are likely to be needed as witnesses at the trial; and
   (b) that the conduct of the applicant's defence at the trial is likely to be substantially prejudiced if the direction is not given,

the judge shall direct that the preceding subsection shall not, by virtue of the accusation alleging the offence aforesaid, apply in relation to the complainant.

2–54   (3)   If at a trial the judge is satisfied that the effect of subsection (1) of this section is to impose a substantial and unreasonable restriction upon the reporting of proceedings at the trial and that it is in the public interest to remove or relax the restriction, he shall direct that that subsection shall not apply to such matter as is specified in the direction; but a direction shall not be given in pursuance of this subsection by reason only of the outcome of the trial.

2–55   (4)   If a person who has been convicted of an offence and given notice of appeal to the Court of Appeal against the conviction, or notice of an application for leave so to appeal, applies to the Court of Appeal for a direction in pursuance of this subsection and satisfies the Court—

(a) that the direction is required for the purpose of obtaining evidence in support of the appeal; and

(b) that the applicant is likely to suffer substantial injustice if the direction is not given,

the Court shall direct that subsection (1) of this section shall not, by virtue of an accusation which alleged a rape offence and is specified in the direction, apply in relation to a complainant so specified.

2–56   (5)   If any matter is published, or included in a relevant programme in contravention of subsection (1) of this section, the following persons, namely—

(a) in the case of a publication in a newspaper or periodical, any proprietor, any editor and any publisher of the newspaper or periodical;

(b) in the case of any other publication, the person who publishes it; and

(c) in the case of matter included in a relevant programme, any body corporate which is engaged in providing the service in which the programme is included and any person having functions in relation to the programme corresponding to those of an editor of a newspaper

shall be guilty of an offence and liable on summary conviction to a fine not exceeding level 5 on the standard scale.

   (5A)   Where a person is charged with an offence under subsection (5) of this section in respect of the publication of any matter or the inclusion of any matter in a relevant programme, it shall be a defence, subject to subsection (5B) below, to prove that the publication, or programme in which the matter appeared was one in respect of which the woman or man had given written consent to the appearance of matter of that description.

   (5B)   Written consent is not a defence if it is proved that any person interfered unreasonably with the peace or comfort of the woman or man with intent to obtain consent.

2–57   (6)   For the purposes of this section a person is accused of a rape offence if—

   (a) an information is laid alleging that he has committed a rape offence; or

   (b) he appears before a court charged with a rape offence; or

   (c) a court before which he is appearing commits him for trial on a new charge alleging a rape offence; or

   (d) a bill of indictment charging him with a rape offence is preferred before a court in which he may lawfully be indicted for the offence, and references in this section and section 7(5) of this Act to an accusation alleging a rape offence shall be construed accordingly; and in this section—

       'complainant', in relation to a person accused of a rape offence or an accusation alleging a rape offence, means the woman or man against whom the offence is alleged to have been committed; and 'relevant programme' means a programme included in a programme service (within the meaning of the Broadcasting Act 1990);

       'written publication' includes a film, a sound track and any other record in permanent form but does not include an indictment or other document prepared for use in particular legal proceedings.

(6A) For the purposes of this section, where it is alleged or there is an accusation that an offence of incitement to rape or conspiracy to rape has been committed, the person who is alleged to have been the intended victim of the rape shall be regarded as the alleged victim of the incitement or conspiracy or, in the case of an accusation, as the complainant.

(7)   Nothing in this section—   2–58

   (a) repealed

   (b) affects any prohibition or restriction imposed by virtue of any other enactment upon a publication, or upon matter included in a relevant programme;

       and a direction in pursuance of this section does not affect the operation of subsection (1) of this section at any time before the direction is given."

A "rape offence" is defined in section 7 as: rape, attempted rape, aiding,   2–59
abetting, counselling and procuring rape or attempted rape, incitement to rape, conspiracy to rape and burglary with intent to rape. The protection does not extend to complainants in other sexual offences such as indecent assault or incest. Child witnesses are of course already protected.

Care must always be taken in reporting rape cases to ensure that reported evidence cannot lead to the identification of the complainant by the public. For example, the disclosure of a nickname or, it is submitted, the citizen band radio call sign of a complainant may offend this provision.

III. COMPLAINANTS IN OTHER SEXUAL CASES

The Sexual Offences (Amendement) Act 1992, s.1 states: 2–60

    "(1) Where an allegation has been made that an offence to which this Act applies has been committed against a person, neither the name nor address, and no still or moving picture, of that person shall during that person's lifetime—

(a) be published in England and Wales in a written publication available to the public; or

(b) be included in a relevant programme for reception in England and Wales,

if it is likely to lead members of the public to identify that person as the person against whom the offence is alleged to have been committed.

2–61   (2) Where a person is accused of an offence to which this Act applies, no matter likely to lead members of the public to identify a person as the person against whom the offence is alleged to have been committed ('the complainant') shall during the complainant's lifetime—

(a) be published in England and Wales in a written publication available to the public; or

(b) be included in a relevant programme for reception in England and Wales.

2–62   (3) Subsections (1) and (2) are subject to any direction given under section 3.

(4) Nothing in this section prohibits the publication or inclusion in a relevant programme of matter consisting only of a report of criminal proceedings other than proceedings at, or intended to lead to, or on an appeal arising out of, a trial at which the accused is charged with the offence."

2–63   Section 2 states:

"(1) This Act applies to the following offences—

(a) any offence under any of the provisions of the Sexual Offences Act 1956 mentioned in subsection (2);

(b) any offence under section 128 of the Mental Health Act 1959 (intercourse with mentally handicapped person by hospital staff, etc);

(c) any offence under section 1 of the Indecency with Children Act 1960 (indecent conduct towards young children);

(d) any offence under section 54 of the Criminal Law Act 1977 (incitement by man of his grand-daughter, daughter or sister under the age of 16 to commit incest with him);

(e) any attempt to commit any of the offences mentioned in paragraphs (a) to (d).

2–64   (2) The provisions of the Act of 1956 are—

(a) section 2 (procurement of a woman by threats);

(b) section 3 (procurement of a woman by false pretences);

(c) section 4 (administering drugs to obtain intercourse with a woman);

(d) section 5 (intercourse with a girl under the age of 13);

(e) section 6 (intercourse with a girl between the ages of 13 and 16);

    (f)   section 7 (intercourse with a mentally handicapped person);

    (g)   section 9 (procurement of a mentally handicapped person);

    (h)   section 10 (incest by a man);

    (i)   section 11 (incest by a woman);

    (j)   section 12 (buggery);

    (k)   section 14 (indecent assault on a woman);

    (l)   section 15 (indecent assault on a man);

    (m) section 16 (assault with intent to commit buggery)."

Section 3 states: **2–65**

"(1) If, before the commencement of a trial at which a person is charged with an offence to which this Act applies, he or another person against whom the complainant may be expected to give evidence at the trial, applies to the judge for a direction under this subsection and satisfies the judge—

    (a)   that the direction is required for the purpose of inducing persons who are likely to be needed as witnesses at the trial to come forward; and

    (b)   that the conduct of the applicant's defence at the trial is likely to be substantially prejudiced if the direction is not given,

         the judge shall direct that section 1 shall not, by virtue of the accusation alleging the offence in question, apply in relation to the complainant.

(2) If at a trial the judge is satisfied—   **2–66**

    (a)   that the effect of section 1 is to impose a substantial and unreasonable restriction upon the reporting of proceedings at the trial, and

    (b)   that it is in the public interest to remove or relax the restriction,

         he shall direct that that section shall not apply to such matter as is specified in the direction.

(3) A direction shall not be given under subsection (2) by reason only of   **2–67**
the outcome of the trial.

(4) If a person who has been convicted of a offence and has given notice   **2–68**
of appeal against the conviction, or notice of an application for leave so to appeal, applies to the appellate court for a direction under this subsection and satisfies the court—

    (a)   that the direction is required for the purpose of obtaining evidence in support of the appeal; and

    (b)   that the applicant is likely to suffer substantial injustice if the direction is not given,

         the court shall direct that section 1 shall not, by virtue of an accusation which alleges an offence to which this Act applies and is specified in the direction, apply in relation to a complainant so specified.

(5) A direction given under any provision of this section does not affect   **2–69**
the operation of section 1 at any time before the direction is given.

(6) In subsections (1) and (2), 'judge' means—   **2–70**

    (a)   in the case of an offence which is to be tried summarily or for which the mode of trial has not been determined, any justice of the peace acting for the petty sessions area concerned; and

(b)   in any other case, any judge of the Crown Court.

2-71   (7)   If, after the commencement of a trial at which a person is charged with an offence to which this Act applies, a new trial of the person for that offence is ordered, the commencement of any previous trial shall be disregarded for the purposes of subsection (1)."

2-72   Section 4 states:

"(1)   in this section—

'section 10 offence' means an offence under section 10 of the Sexual Offences Act 1956 (incest by a man) or an attempt to commit that offence;

'section 11 offence' means an offence under section 11 of that Act (incest by a woman) or an attempt to commit that offence;

'section 12 offence' means an offence under section 12 of that Act (buggery) or an attempt to commit that offence."

Exceptions

2-73   (2)   "Section 1 does not apply to a woman against whom a section 10 offence is alleged to have been committed if she is accused of having committed a section 11 offence against the man who is alleged to have committed the section 10 offence against her.

2-74   (3)   Section 1 does not apply to a man against whom a section 11 offence is alleged to have been committed if he is accused of having committed a section 10 offence against the woman who is alleged to have committed the section 11 offence against him.

2-75   (4)   Section 1 does not apply to a person against whom a section 12 offence is alleged to have been committed if that person is accused of having committed a section 12 offence against the person who is alleged to have committed the section 12 offence against him.

2-76   (5)   Subsection (2) does not affect the operation of this Act in relation to anything done at any time before the woman is accused.

(6)   Subsection (3) does not affect the operation of this Act in relation to anything done at any time before the man is accused.

2-77   (7)   Subsection (4) does not affect the operation of this Act in relation to anything done at any time before the person mentioned first in that subsection is accused."

2-78   Section 5 states:

"(1)   If any matter is published or included in a relevant programme in contravention of section 1, the following persons shall be guilty of an offence and liable on summary conviction to a fine not exceeding level 5 on the standard scale-

(a)   in the case of publication in a newspaper or periodical, any proprietor, any editor and any publisher of the newspaper or periodical;

(b)   in the case of publication in any other form, the person publishing the matter; and

(c) in the case of matter included in a relevant programme—
  (i) any body corporate engaged in providing the service in which the programme is included; and
  (ii) any person having functions in relation to the programme corresponding to those of an editor of a newspaper.

(2) Where a person is charged with an offence under this section in respect of the publication of any matter or the inclusion of any matter in a relevant programme, it shall be a defence, subject to subsection (3), to prove that the publication or programme in which the matter appeared was one in respect of which the person against whom the offence mentioned in section 1 is alleged to have been committed had given written consent to the appearance of matter of that description. **2–79**

(3) Written consent is not a defence if it is proved that any person interfered unreasonably with the peace or comfort of the person giving the consent, with intent to obtain it. **2–80**

(4) Proceedings for an offence under this section shall not be instituted except by or with the consent of the Attorney-General. **2–81**

(5) Where a person is charged with an offence under this section it shall be a defence to prove that at the time of the alleged offence he was not aware, and neither suspected nor had reason to suspect, that the publication or programme in question was of, or (as the case may be) included, the matter in question. **2–82**

(6) Where an offence under this section committed by a body corporate is proved to have been committed with the consent or connivance of, or to be attributable to any neglect on the part of— **2–83**
  (a) a director, manager, secretary or other similar officer of the body corporate, or
  (b) a person purporting to act in any such capacity, he as well as the body corporate shall be guilty of the offence and liable to be proceeded against and punished accordingly.

(7) In relation to a body corporate whose affairs are managed by its members 'director', in subsection (6), means a member of the body corporate." **2–84**

Section 6 states: **2–85**

"(1) In this Act—
'complainant' has the meaning given in section 1(2);
'picture' includes a likeness however produced;
'relevant programme' means a programme included in a programme service, within the meaning of the Broadcasting Act 1990; and
'written publication' includes a film, a sound track and any other record in permanent form but does not include an indictment or other document prepared for use in particular legal proceedings.

(2) For the purposes of this Act— **2–86**
  (a) where it is alleged that an offence to which this act applies has been committed, the fact that any person has consented to an act which, on any prosecution for that offence, would fall to be

proved by the prosecution, does not prevent that person from being regarded as a person against whom the alleged offence was committed; and

(b) where a person is accused of an offence of incest or buggery, the other party to the act in question shall be taken to be a person against whom the offence was committed even though he consented to that act.

2–87   (3) For the purposes of this Act, a person is accused of an offence if—

(a) an information is laid alleging that he has committed the offence,

(b) he appears before a court charged with the offence,

(c) a court before which he is appearing commits him for trial on a new charge alleging the offence, or

(d) a bill of indictment charging him with the offence is preferred before a court in which he may lawfully be indicted for the offence,

and references in section 3 to an accusation alleging an offence shall be construed accordingly.

2–88   (4) Nothing in this Act affects any prohibition or restriction imposed by virtue of any other enactment upon a publication or upon matter included in a relevant programme."

IV. Screens, Television Links And Video Recorded Evidence In Chief

2–89   There has developed, either through statute or case law, a number of ways of reducing the trauma for a witness, especially a child witness, when having to give evidence before a court and in the presence of the defendant. These range from the use of screens, where the witness is hidden from the view of the defendant, to the giving of evidence through the medium of a live television link, thus avoiding the need for the witness to be in the courtroom at all and finally the giving of the evidence in chief of a child witness by means of a pre-recorded video recording.

(a) Screens

2–90   It seems that the first case to consider preventing a child witness from being under the gaze of the defendant when testifying against him, was that of *R v. Smellie* [1919] 14 Cr.App.R. 128, when the court ordered the accused to sit on the stairs leading out of the dock, out of sight of the young witness. On appeal it was held that that was a perfectly proper procedure.

2–91   In 1989, the subject of preventing the witness seeing the defendant was again considered in the case of *D.J.X.,S.C.Y.,G.C.Z.* (1990) 91 Cr.App.R. 36. The applicants, X,Y and Z were all related to the child witnesses (aged between eight and 12) by either blood or marriage and, in the words of the Lord Chief Justice, the former abused the latter: "in almost every permutation of sexual perversion which one can imagine". At first instance, the judge permitted screens to be placed in court to prevent the child witnesses from being able to see those in the dock or to be seen by those in the dock. The judge had received representations from the prosecution that some of the witnesses would be unwilling or unable to speak as to the facts if confronted in court by seeing those against whom they had to give evidence, particularly their own father or relations. Ten days before the trial was due to start, the judge assembled counsel and sought to obtain their views on the use of screens. The judge had had a screen placed in the proposed position in court so that it was apparent that only the defendants would be unable to see the witnesses. Defence counsel objected but the judge decided that the screen should be used. At the outset of the trial, the judge said to the jury that they should not allow the presence of the screens to prejudice them against any of the defendants and that the purpose of the screens was to prevent children from being intimidated by their surroundings.

Following conviction, the appellants (applying for leave to appeal) con-   **2–92**
tended, *inter alia*, that the use of screens was unfair and prejudicial, the suggestion from the presence of the screen being that the jury might have been unduly influenced, unfairly prejudiced against the defendants by seeing the screen there, and the jury might think that there was a suggestion that the person in the dock had already in some way intimidated the child who was going to give evidence. It was held, dismissing the applications that the judge has a duty to see that justice is done and that the system operates fairly not only to the defendants but also to the prosecution and the witnesses. In this case he came to the conclusion that the necessity of trying to ensure that these children would be able to give evidence outweighed any possible prejudice to the defendants by the erection of screens. The Lord Chief Justice said (at 40): "This Court agrees with him in that view. We do not think, even without the warning which the learned judge did give to the jury, that any sensible jury could have been prejudiced against any defendant by the existence of this barrier between the witnesses and the dock. We take the view that what the learned judge here did in his discretion was a perfectly proper, and indeed a laudable attempt to see that this was a fair trial: fair to all."

(b) Other uses for screens

The use of screens need not be restricted to child witnesses. In *R v. Schaub*   **2–93**
and Cooper (Joey), *The Times*, December 3, 1993, the Court of Appeal held that it was permissible to make use of a screen or other similar protective device in the case of any witness if it was otherwise impossible to do justice. However, in the case of an adult witness, such a course should be adopted only in the most exceptional cases.

In *R v.Taylor*, *The Times*, August 17, 1994, the defendant was charged   **2–94**
with perverting the course of justice in that he had been involved in disposing of the body of a murder victim. The only corroborative evidence of three witnesses, who the judge directed the jury were or might be accomplices, was that of a witness whom the judge permitted to give her evidence from behind a screen and whose name and address he ruled should not be disclosed. On appeal, it was held that it was a fundamental right of a defendant to see and

know the identity of his accusers, including witnesses for the Crown, which should only be denied in rare and exceptional cases. Whether such circumstances existed was pre-eminently a decision for the exercise of the trial judge's discretion. In exercising that discretion, first there must be real grounds for fear of the consequences if the evidence were given and the identity of the witness revealed; secondly, the evidence must be sufficiently relevant and important to make it unfair to make the Crown proceed without it; thirdly, the Crown must satisfy the court that the creditworthiness of the witness had been fully investigated and disclosed; fourthly, the court must be satisfied that there would be no undue prejudice to the accused; and fifthly, the court could balance the need for protection of witnesses, including the extent of that protection, against unfairness or the appearance of unfairness.

2-95   In *R v. F* (unreported, October 20, 1994) the witness, who was the defendants step-daughter and the complainant on the charge of rape, was aged 20 by the time she was required to give evidence. The Crown applied successfully for her to testify from behind a screen. F appealed on the ground that it was only in very exceptional cases that screens should be ordered for an adult. It was held that while it was by no means the case that every rape complaint or prosecution for a sexual offence would involve the use of screens, it doubted that the use of screens in this case was prejudicial to the accused.

(c) Television links

2-96   By virtue of section 32 of the Criminal Justice Act 1988, the court can, in certain circumstances, hear the evidence of a child witness through a live television link. The section also enables witnesses, in certain cases, outside the jurisdiction to give live evidence without the need for them physically to attend court.

2-97   Section 32 states:

"(1)   A person other than the accused may give evidence through a live television link in proceedings to which subsection (1A) below applies if—
    (a)   the witness is outside the United Kingdom; or
    (b)   the witness is a child, or is to be cross-examined following the admission under section 32A below of a video recording of testimony from him, and the offence is one to which subsection (2) below applies;
but evidence may not be given without the leave of the court.
(1A)   This subsection applies—
    (a)   to trials on indictment, appeals to the criminal division of the Court of Appeal and hearings of references under section 17 of the Criminal Appeal Act 1968; and
    (b)   to proceedings in youth courts and appeals to the Crown Court arising out of such proceedings.

2-98   (2)   This subsection applies—

(a) to an offence which involves an assault on, or injury or a threat of injury to, a person;

(b) to an offence under section 1 of the Children and Young Persons Act 1933 (cruelty to persons under 16);

(c) to an offence under the Sexual Offences Act 1956, the Indency with Children Act 1960, the Sexual Offences Act 1967, section 54 of the Criminal Law Act 1977 or the Protection of Children Act 1978; and

(d) to an offence which consists of attempting or conspiring to commit, or of aiding, abetting, counselling, procuring or inciting the commission of, an offence falling within paragraph (a), (b) or (c) above.

(3) A statement made on oath by a witness outside the United Kingdom and given in evidence through a link by virtue of this section shall be treated for the purposes of section 1 of the Perjury Act 1911 as having been made in the proceedings in which it is given in evidence.

(3A) Where, in the case of any proceedings before a youth court—

(a) leave is given by virtue of subsection (1)(b) above for evidence to be given through a television link; and

(b) suitable facilities for receiving such evidence are not available at any petty-sessional court-house in which the court can (apart from this subsection) lawfully sit, the court may sit for the purposes of the whole or part of those proceedings at any place at which such facilities are available and which has been appointed for the purposes of this subsection by the justices acting for the petty sessions area for which the court acts.

(3B) A place appointed under subsection (3A) above may be outside the petty sessions area for which it is appointed; but it shall be deemed to be in that area for the purposes of the jurisdiction of the justices acting for that area."

(d) The Criminal Procedure and Investigations Act 1996

The Criminal Procedure and Investigations Act 1996, s. 62 inserts subsections 32(3C), (3D) and (3E) into the 1988 Act. These subsections came into force on January 1, 1997 and apply where the leave concerned is given on or after that date.

2–99

Section 32 states:

"(3C)Where—

(a) the court gives leave for a person to give evidence through a live television link, and

(b) the leave is given by virtue of subsection (1)(b) above, then, subject to subsection (3D) below, the person concerned may not give evidence otherwise than through a live television link.

(3D) In a case falling within subsection (3C) above the court may give permission for the person to give evidence otherwise than through a live television link if it appears to the court to be in the interests of justice to give such permission.

(3E) Permission may be given under subsection (3D) above—
    (a) on an application by a party to the case, or
    (b) of the court's own motion;
but no application may be made under paragraph (a) above unless there has been a material change of circumstances since the leave was given by virtue of subsection (1)(b) above."

(Subsections (4)–(5) not printed.)

2–100   "(6) Subsection (7) of section 32A below shall apply for the purposes of this section as it applies for the purposes of that section, but with the omission of the references to a person being, in the cases there mentioned, under the age of fifteen years or under the age of eighteen years."

2–101   The provision for the evidence of a witness outside the United Kingdom to be given through a television link only applies in respect of proceedings for murder, manslaughter or any other offence consisting of the killing of any person, and proceedings being conducted by the Director of the Serious Fraud Office under section 1(5) of the Criminal Justice Act 1987, or proceedings in which a notice of transfer has been given under section 4 of that Act.

2–102   Pursuant to sections 32(4) and (5) of the 1988 Act, rules were made in respect of applications for evidence to be heard through a television link: rule 23A of the Crown Court Rules 1982 governs applications concerning the evidence of child witnesses, and rule 23B, witnesses outside the United Kingdom.

Rules 23A and 23B state that any party may apply for leave under section 32(1) and (1)(b) of the 1988 Act for evidence to be given through a television link where either the witness is outside the United Kingdom (r. 23B(1)), or where (r. 23 A(1))—

"(a) the offence charged is one to which section 32(2) of the 1988 Act applies; and
(b) the evidence is to be given by a witness who is either—
    (i) in the case of a offence falling within section 32(2)(a) or (b), under the age of 14; or
    (ii) in the case of an offence falling within section 32(2)(c), under the age of 17; or
    (iii) a person who is to be cross-examined following the admission under section 32A of the 1988 Act of a video recording of testimony from him."

2–103   Applications shall be made by giving notice in writing in the prescribed form (r. 23A(2) and r. 23B(3)) (see App. 5), and should be sent by the applicant, to the appropriate officer of the Crown Court and a copy thereof to every other party to the proceedings (r. 23A(4) and r. 23B(6)). An application which relates to a witness outside the United Kingdom and falls to be determined by the Crown Court may be dealt with by any Judge of the Crown Court in chambers (r. 23B(2)).

(e) Time requirement

The application must be made within 28 days after the date of committal, or   2–104
of the preferment of a bill of indictment, or of the giving of a notice of transfer under section 4(1)(c) of the Criminal Justice Act 1987, or (in the case of child witnesses) of the service of notice of transfer under section 53 of the Criminal Justice Act 1991 or of the service of Notice of Appeal from a decision of a youth court or magistrates' court (r. 23A(3) and r. 23B(4)).

This period of 28 days may be extended by the Crown Court, either before   2–105
of after it expires, on an application made in writing, specifying the grounds of the application (r. 23A(8) and r. 23B(5)). The application for extension shall be sent to the appropriate officer of the Crown Court and a copy thereof shall be sent by the applicant to every other party to the proceedings (r. 23A(8) and r. 23B(6)). Such an application shall be determined by a judge of the Crown Court without a hearing unless the judge otherwise directs (r. 23A(9)). The decision of the judge will be notified to the parties by an appropriate officer of the Crown Court (r. 23A(8) and r. 23B(5)).

Where the application is for the evidence of a child to be heard through a   2–106
television link, a party who receives a copy of the notice and wishes to oppose it must notify the applicant and the Court in writing of his opposition within 14 days and specify his reasons for the opposition (r. 23A(5)). The application shall be determined by a judge of the Crown Court without a hearing unless the judge otherwise directs and the appropriate officer of the Crown Court shall notify the parties of the time and place of any such hearing (r. 23A(6)). The appropriate officer of the Crown Court shall notify all the parties and any person who is to accompany the witness of the decision of the judge.

(f) Notification

If the application for the television link is granted, the notification shall   2–107
state—

   (a)   where the witness is to give evidence on behalf of the prosecutor, the name of the witness, and, if known, the name, occupation and relationship (if any) to the witness of any person who is to accompany the witness, and
   (b)   the location of the Crown Court at which the trial should take place (r. 23A(7)). The witness can only be accompanied by a person who is acceptable to the judge, and unless the judge otherwise directs, by no other person (r. 23A(10)).

Where the application for the television link is in respect of a witness   2–108
outside the United Kingdom, any party receiving a copy of the application for the link has 28 days within which to notify the applicant and the Court in writing whether or not he opposes the application, giving his reason, and

whether or not he wishes to be represented at any hearing of the application (r. 23B(7)). After the expiry of the 28 days, the Court shall determine whether the application is to be dealt with without a hearing, or at a hearing at which the applicant and such other party as the court may direct may be represented, the Court notifying the parties of the time and place (r. 23B(8)).

2–109   If the application for the link is granted, the Court shall notify the parties and the notification shall state:

(a) the country in which the witness will give evidence;
(b) if known, the place where the witness will give evidence;
(c) where the witness is to give evidence on behalf of the prosecutor, or where disclosure is required by section 11 of the Criminal Justice Act 1967 (alibi) or by rules under section 81 of the Police and Criminal Evidence Act 1984 (expert evidence), the name of the witness;
(d) the location of the Crown Court at which the trial should take place; and
(e) any conditions specified by the Crown Court in accordance with paragraph (10) (r. 23B(9)).

2–110   Where the Court grants an application under rule 23B(1), it may specify that as a condition of the grant, the witness should give the evidence in the presence of a specified person who is able and willing to answer under oath or affirmation any question the trial judge may put as to the circumstances in which the evidence is given, including questions about any persons who are present when the evidence is given and any matters which may affect the giving of the evidence (r. 23B(10)).

2–111   Rules concerning the hearing of the evidence of a child witness through a television link before the magistrates' court are governed by the Magistrates' Court (Children and Young Persons) Rules 1992, s. 23 which are in essence the same as those for the Crown court except that all applications are made to the clerk to the justices and decisions are made by a justice of the peace.

2–112   The Criminal Appeal Rules 1968, rr.9A and 9B, govern the procedure for the use of the television link where the party to an appeal applies for leave to call witnesses.

(g) Video evidence

2–113   The ability of the testimony of a child to be given to the court through the medium of a previously made video recording is subject to the Sexual Offences (Protected Material) Act 1997 and is governed by section 32A of the Criminal Justice Act 1988:

"(1) This section applies in relation to the following proceedings, namely—
(a) trials on indictment for any offence to which section 32(2) applies;

    (b) appeals to the criminal division of the Court of Appeal and hearings of references under section 17 of the Criminal Appeal Act 1968 in respect of any such offence; and

    (c) proceedings in youth courts for any such offence and appeals to the Crown Court arising out of such proceedings.

(2) in any such proceedings a video recording of an interview which—   **2–114**

    (a) is conducted between an adult and a child who is not the accused or one of the accused ('the child witness'); and

    (b) relates to any matter in issue in the proceedings, may, with the leave of the court, be given in evidence in so far as it is not excluded by the court under subsection (3) below.

(3) Where a video recording is tendered in evidence under this section,   **2–115** the court shall (subject to the exercise of any power of the court to exclude evidence which is otherwise admissible) give leave under subsection (2) above unless—

    (a) it appears that the child witness will not be available for cross-examination;

    (b) any rules of court requiring disclosure of the circumstances in which the recording was made have not been complied with to the satisfaction of the court; or

    (c) the court is of the opinion, having regard to all the circumstances of the case, that in the interests of justice the recording ought not to be admitted;

and where the court gives such leave it may, if it is of the opinion that in the interests of justice any part of the recording ought not to be admitted, direct that that part shall be excluded.

(4) In considering whether any part of a recording ought to be excluded   **2–116** under subsection (3) above, the court shall consider whether any prejudice to the accused, or one of the accused, cwhich might result from the admission of that part is outweighed by the desirability of showing the whole, or substantially the whole, of the recorded interview.

(5) Where a video recording is admitted under this section—   **2–117**

    (a) the child witness shall be called by the party who tendered it in evidence;

    (b) that witness shall not be examined in chief on any matter which, in the opinion of the court, has been dealt with in his recorded testimony.

(6) Where a video recording is given in evidence under this section, any   **2–118** statement made by the child witness which is disclosed by the recording shall be treated as if given by that witness in direct oral testimony; and accordingly—

    (a) any such statement shall be admissible evidence of any fact of which such testimony from him would be admissible;

    (b) no such statement shall be capable of corroborating any other evidence given by him;

and in estimating the weight, if any, to be attached to such a statement, regard shall be had to all the circumstances from which any inference can reasonably be drawn (as to its accuracy or otherwise)."

2-119   The Criminal Procedure and Investigations Act 1996, s. 62 inserts subsections (6A) to (6D) into the 1988 Act. The subsections came into force January 1, 1997 and apply where the leave concerned is given on or after that date:

"(6A)Where the court gives leave under subsection (2) above the child witness shall not give relevant evidence (within the meaning given by subsection (6D) below) otherwise than by means of the video recording; but this is subject to subsection (6B) below.

(6B) In a case falling within subsection (6A) above the court may give permission for the child witness to give relevant evidence (within the meaning given by subsection (6D) below) otherwise than by means of the video recording if it appears to the court to be in the interests of justice to give such permission.

(6C) Permission may be given under subsection (6B) above—

(a) on an application by a party to the case, or

(b) of the court's own motion;

but no application may be made under paragraph (a) above unless there has been a material change of circumstances since the leave was given under subsection (2) above.

(6D) For the purposes of subsections (6A) and (6B) above evidence is relevant evidence if—

(a) it is evidence in chief on behalf of the party who tendered the video recording, and

(b) it relates to matter which, in the opinion of the court, is dealt with in the recording and which the court has not directed to be excluded under subsection (3) above.

2-120   (7) In this section 'child' means a person who—

(a) in the case of an offence falling within section 32(2)(a) or (b) above, is under fourteen years of age or, if he was under that age when the video recording was made, is under fifteen years of age; or

(b) in the case of an offence falling within section 32(2)(c) above, is under seventeen years of age or, if he was under that age when the video recording was made, is under eighteen years of age.

2-121   (8) Any reference in subsection (7) above to an offence falling within paragraph (a), (b) or (c) of section 32(2) above includes a reference to an offence which consists of attempting or conspiring to commit, or of aiding, abetting, counselling, procuring or inciting the commission of, an offence falling within that paragraph.

(9) In this section—

'statement' includes any representation of fact, whether made in words or otherwise;

'video recording' means any recording, on any medium, from which a moving image may by any means be produced and includes the accompanying sound-track.

2-122   (10) A magistrates' court inquiring into an offence as examining justices

under section 6 of the Magistrates' Courts Act 1980 may consider any video recording as respects which leave under subsection (2) above is to be sought at the trial, notwithstanding that the child witness is not called at the committal proceedings."
(Subsection (11) not printed.)

"(12) Nothing in this section shall prejudice the admissibility of any video   **2–123**
recording which would be admissible apart from this section.

Pursuant to section 32A(11) of the 1988 Act, rules were made governing   **2–124**
the procedure for the use of video recordings of testimony in the Crown Court, magistrates' court and appellate courts."

Section 23C(1) of the Crown Court Rules 1982 states that: **2–125**

"any party may apply for leave under section 32A of the 1988 Act to tender in evidence a video recording of testimony from a witness where—
  (a) the offence charged is one to which section 32(2) of that Act applies;
  (b) in the case of an offence falling within section 32(2)(a) or (b), the proposed witness is under the age of 14 or, if he was under 14 when the video recording was made, is under the age of 15;
  (c) in the case of an offence falling within section 32(2)(c), the proposed witness is under the age of 17 or, if he was under 17 when the video recording was made, is under the age of 18; and
  (d) the video recording is of an interview conducted between an adult and a person coming within sub-paragraph (b) or (c) above (not being the accused or one of the accused) which relates to any matter in issue in the proceedings."

(h) Requirements

Section 23C(2) states: **2–126**

"An application under paragraph (1) shall be made by giving notice in writing which shall be in the form prescribed in Schedule 7 or a form to the like effect. The application shall be accompanied by the video recording which it is proposed to tender in evidence and shall include the following namely—
  (a) the name of the defendant and the offence or offences charged;
  (b) the name and date of birth of the witness in respect of whom the application is made;
  (c) the date on which the video recording was made;
  (d) a statement that in the opinion of the applicant the witness is willing and able to attend the trial for cross-examination;
  (e) a statement of the circumstances in which the video recording was made which complies with paragraph (4); and
  (f) the date on which the video recording was disclosed to the other party or parties."

If it is proposed to tender only part of a video recording, the application must specify which part and be accompanied by the whole video recording" (s.23C(3)). (See App. 6.)

2–127   Section 23C(4) states:

"The statement of the circumstances in which the video recording was made referred to in paragraphs (2)(e) and (3) above shall include the following information, except in so far as it is contained in the recording itself, namely—
    (a) the times at which the recording commenced and finished, including details of any interruptions;
    (b) the location at which the recording was made and the usual function of the premises;
    (c) the name, age and occupation of any person present at any point during the recording; the time for which he was present; his relationship (if any) to the witness and to the defendant;
    (d) a description of the equipment used including the number of cameras used and whether they were fixed or mobile; the number and location of microphones; the video format used and whether there were single or multiple recording facilities;
    (e) the location of the mastertape if the video recording is a copy and details of when and by whom the copy was made."

2–128   The application must be made within 28 days of the date of the committal for trial, or the giving of a notice of transfer under section 53 of the Criminal Justice Act 1991, or of consent to the preferment of a bill of indictment in relation to the case, or of the service of Notice of Appeal from a decision of a youth court or magistrates' court (s.23C(5)). This period of 28 days may be extended by a judge of the Crown Court either before or after it expires on an application made in writing specifying the grounds of the application (s.23C(6)).

2–129   Notices under sections 23C(2) or (6) must be sent by the applicant, to the appropriate officer of the Crown Court with copies thereof to every other party to the proceedings. The notice shall be accompanied by copies of the video recording, if copies have not already been supplied. Where the defendant is unrepresented, a copy of the recording shall be made available for viewing by him (s.23C(7)).

2–130   Section 23C(8) states:

"A party who receives a copy of the notice under paragraph (2) shall, within 14 days of service of the notice, notify the applicant and the appropriate officer of the Crown Court in writing—
    (a) whether he objects to the admission of any part of the recording or recordings disclosed, giving his reasons why it would not be in the interests of justice for it to be admitted; and
    (b) whether he would agree to the admission of part of the video recording or recordings disclosed and if so, which part or parts; and
    (c) whether he wishes to be represented at any hearing of the application."

Section 23C(9) states: 2–131

"After the expiry of the period referred to in paragraph (8), a judge of the Crown Court shall determine whether an application under paragraph (1) is to be dealt with—

(a) without a hearing; or

(b) where any party notifies the appropriate officer of the Crown Court pursuant to paragraph (8) that he objects to the admission of any part of the video recording and that he wishes to be represented at any hearing, or in any other case where the judge so directs, at a hearing at which the applicant and such other party or parties as the judge may direct may be represented, and the appropriate officer of the Crown Court shall notify the applicant and, where necessary, the other party or parties of the time and place of any such hearing."

Once the judge has made a decision in respect of an application for leave to   2–132
tender a video recording, the appropriate officer of the Court has three days within which to notify all the parties of the decision. If leave is granted, the notification shall state whether the whole or specified parts only of the recordings are to be admitted in evidence (s.23C(10)).

(i) Other provisions

The Magistrates' Court (Children and Young Persons) Rules 1992, s. 24   2–133
governs the procedure for an application for leave to tender in evidence a video recording of testimony. They are in essence the same as the rules in respect of the Crown Court except that notices must be sent to the clerk to the justices and any decisions are made by a justice of the peace.

The Criminal Appeal Rules 1968, r.9C determines the procedure to be   2–134
used when a party to an appeal applies for leave to tender in evidence a video recording of testimony from a witness.

The *Practice Direction (Crime: Child's Video Evidence)* [1992] 1 W.L.R.   2–135
839, states that "where a court grants leave to admit a video recording in evidence under section 32A(2) of the 1988 Act, it may direct that any part of the recording be excluded. When such a direction is given, the party who made the application to admit the recording must edit the recording in accordance with the judge's direction and send a copy of the edited recording to the appropriate officer of the Crown Court and to every other party to the proceedings".

During proceedings, the recording should be produced and proved by the   2–136
interviewer, or any other person who was present at the interview at which the recording was made, either by live testimony or by a written statement accepted by the parties.

It is for the party adducing the recording to make arrangements for the   2–137
operation of the video playing equipment during the trial. Once a trial has begun, if by reason of faulty or inadequate preparation or for some other cause, the procedures set out have not been properly complied with, and an application is made to edit the recording thus requiring an adjournment, the court may make at its discretion an appropriate award of costs.

(j) R v. Day

2–138   It was held in *R v. Day (Barry Ronald)*, *The Times*, March 8,1996, that the video recording of an unsworn interview might be put before the court even if by the time of the trial, the witness was old enough to be sworn.

2–139   When a video recording is to be admitted as evidence in chief, the judge has a power (although he is not under any duty to do so) to conduct a preliminary investigation of the child's competence to give evidence where he considered that there was a question as to the child's knowledge of the difference between truth and falsehood and the importance of telling the truth (*R v. Hampshire* [1995] 2 All E.R. 1019).

In this case, the appellant was charged with two counts of indecent assault upon a nine-year old girl, S. The police videotaped an interview with S, at the end of which the interviewer discussed with her the difference between telling a lie and telling the truth. The prosecution applied for leave under section 32A of the 1988 Act for the video recording to be played as her evidence in chief. The recorder watched the video before the trial, concluded that S was competent to give evidence and that there was no other interest of justice which prevented him from granting leave for her to do so in chief through the medium of the video. At trial, the video recording was shown to the jury. On conclusion of S's evidence the recorder realised that he had not investigated S's competence as a witness in the presence of the jury by asking her whether she understood the difference between telling the truth and lies and the importance of telling the truth. S was therefore recalled and, in the presence of the jury, the recorder satisfied himself as to her competence to give the evidence that she had already given.

2–140   Appealing against conviction, the appellant contended that the recorder's failure to establish for himself, in the presence of the jury and before the video recording was played to them, S's understanding of the truth and the importance of telling it, was a material irregularity which vitiated the conviction and was not cured by the recorder's subsequent actions. Held, dismissing the appeal, that although a judge was under no duty to conduct a preliminary investigation of a child's competence to give evidence, he retained the power to do so where he considered that there was a question as to the child's knowledge of the difference between truth and falsehood and the importance of telling the truth. In those cases where a judge considered it necessary to investigate a child's competence to give evidence in addition to or without the benefit of an earlier view of the videotaped interview, he should do so in open court in the presence of the accused because it was a part of the trial, but need not do so in the presence of the jury. The jury's function was to assess the child's evidence, including its weight, from the evidence he or she gave on the facts of the case after the child had been found competent to give it, and the exercise of determining competence was not a necessary aid to that function. On the facts, the recorder was justifiably satisfied from his pre-trial view of the video recording as to S's competence to give evidence. Accordingly, he had no duty to investigate the matter again with her at all or in the presence of the jury.

2–141   In *R v. Springer* [1996] Crim.L.R. 903, the appellant was convicted of two counts of indecent assault and one count of rape. The victim was aged four years when the appellant's conduct started and nine at the time of the trial. Her evidence-in-chief was given by way of video-recorded interview, of which the jury were given a transcript. The defence applied, unsuccessfully, to the trial judge for the video to be excluded on the ground that the substance of her evidence was hearsay. That the child was repeating what she had been told by her mother.

On appeal, the court held that although the judge could not be criticised for having permitted the jury to see the video, he had failed to give them any warning about the risks of attaching undue weight to the transcript of that evidence. He had also in his summing-up failed to refer to the defence submission that there was a least a risk that the account given by the victim was not her own. The judge should give a balanced, clear summing up adverting, where necessary, to specific problems that could arise when video evidence was sought to be adduced before the jury. The conviction was unsafe, the appeal was therefore allowed but a retrial was ordered.

In civil cases, it is worth noting that a different approach is taken. In *R N (a Minor) (Child abuse: Evidence) The Times*, March 3, 1996, it was held that where a video recording was admitted into court as a form of hearsay evidence the judge could hear expert evidence to help him decide its weight and credibility and whether or not the child should be believed.

If the child retracts its allegations following a recorded interview, the video recording should not be tendered as the child's evidence-in-chief, but the child should be called to give its evidence before the jury (*R v. Parker*, unreported, December 18, 1995, C.A.). **2–142**

(k) Jury requests

There are occasions when the jury, following retirement, asks that they be permitted a second viewing of the video recording. In *R v. Rawlings and Broadbent* [1995] 2 Cr.App.R. 222, it was held, Lord Taylor C.J giving the judgment of the Court, that it was a matter for the judge's discretion whether the jury's request should be granted or refused, bearing in mind the need to guard against unfairness deriving from the replay of only the evidence in chief of the complainant. Usually, if the jury simply wished to be reminded of what the witness had said, it would be sufficient and most expeditious to remind them from the judge's own note. However, if the jury indicated that how the words were spoken was of importance to them, the judge might in his discretion, allow the video or the relevant part of it to be replayed. The judge should enquire of the jury their reasons for wanting to see the recordings again. Where a replay was permitted the judge should comply with three requirements: **2–143**

    (a)   the replay should be in court with judge, counsel and defendant present;

    (b)   the judge should warn the jury, because it was hearing the evidence in chief of the complainant a second time after all the other evidence, to guard against giving it disproportionate weight and to bear in mind the other evidence; and

> (c) the judge should remind the jury of the cross-examination and re-examination from his notes.

2-144   In *R v. M* unreported, April 10, 1994, a case which was heard at first instance before the decision in *R v. Rawlings and Broadbent*, the Court of Appeal held that where the judge had allowed a replay of the video recording but had failed to observe what became the third of the requirements given in *R v. Rawlings and Broadbent*, the appeal should be allowed.

2-145   *R v. Rawlings and Broadbent* was distinguished in *R v. Dennis Saunders* [1995] 2 Cr.App.R 313. In this case, during the summing-up, the jury sent a note to the judge seeking a transcript of the video evidence of the complainant. The judge refused, but reminded the jury that the whole or part of the video evidence could be shown if so requested. The jury asked to see the video again. The judge told the jury that they could ask to be reminded of the cross-examination, but no request was made. On appeal, it was argued that the judge should have reminded the jury of the cross-examination and re-examination of the complainant from his notes, whether or not the jury asked him to do so. Held dismissing the appeal, that the judge had referred in detail to the cross-examination of the complainant in summing-up. The jury had not requested any further assistance although they were expressly told that they could have it if they wished. No useful purpose would have been served by further repetition of the cross-examination. As far as the third requirement in *R v. Rawlings and Broadbent* was concerned the Court did not accept (at 318)," that the Lord Chief Justice could ever have intended to require a judge to remind the jury yet again of cross-examination after that judge had taken the care that [the judge at first instance] did in this case."

2-146   In *R v. M (Criminal evidence: Replaying video)*, *The Times*, November 29, 1995, the Court of Appeal held that generally speaking an application for a video of a complainant's evidence to be played for a second time should be granted only if it was made specifically by the jury (in this case it was made by counsel for the Crown). A replay should be discouraged as being a departure from the normal course of the way in which evidence at a criminal trial was heard and in general any departure should only be made if there were exceptional circumstances.

2-147   Despite the judge at first instance in *R v. Dennis Saunders* (above) being of the opinion that a jury could not have a transcript of the video recording, there have been occasions when it has been permitted.
    In *R v. Coshall*, *The Times*, February 17, 1995, the Court of Appeal held that the safeguards imposed for the replaying of the recording applied equally to the transcript since there was a serious risk of disproportionate weight being attached to the complainant's evidence in chief, as against the rest of the evidence including the cross-examination and the evidence of the defendant and his witnesses. Where both defence and prosecution agree, there could be no objection to supplying the jury with the transcript provided the jury were reminded of the other evidence and the status of the transcript in the context of the evidence as a whole. In the face of defence objections, it would not normally be appropriate to supply the transcript to the jury.

2-148   The matter was further considered in *R v. Welstead* (unreported, 1995) where it was decided that it was permissible for the jury to be supplied with a transcript of the video recording provided that:

(a) the transcript will be likely to assist the jury in following the evidence of the witness;

(b) the judge makes clear to the jury that the transcript is made available to them only for that limited purpose and that they should concentrate primarily on the oral evidence; and

(c) the judge gives the jury such directions, both when the transcript is made available and in the summing-up, as will be likely to be effective safeguards against the risk of disproportionate weight being given to the transcript. (See also *R v. Springer*, at para. 2–133 above.)

E. PROTECTION FROM CROSS-EXAMINATION

I. CHILDREN

Children are protected from cross-examination. The calling of children to give evidence at committal proceedings is governed by section 103 of the Magistrates Court Act 1980, which provides: 2–149

"(1) In any proceedings before a magistrates' court inquiring into an offence to which this section applies as examining justices—

    (a) a child shall not be called as a witness for the prosecution; but

    (b) any statement made by or taken from a child shall be admissible in evidence of any matter of which his oral testimony would be admissible,

    except in a case where the application of this subsection is excluded under subsection (3) below.

(2) This section applies—   2–150

    (a) to an offence which involves an assault, or injury or a threat of injury to, a person;

    (b) to an offence under section 1 of the Children and Young Persons Act 1933 (cruelty to persons under 16);

    (c) to an offence under the Sexual Offences Act 1956, the Indecency with Children Act 1960, the Sexual Offences Act 1967, section 54 of the Criminal Law Act 1977 or the Protection of Children Act 1978; and

    (d) to an offence which consists of attempting or conspiring to commit, or of aiding, abetting, counselling, procuring or inciting the commission of, an offence falling within paragraph (a), (b) or (c) above.

(3) The application of subsection (1) above is excluded—   2–151

    (b) where the prosecution requires the attendance of the child for the purpose of establishing the identity of any person; or

       (c)   where the court is satisfied that it has not been possible to obtain from the child a statement that may be given in evidence under this section; or

       (d)   where the inquiry into the offence takes place after the court has discontinued to try it summarily and the child has given evidence in the summary trial.

2–152   (4)   Section 28 above shall not apply to any statement admitted in pursuance of subsection (1) above.

2–153   (5)   In this section 'child' has the same meaning as in section 53 of the Criminal Justice Act 1991.

2–154   It should be noted that in sexual cases the prosecution have to submit the child's statement under section 103(1) unless one of the exceptions in section 103(3) applies."

2–155   The Criminal Justice Act 1988, s.34A states that no person who is charged with an offence to which section 32(2) applies (which includes an offence under the Sexual Offences Act 1956; Indecency with Children Act 1960; Sexual Offences Act 1967, Criminal Law Act 1977, s.54; Protection of Children Act 1978 and offences of attempting, conspiring, aiding, abetting, counselling, procuring or inciting the commission of them: s.32(2)(c) and (a)):

"shall cross-examine in person any witness who—
     (a)   is alleged—
        (i)   to be a person against whom the offence was committed; or
       (ii)   to have witnessed the commission of the offence; and
     (b)   is a child, or is to be cross-examined following the admission under section 32A of a video recording of testimony from him."

The child must be under 17 years in this case (ss.34A(2), 32A and 32(2)(c)).

II. Cross-Examination As To Sexual Matters

There are a number of restrictions upon the cross-examination of complainants and witnesses concerning sexual matters.

2–156   The Bar Code states that no barrister may be used by a client as a tool or device to make allegations against any other party, whether witness, complainant or person who has had no specific connection with the trial, unless he or she has satisfied himself or herself, first, that there is reasonable foundation, and secondly, that it is proper in the general administration of justice.

(a) Common law

2–157   At common law, the basic rule is that no evidence is admissible unless it is relevant to the proceedings.

The complainant may be cross-examined as to his or her sexual history in some circumstances and contradictory evidence may be called by the defence where the matters relate to a fact in issue, such as consent, but contradictory evidence may not be called where the matters are collateral or go only to credit.

The complainant can always be cross-examined about previous sexual   2-158
intercourse with the defendant as it directly affects the issue of consent on the occasion complained of—R v. Riley [1887] 18 Q.B.D. 481.

His or her history of sexual intercourse with other men may be the subject   2-159
of cross-examination but the answers are normally final and cannot be the subject of rebuttal evidence, subject to a number of exceptions—R v. Holmes [1871] L.R. 1 C.C.R. 334. The exceptions relate to the question of consent with the defendant on the occasion complained of.

So, in R v. Ahmed [1994] Crim.L.R. 669, the defence disputed that an act   2-160
of buggery with the complainant was non-consensual. It was held that the defence could cross-examine the complainant as to her previous sexual history with other men which excluded buggery but that the defence were bound by her answers and could not call rebuttal evidence. Her previous history did not affect the question of consent to buggery. (Note that the case pre-dated the Criminal Justice and Public Order Act 1994—non-consensual buggery is now rape and would therefore be subject to s. 2 of the Sexual Offences (Amendment) Act 1976, below).

If a young girl, the complainant in an indecent assault allegation gives   2-161
details of sexual knowledge of which, the jury may assume, she would not have knowledge unless the defendant was guilty of the offence she may be cross-examined on her previous sexual activities with others to show that her knowledge may have been obtained pre-him, rather than from the defendant—R v. Walker [1994] Crim.L.R. 763.

If the description given by the complainant sounds so much like a descrip-   2-162
tion of the loss of her virginity the jury should not be left with this impression. If it appears that the act complained of—unlawful sexual intercourse is itself the loss of virginity then that matter goes to the issues in the case and not merely as to credit—R v. Funderburk [1990] 2 All E.R. 482.

The exceptions to the basic rule were set out in R v. Krausz (1973) 57   2-163
Cr.App.R. 466 at 472. It is settled (common) law that she who complains of rape or attempted rape can be cross-examined about:

(a) her general reputation and moral character;
(b) sexual intercourse between herself and the defendant on other occasions; and
(c) sexual intercourse between herself and other men.

Evidence can be called to contradict her on (a) and (b) but no evidence can be called to contradict her denials of (c). In the previous case of R v. Bashir (1970) 54 Cr.App.R. 1, she could be cross-examined to establish that she was a prostitute as it went to consent. In Krausz, it was held that the rule extended to prostitution or at least of notoriously immoral character and reputation:

"In an age of changing standards of morality it may be harder to say where promiscuity ends and prostitution begins, and it may be unnecessary to decide on which side of the dividing line the particular conduct falls which a man charged with rape may wish to prove. Evidence which proves that a woman is in the habit of submitting her body to different men without discrimination whether for pay or not, would seem to be admissible".

2–164   Somewhat different is cross-examination that the complainant has previously had sexual activity with another person and transferred that conduct in fantasy from the third party to the defendant. The defence was not allowed to call the third party to give evidence. His evidence would have gone mainly to credit and been collateral and therefore could not be called. The jury may have further been distracted into other matters not directly related to the defendant's guilt or innocence. The court would in fact have been reduced to trying both the present issue and the previous allegation at the same time. Finally, it was not right to call evidence to rebut evidence that the defence had adduced themselves in cross-examination (*R v. S* [1992] Crim.L.R. 307—the final reason is described as "rather less convincing" by Professor Smith in his commentary to the case).

(b) Statute

2–165   The Sexual Offences (Amendment) Act 1976, s.2 states:

"(1)   If at a trial any person is for the time being charged with a rape offence to which he pleads not guilty, then, except with the leave of the judge, no evidence and no question in cross-examination shall be adduced or asked at the trial, by or on behalf of any defendant at the trial, about any sexual experience of a complainant with a person other than the defendant.

(2)   The judge shall not give leave in pursuance of the preceding subsection for any evidence or question except on an application made to him in the absence of the jury by or on behalf of a defendant; and on such an application the judge shall give leave if and only if he is satisfied that it would be unfair to that defendant to refuse to allow the evidence to be adduced or the question to be asked.

(3)   In subsection (1) of this section 'complainant' means a woman upon whom, in a charge for a rape offence to which the trial in question relates, it is alleged that rape was committed, attempted or proposed.

(4)   Nothing in this section authorises evidence to be adduced or a question to be asked which cannot be adduced or asked apart from this section."

(i) Sexual experience

2–166   The term "sexual experience" clearly goes beyond sexual intercourse. It is however limited to sexual experience with another person. In *R v. Barnes* unreported, January 18, 1994, the defendant was charged with rape of his step-daughter. Medical evidence was adduced concerning the condition of her hymen. It was held on appeal that evidence that she had a vibrator in her bedroom should have been admitted. It was not a sexual experience excluded by the section and was relevant to explain the medical evidence.

Two aspects are of fundamental importance: first the section applies only   2-167
to rape offences as defined by section 7—the common law rules continue to apply therefore to indecent assault, and other sexual offences; secondly, subsection 4 specifically states that the common law limitations continue to apply to rape cases. Section 2 imposes additional restrictions in rape cases.

The section seeks to exclude all evidence of previous sexual experience of the complainant save that involving the defendant himself.

Prior to 1976 there had been much criticism of the common law rules for   2-168
cross-examination and calling of rebuttal evidence in rape cases. The effect of the common law rules was that the interests of justice were not advanced and in effect the woman was put on trial. Public concern was addressed by the Heilbron Committee in 1975 which was highly critical of the common law rules. The Committee recommended that evidence relating to the woman's previous sexual history should be excluded unless there was a striking similarity between the sexual conduct of the complainant on a previous occasion and on the occasion complained of. In these rare cases the judge could admit the evidence if it was so strikingly similar that it would be unfair to the defendant to exclude it.

(ii) Sexual Offences (Amendment) Act 1976

As a result of the Heilbron Committee's recommendations, section 2 of the   2-169
Sexual Offences (Amendment) Act 1976 was enacted. However the detailed test of strikingly similar evidence was omitted in favour of a judgment by the court as to the unfairness to the defendant of excluding the evidence.

However the section quite clearly was intended to place further restric-   2-170
tions in addition to the pre-existing limitations imposed on the defence attacks upon the complainant.

Section 2 has not been interpreted by the courts in accordance with its   2-171
obvious intent and has been the subject of much criticism by academic writers (see, for example, Professor Temkin [1993] Crim.L.R. 3). Professor Birch has recommended that the courts revert to a strict, rather than a generous interpretation and adopt a test analogous to similar fact evidence admitting reference to the complainant's previous sexual history only where its positive probative value is so great that it would be an affront to common sense to exclude it (see [1990] Crim.L.R. at p.719).

Instead the courts have used the section to admit evidence which would   2-172
have been excluded at common law, contrary to both the intent and the wording of section 2. It is respectfully submitted that the interpretation of section 2 by the Court of Appeal is inappropriate and that the approach suggested by Professor Birch is indeed the correct one. Questions and evidence will be prohibited if their intent is to suggest to the jury that the woman is agreeable to intercourse outside marriage and therefore cannot be worthy of belief.

Evidence will be allowed if she states as a fact she was prior to the events   2-173
complained of a virgin and it is demonstrable that this is untrue as it is part

of the *res gestae*. It is comparable to her saying that her clothes were ripped open if it can be proved that in fact her clothes were still intact.

2–174   However, it is submitted that the correct use of section 2 should be that where the defence is one of consent, the fact that she may have consented to intercourse with a man other than the defendant on a different occasion has no relevance to the question as to her consent to intercourse with this man on this occasion unless the facts are so strikingly similar it would be an affront to good sense, and therefore unfair to the defendant to exclude it. If a woman who is homeless is prepared to sleep with a man upon being offered a bed for the night and then moves in to co-habit with him, it has no relevance to a subsequent occasion when, being homeless she stays with a man and is subsequently found sobbing and heartbroken and complains of rape. It cannot be unfair to distinguish between unrelated situations when all the surrounding circumstances are taken into account. Such an argument—that the person has done it before and therefore probably did it on this occasion—is excluded from evidence against the defendant because it is unfair. The argument is invalid. It is submitted that an invalid argument should not be admitted under section 2 to assist the defendant. If a girl complains of rape by a man twice her age who has a false eye and one hand, it matters not how many other men she has consented to have sex with. The only ones relevant to the question of consent in this case are previous men who are twice her age with false eyes and a missing hand.

(iii) The interpretation in practice

2–175   The courts are however, more generous to defendants in practice.

2–176   Section 2 was first considered in a Crown Court case of *R v. Lawrence and Another* [1977] Crim.L.R. 492. The Court's approach was summed up in a much quoted judgment by May J.:

> "The important points of the statute which I think needs construction are the words 'if and only if he [the judge] is satisfied that it would be unfair to the defendant to refuse to allow the evidence to be adduced on the question to be asked'. And, in my judgment, before a judge is satisfied or may be said to be satisfied that to refuse to allow a particular question or a series of questions in cross-examination would be unfair to a defendant he must take the view that it is more likely than not that the particular question or line of cross-examination if allowed, might reasonably lead the jury, properly directed in the summing-up, to take a different view of the complainant's evidence from that which they might take if the question or series of questions was or were not allowed."

2–177   If the intention of the question, or series of questions is to suggest to the jury the unspoken comment "that is the sort of girl she is" it should be excluded. The judgment states that in distinguishing between cross-examination designed to blacken the complainant's sexual character so as to leave such a comment, and cross-examination as to the trustworthiness of her evidence, only the latter going to credit, properly so called, was permissible. The commentary to the case suggests that the case reflects the common-law principles. It is suggested that cross-examination will be allowed only in rare cases where her behaviour on another occasion or occasions suggests that the story she has told in the witness box is untrue.

The judgment in *Lawrence* was approved in *R v. Mills* (1979) 68 Cr.App.   2–178
R. 327 where the defence application was refused. In *Mills* the facts of the case are not reported. It will be noticed that in *Mills* it was said that the application of section 2 is a matter for the judge's discretion which the Appeal Court should not in the circumstances disturb. The use of the word "discretion" was corrected in *R v. Viola* [1982] 3 All E.R. 73 at 77 C and D. The judge has to make a judgment as to whether the terms of section 2 are satisfied. Having so decided it would be unfair to the defendant to exclude evidence, then he has no discretion. The questions must be allowed.

Lawrence was again approved in *R v. Viola* (above) where the "sexual   2–179
promiscuity" of the complainant with third parties was held to be relevant and should have been admitted. It was held that:

"there is a grey area which exists between the two types of relevance, namely relevance to credit and relevance to an issue in the case. On the one hand evidence of sexual promiscuity may be so strong or so closely contemporaneous in time to the event in issue as to come near to, or indeed to reach the border between credit and issue in the case. Conversely, the relevance of the evidence to an issue in the case may be so slight as to lead the judge to the conclusion that he is far from satisfied that the exclusion of the evidence or the questions from the consideration of the jury would be unfair to the defendant."

In this case the complainant was a woman of 22 who alleged rape by a slight acquaintance half an hour before midnight on Tuesday, September 8. The defence wished to call evidence of three matters:

(a)   during the afternoon and evening of Tuesday, she had made sexual advances to two men in her flat offering to let them try her new bed;
(b)   on the afternoon of September 9, she had intercourse with her boyfriend; and
(c)   on the morning of September 9, a visitor had discovered a man in her flat naked except for a pair of slippers.

The Court of Appeal held that item (b) was correctly excluded but that not only was the incident with the two men prior to the alleged rape relevant but also the subsequent sighting of the man in the slippers was relevant to questions of whether the complainant had consented to intercourse with the defendant the previous day.

(iv) Bolstered evidence

Evidence of the complainant's previous and subsequent sex life has been   2–180
admitted where the court felt that the complainant had bolstered her evidence by adding significance to surrounding circumstances.

In *R v. Redguard* [1991] Crim.L.R. 213, the complainant stated she would   2–181
not allow a man other than her boyfriend to stay over night. The Court of Appeal stated that she should have been cross-examined on an allegation

that a man, not her boyfriend, had stayed overnight and had consensual sex with her two weeks after the alleged rape.

2–182   In *R v. Riley* [1991] Crim.L.R. 460, the complainant stated in evidence that she would not agree to intercourse with her child sleeping in the bedroom. However a former boyfriend H later gave evidence that this had occurred. The defence wished to cross-examine her to the effect that this had also occurred with a further previous boyfriend C at an even earlier time. The complainant had not been cross-examined about the statement made by H. The court also held that the other man C should also have been called.

2–183   In *R v. Ellis* [1990] Crim.L.R. 717, the complainant said on oath that after the alleged rape she had bathed more than once. She had been cross-examined on the basis she had previously had intercourse with S and told a friend G that afterwards she had felt dirty and had a bath. She denied she had had intercourse with S. The Court of Appeal held that G should have been called as her evidence was material to whether the complainant had consented to intercourse with Ellis.

2–184   In *R v. Cleland* [1995] Crim.L.R. 742, a rape victim claimed that she never had unprotected sex with her boyfriend. She also said that an abortion she underwent after the alleged rape was of a pregnancy attributable to the rape. It was held, on appeal, that the defence should have been allowed to cross-examine her on an abortion prior to the rape and on the fact that she menstruated after the attack and prior to the second abortion. Both went to the heart of the complainant's credibility.

The Court of Appeal has held that cross-examination of sexual experience should be allowed even where the complainant cannot be said to have bolstered her evidence but where the matter in issue has been raised by the defence.

2–185   In *R v. SMS* [1992] Crim.L.R. 310, it was alleged that a 14 year old white girl had been raped by a 26 year old coloured man with a false eye and one hand. In evidence-in-chief she stated that intercourse had been painful. Medical evidence was inconclusive as to her prior virginity. It was held on appeal that the defence should have been allowed to cross-examine her on previous sexual experience because a jury may have concluded that she had been a virgin and may have found it impossible to believe that as a virgin she would have consented to her first act of sexual intercourse in these circumstances with a man of these characteristics. It went to consent. The court felt that the jury may not have come to that conclusion if they did not believe she was a virgin. Presumably, having lost her virginity, a 14 year old girl is more likely to consent to a man with a false eye and one hand.

2–186   In *R v. Said* [1992] Crim.L.R. 433, another 14 year old girl was alleged to have been raped in sordid circumstances by a man "not of the same ethnic origin" and with limitations which did not add to his physical attractions. After intercourse the defendant wiped his penis on the curtain. It was alleged by the defence that this had occurred at her suggestion and that opened the way to cross-examine her as to her previous sexual experiences.

The Court of Appeal has experienced difficulty distinguishing between evidence going to credit and evidence going to the issues.

2–187   In *R v. Funderburk* [1990] 2 All E.R. 482, it was said that where the disputed issue is a sexual one between two person in private, the difference between questions going to credit and questions going to issue is reduced to vanishing-point because sexual intercourse, whether or not consensual, most often takes place in private and leaves few visible traces of having occurred, so that the evidence is often effectively limited to that of the parties, and much is likely to depend upon the balance of credibility between them. The court held that the general principles set out in section 2 should be considered even in cases other than rape (in this case unlawful sexual intercourse), *i.e.* should extend to common law.

It was stated that the defence should have been allowed to put the disputed questions as to the admissions made to the defendant's co-habitee of intercourse with married men. The Court of Appeal held that the jury might well have reappraised the complainant's evidence about the loss of her virginity and her credibility had they heard of her previous statement regarding her earlier sexual experiences.

In *R v. C* [1992] Crim.L.R. 648, it was held that just because there were 2–188 further charges in addition to rape, in this case two allegations of buggery, the restrictions imposed on cross-examination are not removed.

The jury was left in no doubt as to C's case regarding sexual promiscuity on the part of the complainant, his daughter. The summing-up properly reminded the jury of the issues concerning the complainant's character. Cross-examination concerning subsequent acts of buggery was not allowed however. The judge in deciding whether it was fair to permit cross-examination would have to take into account the existence of other charges.

In both these cases, the defence was not one of consent but a denial of the 2–189 incidents and a claim that the girl was promiscuous and blaming the defendant for her medical condition (either lack of virginity or evidence of buggery). In both cases, the judge had to consider to what extent the allegations as to the girl's promiscuity should be explored by the defence.

In cases where the defence is not one of consent but an allegation that the complainant is transferring to the defendant incidents committed with others, cross-examination will have to be allowed pursuant to, but limited to that possibility. In *R v. Bogie* [1992] Crim.L.R. 301, a young woman found herself with nowhere to sleep one night. She went to a house of which the defendant was a caretaker and it was alleged that she was raped. She was found later "in quite a state, sobbing as if broken-hearted" and showing some injuries. The trial court held that she could be cross-examined by the defence as to an incident where she was again homeless and spent the night with a man and the following day moved in with him. However, the two incidents, one resulting in her co-habiting, the other in her being broken-hearted, injured and alleging rape, are hardly similar.

The Court of Appeal held that other evidence, (a) that she had massaged a man's back and subsequently had sex with him in the kitchen and (b) that she had had intercourse and oral sex with another man in the bathroom, should also have been admitted.

The Court said that these items of evidence would have been admitted at common law and that the judge had been wrong to exclude them. It has been pointed out by Professor Temkin ([1993] Crim.L.R. 3 at p.9) that the purpose of the section was to prevent such cross-examination, not endorse it.

(c) Defendant's belief in consent

2-190   The defendant may allege that, whether or not the woman was consenting, he genuinely believed that she was consenting and that his belief was based upon her reputation. This situation is, in rape cases, also subject to section 2.

Distinguishing between consent, and a genuine but mistaken belief in consent is often difficult. However, it was held in *R v. Barton* (1987) 85 Cr.App.R. 5, that in the later case no attack is being made upon the woman's credit. Common sense should be applied by the court.

F. SEXUAL OFFENCES (PROTECTED MATERIAL) ACT 1997

2-191   This Act regulates access by the defendant and others to victim statements and certain other material disclosed by the prosecution in connection with proceedings relating to specific sexual offences, and makes appropriate amendments to the Magistrates' Courts Act 1980 and the Criminal Procedure and Investigations Act 1996.

2-192   Section 3 provides that:

"when statements or material covered by the Act which fall to be disclosed by the prosecutor to the defendant—
  (a) the prosecutor shall not disclose that material to the defendant; and
  (b) it shall instead be disclosed under the Act in accordance with whichever of subsection (2) and (3) below is appropriate."

2-193   Subsection (2) states—

"If—(a) the defendant has a legal representative, and
  (b) the defendant's legal representative gives the prosecutor the undertaking required by section 4 (disclosure to defendant's legal representative), the prosecutor shall disclose the material in question by giving a copy of it to the defendant's legal representative."

2-194   Subsection (3) states:

"If subsection 2 is not applicable the prosecutor shall disclose the material in question by giving a copy of it to the appropriate person for the purposes of section 5 (disclosure to unrepresented defendants) in order for that person to show that copy to the defendant under that section."

2-195   Subsection (4) provides that:

"where a copy of any material falls to be given to any person by the prosecutor, any such copy—
(a) may be in such form as the prosecutor thinks fit, and
(b) where the material consists of information which has been recorded in any form, need not be in the same form as that in which the information has already been recorded."

A video recording may therefore be disclosed as a written transcript. By subsection 5, once a copy of any material is given to any person under the Act by the prosecutor, the copy is protected material.

I. Disclosure To The Defendant's Legal Representative

The defendant's legal representative is required by section 4 to give, in relation to any protected material given to him under the Act, an undertaking to discharge various obligations set out in the section. These are contained in subsections (2) to (7).   **2–196**

Subsection (2) states: **2–197**

"He must take reasonable steps to ensure—
(a) that the protected material, or any copy of it, is only shown to the defendant in circumstances where it is possible to prevent the defendant retaining possession of the material, or copy, or making a copy of it, and
(b) that the protected material is not shown and no copy of it is given and its contents are not revealed, to any person other than the defendant, except so far as it appears to him necessary to show the material or give a copy of it to any such person—
    (i)   in connection with any relevant proceeding, or
    (ii) for the purposes of any assessment or treatment of the defendant (whether before or after conviction)."

It may of course therefore be copied to the defendant's Counsel in the brief.

Subsection (3) states: **2–198**

"He must inform the defendant—
(a) that the protected material is such material for the purposes of this Act,
(b) that the defendant can only inspect that material, or any copy of it, in circumstances such as are described in subsection (2)(a) above,
(c) that it would be an offence for the defendant—
    (i)   to have that material, or any copy of it, in his possession otherwise than while inspecting it or the copy in such circumstances or
    (ii) to give that material, or any copy of it, or otherwise reveal its contents, to any other person."

Subsection (4) states: **2–199**

"He must, where the protected material or a copy of it has been shown or given in accordance with subsection (2)(b)(i) or (ii) to a person other than the defendant, inform that person—

    (a) that that person must not give any copy of that material or otherwise reveal its contents—

        (i) to any other person other than the defendant, or

        (ii) to the defendant otherwise than in circumstances such as are described in subsection 2(a); and

    (b) that it would be an offence for that person to do so."

2–200   Subsection (5) and (6) make provisions for the situation where one legal representative ceases to represent the defendant. He must inform the prosecutor. If he is informed by the prosecutor that the new legal representative has given the prosecutor the required undertaking he must give the protected material and any copies of it in his possession to the defendant's new legal representative. When this occurs he must inform that new legal representative—

    (a) that that material is protected material for the purposes of the Act and

    (b) of the extent to which—

        (i) that material has been shown by him; and

        (ii) any copies of it have been given by him to any other person (including the defendant).

2–201   Subsection (7) states that: "He must keep an record of every occasion on which the protected material was shown, or a copy of it was given as mentioned in subsection 6(b)."

Section 6 provides for further disclosure where the defendant's legal representative ceases to act for him, dies or becomes incapacitated, and where the disclosure has been made to an unrepresented defendant who then acquires a legal representative.

II. DISCLOSURE TO UNREPRESENTED DEFENDANTS

2–202   Section 5 of the Sexual Offences (Protected Material) Act 1997 covers the situation described in section 3(3). The appropriate person in such a case is—

    (a) if the defendant is in prison, the governor of the prison, or any person nominated by the governor for the purposes of the section; and

    (b) otherwise the officer in charge of such police station as appears *to the prosecutor* to be suitable for enabling the defendant to have access to the material in accordance with this section, or any person nominated by that officer for the purposes of this section.

The Secretary of State may however, by regulations provide the appropriate person.

2–203   The appropriate person shall, by subsection (4):

"take reasonable steps to ensure—

(a) that the protected material, or any copy of it, is only shown to the defendant in circumstances where it is possible to exercise adequate supervision to prevent the defendant retaining possession of the material or copy, or making a copy of it,

(b) that, subject to paragraph (a)(above) the defendant is given such access to that material, or a copy of it, as he reasonably requires in connection with any relevant proceeding and

(c) that that material is not shown and no copy of it is given, and its contents are not otherwise revealed, to any person other than the defendant."

Subsections (5) and (6) detail the information which the prosecutor shall, at the time of giving the protected material to the appropriate person, provide to that person and the defendant: **2–204**

"The defendant shall be informed—

(a) that that material is protected material

(b) that the defendant can only inspect that material, or any copy of it in circumstances such as are described in subsection (4) (a) and

(c) that it would be an offence for the defendant—

  (i) to have that material, or any copy of it, in his possession otherwise than while inspecting it, or the copy in such circumstances, or

  (ii) to give that material, or any copy of it, or otherwise reveal its contents to any other person."

The prosecutor must also inform the defendant of his right to request the prosecutor in writing to give a further copy of the material to some other person and that if it appears to the prosecutor to be necessary to do so—

(i) in connection with the relevant proceedings or

(ii) for the purposes of any assessment or treatment of the defendant (before or after conviction)

the prosecutor shall give such a copy to that person.

If the prosecutor receives such a request but does not consider it necessary he may refuse the request and shall inform the defendant of his refusal (subs. (10)). The prosecutor may give such a copy to some other person where the request has been made by the defendant where it appears to him that it is necessary in the interests of the defendant (sub. (8)). This would appear to cover disclosure to a probation officer or social worker for the purposes of preparing pre-sentence reports where such disclosure is in the interests of the defendant.

When the prosecutor provides such disclosure whether requested by the defendant or not he shall inform the person to whom the copy is given—   **2–205**

(a) that the copy is protected material for the purposes of the Act

(b) that he must not give any copy of the protected material or otherwise reveal its contents—

  (i) to any person other than the defendant, or

    (ii) to the defendant otherwise than in circumstances such as are described in subsection (4)(a), and

    (iii) that it would be an offence for him to do so.

III. "PROTECTED MATERIAL"

2–206 Section 1 of the Act defines protected material as:

"(a) any statements relating to that or any other sexual offence made by any victim of the offence (whether the statement is recorded in writing or in any other form),

(b) a photograph or pseudo-photograph of any such victim,

(c) a report of a medical examination of the physical condition of any such victim

which is a copy given by the prosecutor to any person under the Act."

A person is a victim of an offence if—

(a) the charge, summons or indictment by which the proceedings are instituted names that person as a person in relation to whom that offence was committed or

(b) that offence can, in the prosecutor's opinion be reasonably regarded as having been committed in relation to that person and a person is in relation to any such proceedings, a victim of any other sexual offence if that offence can, in the prosecutor's opinion, be reasonably regarded as having been committed in relation to that person.

The Act does not therefore protect detailed descriptions of an offence as described by an eyewitness who is not also a victim. References to material and copies include any part of that material or copy.

2–207 There is an important protection for the defendant. References to a copy made by the defendant does not apply to a manuscript copy which is not a verbatim copy of the whole of that material, or having in his possession a copy which is not a verbatim copy of the whole of that material. The defendant may therefore copy a person's notes of, including direct lengthy quotes from the protected material.

2–208 Disclosure of material does not include:

(a) any disclosure made in the course of any proceedings before a Court or in any report of any such proceedings, or

(b) any disclosure made or copy given by a person when returning any protected material, or a copy to the prosecutor or the defendant's legal representative (section 8(7)).

2–209 The sexual offences covered by the Act are:
Sexual Offences Act 1956: s. 1: rape;
s. 2: procurement of a woman by threats;
s. 3: procurement of a woman by false pretences;
s. 4: administering drugs to obtain sexual intercourse;
s. 5: USI with a girl under 13;

s. 6: USI with a girl between 13 and 16;
s. 7: sexual intercourse with a mentally handicapped person;
s. 9: procurement of a mentally handicapper person;
s. 10: incest by a man;
s. 11: incest by a woman;
s. 12: buggery;
s. 14: indecent assault on a woman;
s. 15: indecent assault on a man;
s. 16: assault with intent to commit buggery.
Mental Health Act 1959: s. 128: intercourse with mentally handicapped person by hospital staff.
Indecency with Children Act 1966: s. 1: indecent conduct towards a young child.
Criminal Law Act 1977: s. 54: incitement by a man of his grand-daughter, daughter or sister under 16 to commit incest with him.
Protection of Children Act 1978, section 1 and **Criminal Justice Act 1988**, s. 160: indecent photographs of children.
Criminal Law Act 1977, s. 1 (conspiracy) and **Criminal Attempts Act 1981** (attempts) and any offences of inciting another to commit any of these offences.

Sexual offence proceedings include: **2–210**

(a)   any appeal or application for leave to appeal brought or made by or in relation to a defendant in such proceedings;
(b)   any application made to the Criminal Cases Review Commission for the reference under section 9 or 11 of the Criminal Appeal Act 1995 of any conviction, verdict, finding or sentence recorded or imposed to any such defendant, or
(c)   any petition to the Secretary of State requesting him to recommend the exercise of Her Majesty's prerogative of mercy in relation to any such defendant.

IV. OFFENCES

Section 8 provides that it is an offence: **2–211**

"(1)   where material has been disclosed under the Act for the defendant—
    (a)   to have the protected material, or any copy of it in his posses-sion, otherwise than while inspecting it or the copy as permitted;
    (b)   to give that material or any copy of it, or otherwise reveal its contents to any other person
(2)   where material has been disclosed to another person under section 4(2)(b)(i) or 5(7) or (8) for that person to reveal its contents—
    (a)   to any person other than the defendant
    (b)   to the defendant otherwise than in circumstances as are descri-bed in section 4(2)(a) or 5(4)(a)."

The proceedings may be current or contemplated.

A person guilty of an offence is liable:

(a) on summary conviction to imprisonment for a term not exceeding six months or a fine not exceeding the statutory maximum or both

(b) on conviction on indictment for a term not exceeding two years or a fine or both.

2–212 It is a defence to the charge to prove that at the time of the alleged offence he was not aware, and neither suspected nor had reason to suspect, that the material or copy in question was protected material or (as the case may be) a copy of such material. It is clear that the onus of proof lies with the defendant to the normal standard of proof.

2–213 A court before which a person is tried for an offence may (whether or not he is convicted of that offence) make an order requiring him to return any protected material.

Chapter 3
Procedure

The basic rules of procedure apply to sexual offences as they do to any other criminal allegation. There are however some provisions which it may be helpful to discuss specifically because they relate to offences involving children or because they deal with particularly serious offences.

A. TRANSFERS TO THE CROWN COURT

Section 53 of the Criminal Justice Act 1991 enables cases involving child **3–01** witnesses, that are destined for the Crown court, to be transferred from the magistrates' court to the Crown court without the need for committal proceedings. The object of the exercise, along with the provisions for television links and video recorded evidence in chief, being to ensure that the distress and disturbance suffered by the child as a result of the proceedings, is kept to a minimum.

Section 53 of the 1991 Act states: **3–02**

"(1) If a person has been charged with an offence to which section 32(2) of the 1988 Act applies (sexual offences and offences involving violence or cruelty) and the Director of Public Prosecutions is of the opinion:

(a) that the evidence of the offence would be sufficient for the persons charged to be committed for trial;

(b) that a child who is alleged:

(i) to be a person against whom the offence was committed; or

(ii) to have witnessed the commission of the offence,

will be called as a witness at the trial; and

(c) that, for the purpose of avoiding any prejudice to the welfare of the child, the case should be taken over and proceeded with without delay by the Crown Court,

a notice ('notice of transfer') certifying that opinion may be given by or on behalf of the Director to the magistrates' court in whose jurisdiction the offence has been charged.

3–03   (2)   A notice of transfer shall be given before the magistrates' court begins to inquire into the case as examining justices.

3–04   (3)   On the giving of a notice of transfer the functions of the magistrates' court shall cease in relation to the case except as provided by paragraphs 2 and 3 of Schedule 6 to this Act or by section 20(4) of the Legal Aid Act 1988.

3–05   (4)   The decision to give a notice of transfer shall not be subject to appeal or liable to be questioned in any court.

3–06   (5)   Schedule 6 to this Act (which makes further provision in relation to notices of transfer) shall have effect.

3–07   (6)   In this section 'child' means a person who:

       (a)   in the case of an offence falling within section 32(2)(a) or (b) of the 1988 Act, is under fourteen years of age or, if he was under that age when any such video recording as is mentioned in section 32A(2) of that Act was made in respect of him, is under fifteen years of age; or

       (b)   in the case of an offence falling within section 32(2)(c) of that Act, is under seventeen years of age or, if he was under that age when any such video recording was made in respect of him, is under eighteen years of age.

3–08   (7)   Any reference in subsection (6) above to an offence falling within paragraph (a), (b) or (c) of section 32(2) of that Act includes a reference to an offence which consists of attempting or conspiring to commit, or of aiding, abetting, counselling, procuring or inciting the commission of, an offence falling within that paragraph."

I. Criminal Justice Act 1991, Sched. 6

3–09   Schedule 6 of the 1991 Act states:

"1(1)   A notice of transfer shall specify the proposed place of trial; and in selecting that place the Director of Public Prosecutions shall have regard to the considerations to which a magistrates' court committing a person for trial is required by section 7 of the 1980 Act to have regard when selecting the place at which he is to be tried.

      (2)   A notice of transfer shall specify the charge or charges to which it relates and include or be accompanied by such additional material as regulations under paragraph 4 below may require.

3–10   2(1)   If a magistrates' court has remanded in custody a person to whom a notice of transfer relates, it shall have power, subject to section 4 of the Bail Act 1976, and regulations under section 22 of the Prosecution of Offences Act 1985:

       (a)   to order that he shall be safely kept in custody until delivered in due course of law; or

       (b)   to release him on bail in accordance with the Bail Act 1976, that is to say, by directing him to appear before the Crown Court for trial.

(2) Where:
  (a) a person's release on bail under paragraph (b) of sub-paragraph (1) above is conditional on his providing one or more sureties; and
  (b) in accordance with subsection (3) of section 8 of the Bail Act 1976, the court fixes the amount in which a surety is to be bound with a view to his entering into his recognizance subsequently in accordance with subsections (4) and (5) or (6) of that section,
  the court shall in the meantime make an order such as is mentioned in paragraph (a) of that sub-paragraph.

(3) If the conditions specified in sub-paragraph (4) below are satisfied, a court may exercise the powers conferred by sub-paragraph (1) above in relation to a person charged without his being brought before it in any case in which by virtue of subsection (3A) of section 128 of the 1980 Act it would have the power further to remand him on an adjournment such as is mentioned in that subsection.

(4) The conditions referred to in sub-paragraph (3) above are:
  (a) that the person in question has given his written consent to the powers conferred by sub-paragraph (1) above being exercised without his being brought before the court; and
  (b) that the court is satisfied that, when he gave his consent, he knew that the notice of transfer had been issued.

(5) Where a notice of transfer is given after a person to whom it relates has been remanded on bail to appear before a magistrates' court on an appointed day, the requirement that he shall so appear shall cease on the giving of the notice unless the notice states that it is to continue.

(6) Where that requirement ceases by virtue of sub-paragraph (5) above, it shall be the duty of the person in question to appear before the Crown Court at the place specified by the notice of transfer as the proposed place of trial or at any place substituted for it by a direction under section 76 of the Supreme Court Act 1981.

(7) If, in a case where the notice states that the requirement mentioned in sub-paragraph (5) above is to continue, a person to whom the notice relates appears before the magistrates' court, the court shall have:
  (a) the powers and duties conferred on a magistrates' court by sub-paragraph (1) above but subject as there provided; and
  (b) power to enlarge, in the surety's absence, a recognizance conditioned in accordance with section 128(4)(a) of the 1980 Act so that the surety is bound to secure that the person charged appears also before the Crown Court."

Schedule 6 goes on to state: **3–11**

"3. For the purposes of the Criminal Procedure (Attendance of Witnesses) Act 1965:
  (a) any magistrates' court for the petty sessions area for which the court from which a case was transferred sits shall be treated as examining magistrates; and

  (b) a person indicated in the notice of transfer as a proposed witness shall be treated as a person who has been examined by the court."

(Paragraph 4 not printed.)

"5(1) Where a notice of transfer has been given, any person to whom the notice relates may, at any time before he is arraigned (and whether or not an indictment has been preferred against him), apply orally or in writing to the Crown Court sitting at the place specified by the notice of transfer as the proposed place of trial for the charge, or any of the charges, in the case to be dismissed.

 (2) The judge shall dismiss a charge (and accordingly quash a count relating to it in any indictment preferred against the applicant) which is the subject of any such application if it appears to him that the evidence against the applicant would not be sufficient for a jury properly to convict him.

 (3) No oral application may be made under sub-paragraph (1) above unless the applicant has given the Crown Court mentioned in that sub-paragraph written notice of his intention to make the application.

 (4) Oral evidence may be given on such an application only with the leave of the judge or by his order; and the judge shall give leave or make an order only if it appears to him, having regard to any matters stated in the application for leave, that the interests of justice require him to do so.

 (5) No leave or order under sub-paragraph (4) above, shall be given or made in relation to oral evidence from a child (within the meaning of section 53 of this Act) who is alleged:

  (a) to be a person against whom an offence to which the notice of transfer relates was committed; or

  (b) to have witnessed the commission of such an offence.

 (6) If the judge gives leave permitting, or makes an order requiring, a person to give oral evidence, but that person does not do so, the judge may disregard any document indicating the evidence that he might have given.

 (7) Dismissal of the charge, or all the charges, against the applicant shall have the same effect as a refusal by examining magistrates to commit for trial, except that no further proceedings may be brought on a dismissed charge except by means of the preferment of a voluntary bill of indictment.

 (8) Crown Court Rules may make provision for the purposes of this paragraph and, without prejudice to the generality of this sub-paragraph, may make provision:

  (a) as to the time or stage in the proceedings at which anything required to be done is to be done (unless the court grants leave to do it at some other time or stage);

  (b) as to the contents and form of notices or other documents;

  (c) as to the manner in which evidence is to be submitted; and

  (d) as to persons to be served with notices or other material.

6(1) Except as provided by this paragraph, it shall not be lawful:

    (a) to publish in Great Britain a written report of an application under paragraph 5(1) above; or

    (b) to include in a relevant programme for reception in Great Britain a report of such an application,

if (in either case) the report contains any matter other than that permitted by this paragraph.

(2) An order that sub-paragraph (1) above shall not apply to reports of an application under paragraph 5(1) above may be made by the judge dealing with the application.

(3) Where in the case of two or more accused one of them objects to the making of an order under sub-paragraph (2) above, the judge shall make the order if, and only if, he is satisfied, after hearing the representations of the accused, that it is in the interests of justice to do so.

(4) An order under sub-paragraph (2) above shall not apply to reports of proceedings under sub-paragraph (3) above, but any decision of the court to make or not to make such an order may be contained in reports published or included in a relevant programme before the time authorised by sub-paragraph (5) below.

(5) It shall not be unlawful under this paragraph to publish or include in a relevant programme a report of an application under paragraph 5(1) above containing any matter other than that permitted by sub-paragraph (8) below where the application is successful.

(6) Where:

    (a) two or more persons were jointly charged; and

    (b) applications under paragraph 5(1) above are made by more than one of them,

sub-paragraph (5) shall have effect as if for the words 'the application is' there were substituted the words 'all the applications are'.

(7) It shall not be unlawful under this paragraph to publish or include in a relevant programme a report of an unsuccessful application at the conclusion of the trial of the person charged, or of the last of the persons charged to be tried.

(8) The following matters may be contained in a report published or included in a relevant programme without an order under sub-paragraph (2) above before the time authorised by sub-paragraphs (5) and (6) above, that is to say:

    (a) the identity of the court and the name of the judge;

    (b) the names, ages, home addresses and occupations of the accused and witnesses;

    (c) the offence or offences, or a summary of them, with which the accused is or are charged;

    (d) the names of counsel and solicitors engaged in the proceedings;

    (e) where the proceedings are adjourned, the date and place to which they are adjourned;

    (f) the arrangements as to bail;

(g) whether legal aid was granted to the accused or any of the accused.

(9) The addresses that may be published or included in a relevant programme under sub-paragraph (8) above are addresses:
(a) at any relevant time; and
(b) at the time of their publication or inclusion in a relevant programme.

(10) If a report is published or included in a relevant programme in contravention of this paragraph the following persons, that is to say:
(a) in the case of a publication of a written report as part of a newspaper or periodical, any proprietor, editor or publisher of the newspaper or periodical;
(b) in the case of a publication of a written report otherwise than as part of a newspaper or periodical, the person who publishes it;
(c) in the case of the inclusion of a report in a relevant programme, any body corporate which is engaged in providing the service in which the programme is included and any person having functions in relation to the programme corresponding to those of the editor of a newspaper;
shall be liable on summary conviction to a fine not exceeding level 5 on the standard scale.

(11) Proceedings for an offence under this paragraph shall not, in England and Wales, be instituted otherwise than by or with the consent of the Attorney-General.

(12) Sub-paragraph (1) above shall be in addition to, and not in derogation from, the provisions of any other enactment with respect to the publication of reports of court proceedings.

(13) In this paragraph:
'publish', in relation to a report, means publish the report, either by itself or as part of a newspaper or periodical, for distribution to the public;
'relevant programme' means a programme included in a programme service (within the meaning of the Broadcasting Act 1990);
'relevant time' means a time when events giving rise to the charges to which the proceedings relate occurred.

3-14   7(1) Where a notice of transfer has been given in relation to any case:
(a) the Crown Court before which the case is to be tried; and
(b) any magistrates' court which exercises any functions under paragraph 2 or 3 above or section 20(4) of the Legal Aid Act 1988 in relation to the case,
shall, in exercising any of its powers in relation to the case, have regard to the desirability of avoiding prejudice to the welfare of any relevant child witness that may be occasioned by unnecessary delay in bringing the case to trial.

(2) In this paragraph 'child' has the same meaning as in section 53 of this Act and 'relevant witness' means a child who will be called as a witness at the trial and who is alleged:

(a) to be a person against whom an offence to which the notice of transfer relates was committed; or

(b) to have witnessed the commission of such an offence."

II. Criminal Justice Act 1991 (Notice of Transfer Regulations 1992)

The Criminal Justice Act 1991 (Notice of Transfer) Regulations 1992 require that the notice of transfer shall be in the prescribed form (see Appendix 7), and that a copy of the notice shall be given to any person to whom it relates (or, if represented, to his solicitor) together with a notice in Form 2 in the Schedule (see Appendix 8) and a statement of the evidence on which any charge to which the notice of transfer relates is based. A copy of the notice should also be given to the Crown Court together with a copy of the notice and statement given to the defence. If the defendant is in custody, copies of the notices should also be sent to the prison governor.   3–15

The Criminal Justice Act 1991 (Dismissal of Transferred Charges) Rules 1992 require that where a notice of transfer has been given by the prosecution and the person to whom it relates wishes to apply orally for any charge to be dismissed, he must give written notice to the Crown Court not later than 14 days after the day on which the notice of transfer was given, with a copy to the prosecution and any other person to whom the notice of transfer relates. The time for giving such a notice of intention to make oral application may be extended following an application in writing to the Crown Court, again with copies going to the other parties involved. A notice of intention to make oral application must be accompanied by a copy of any material on which the applicant relies including a list of the witnesses it is proposed to call. The judge's decision, indicating what witnesses are to be called if leave to make the application is granted, will be given by the Crown Court to the prosecution and other parties to whom the notice of transfer relates. If leave is granted, the matter will be listed before a judge of the Crown Court.   3–16

III. Dismissal

A written application for dismissal must be made on the appropriate form and sent to the Crown Court (with accompanying documents in support) with copies of everything being given to the prosecution and other parties to whom the notice of transfer relates. The application must be made not later than 14 days after the day on which notice of transfer was given unless an extension is applied for and obtained.   3–17

Within seven days of the date of service of a notice of intention to apply orally, or the receiving of a copy of the written application for dismissal, the prosecution may apply to the Crown Court to adduce oral evidence or for an oral hearing. The application by the prosecution must be on the correct form and specify the grounds of the application and, where leave is sought to adduce oral evidence, indicating what witnesses it is proposed to call and   3–18 confirming that they are not children. Where the prosecution has received the material accompanying the defence applications, and it proposes to adduce in reply thereto any written comments or further evidence, such comments or evidence must be served on the Crown Court (with copies to the other parties) not later than 14 days from the date of receiving the said material. Both the seven day and the 14 day time limits may be extended on written application.

3–19   A judge may grant leave for a witness to give oral evidence on an application for dismissal notwithstanding that the notice of intention to call that witness has not been given in the appropriate manner.

3–20   Where a written application for dismissal has been made, the Court should inform all the parties as soon as is practicable of the result.

3–21   Notices required to be given by these Rules can be served personally, or sent by post at the recipient's usual or last known address or place of business or to that person's solicitor. The Magistrates' Courts (Notice of Transfer) (Children's Evidence) Rules 1992 require the clerk of the magistrates' court, where a person in respect of whom a notice of transfer has been given is granted bail, to give written notice thereof to the governor of the prison or remand centre to which the person would have been committed by that court if he had not been granted bail. Where a notice of transfer is given in respect of a person removed to a hospital under section 47 or 48 of the Mental Health Act 1983, the clerk of the magistrates' court shall give written notice to the governor of the prison where that person would have been if committed in custody and to the managers of the hospital where he is detained.

3–22   Where by virtue of Schedule 6 a person is no longer required to appear before a magistrates' court, the court shall fix a date on which it will exercise its functions under paragraph 3 of Schedule 6 and give notice thereof to the defendant and the prosecution.

3–23   As soon as practicable after a magistrates' court to which notice of transfer has been given, has discharged its functions under section 53(3), the clerk of the court shall send to the Crown Court:

(a) a list of the names, addresses and occupations of the witnesses in respect of whom witness orders have been made;

(b) a copy of the record made in pursuance of section 5 of the Bail Act 1976 relating to the grant or withholding of bail in respect of the accused;

(c) any recognizance entered into by any person as surety for the accused together with a statement of any enlargement thereof;

(d) a copy of any legal aid order previously made in the case;

(e) a copy of any contribution order previously made in the case under section 23 of the Legal Aid Act 1988;

(f) a copy of any legal aid application previously made in the case which has been refused;

(g) any statement of means already submitted.

3–24   Where a defendant faces a number of charges, all those charges which can appear on the same indictment (because there is a sufficient nexus between them) may be transferred under section 53 even if some of them would not, of themselves, have qualified for transfer under section 53 (*R v. Peter Wrench*, unreported, May 23, 1995).

The fact that an offence is an indictable offence, triable either way does not invalidate the decision of the DPP to issue a notice of transfer where a magistrates' court has not determined mode of trial (*R v. DPP, ex p. Brewer* [1995] Crim.L.R. 68). 3–25

It appears that there is no provision for the Crown Court to deal with summary related matters transferred under section 53—unlike offences committed under section 40 or 41 of the Criminal Justice Act 1988. In *R v. Wrench* [1996] Crim.L.R. 265, the defendant was convicted of conduct outraging public decency (count one), attempted abduction of a girl (count two), and common assault on that girl (count three). Count two was the subject of a notice of transfer under section 53. It was contended on appeal that the proceedings were a nullity. Held: 3–26

(a) that once the transfer procedure applies, it applies to the whole case against the accused;

(b) counts one and two were properly joined in the same indictment because they were offences of a similar character; and

(c) even if counts one and three were wrongly added to the indictment (since in relation to count three, section 40(1) of the Criminal Justice Act 1988 did not apply as there had been no "examination or deposition taken before a justice"), no application had been made at trial to quash them or the indictment, and there could be no quashing on appeal (Administration of Justice (Miscellaneous Provisions) Act 1933, s.2(3)(b)).

B. DISCLOSURE OF UNUSED MATERIAL

Interviews, reports and medical notes may be disclosed to the defence. The Attorney-General set out *Guidelines for Disclosure* in 1981 ((1981) 74 Cr.App.R. 302), which have subsequently been replaced by case law and statute and are no longer an adequate statement of the law (see *R. v. Mills; R. v. Poole, The Times*, July 30, 1997). 3–27

I. The Criminal Procedure And Investigations Act 1996

At common law the prosecution team included the police, experts instructed by the prosecution and the Crown Prosecution Service. The Criminal Procedure and Investigations Act 1996, s. 21 disapplies all the common law rules relating to disclosure by the prosecution and replaces them with a statutory scheme supported by new Codes of Practice. The prosecution team will no longer exist and expert witnesses will have the duties placed on them by the advance notice of expert evidence rules which are extended to the Magistrates' Court. Everyone else is a third party. 3–28

It is important that full and accurate notes of the examination be taken and preserved. The police surgeon will, as a matter of good clinical practice, 3–29 obtain from the victim a full medical history. The victim often also gives details of previous sexual experience and possibly of past psychiatric problems. Such information is normally not recorded on the doctor's Criminal Justice Act 1967 statement. It will however be recorded in his notes.

3–30   The prosecution is required to disclose to the defence unused material held by the prosecution. A police surgeon or other doctor employed by or on behalf of the police will fall within the definition of the prosecution. Only such information as is material to the case needs to be disclosed (*R v. Keane* [1994] 2 All E.R. 478).

3–31   Nonetheless, all information must be recorded and revealed to the investigating officer, especially evidence which may effect the strength of a future prosecution or which may be of assistance to the defence.

3–32   There is no form of privilege which applies to information passed to the police surgeon, and that which is material to a case must be disclosed.

There is no legal privilege covering matters disclosed by a patient to a doctor, nor to his medical records (*Hunter v. Mann* [1974] 2 All E.R. 414). There is no privilege covering confessions made to clergymen even if made in the confessional (*Wheeler v. Le Marchant* (1881) 45 J.P. 728). A judge may order the information to be disclosed to the court if it is relevant, proper and necessary for the question to be answered (Lord Denning in *Attorney-General v. Mulholland; Attorney-General v. Foster* [1963] 1 All E.R. 767; [1963] 2 Q.B. 477, approved by Lord Wilberforce and Lord Dilhorne in *BSC v. Granada Television* [1981] 1 All E.R. 452, H.L.).

3–33   The duty of disclosure extends beyond the items set out in rule 3(1)(b) of the Crown Court (Advance Notice of Expert Evidence) Rules 1987 (*R v. Ward* (1992) 96 Cr.App.R.1).

3–34   Disclosable material will include:

(a) laboratory submission forms, details of packaging and sealing of items, dates and times of examinations, records of continuity of items and records of material not examined;

(b) notes made at the scene, notes of assistants and checkers, records of laboratory notes and photographs, draft statements and copies of witness statements provided by the police; and

(c) documentation concerning procedure, technical methods, databases and surveys.

3–35   In the event of a dispute concerning what is material, application must be made to the court of trial for disclosure. However, notes held by a doctor who cannot be said to be part of the prosecution, in some cases for example, a G.P. who is not a prosecution witness, are not subject to disclosure by the prosecution. In such cases, a witness summons would be required by the defence to obtain access to the patient's notes.

3–36   If the documents are being used in civil proceedings the application must be made to the judge hearing the case. The proceedings will be by summons supported by an affidavit setting out the grounds for disclosure. The summons will be *ex parte*. An *inter partes* hearing will allow the party resisting disclosure to reply.

3–37   If the civil proceedings are not extant, a witness summons can be issued against the person holding the required documentation. The person upon whom the witness summons has been issued can apply to the criminal trial judge to have the summons set aside by claiming either that the material is irrelevant or that it is subject to public interest immunity.

Caution dictates however that the Court is aware that the application is 3–38 not a mere fishing exercise or costs may be awarded against the solicitor making the application. In *Re a Solicitor (Wasted Costs Order)* (1996) 160 J.P. 29, C.A., the solicitor represented a man charged with indecent assault on a girl who was in accommodation provided by the local authority namely supported lodgings. After committal the solicitor sought disclosure of the complete local authority file relating to the girl. The authority produced the file to the judge but contended that its contents were confidential. The judge found in favour of the local authority holding that the files were indeed confidential and that the application was a speculative manoeuvre without any merit. He made a wasted costs order against the defendant's solicitor in the sum of £727.88 in respect of the authority's attendance at court. On appeal, the Court of Appeal upheld the order. By section 18A (1) of the Prosecution of Offences Act 1985 the Court could make an order for wasted costs "in any criminal proceedings", an expression which covered proceedings initiated by summons for the attendance of a witness to produce a document. Further, a solicitor acting for a defendant in a criminal case was expected to possess the skill of the competent practitioner. It was not proper to issue a witness summons for the disclosure of a document or documents, still less the whole contents of a file or files, for the speculative purpose that material might come to light which could discredit a complainant. The law was sufficiently clear to provide adequate guidance for the competent solicitor who had applied his mind to it.

II. Civil Proceedings

The reverse situation may arise whereby parties to a civil case may require 3–39 information in the hands of those conducting a criminal investigation or prosecution, *i.e.* the police or the Crown Prosecution Service. Again, public interest immunity may well be claimed. The situation was discussed in *Nottinghamshire C.C. v. H (Minors)* [1995] 2 F.C.R. 366. A summons was issued requiring the attendance of a senior member of the Crown Prosecution Service to produce documents submitted to it by the police. An order was made to disclose two documents but disclosure was subject to stringent restriction as to copying and further disclosure of those documents.

Normally, the application should be directed to the Chief Constable and 3–40 not to the Crown Prosecution Service (*Nottinghamshire C.C. v.H* (above) at 369). A judge should not inspect the documents until he is satisfied that they contain material which would give substantial support to the contentions of the party seeking disclosure. This situation normally occurs where for example, the parents seek disclosure of social work records of the local authority (*Air Canada and Others v. Secretary of State for Trade* [1983] A.C. 394).

3–41   If the case is to be heard in the Crown Court, application concerning disclosure should be heard by that court, not the magistrates court (*R v. Crown Prosecution Service, ex p. Warby, The Independent*, September 16, 1993).

3–42   Guidance on the procedures to be followed in making applications to withhold material on the grounds of public interest immunity were set out in *R v. Davis, Johnson and Rowe* [1993] 2 All E.R. 643.

3–43   In *R v.H (a minor)* [1995] 2 F.C.R. 711, a defendant in a rape case issued a summons to the Local Authority seeking disclosure of files relating to adoption proceedings held by the Authority (as previously set out in [1990] 1 All E.R. 639). The Authority successfully applied for the summons to be set aside on the grounds that the information was confidential and should not be disclosed. The Authority then issued an originating summons seeking the assistance of the Family Court. The court held that whether the documents should be disclosed was a matter entirely for the judge in the criminal proceedings. Adoption papers do not now need to be passed to the Attorney-General for advice. The case may have implications for the prosecution of incest and rape cases.

Applications against third parties were further considered in *R v. W(G); R v. W(E), The Times*, July 12, 1996. G was charged with cruelty, indecent assault, rapes and buggery of two of his daughters, his wife E was charged with indecent assault, and aiding and abetting the rapes and buggery. An application was made by them against the Borough Council for numerous documents to be disclosed. The estimated time needed just to read the documents was 72 hours. The solution reached was that the Local Authority appointed seperate counsel to sort out the relevant from the irrelevant documents. The prosecution then claimed public interest immunity over 20 of them. It was held that the procedure adopted by the judge was acceptable. The possessor of the documents was entitled to go to the court and say that they were irrelevant. The judge could either read or look at the documents himself, or he may accept that assertion. If the assertion was suspect or implausable the judge would no doubt look at the documents himself. An assertion from an independant competent member of the Bar was sufficient reason to draw the conclusion that they were irrelevant, and the judge's acceptance of the Local Authority's assurance based upon Counsel's opinion was perfectly proper. Judges do not need to examine the documents themselves.

3–44   In the case of *Re M (Minors) (Care proceedings: police videos)*, unreported July 7, 1995, H.L., it was held that it might be appropriate for a party to care proceedings to have copies of the videos of police interviews with his children. The father was alleged to have sexually abused the children. A *subpoena duces tecum* was appropriately issued against the police and an order was made for one copy of the videos to be made available each to the father and the local authorities. However, the order did not intend a copy should be supplied to the father himself, but to the father's solicitor. Allowances were given to the Court to secure confidentiality and integrity of the copies and to prevent further copying or dissemination.

Criminal Procedure and Investigations Act 1996, s. 17 protects unused material disclosed by the prosecution to the accused or his legal advisor under the new disclosure scheme set out in Part 1. Such material must be treated as confidential and, without the permission of the court, it cannot be used for any other purposes than the criminal proceedings to which it relates (or subsequent proceedings such as an appeal). If the material is displayed or read out in court it loses this status as confidential.

C. VICTIM IMPACT CASES

In the unreported case of *R v. Summerfield: Attorney-General's Reference*   3–45
(No. 2) (1995) the defendant had abused his own daughter over a prolonged period of time commencing when she was between five and six years old. There were a number of aggravating features. Prior to sentence, a statement was taken from her showing the impact of the abuse upon her, which had included an attempt to take her own life and the necessity for counselling. The trial judge had felt that it was "inappropriate for a judge to receive evidence which sought to aggravate the impact which the offending had had upon the victim". The Court of Appeal disagreed and felt that it was wholly appropriate that a judge should receive factual information as to the impact of the offending upon the victim. In this case, the conduct had a clear effect upon the victim.

However, the evidence must be in proper form and it is wholly improper   3–46
for counsel for the Crown to inform the court of the effects of an indecent assault upon the complainant without submitting supporting evidence to the court in the appropriate form (*R v. Hobstaff* (1993) 14 Cr.App.R(S) 605). Counsel for the Crown described that the victims of indecent assaults were now sleep walking, suffering from nightmares and were being seen by a child psychologist. The defence had received no notice of this and had not been able to take instructions. It was held that the remarks were improper. Counsel should have followed guidance in *Attorney-General's Reference (No. 1)* [1989] 1 W.L.R. 1117, the evidence should be in proper form as witness statements. This served two essential purposes: first, the evidence had to be served in advance on the defence to deal with; and secondly, the evidence had to form part of the judge's papers who would then be fully informed and his judgment would not be influenced by the prosecution's information alone.

D. BAIL IN SEXUAL CASES

Where a court grants bail to a defendant charged with rape or attempted rape   3–47
(murder, manslaughter, or attempted murder), after the Crown has made representations that the defendant would a) fail to surrender; b) commit an offence while on bail; or c) interfere with witnesses or otherwise obstruct the

course of justice, the court shall state the reasons for its decisions and shall cause their reasons to be included in the record of the proceedings (Bail Act 1976, Sched., 1, para. 9A)

3-48   However, where a person is charged with, or convicted of rape or attempted rape (murder, manslaughter or attempted murder), if that person has been previously convicted in any part of the United Kingdom of any such offence or culpable homicide, he shall not be granted bail (in the case of manslaughter or culpable homicide, the conviction must have attracted a custodial sentence): Criminal Justice and Public Order Act 1994, s. 25. The reference to "any such offence" indicates that it need not be a like offence.

3-49   It is submitted that this is an absolute prohibition upon the grant of bail and still applies even if the normal custody time limit has expired without extension—section 25 of the Criminal Justice and Public Order Act 1994 post–dates the Prosecution of Offences Act 1985, s. 22 and is mandatory. Custody time limits do not apply therefore to cases covered by section 4(8) of the Bail Act 1976, Sched. 10, para. 32.

E. SERIES OF OFFENCES

3-50   A series of offences joined on an indictment under rule 9 of the Indictment Rules (S.I. 1971 No. 1253) should not be approached by consideration of the ordinary dictionary definition of "series".

3-51   In R v. Baird, The Times, January 12, 1993, the defendant was charged with two indecent assaults on boy A, nine years prior to an indecent assault on boy B. The court accepted that the similarities between the two sets of offences were "truly remarkable" although there was no coincidence in time, or in place. The defendant had developed a casual encounter in the street to build a degree of friendship and familiarity with the boys and to gain their parents' confidence. The similarity justified their joinder on the indictment and the refusal to sever under the discretion given by section 5(3) of the Indictments Act 1915. In addition, the similarity was sufficient for each boy to corroborate the other.

3-52   In R v. Christou (George) [1996] Crim.L.R.911, the court considered rule 9 of the 1971 Indictment Rules and section 5 of the Indictments Act 1915 as they apply to child abuse cases. The Court held that the trial judge had a discretion to decide severance and his discretion should not be faltered in any particular class of case. The defendant was alleged to have indecently assaulted two young female cousins. There was no rule that where the evidence of one child was not admissible to support the evidence of the other as laid down in DPP v. P [1991] 2 A.C. 447 the indictment should always be severed. The allegation was of a continuous course of conduct within one household involving two or more children over the same period and in similar circumstances. A joint trial may well be appropriate. Joinder had been allowed in a number of cases such as R v. Dixon (1989) Cr.App.R. 43; R v. Tickner [1992] Crim.L.R. 44; R v. Smith [1992] Crim.L.R. 445 and R v. Cannan (1990) 92 Cr.App.R. 16. Both cases reviewed previous authorities.

In the later it was said that the Indictments Act 1915 allows the judge a discretion and the appeal courts will not interfere unless it is shown that the judge has failed to exercise his descretion upon the usual and proper principles, namely taking into account all things he should and not taking into account anything he should not. The question will of course be resolved if the evidence of the victims is mutually corroborative.

Severence has been allowed on the principles set out in *R v. Sims* [1946] K.B. 531 that it is asking too much to expect any jury when considering one charge to disregard the evidence on the others, and if such evidence is inadmissable the prejudice created by it would be improper and would be too great for any direction to overcome, subsequently described as 'asking too much of any jury to tell them to perform mental gymnastics of this sort'. *R v. Boardman* [1975] A.C. at 459. The comments made in Boardman are however *obiter dicta* (see Russell L.J. in *R v. Dixon* (above)). In the Australian case of *De Jesus v. The Queen* (1987) 68 A.E.R. 1, it was said 'when the admission of the evidence admissible on the charges joined in an indictment carries the risk of impermissible prejudice to the accused if the charges are tried together, seperate trials should be ordered'.

When applying his discretion it was said in *R v. Christou* (above) that a number of factors should be taken into account:

(i)   how disparate or interrelated are the facts giving rise to the counts? In that case the allegation was of a continuous course of conduct within one household involving two or more children over the same period and in similar circumstances;

(ii) the impact of ordering two or more trials on the defendant and his family. If two trials are more favourable to the defendant this is likely to weigh in favour of severance;

(iii) the impact of ordering two or more trials on the victims and their families. This will be of relevance only to those witnesses whose evidence is admissible in the two or more trials;

(iv) the impact of ordering two or more trials on press publicity. There are of course provisions for preventing unsatisfactory implications of press coverage, the most famous perhaps being seen in *R v. West, The Times*, April 3, 1996; and

(v)   importantly, whether directions the judge can give the jury will suffice to secure a fair trial if the counts are tried together.

For a discussion of similar fact evidence, see Chapter 2, paras. 2–25—2–41.

F. DELAY

It is not a matter of law, nor of invariable practise that a judge should give to   **3–53**
the jury a direction about the difficulty in which the defence may find itself
when there is a delay in bringing to court an allegation of sexual abuse. Much

depends upon the length of the delay, the cogency of the evidence and the circumstances of the case.

3-54   In *R v. E (Sexual abuse: delay) The Times*, July 6, 1995, the defendant was alleged to have committed indecent assaults and an incident of attempted buggery on male relatives, 17 to 23 years previously when the boys were aged between three and seven. The trial judge had made no reference to the difficulties caused by the lapse of time. The Court of Appeal held that in cases of such antiquity, especially where the evidence was uncorroborated, a failure to give such a direction to the jury would amount to a misdirection.

3-55   In unreported, *R v. H* (November 24, 1995, C.A.) delay was also discussed. The arguments were first, that the trial judge having ruled against an abuse of process submission should have warned the jury of the difficulties faced by the defence after a lapse of time which would handicap the obtaining of exculpatory evidence; secondly, that the conviction would be unsafe partially because there had been long term therapy.

3-56   Long term therapy of its very nature may involve the use of leading questions and the suggestion of answers. Although notes of the therapy should be available to the defence, they will be of minimal value and therapy sessions will generally not be taped, videoed or subject to any Code of Best Practice. The danger anticipated is that as a result the evidence of the victim may be tainted, if not positively constructed but genuinely believed as a "recovered memory".

G. SENTENCING ON SPECIMEN COUNTS

3-57   In some examples of sexual offences committed over a substantial period of time, for example, in cases of child abuse, it may be necessary to select specimen counts to avoid overloading the indictment. The specimen charges chosen should be sufficient to allow the sentencing court to reflect fairly the criminality of the offending.

3-58   The principle laid down in *Anderson v. DPP* [1978] A.C. 964, is of general application in the criminal law. The defendant cannot be sentenced for a crime which he has neither admitted nor been convicted.

3-59   In *R v. Clark* (unreported, February 28, 1996, C.A.), the Crown attempted to reflect indecent assaults occurring on a weekly basis over a two year period by a single specimen count. The defendant was sentenced to five years' imprisonment. On appeal, the sentence was reduced to two years. The Court of Appeal confirmed that the defendant could only be sentenced for the offence of which he had been convicted, *i.e.* a single incident.

H. SENTENCING OF SERIOUS SEXUAL OFFENCES— PROTECTION OF THE PUBLIC

Criminal Justice Act 1991, s.1, amended by the Criminal Justice and Public   3–60
Order Act 1994, s.66(1) states in subsection 2 that:

"Subject to subsection (3) (where an offender refuses to give his consent to
a community sentence) the court shall not pass a custodial sentence on the
offender unless it is of the opinion:
  (a) that the offence or the combination of the offence and one or
       more other offences associated with it, was so serious that only
       such a sentence can be justified for the offence; or
  (b) where the offence is a violent, or sexual offence, that only such a
       sentence would be adequate to protect the public from serious
       harm from him."

The court must state that either or both paragraphs (a) and (b) apply and
why the court is of that opinion and must explain to the offender in open
court and in ordinary language why it is passing a custodial sentence on him
(subs. 4).

The Criminal Justice Act, s.2(2) states: 3–61

"The custodial sentence shall be:
  (a) for such term (and not exceeding the permitted maximum) as in
       the opinion of the court is commensurate with the seriousness of
       the offence, or the combination of the offence and one or more
       offences associated with it; or
  (b) where the offence is a violent, or sexual offence, for such longer
       term (not exceeding the permitted maximum) as in the opinion
       of the court is necessary to protect the public from serious harm
       from the offender."

Subsection 3 obliges the court to state in open court that subsection 2(b)   3–62
(above) applies and why it is of that opinion and to explain to the offender in
open court and in ordinary language why the sentence is for such a term.

Subsection 4 states that a custodial sentence for an indeterminate period   3–63
shall be regarded as a custodial sentence for a term longer than any actual
term.

Under section 2(2) the sentence *shall* be as described, *i.e.* the section is   3–64
mandatory not discretionary. The protection of the public becomes of
primary importance taking precedence over mitigation.

I. "SEXUAL OFFENCE"

The Criminal Justice and Public Order Act 1994, Sched. 9, para.45 intro-   3–65
duced a new definition of "sexual offence". Now a sexual offence is defined
as:

"(a) an offence under the Sexual Offences Act 1956, other than an offence
       under sections 30, 31, or 33 to 36;

(b)   an offence under section 128 of the Mental Health Act 1959;

(c)   an offence under the Indecency with Children Act 1960;

(d)   an offence under section 9 of the Theft Act 1968 of burglary with intent to commit rape;

(e)   an offence under section 54 of the Criminal Law Act 1977;

(f)   an offence under the Protection of Children Act 1978;

(g)   an offence under section 1 of the Criminal Law Act 1977 of conspiracy to commit any of the offence in (a) to (f) above;

(h)   an offence under section 1 of the Criminal Attempts Act 1981 of attempting to commit any of those offences; and

(i)   an offence of inciting another to commit any of those Acts."

Counsel should always be warned that the sentencer is considering invoking the use of the section. Failure to comply will not however invalidate the sentence. It will be very rare for a magistrates' court to make use of the section (*R v. Baverstock* [1993] 1 W.L.R. 202).

3–66   Section 2(2)(b) is mandatory and not limited to cases where the danger of serious harm is obvious, nor where the serious harm has already been caused. The court may take into account all reports it has received and the details of previous offences. The present offence need not be the most serious especially where the defendant has previous convictions for similar offences and reports indicate that there remains a possibility of further future attacks (*R v. Bowler* (1993) 15 Cr.App.R(S) 78; *Att-Gen's Ref (No.4 of 1993)*; *R v. Bingham* 15 Cr.App.R(S) 205; *R v. Williams* 15 Cr.App.R(S) 330; *R v. Apelt* 15 Cr.App.R(S) 420; *R v. Meikle* 15 Cr.App.R(S) 311; *R v. Lyons* 15 Cr.App.R(S) 460).

3–67   The harm envisaged must however be serious and not merely unpleasant or distressing (*R v. Creasy* 15 Cr.App.R(S) 671). What is important is the seriousness of the harm not the seriousness of the risk.

II. THE CORRECT APPROACH

3–68   The correct approach is for the court first to calculate the sentence which would be commensurate with the facts of the case under section 2(2)(a) and then add to it the additional period to protect the public under section 2(2)(b) (*R v. Mansell* (1994) 15 Cr.App.R(S) 771; *R v. Crow and Pennington* (1995) 16 Cr.App.R.(S) 409). The judge is not required to indicate to the defendant the sentence he would have passed had he not intended to use the powers under section 2(2)(b) (*R v. Powell*, The Times, August 9, 1996).

3–69   In doing so the sentencer has to perform a balancing exercise. On the one hand the sentencer has to give priority to the protection of the public. On the other hand, regard must also be had to any mitigation and the need to see that the totality of the sentence is not out of all proportion to the nature of the offending (*R v. Mansell*, above). If a commensurate sentence would have been relatively short some circumstances may justify an enhanced sentence of much greater length. In *R v. Fisher* (1994) 16 Cr.App.R. (S) 643 a minor indecent assault on a small child attracted a sentence of six years' imprisonment to provide additional protection to the public.

One danger in this balance is that some guideline sentencing cases already   **3–70**
have a weighting for protection of the public because of the serious risk. *R v.*
Billam (1986) 82 Cr.App.R. 347, the guideline judgment for rape is such an
example. Where the guideline case recommends a higher starting point for a
custodial sentence the court must guard against the danger of effectively
imposing an element of the sentence twice over when applying section
2(2)(b) (*R v. Christie* (1995) 16 Cr.App.R(S) 469, which involved the aspect
of violence, not a sexual offence, in an armed robbery).

The problem was addressed by the Court of Appeal in *R v. Campbell*
(*James Alexander*), *The Times*, July 18, 1996. It was advised that the judge
should first make up his mind as to the appropriate commensurate sentence
and leave out of the account the element of enhancement to protect the
public. Having thus arrived at this starting point, the sentencer should then
add the greater element needed to protect the public. This approach would
avoid the danger of imposing an element of the sentence twice over.

Strictly interpreted the court is not required to obtain medical reports   **3–71**
before applying section 2(2)(b): *R v. Hashi* (1995) 16 Cr.App.R(S) 121.
Nonetheless, it was stated in *R v. Fawcett* (1995) 16 Cr.App.R(S) 55 that "if
the danger is due to a mental or personality problem, the sentencing court
should, in our view always call for a medical report before passing sentence
under section 2(2)(b)". The court should ascertain if a medical disposal
would be more appropriate. A hospital order (with or without a restriction
order) may only be made however if:

(a)   the condition is held to be treatable; and
(b)   a hospital is willing to accept the offender as a patient (Mental
       Health Act 1983, s.37)

A sentence under section 2(2)(b) should be based upon and by reference to   **3–72**
previous convictions and conduct particularly irrational acts or lack of
remorse (*R v. Fawcett*, above). It should not be based solely upon the facts of
the current offence (where the offender has no past history of similar
offences) and the medical evidence is equivocal (*R v. Thomas* (1995) 16
Cr.App.R(S) 671).

The Criminal Justice Act 1991, s.44 states that if a sentencing court so   **3–73**
specifies, an offender may, after he has been released on licence, be required
to serve out the full term of his sentence under supervision in the community
instead of receiving unconditional release after he has served three quarters
of his term where the whole or part of his custodial sentence was imposed for
a sexual offence.

The Court must have regard to the need to protect the public from serious   **3–74**
harm, the desirability of preventing further offences and of securing the
offender's rehabilitation.

The section refers to the case of long or short term prisoners. A long term   **3–75**
prisoner is a person serving a sentence of four years or more and a short term
prisoner is a person who is serving a sentence of less than four years
(s. 33(5)). A short term prisoner who serves a sentence of less than 12
months, however, is to be released automatically after having served half his
sentence and is to be released unconditionally. It is submitted therefore that

section 44 only refers to a prisoner conditionally released (as in ss.33 and 37) and not to one released unconditionally and automatically and therefore does not apply to short term sentences of less than 12 months.

III. DISCRETIONARY LIFE PRISONERS

3-76 The Criminal Justice Act 1991, s.34 deals with the duty to release discretionary life prisoners. It states:

"(1) a life prisoner is a discretionary life prisoner for these purposes if:
  (a) his sentence was imposed for a violent or sexual offence the sentence for which is not fixed by law; and
  (b) the court by which he was sentenced for that offence ordered that this section should apply to him as soon as he has served a part of his sentence specified in the order."

(Subsection (2) not printed.)

"(3) If, in the case of a discretionary life prisoner:
  (a) he has served the part of his sentence specified in the order ('the relevant part'); and
  (b) the Board has directed his release under this section, it shall be the duty of the Secretary of State to release him on licence."

The Board must be satisfied that it is no longer necessary for the protection of the public that the prisoner should be confined (s.34(4)).

3-77 The sentencer's decision as to the relevant part is an order of the court and it is inappropriate to refer to it as a recommendation.

As an order it is subject to appeal by the defendant under section 9(1) of the Criminal Appeal Act 1968. It is not necessary to appeal against the whole sentence, an appeal against the order, against the relevant part, alone may be undertaken (*R v. Frank George Dalton* (1995) 2 Cr.App.R 340, applying *R v. Billam* (1986) Cr.App.R. 347 reducing the relevant period from 12 years to 10 years).

3-78 The judge need not of course apply section 34 if he forms the view that the gravity of the offending was such that "life" should mean life (*Practice Direction (Discretionary life sentences)* [1993] 1 W.L.R. 223).

IV. MANDATORY SENTENCES

3-78A The Crime (Sentences) Act 1997, Pt. 1, s. 2 specifies that where a person is convicted of a serious offence after the commission of the section and at the time when that offence was committed he was 18 or over and had been convicted in any part of the United Kingdom of a serious offence, the court shall impose a life sentence unless the court is of the opinion that there are exceptional circumstances relating to either offence or to the offender which justify its not doing so. Where the court does not impose a life sentence, it shall state in open court that it is of that opinion and what the exceptional circumstances are (subs. 1(c)).

The term "life sentence" means where the person is 21 or over a sentence   **3-78B**
of imprisonment for life and where he is over 18 and under 21 a sentence
under section 8(2) of the Criminal Justice Act 1982.

Two of the serious offences listed are rape or attempted rape, and an   **3-78C**
offence under section 5 of the Sexual Offences Act 1956 (intercourse with a
girl under 13). The offence for which the life sentence is imposed shall not be
regarded as an offence the sentence for which is fixed by law. The "other
serious offence" may have been committed prior to the commencement of
the Act and need not be the same type of serious offence as that for which
sentence is now being passed.

I. POWERS OF FORFEITURE AND CONFISCATION

In addition to powers of forfeiture and confiscation contained within specific   **3-79**
statutes, the courts have powers under ancillary acts to order confiscation
and forfeiture.

Section 43 of the Powers of Criminal Courts Act 1973 states:

(1)   subject to the following provisions of this section, where a person is   **3-80**
      convicted of an offence, and:
      (a)   the court by or before which he is convicted is satisfied that any
            property which has been lawfully seized from him or which was
            in his possession or under his control at the time when he was
            apprehended for the offence or when a summons in respect of it
            was issued:
            (i)   has been used for the purposes of committing, or facilitating
                  the commission of, any offence; or
            (ii) was intended by him to be used for that purpose; or
      (b)   the offence, or an offence which the court has taken into con-
            sideration in determining his sentence, consists of unlawful
            possession of property which:
            (i)   has been lawfully seized from him; or
            (ii) was in his possession or under his control at the time when
                  he was apprehended for the offence of which he has been
                  convicted or when a summons in respect of that offence was
                  issued, the court may make an order under this section in
                  respect of that property, and may do so whether or not it
                  also deals with the offender in respect of the offence in any
                  other way and without regard to any restriction on for-
                  feiture in an enactment contained in an Act passed before
                  the Criminal Justice Act 1988.
(1A) In considering whether to make such an order in respect of any   **3-81**
      property a court shall have regard:
      (a)   to the value of the property; and
      (b)   to the likely financial and other effects on the offender of the
            making of the order (taken together with any other order that
            the court contemplates making)."

I. OTHER CONSIDERATIONS

3–82   Property does not include real property such as the offender's home (*R v. Khan* [1982] 1 W.L.R. 1405), nor can the court order forfeiture of property which appears to be the proceeds of an earlier offence (*R v. Neville* (1987) 9 Cr.App.R.(S) 222), or associated with an offence committed by a person other than the defendant (*R v. Slater* [1986] 1 W.L.R. 1340, distinguished in *R v. Coleville-Scott* (1990) 12 Cr.App.R.(S) 238). However, it is not necessary that the defendant should have used the property to facilitate the offence of which he has been convicted.

3–83   Possession may be either physical possession or an entitlement to an immediate right to possession but forfeiture orders should only be made in simple, uncomplicated cases and not for example where the property is jointly owned (*R v. Troth* (1980) Crim.L.R. 249).

3–84   Where the court is considering making a forfeiture order, evidence must be laid before the judge on the issue of forfeiture and a full and proper investigation must be made into the prosecution's application (*R v. Pemberton* (1982) 4 Cr.App.R.(S) 328; *R v. Richards* (1992) 2 All E.R. 572). An order depriving a defendant of his rights in property should be viewed as part of the total penalty imposed for the offence (*R v. Buddo* (1982) 4 Cr.App.R.(S) 268).

3–85   Section 43 of the Powers of Criminal Courts Act 1973 states:

"(2) Facilitating the commission of an offence shall be taken for the purposes of this section and section 44 of this Act to include the taking of any steps after it has been committed for the purpose of disposing of any property to which it relates or of avoiding apprehension or detection, and references in this or that section to an offence punishable with imprisonment shall be construed without regard to any prohibition or restriction imposed by or under any enactment on the imprisonment of young offenders.

3–86   (3) An order under this section shall operate to deprive the offender of his rights, if any, in the property to which it relates and the property shall (if not already in their possession) be taken into the possession of the police.

3–87   (4) The Police (Property) Act 1897 shall apply, with the following modifications, to property which is in the possession of the police by virtue of this section:

(a) no application shall be made under section 1(1) of that Act by any claimant of the property after the expiration of six months from the date on which the order in respect of the property was made under this section; and

(b) no such application shall succeed unless the claimant satisfies the court either that he had not consented to the offender having possession of the property or, where an order is made under subsection (1)(a) above, that he did not know, and had no reason to suspect, that the property was likely to be used for the purpose mentioned in that paragraph.

3–88   (5) In relation to property which is in the possession of the police by virtue of this section, the power to make regulations under section 2(1) of the Police (Property) Act 1897 (disposal of property in cases where the owner of the property has not been ascertained and no order of a competent court has been made with respect thereto) shall include power to make regulations for disposal in cases where no application by a claimant of the property has been made within the period specified in subsection 4(a) above or no such application has succeeded."

II. CRIMINAL JUSTICE ACT 1988

The provisions under the 1988 Act have been amended by the Proceeds of Crime Act 1995. Section 71 as amended applies to proceedings for offences committed after November 1, 1995. Sections 75(5A) and 75A apply to offences, in respect of which a confiscation order is made, which are committed after November 1,1995.   3–89

The Act as amended, provides two different procedures for the making of a confiscation order in relation to the benefit derived by an offender from certain crimes. It specifically refers to offences in relation to sex establishments and under the Video Recordings Act 1984. The court may also consider offences which have been taken into consideration but may not take account of offences of which the defendant has not been convicted, *i.e.* those represented by specimen counts.   3–90

Section 71 states: 3–91

"(1) Where an offender is convicted, in any proceedings before the Crown Court or a magistrates' court, of an offence of a relevant description, it shall be the duty of the court:
   (a) if the prosecutor has given written notice to the court that he considers that it would be appropriate for it so to proceed under this section, or
   (b) if the court considers, even though it has not been given such notice, that it would be appropriate for it so to proceed, to act as follows before sentencing or otherwise dealing with the offender in respect of that offence or any other relevant criminal conduct".

(a) Benefits

"(1A) The court shall first determine whether the offender has benefited from any relevant criminal conduct.   3–92
   (1B) Subject to subsection (1C) below, if the court determines that the offender has benefited from any relevant criminal conduct, it shall then:
   (a) determine in accordance with subsection (6) below the amount to be recovered in his case by virtue of this section, and
   (b) make an order under this section ordering the offender to pay that amount.

(1C) If, in any case falling within subsection (1B) above, the court is satisfied that a victim of any relevant criminal conduct has instituted, or intends to institute, civil proceedings against the defendant in respect of loss, injury or damage sustained in connection with that conduct:

(a) the court shall have a power, instead of a duty, to make an order under this section; and

(b) subsection (6) below shall not apply for determining the amount to be recovered in that case by virtue of this section; and

(c) where the court makes an order in exercise of that power, the sum required to be paid under that order shall be of such amount, not exceeding the amount which (but for paragraph (b) above) would apply by virtue of subsection (6) below, as the court thinks fit.

3-93 (1D) In this part of this Act 'relevant criminal conduct', in relation to a person convicted of an offence in any proceedings before a court, means (subject to section 72AA(6) below) that offence taken together with any other offences of a relevant description which are either:

(a) offences of which he is convicted in the same proceedings, or

(b) offences which the court will be taking into consideration in determining his sentence for the offence in question."

(b) The offence

3-94 "(1E) For the purposes of this part of this Act an offence is an offence of a relevant description:

(a) in the case of an offence of which a person is convicted in any proceedings before the Crown Court or which is or will be taken into consideration by the Crown Court in determining any sentence, if it is an offence to which this part of this Act applies; and

(b) in the case of an offence of which a person is convicted in any proceedings before a magistrates' court or which is or will be taken into consideration by a magistrates' court in determining any sentence, if it is an offence listed in schedule 4 to this Act.
(Subsections 2–3 not printed.)

3-95 (4) For the purposes of this part of this Act a person benefits from an offence if he obtains property as a result of or in connection with its commission and his benefit is the value of the property so obtained.

(5) Where a person derives a pecuniary advantage as a result of or in connection with the commission of an offence, he is to be treated for the purposes of this part of this Act as if he had obtained as a result of or in connection with the commission of the offence a sum of money equal to the value of the pecuniary advantage.

3-96 (6) Subject to subsection (1C) above the sum which an order made by a court under this section requires an offender to pay shall be equal to:

(a) the benefit in respect of which it is made; or

(b)   the amount appearing to the court to be the amount that might
be realised at the time the order is made,
whichever is the less.

(7A) The standard of proof required to determine any question arising   3–97
under this part of the Act as to:
(a)   whether a person has benefited from any offence; or
(b)   the amount of to be recovered in his case, shall be that applicable
in civil proceedings."
(Subsection (8) not printed)

(c) Definitions

"(9) In this Part of this Act: 3–98
(a)   an order made by a court under this section is referred to as a
'confiscation order';
(b)   'drug trafficking offence' has the same meaning as in the Drug
Trafficking Offences Act 1986;
(c)   references to an offence to which this Part of this Act applies are
references to any offence which:
(i)   is listed in Schedule 4 to this Act; or
(ii) if not so listed, is an indictable offence, other than a drug
trafficking offence or an offence under Part III of the Prevention of Terrorism (Temporary Provisions) Act 1989;
and
(d)   a person against whom proceedings have been instituted for an
offence to which this Part of this Act applies is referred to
(whether or not he has been convicted) as 'the defendant'."

(d) Schedule 4 offences:

1.   Local Government (Miscellaneous Provisions) Act 1982, Sched. 3,
paras. 20 and 21 (offences relating to sex establishments);
2.   Video Recordings Act 1984, ss. 9 and 10 (supplying video recording of unclassified work and possession of video recording of
unclassified work for the purposes of supply);
3.   Cinemas Act 1985, s. 10(1)(a) (use of unlicensed premises for
exhibition which requires a licence);
4.   Local Government Act 1963, Sched. 12, paras 10(1) and (2);
Private Places of Entertainment (Licensing) Act 1967, s. 4(1) and
(2); Local Government (Miscellaneous Provisions) Act 1982,
Sched. 1, paras 12(1) and (2) (offences relating to the use of places
for dancing, music or other entertainment);
5.   Copyright, Designs and Patents Act 1988, ss. 107(1), (2) or (3) and
198(1) or (2) (making or dealing with infringing articles etc. and
making, dealing with or using illicit recordings);
6.   Trade Marks Act 1994, s. 92(1), (2) or (3) (unauthorised use of
trade marks, etc., in relation to goods).

(e) **Sentencing**

3–99   (Section 72(1)–(4) not printed.)
         Section 72(5) states:

"Where a court makes a confiscation order against a defendant in any proceedings, it shall be its duty, in respect of any offence of which he is convicted in those proceedings, to take account of the order before:
  (a) imposing any fine on him, or
  (b) making any order involving any payment by him, other than an order under section 35 of the Powers of Criminal Courts Act 1973 (compensation orders); or
  (c) making any order under:
       (i) section 27 of the Misuse of Drugs Act 1971 (forfeiture orders); or
       (ii) section 43 of the Powers of Criminal Courts Act 1973 (deprivation orders), but subject to that shall leave the order out of account in determining the appropriate sentence or other manner of dealing with him.

3–100   (6) No enactment restricting the power of a court dealing with an offender in a particular way from dealing with him also in any other way shall by reason only of the making of a confiscation order restrict the court from dealing with an offender in any way it considers appropriate in respect of an offence to which this part of this Act applies.

3–101   (7) Where:
         (a) a court makes both a confiscation order and an order for the payment of compensation under section 35 of the Powers of Criminal Courts Act 1973 against the same person in the same proceedings; and
         (b) it appears to the court that he will not have sufficient means to satisfy both the orders in full, it shall direct that so much of the compensation as will not in its opinion be recoverable because of the insufficiency of his means shall be paid out of any sums recovered under the confiscation order."

3–102   Section 72AA states:

"(1) This section applies in a case where an offender is convicted, in any proceedings before the Crown Court or a magistrates' court, of a qualifying offence which is an offence of a relevant description, if:
      (a) the prosecutor gives written notice for the purposes of subsection (1)(a) of section 71 above;
      (b) that notice contains a declaration that it is the prosecutor's opinion that the case is one in which it is appropriate for the provisions of this section to be applied; and (c) the offender:
           (i) is convicted in those proceedings of at least two qualifying offences (including the offence in question); or
           (ii) has been convicted of a qualifying offence on at least one previous occasion during the relevant period.

(2)   In this section 'qualifying offence', in relation to proceedings before   **3–103**
the Crown Court or a magistrates' court, means any offence in
relation to which all the following conditions are satisfied, that is to
say:
(a)   it is an offence to which this part of this Act applies;
(b)   it is an offence which was committed after the commencement of
section 2 of the Proceeds of Crime Act 1995 (November 1,
1995); and
(c)   that court is satisfied that it is an offence from which the
defendant has benefited."

(f) Assumptions

"(3)   When proceeding under section 71 above in pursuance of the notice   **3–104**
mentioned in subsection (1)(a) above, the court may, if it thinks fit,
determine that (subject to subsection (5) below) the assumptions
specified in subsection (4) below are to be made for the purpose:
(a)   of determining whether the defendant has benefited from relevant criminal conduct; and
(b)   if he has, of assessing the value of the defendant's benefit from
such conduct.
(4)   Those assumptions are:
(a)   that any property appearing to the court:
(i)   to be held by the defendant at the date of conviction or at
any time in the period between that date and the determination in question, or
(ii)   to have been transferred to him at any time since the
beginning of the relevant period, was received by him, at the
earliest time when he appears to the court to have held it, as
a result of or in connection with the commission of offences
to which this part of this Act applies;
(b)   that any expenditure of his since the beginning of the relevant
period was met out of payments received by him as a result of or
in connection with the commission of offences to which this part
of this Act applies; and
(c)   that, for the purposes of valuing any benefit which he had or
which he is assumed to have had at any time, he received the
benefit free of any other interests in it.
(5)   Where the court has determined that the assumptions specified in   **3–105**
subsection (4) above are to be made in any case it shall not in that case
make any such assumption in relation to any particular property or
expenditure if:
(a)   that assumption, so far as it relates to that property or expenditure, is shown to be incorrect in the defendant's case;
(b)   that assumption, so far as it relates, is shown to be correct in
relation to an offence the defendant's benefit from which has
been the subject of a previous confiscation order; or
(c)   the court is satisfied that there would (for any other reason) be a

serious risk of injustice in the defendant's case if the assumption were to be made in relation to that property or expenditure.

(6) Where the assumptions specified in subsection (4) above are made in any case, the offences from which, in accordance with those assumptions, the defendant is assumed to have benefited shall be treated as if they were comprised, for the purposes of this part of this Act, in the conduct which is to be treated, in that case as relevant criminal conduct in relation to the defendant.

3-106   (7) In this section 'the date of conviction' means:

(a) in a case not falling within paragraph (b) below, the date on which the defendant is convicted of the offence in question, or

(b) where he is convicted of that offence and one or more other offences in the proceedings in question and those convictions are not all on the same date, the date of the latest of those convictions; and

'the relevant period' means the period of six years ending when the proceedings in question were instituted against the defendant".

(g) Further information

3-107   Section 72A states:

"(1) Where a court is acting under section 71 above but considers that it requires further information before:

(a) determining whether the defendant has benefited as mentioned in section 71(2)(b)(i) above; or

(b) [*Repealed.*]

(c) determining the amount to be recovered in his case,

it may, for the purpose of enabling that information to be obtained, postpone making that determination for such period as it may specify.

(2) More than one postponement may be made under subsection (1) above in relation to the same case.

(3) Unless it is satisfied that there are exceptional circumstances, the court shall not specify a period under subsection (1) above which:

(a) by itself; or

(b) where there have been one or more previous postponements under subsection (1) above or (4) below, when taken together with the earlier specified period or periods,

exceeds six months beginning with the date of conviction.

(4) Where the defendant appeals against his conviction, the court may, on that account:

(a) postpone making any of the determinations mentioned in subsection (1) above for such period as it may specify; or

(b) where it has already exercised its powers under this section to postpone, extend the specified period.

3-108   (5) A postponement or extension under subsection (1) or (4) above may be made:

(a) on application by the defendant or the prosecutor; or

    (b) by the court of its own motion.

(6) Unless the court is satisfied that there are exceptional circumstances, any postponement or extension under subsection (4) above shall not exceed the period ending three months after the date on which the appeal is determined or otherwise disposed of.

(7) Where the court exercises its power under subsection (1) or (4) above, it may nevertheless proceed to sentence, or otherwise deal with, the defendant in respect of the offence or any of the offences concerned.   **3–109**

(8) Where the court has so proceeded:

    (a) subsection (1) of section 71 above shall have effect as if the words from 'before sentencing' onwards were omitted;

    (b) that section shall further have effect as if references to an offence that will be taken into consideration in determining any sentence included references to an offence that has been so taken into account; and

    (c) section 72(5) above shall have effect as if after 'determining' there were inserted 'in relation to any offence in respect of which he has not been sentenced or otherwise dealt with'.

(9) In sentencing, or otherwise dealing with, the defendant in respect of the offence, or any of the offences, concerned at any time during the specified period, the court shall not: **3–110**

    (a) impose any fine on him; or

    (b) make any such order as is mentioned in section 72(5)(b) or (c) above.

(9A) Where the court has sentenced the defendant under subsection (7) above during the specified period it may, after the end of that period, vary the sentence by imposing a fine or making any such order as is mentioned in section 72(5)(b) or (c) above so long as it does so within a period corresponding to that allowed by section 47(2) or (3) of the Supreme Court Act 1981 (time allowed for varying a sentence) but beginning with the end of the specified period.

(10) In this section, references to an appeal include references to an application under section 111 of the Magistrates Court Act 1980 (statement of case by magistrates' court).   **3–111**

(11) In this section 'the date of conviction' means:

    (a) the date on which the defendant was convicted of the offence concerned, or

    (b) where he was convicted in the same proceedings, but on different dates, of two or more offences which are comprised in relevant criminal conduct, the date of the latest of those convictions".

(h) Prosecution statement of benefit

Section 73 states: **3–112**

"(1) Subsection (1A) below applies in a case where a person has been convicted of an offence of a relevant description if:

(a) the prosecutor has given written notice to the court for the purposes of subsection (1)(a) of section 71 above; or

(b) the court is proceedings in pursuance of subsection (1)(b) of that section and requires a statement under this section from the prosecutor.

(1A) Where this subsection applies, the prosecutor shall, within such period as the court may direct, tender to the court a statement as to any matters relevant:

(a) to determining whether the defendant has benefited from any relevant criminal conduct; or

(b) to an assessment of the value of the defendant's benefit from that conduct;

and, where such a statement is tendered in a case in which a declaration has been made for the purposes of subsection (1)(b) of section 72AA above, that statement shall also set out all such information available to the prosecutor as may be relevant for the purposes of subsections (4) and (5)(b) or (c) of that section.

3–113 (1B) Where a statement is tendered to the court under this section:

(a) the prosecutor may at any time tender to the court a further statement as to the matters mentioned in subsection (1A) above; and

(b) the court may at any time require the prosecutor to tender a further such statement within such period as it may direct''.

3–114 (1C) Where:

(a) any statement has been tendered to any court by the prosecutor under this section, and

(b) the defendant accepts to any extent any allegation in the statement,

the court may, for the purpose of determining whether the defendant has benefited from any relevant criminal conduct, treat his acceptance as conclusive of the matters to which it relates.

(2) Where:

(a) a statement is tendered by the prosecutor under this section; and

(b) the court is satisfied that a copy of that statement has been served on the defendant,

the court may require the defendant to indicate to what extent he accepts each allegation in the statement and, so far as he does not accept any such allegation, to indicate any matters he proposes to rely on.

(3) If the defendant fails in any respect to comply with a requirement under subsection (2) above, he may be treated for the purposes of this section as accepting every allegation in the statement apart from:

(a) any allegation in respect of which he has complied with the requirement; and

(b) any allegation that he has benefited from an offence or that any property was obtained by him as a result of or in connection with the commission of an offence.

(5) An allegation may be accepted or a matter indicated for the purposes of this section either:
   (a) orally before the court; or
   (b) in writing in accordance with rules of court.

(6) If the court is satisfied as to any matter relevant for determining the amount that might be realised at the time the confiscation order is made (whether by an acceptance under this section or otherwise), the court may issue a certificate giving the court's opinion as to the matters concerned and shall do so if satisfied that the amount that might be realised at the time the confiscation order is made is less than the amount the court assesses to be the value of the defendant's benefit from any relevant criminal conduct.   **3–115**

(7) Where the court has given a direction under this section, it may at any time vary the direction by giving a further direction".

(i) Defence information

Section 73A states: **3–116**

"(1) This section applies in a case where a person has been convicted of an offence of a relevant description if:
   (a) the prosecutor has given written notice to the court for the purposes of subsection (1)(a) of section 71 above; or
   (b) the court is proceeding in pursuance of subsection (1)(b) of that section or is considering whether so to proceed.

(2) For the purpose of obtaining information to assist it in carrying out its functions under this Part of this Act, the court may at any time order the defendant to give it such information as may be specified in the order.   **3–117**

(3) An order under subsection (2) above may require all, or any specified part, of the required information to be given to the court in such a manner, and before such date, as may be specified in the order.

(4) Rules of court may make provision as to the maximum or minimum period that may be allowed under subsection (3) above.

(5) If the defendant fails, without reasonable excuse, to comply with any order under this section, the court may draw such inference from that failure as it considers appropriate.

(6) Where the prosecutor accepts to any extent any allegation made by the defendant: **3–118**
   (a) in giving to the court information required by an order under this section, or
   (b) in any other statement tendered to the court for the purposes of this Part of this Act,
   the court may treat that acceptance as conclusive of the matters to which it relates.

(7) For the purposes of this section an allegation may be accepted in such manner as may be prescribed by rules of court or as the court may direct".

101

(j) The property

3–119   Section 74 states:

"(1) In this Part of this Act, 'realisable property' means, subject to subsection (2) below:

(a) any property held by the defendant; and

(b) any property held by a person to whom the defendant has directly or indirectly made a gift by this Part of this Act.

(2) Property is not realisable property if:

(a) an order under section 43 of the Powers of Criminal Courts Act 1973 (deprivation orders);

(b) an order under section 27 of the Misuse of Drugs Act 1971 (forfeiture orders);

(c) an order under section 13(2), (3) or (4) of the Prevention of Terrorism (Temporary Provisions) Act 1989 (forfeiture orders), is in force in respect of the property.

3–120   (3) For the purposes of this Part of this Act the amount that might be realised at the time a confiscation order is made is:

(a) the total of the values at that time of all the realisable property held by the defendant, less

(b) where there are obligations having priority at that time, the total amounts payable in pursuance of such obligations, together with the total of the values at that time of all gifts caught by this Part of this Act.

3–121   (4) Subject to the following provisions of this section, for the purposes of this Part of this Act the value of property (other than cash) in relation to any person holding the property:

(a) where any other person holds an interest in the property, is:

(i) the market value of the first-mentioned person's beneficial interest in the property, less

(ii) the amount required to discharge any encumbrance (other than a charging order) on that interest; and

(b) in any other case, is its market value.

(5) References in this Part of this Act to the value at any time (referred to in subsection (6) below as 'the material time') of any property obtained by a person as a result of or in connection with the commission of an offence are references to:

(a) the value of the property to him when he obtained it adjusted to take account of subsequent changes in the value of money; or

(b) where subsection (6) below applies, the value there mentioned, whichever is the greater.

3–122   (6) If at the material time he holds:

(a) the property which he obtains (not being cash); or

(b) property which, in whole or in part, directly or indirectly represents in his hands the property which he obtained,

the value referred to in subsection (5)(b) above is the value to him at the material time of the property mentioned in paragraph (a) above or, as the case may be, of the property mentioned in paragraph (b) above, so far as it so represents the property which he obtains, but disregarding any charging order.

(7)   Subject to subsection (12) below, references in this Part of this Act to the value at any time (referred to in subsection (8) below as 'the material time') of a gift caught by this Part of this Act are references to:
   (a)   the value of the gift to the recipient when he received it adjusted to take account of subsequent changes in the value of money; or
   (b)   where subsection (8) below applies, the value there mentioned, whichever is the greater.

(8)   Subject to subsection (12) below, if at the material time he holds:
   (a)   the property which he received (not being cash); or
   (b)   property which, in whole or in part, directly or indirectly represents in his hands the property which he received;
the value referred to in subsection (7) above is the value to him at the material time of the property mentioned in paragraph (a) above or, as the case may be, of the property mentioned in paragraph (b) above so far as it so represents the property which he received, but disregarding any charging order.

(9)   For the purposes of subsection (3) above, an obligation has priority at any time if it is an obligation of the defendant to: **3–123**
   (a)   pay any amount due in respect of a fine, or other order of a court, imposed or made on conviction of an offence, where the fine was imposed or order made before the confiscation order; or
   (b)   pay any sum which would be included among the preferential debts (within the meaning given by section 386 of the Insolvency Act 1986) in the defendant's bankruptcy commencing on the date of the confiscation order or winding up under an order of the court made on that date."

(k) A gift

"(10) A gift (including a gift made before the commencement of this Part of this Act), is caught by this Part of this Act if: **3–124**
   (a)   it was made by the defendant at any time after the commission of the offence or, if more than one, the earliest of the offences to which the proceedings for the time being relate; and
   (b)   the court considers it appropriate in all the circumstances to take the gift into account.

(11)   The reference in subsection (10) above to an offence to which the proceeding for the time being relate includes, where the proceedings have resulted in the conviction of the defendant, a reference to any offence which the court takes into consideration when determining his sentence.

(12)   For the purposes of this Part of this Act: **3–125**
   (a)   the circumstances in which the defendant is to be treated as

making a gift include those where he transfers property to another person directly or indirectly for a consideration the value of which is significantly less than the value of the consideration provided by the defendant; and

(b) in those circumstances, the preceding provisions of this section shall apply as if the defendant had made a gift of such share in the property as bears to the whole property the same proportion as the difference between the values referred to in paragraph (a) above bears to the value of the consideration provided by the defendant."

(l) Subsequent information

3–126   Section 74A states:

"(1) This section applies in any case where:
(a) a person has been convicted, in any proceedings before the Crown Court or a magistrates' court, of an offence of a relevant description;
(b) the prosecutor did not give written notice for the purposes of subsection (1)(a) of section 71 above; and
(c) a determination was made for the purposes of subsection (1)(b) of that section not to proceed under that section or no determination was made for those purposes.

(2) If the prosecutor has evidence:
(a) which, at the date of conviction or, if later, when any determination not to proceed under section 71 above was made, was not available to the prosecutor (and, accordingly, was not considered by the court); but
(b) which the prosecutor believes would have led the court to determine if:
(i) the prosecutor had given written notice for the purposes of subsection (1)(a) of that section, and
(ii) the evidence had been considered by the court, that the defendant had benefited from relevant criminal conduct, the prosecutor may apply to the relevant court for it to consider the evidence.

3–127   (3) If, having considered the evidence, the relevant court is satisfied that it is appropriate to do so, it shall proceed under section 71 above as if it were doing so before sentencing or otherwise dealing with the defendant in respect of any relevant criminal conduct and section 72A above shall apply accordingly.

(4) In considering whether it is appropriate to proceed under section 71 above in accordance with subsection (3) above, the court shall have regard to all the circumstances of the case.

3–128   (5) Where, having decided in pursuance of subsection (3) above to proceed under section 71 above, the relevant court determines that the defendant did benefit from relevant criminal conduct:
(a) subsection (1B)(b) of that section shall not apply and subsection

(6) of that section shall not apply for determining the amount to be recovered in that case;

(b) that court shall have a power, instead of a duty, to make a confiscation order; and

(c) if the court makes an order in exercise of that power, the sum required to be paid by that order shall be of such amount, not exceeding the amount which (but for paragraph (a) above) would apply by virtue of subsection (6) of that section, as the court thinks fit.

(6) In considering the circumstances of any case either under subsection (4) above or for the purposes of subsection (5)(b) and (c) above, the relevant court shall have regard, in particular, to: **3–129**

(a) any fine imposed on the defendant in respect of any relevant criminal conduct; and

(b) any order made in connection with any such conduct under section 35 of the Powers of Criminal Courts Act 1973 (compensation orders).

(7) In making any determination under or for the purposes of this section the relevant court may take into account, to the extent that they represent respects in which the defendant has benefited from any relevant criminal conduct, any payments or other rewards which were not received by him until after the time when he was sentenced or otherwise dealt with in the case in question. **3–130**

(8) Where an application under this section contains such a declaration as is mentioned in paragraph (b) of subsection (1) of section 72AA above, that section shall apply (subject to subsection (9) below) in the case of any determination on the application as if it were a determination in a case in which the requirements of paragraphs (a) and (b) of that subsection had been satisfied.

(9) For the purposes of any determination to which section 72AA above applies by virtue of subsection (8) above, none of the assumptions specified in subsection (4) of that section shall be made in relation to any property unless it is property held by or transferred to the defendant before the time when he was sentenced or otherwise dealt with in the case in question.

(10) No application shall be entertained by the court under this section if it is made after the end of the period of six years beginning with the date of conviction. **3–131**

(11) Sections 73 and 73A above shall apply where the prosecutor makes an application under this section as they apply in a case where the prosecutor has given written notice to the court for the purposes of subsection (1)(a) of section 71 above, but as if the reference in section 73(1A) to a declaration made for the purposes of subsection (1)(b) of section 72AA above were a reference to a declaration for the purposes of subsection (8) above.

(12) In this section: **3–132**
'the date of conviction' means:
(a) in a case not falling within paragraph (b) below, the date on

which the defendant was convicted of the offence in question, or

(b) where he was convicted of that offence and one or more other offences in the same proceedings and those convictions were not all on the same date, the date of the latest of those convictions;

and 'the relevant court' means:

(a) where the defendant was convicted in proceedings before the Crown Court, that Court; and

(b) where he was convicted in proceedings before a magistrates' court, any magistrates' court for the same area."

(m) Information not originally considered

3-133 Section 74B states:

"(1) This section applies where in any case there has been a determination under subsection (1A) of section 71 above ('the original determination') that the defendant in that case had not benefited from any relevant criminal conduct.

(2) If the prosecutor has evidence:

(a) which was not considered by the court which made the original determination, but

(b) which the prosecutor believes would have led that court (if it had been considered) to determine that the defendant had benefited from relevant criminal conduct,

the prosecutor may apply to the relevant court for it to consider that evidence.

3-134 (3) If, having considered the evidence, the relevant court is satisfied that (if that evidence had been available to it) it would have determined that the defendant had benefited from relevant criminal conduct, that court:

(a) shall proceed, as if it were proceeding under section 71 above before sentencing or otherwise dealing with the defendant in respect of any relevant criminal conduct:

(i) to make a fresh determination of whether the defendant has benefited from any relevant criminal conduct; and

(ii) then to make such a determination as is mentioned in subsection (1B)(a) of that section;

and

(b) subject to subsection (4) below, shall have a power, after making those determinations, to make an order requiring the payment of such sum as it thinks fit;

and an order under paragraph (b) above shall be deemed for all purposes to be a confiscation order.

(4) The court shall not, in exercise of the power conferred by paragraph (b) of subsection (3) above, make any order for the payment of a sum which is more than the amount determined in pursuance of paragraph (a)(ii) of that subsection.

3-135 (5) In making any determination under or for the purposes of subsection

(3) above the relevant court may take into account, to the extent that they represent respects in which the defendant has benefited from any relevant criminal conduct, any payments or other rewards which were not received by him until after the making of the original determination.

(6) Where, in a case in which section 72AA above does not otherwise **3-136** apply, an application under this section contains such a declaration as is mentioned in paragraph (b) of subsection (1) of that section, that section shall apply (subject to subsection (7) below) in the case of any determination on the application as if it were a determination in a case in which the requirements of paragraphs (a) and (b) of that subsection had been satisfied.

(7) For the purposes of any determination under or for the purposes of subsection (3) above to which section 72AA above applies, none of the assumptions specified in subsection (4) of that section shall be made in relation to any property unless it is property held by or transferred to the defendant before the time when he was sentenced or otherwise dealt with in the case in question."

(Subsection (8) not printed.)

"(9) Section 72A above shall apply where the court is acting under this **3-137** section as it applies where the court is acting under section 71 above.

(10) Sections 73 and 73A above shall apply where the prosecutor makes an application under this section as they apply in a case where the prosecutor has given written notice to the court for the purposes of subsection (1)(a) of section 71 above but:

(a) as if the reference in section 73(1A) to a declaration made for the purposes of subsection (1)(b) of section 72AA above included a reference to a declaration for the purposes of subsection (6) above; and

(b) as if any reference in section 73(6) to the time the confiscation order is made were a reference to the time the order is made on that application.

(11) In this section: **3-138**
'the date of conviction' has the same meaning as in section 74A above; and
'the relevant court' means:

(a) where the conviction by reference to which the original determination was made was in proceedings before the Crown Court, that Court; and

(b) where the conviction was in proceedings before a magistrates' court any magistrates' court for the same area."

(n) Information of greater value

Section 74C states: **3-139**

"(1) This section applies where, in the case of a person convicted of any offence, there has been a determination under this Part of this Act ('the current determination') of any sum required to be paid in his case under any confiscation order.

(2) Where the prosecutor is of the opinion that the value of any benefit to the defendant from any relevant criminal conduct was greater than the value at which that benefit was assessed by the court on the current determination, the prosecutor may apply to the relevant court for the evidence on which the prosecutor has formed his opinion to be considered by the court.

3-140 (3) If, having considered the evidence, the relevant court is satisfied that the value of the benefit from any relevant criminal conduct is greater than the value so assessed by the court (whether because its real value was higher at the time of the current determination than was thought or because the value of the benefit in question has subsequently increased), the relevant court:

  (a) subject to subsection (4) below, shall make a fresh determination, as if it were proceeding under section 71 above before sentencing or otherwise dealing with the defendant in respect of any relevant criminal conduct, of the following amounts, that is to say:

    (i) the amount by which the defendant has benefited from such conduct; and

    (ii) the amount appearing to be the amount that might be realised at the time of the fresh determination; and

  (b) subject to subsection (5) below, shall have a power to increase, to such extent as it thinks just in all the circumstances of the case, the amount to be recovered by virtue of that section and to vary accordingly any confiscation order made by reference to the current determination.

3-141 (4) Where:

  (a) the court is under a duty to make a fresh determination for the purposes of subsection (3)(a) above in any case, and

  (b) that case is a case to which section 72AA above applies, the court shall not have power, in determining any amounts for those purposes, to make any of the assumptions specified in subsection (4) of that section in relation to any property unless it is property held by or transferred to the defendant before the time when he was sentenced or otherwise dealt with in the case in question.

(5) The court shall not, in exercise of the power conferred by paragraph (b) of subsection (3) above, vary any order so as to make it an order requiring the payment of any sum which is more than the lesser of the two amounts determined in pursuance of paragraph (a) of that subsection.

3-142 (6) In making any determination under or for the purposes of subsection (3) above the relevant court may take into account, to the extent that they represent respects in which the defendant has benefited from any relevant criminal conduct, any payments or other rewards which were not received by him until after the making of the original determination.

(7) Where the Crown Court varies a confiscation order under subsection **3–143**
(3) above, it shall substitute for the term of imprisonment or of
detention fixed under subsection (2) of section 31 of the Powers of
Criminal Courts Act 1973 in respect of the amount to be recovered
under the order a longer term determined in accordance with that
section (as it has effect by virtue of section 75 below) in respect of any
greater amount substituted under subsection (3) above.

(8) Subsection (7) above shall apply only if the effect of the substitution
is to increase the maximum period applicable in relation to the order
under section 31(3A) of that Act of 1973.

(9) No application shall be entertained by a court under this section if it
is made after the end of the period of six years beginning with the date
of conviction.

(10) Section 72A above shall apply where the court is acting under this **3–144**
section as it applies where the court is acting under section 71
above.

(11) Sections 73 and 73A above shall apply where the prosecutor makes
an application under this section as they apply in a case where the
prosecutor has given written notice to the court for the purposes of
subsection (1)(a) of section 71 above, but as if any reference in section
73(6) to the time the confiscation order is made were a reference to
the time of the determination to be made on that application.

(12) 'the date of conviction' has the same meaning as in section 74A **3–145**
above; and
'the relevant court' means:
(a) where the court which made the current determination is the
Crown Court, that Court; and
(b) where the court which made that determination is a magistrates'
court, any magistrates' court for the same area."

Section 75 states: **3–146**

"(1) Where the Crown Court orders the defendant to pay an amount
under this Part of this Act, sections 31(1) to (3C) and 32(1) and (2) of
the Powers of Criminal Courts Act 1973 (powers of Crown Court in
relation to fines and enforcement of Crown Court fines) shall have
effect as if that amount were a fine imposed on him by the Crown
Court.

(2) Where a magistrates' court orders the defendant to pay an amount
under this Part of this Act, that amount shall be treated as a fine for
the purposes of section 31(3) of the Magistrates' Courts Act 1980
(general limit on the power of a magistrates' court to impose imprisonment not to apply in the case of imprisonment in default).

(3) Where: **3–147**
(a) a warrant of commitment is issued for default in payment of an
amount ordered to be paid under this Part of this Act in respect
of an offence; and
(b) at the time the warrant is issued, the defendant is liable to serve
a term of custody in respect of the offence;

the term of imprisonment or of detention under section 9 of the Criminal Justice Act 1982 (detention of persons aged 17 to 20 for default) to be served in default of payment of the amount shall not begin to run until after the term mentioned in paragraph (b) above.

(4) The references in subsection (3) above to term of custody which the defendant is liable to serve in respect of the offence is a reference to the term of imprisonment or detention in a young offender institution which he is liable to serve in respect of the offence; and for the purposes of this subsection:

(a) consecutive terms and terms which are wholly or partly concurrent shall be treated as a single term; and

(b) there shall be disregarded:

(i) any sentence suspended under section 22(1) of the Powers of Criminal Courts Act 1973 which has not taken effect at the time the warrant is issued;

(ii) in the case of a sentence of imprisonment passed with an order under section 47(1) of the Criminal Law Act 1977, any part of the sentence which the defendant has not at that time been required to serve in prison; and

(iii) any term of imprisonment or detention fixed under section 31(2) of the Powers of Criminal Courts Act 1973 for which a warrant of commitment has not been issued at the time.

3–148 (5) In the application of Part III of the Magistrates' Courts Act 1980 to amounts payable under confiscation orders:

(a) such an amount is not a sum adjudged to be paid by a conviction for the purposes of section 81 (enforcement of fines imposed on young offenders) or a fine for the purposes of section 85 (remission of fines); and

(b) in section 87 (enforcement by High Court or county court), subsection (3) shall be omitted.

3–149 (5A) Where the defendant serves a term of imprisonment or detention in default of paying any amount due under a confiscation order, his serving that term does not prevent the confiscation order from continuing to have effect, so far as any other method of enforcement is concerned.

3–150 (6) This section applies in relation to confiscation order made by the criminal division of the Court of Appeal, or by the House of Lords on appeal from that division, as it applies in relation to confiscation orders made by the Crown Court and the creference in subsection (1) above to the Crown Court shall be construed accordingly."

(o) Non-payment of sum

3–151 Section 75A

"(1) If any sums required to be paid by a person under a confiscation order is not paid when it is required to be paid (whether forthwith on the making of the order or at a time specified under section 31(1) of the

Powers of Criminal Courts Act 1973 or for the purposes of section 75(1) or (2) of the Magistrates' Court Act 1980):

    (a) that person should be liable to pay interest on that sum for the period for which it remains unpaid, and

    (b) the amount of the interest shall, for the purposes of enforcement, be treated as part of the amount to be recovered from him under the confiscation order.

(2) The Crown Court may, on the application of the prosecutor, increase the term of imprisonment or detention fixed in respect of the confiscation order under section 31(2) of that Act of 1973 (as it has effect by virtue of section 75 above) if the effect of subsection (1) above is to increase the maximum period applicable in relation to the order under section 31(3A) of that Act of 1973.   **3-152**

(3) The rate of interest under subsection (1) above shall be that for the time being applying to a civil judgment debt under section 17 of the Judgments Act 1838."   **3-153**

(p) The High Court

Section 76 states: **3-154**

"(1) The powers conferred on the High Court by sections 77(1) and 78(1) below are exercisable where:

    (a) proceedings have been instituted in England and Wales against the defendant for an offence to which this Part of this Act applies;

    (b) the proceedings have not been concluded; and

    (c) either a confiscation order has been made or it appears to the court that there are reasonable grounds for thinking that a confiscation order may be made in them.

(2) Those powers are also exercisable where:

    (a) the court is satisfied that, whether by the laying of an information or otherwise, a person is to be charged with an offence to which this Part of this Act applies; and

    (b) it appears to the court that a confiscation order may be made in proceedings for the offence.

(3) For the purposes of sections 77, 78 and 92 below at any time when those powers are exercisable before proceedings have been instituted: **3-155**

    (a) references in this Part of this Act to the defendant shall be construed as references to the person referred to in subsection (2)(a) above;

    (b) references in this Part of this Act to the prosecutor shall be construed as references to the person who the High Court is satisfied is to have the conduct of the proposed proceedings; and

    (c) references in this Part of this Act to realisable property shall be construed as if, immediately before that time, proceedings had been instituted against the person referred to in subsection (2)(a) above for an offence to which this Part of this Act applies.

3–156   (4)   Where the court has made an order under section 77(1) or 78(1) below by virtue of subsection (2) above, the court shall discharge the order if proceedings in respect of the offence are not instituted (whether by the laying of an information or otherwise) within such time as the court considers reasonable."

(q) A restraint order

3–157   Section 77 states:

"(1)   The High Court may by order (referred to in this Part of this Act as a 'restraint order') prohibit any person from dealing with any realisable property, subject to such conditions and exceptions as may be specified in the order.

(2)   Without prejudice to the generality of subsection (1) above, a restraint order may make such provision as the court thinks fit for living expenses and legal expenses.

(3)   A restraint order may apply:
    (a)   to all realisable property held by a specified person, whether the property is described in the order or not; and
    (b)   to realisable property held by a specified person, being property transferred to him after the making of the order.

(4)   This section shall not have effect in relation to any property for the time being subject to a charge under section 78 below.

3–158   (5)   A restraint order:
    (a)   may be made only on an application by the prosecutor;
    (b)   may be made on an *ex parte* application to a judge in chambers; and
    (c)   shall provide for notice to be given to persons affected by the order.

(6)   A restraint order:
    (a)   may be discharged or varied in relation to any property; and
    (b)   shall be discharged when proceedings for the offence are concluded.

(7)   An application for the discharge or variation of a restraint order may be made by any person affected by it.

3–159   (8)   Where the High Court has made a restraint order, the court may at any time appoint a receiver:
    (a)   to take possession of any realisable property, and
    (b)   in accordance with the court's directions, to manage or otherwise deal with any property in respect of which he is appointed,
subject to such exceptions and conditions as may be specified by the court; and may require any person having possession of property in

respect of which a receiver is appointed under this section to give possession of it to the receiver.

(9) For the purposes of this section, dealing with property held by any person includes (without prejudice to the generality of the expression):

   (a) where a debt is owed to that person, making a payment to any person in reduction of the amount of the debt; and

   (b) removing the property from Great Britain.

(10) Where the High Court has made a restraint order, a constable may for the purposes of preventing any realisable property being removed from Great Britain, seize the property.

(11) Property seized under subsection (10) above shall be dealt with in accordance with the court's directions.

(12) The Land Charges Act 1972 and the Land Registration Act 1925 shall apply: 3–160

   (a) in relation to restraint orders, as they apply in relation to orders affecting land made by the court for the purpose of enforcing judgments or recognizances; and

   (b) in relation to applications for restraint orders, as they apply in relation to other pending land actions.

(13) The prosecutor shall be treated for the purposes of section 57 of the Land Registration Act 1925 (inhibitions) as a person interested in relation to any registered land to which a restraint order or an application for such an order relates."

(r) A charging order

Sections 78 and 79 cover the power of the High Court to make a charging   3–161
order on realisable property to secure the payment to the Crown; and supplementary provisions thereto.

(s) Realisation of property

Section 80 deals with the court's powers in respect of the realisation of   3–162
property once a confiscation order has been made, when the order is not subject to appeal and the proceedings in which it was made have not been concluded.

Section 81 covers the application of proceeds of realisation and other   3–163
sums.

Section 82 states that the powers conferred on the High Court by sections   3–164
77 to 81, or on an appointed receiver, shall be exercised with a view to making available for satisfying the confiscation order, the value for the time being of realisable property held by any person by the realisation of such property.

Section 83 states: 3–165

"(1) If, on an application made in respect of a confiscation order:

    (a) by the defendant, or

    (b) by a receiver appointed under section 77, r. 80 above, or in pursuance of a charging order,

        the High Court is satisfied that the realisable property is inadequate for the payment of any amount remaining to be recovered under the order the court shall issue a certificate to that effect, giving the court's reasons.

(2) For the purposes of subsection (1) above:

    (a) in the case of realisable property held by a person who has been adjudged bankrupt or whose estate has been sequestrated the court shall take into account the extent to which any property held by him may be distributed among creditors; and

    (b) the court may disregard any inadequacy in the realisable property which appears to the court to be attributable wholly or partly to anything done by the defendant for the purpose of preserving any property held by a person to whom the defendant had directly or indirectly made a gift caught by this Part of this Act from any risk of realisation under this Part of this Act.

3–166   (3) Where a certificate has been issued under subsection (1) above, the person who applied for it may apply:

    (a) where the confiscation order was made by the Crown Court, to that court; and

    (b) where the confiscation order was made by a magistrates' court, to a magistrates' court for the same area, for the amount to be recovered under the order to be reduced.

    (4) The Crown Court shall, on an application under subsection (3) above:

    (a) substitute for the amount to be recovered under the order such lesser amount as the court thinks just in all the circumstances of the case; and

    (b) substitute for the term of imprisonment or of detention fixed under subsection (2) of section 31 of the Powers of Criminal Courts Act 1973 in respect of the amount to be recovered under the order a shorter term determined in accordance with that section in respect of the lesser amount.

    (5) A magistrates' court shall, on an application under subsection (3) above, substitute for the amount to be recovered under the order such lesser amount as the court thinks just in all the circumstances of the case.

3–167   (6) Rules of court may make provision:

    (a) for the giving of notice of any application under this section; and

    (b) for any person appearing to the court to be likely to be affected by any exercise of its powers under this section to be given an opportunity to make representations to the court."

3–168   Sections 84 to 88 deal with: the position where the defendant is adjudged bankrupt (s.84); sequestration in Scotland (s.85); winding up of a company holding realisable property (s.86); insolvency officers dealing with property subject to a restraint order (s.87) and supplementary provisions in respect of receivers (s.88).

(t) Compensation

Section 89 states: 3–169
"(1) if proceedings are instituted against a person for an offence or offences to which this Part of this Act applies and either:
   (a) the proceedings do not result in his conviction for any such offence, or
   (b) where he is convicted of one or more such offences:
      (i) the conviction or convictions concerned are quashed, or
      (ii) he is pardoned by Her Majesty in respect of the conviction or convictions concerned,
      the High Court may, on an application by a person who held property which was realisable property, order compensation to be paid to the applicant if, having regard to all the circumstances, it considers it appropriate to make such an order.
(2) The High Court shall not order compensation to be paid in any case   3–170
unless the court is satisfied:
   (a) that there has been some serious default on the part of the person concerned in the investigation or prosecution of the offence concerned, being a person mentioned in subsection (5) below; and
   (b) that the applicant has suffered loss in consequence of anything done in relation to the property by or in pursuance of an order under this Part of this Act.
(3) The Court shall not order compensation to be paid in any case where it appears to the Court that the proceedings would have been instituted or continued even if the serious default had not occurred.
(4) The amount of compensation to be paid under this section shall be   3–171
such as the High Court thinks just in all the circumstances of the case.
(5) Compensation payable under this section shall be paid:
   (a) where the person in default was or was acting as a member of a police force, out of the police fund out of which the expenses of that police force are met;
   (b) where the person in default was a member of the Crown Prosecution Service or acting on behalf of the service, by the Director of Public Prosecutions;
   (c) where the person in default was a member of the Serious Fraud Office, by the Director of that Office;
   (d) where the person in default was an officer within the meaning of the Customs and Excise Management Act 1979, by the Commissioners of Customs and Excise; and
   (e) where the person in default was an officer of the Commissioners of Inland Revenue, by those Commissioners."

(u) Arrangement to facilitate concealment of benefits

3–172   Section 93A states:

"(1)   Subject to subsection (3) below, if a person enters into or is otherwise concerned in an arrangement whereby:

(a)   the retention or control by or on behalf of another (A) of A's proceeds of criminal conduct is facilitated (whether by concealment, removal from the jurisdiction, transfer to nominees or otherwise); or

(b)   A's proceeds of criminal conduct:

(i)   are used to secure that funds are placed at A's disposal; or

(ii)   are used for A's benefit to acquire property by way of investment,

knowing or suspecting that A is a person who is or has been engaged in criminal conduct or has benefited from criminal conduct, he is guilty of an offence.

(2)   In this section, references to any person's proceeds of criminal conduct include a reference to any property which in whole or in part directly or indirectly represented in his hands his proceeds of criminal conduct.

3–173   (3)   Where a person discloses to a constable a suspicion or belief that any funds or investments are derived from or used in connection with criminal conduct or discloses to a constable any matter on which such a suspicion or belief is based:

(a)   the disclosure shall not be treated as a breach of any restriction upon the disclosure of information imposed by statute or otherwise; and

(b)   if he does any act in contravention of subsection (1) above and the disclosure relates to the arrangement concerned, he does not commit an offence under this section if:

(i)   the disclosure is made before he does the act concerned and the act is done with the consent of the constable; or

(ii)   the disclosure is made after he does the act, but is made on his initiative and as soon as it is reasonable for him to make it.

3–174   (4)   In proceedings against a person for an offence under this section, it is a defence to prove:

(a)   that he did not know or suspect that the arrangement related to any person's proceeds of criminal conduct; or

(b)   that he did not know or suspect that by the arrangement the retention or control by or on behalf of A of any property was facilitated or, as the case may be, that by the arrangement any property was used, as mentioned in subsection (1) above; or

(c)   that:

(i)   he intended to disclose to a constable such a suspicion, belief or matter as is mentioned in subsection (3) above in relation to the arrangement; but

(ii) there is reasonable excuse for his failure to make disclosure in accordance with subsection (3)(b) above.

(5) In the case of a person who was in employment at the relevant time, subsections (3) and (4) above shall have effect in relation to disclosures, and intended disclosures, to the appropriate person in accordance with the procedure established by his employer for the making of such disclosures as they have effect in relation to disclosures, and intended disclosures, to a constable.   **3–175**

(6) A person guilty of an offence under this section shall be liable: **3–176**
    (a) on summary conviction, to imprisonment for a term not exceeding six months or a fine not exceeding the statutory maximum or to both; or
    (b) on conviction on indictment, to imprisonment for a term not exceeding fourteen years or a fine or to both.

(7) In this Part of this Act 'criminal conduct' means conduct which constitutes an offence to which this Part of this Act applies or would constitute such an offence if it had occurred in England and Wales or (as the case may be) Scotland".

(v) Use of the proceeds of crime

Section 93B states: **3–177**

"(1) A person is guilty of an offence if, knowing that any property is, or in whole or in part directly or indirectly represents, another person's proceeds of criminal conduct, he acquires or uses that property or has possession of it.

(2) It is a defence to a charge of committing an offence under this section that the person charged acquired or used the property or had possession of it for adequate consideration.   **3–178**

(3) For the purposes of subsection (2) above:
    (a) a person acquires property for inadequate consideration if the value of the consideration is significantly less than the value of the property; and
    (b) a person uses or has possession of property for inadequate consideration if the value of the consideration is significantly less than the value of his use or possession of the property.

(4) The provision for any person of services or goods which are of assistance to him in criminal conduct shall not be treated as consideration for the purposes of subsection (2) above.

(5) Where a person discloses to a constable a suspicion or belief that any property is, or in whole or in part directly or indirectly represents another person's proceeds of criminal conduct or discloses to a constable any matter on which such a suspicion or belief is based: **3–179**
    (a) the disclosure shall not be treated as a breach of any restriction upon the disclosure of information imposed by statute or otherwise; and
    (b) if he does any act in relation to that property in contravention of

subsection (1) above, he does not commit an offence under this section if:

(i) the disclosure is made before he does the act concerned and the act is done with the consent of the constable; or

(ii) the disclosure is made after he does the act, but on his initiative and as soon as it is reasonable for him to make it.

3–180 (6) For the purposes of this section, having possession of any property shall be taken to be doing an act in relation to it.

3–181 (7) In proceedings against a person for an offence under this section, it is a defence to prove that:

(a) he intended to disclose to a constable such a suspicion, belief or matter as is mentioned in subsection (5) above; but

(b) there is reasonable excuse for his failure to make the disclosure in accordance with paragraph (b) of that subsection.

3–182 (8) In the case of a person who was in employment at the relevant time, subsections (5) and (7) above shall have effect in relation to disclosures, and intended disclosures, to the appropriate person in accordance with the procedure established by his employer for the making of such disclosures as they have effect in relation to disclosures, and intended disclosures, to a constable.

3–183 (9) A person guilty of an offence under this section is liable:

(a) on summary conviction, to imprisonment for a term not exceeding six months or a fine not exceeding the statutory maximum or to both; or

(b) on conviction on indictment, to imprisonment for a term not exceeding fourteen years or a fine or to both.

3–184 (10) No constable or other person shall be guilty of an offence under this section in respect of anything done by him in the course of acting in connection with the enforcement, or intended enforcement, of any provision of this Act or of any other enactment relating to criminal conduct or the proceeds of such conduct."

3–185 **(w) Concealing property**

Section 93C states:

"(1) A person is guilty of an offence if he:

(a) conceals or disguises any property which is, or in whole or in part directly or indirectly represents, his proceeds of criminal conduct; or

(b) converts or transfers that property or removes it from the jurisdiction,

for the purpose of avoiding prosecution for an offence to which this Part of this Act applies or the making or enforcement in his case of a confiscation order.

(2) A person is guilty of an offence if, knowing or having reasonable grounds to suspect that any property is, or in whole or in part directly

or indirectly represents, another person's proceeds of criminal conduct, he:

(a) conceals or disguises that property; or

(b) converts or transfers that property or removes it from the jurisdiction,

for the purpose of assisting any person to avoid prosecution for an offence to which this Part of this Act applies or the making or enforcement in his case of a confiscation order.

(3) In subsections (1) and (2) above, the references to concealing or disguising any property include references to concealing or disguising its nature, source, location, disposition, movement or ownership or any rights with respect to it.

(4) A person guilty of an offence under this section is liable: 3–186

    (a) on summary conviction, to imprisonment for a term not exceeding six months or a fine not exceeding the statutory maximum or to both; or

    (b) on conviction on indictment, to imprisonment for a term not exceeding fourteen years or a fine or to both."

(x) Disclosing prejudicial information

Section 93D states: 3–187

"(1) A person is guilty of an offence if:

    (a) he knows or suspects that a constable is acting, or is proposing to act, in connection with an investigation which is being, or is about to be, conducted into money laundering; and

    (b) he discloses to any other person information or any other matter which is likely to prejudice that investigation, or proposed investigation.

(2) A person is guilty of an offence if:

    (a) he knows or suspects that a disclosure (the disclosure) has been made to a constable under section 93A or 93B above; and

    (b) he discloses to any other person information or any other matter which is likely to prejudice any investigation which might be conducted following the disclosure.

(3) A person is guilty of an offence if:

    (a) he knows or suspects that a disclosure of a kind mentioned in section 93A(5) or 93B(8) above ('the disclosure') has been made; and

    (b) he discloses to any person information or any other matter which is likely to prejudice any investigation which might be conducted following the disclosure.

(4) Nothing in subsection (1) to (3) above makes it an offence for a   3–188
professional legal adviser to disclose any information or other matter:

    (a) to, or to a representative of, a client of his in connection with the giving by the adviser of legal advice to the client; or

    (b) to any person:

       (i)   in contemplation of, or in connection with, legal proceedings; and

      (ii) for the purpose of those proceedings.

(5) Subsection (4) above does not apply in relation to any information or other matter which is disclosed with a view to furthering any criminal purpose.

3–189 (6) In proceedings against a person for an offence under subsection (1),(2) or (3) above, it is a defence to prove that he did not know or suspect that the disclosure was likely to be prejudicial in the way mentioned in that subsection.

(7) In this section 'money laundering' means doing any act which constitutes an offence under section 93A, 93B or 93C above or, in the case of an act done otherwise than in England and Wales or Scotland, would constitute such an offence if done in England and Wales or (as the case may be) Scotland.

(8) For the purposes of subsection (7) above, having possession of any property shall be taken to be doing an act in relation to it.

3–190 (9) A person guilty of an offence under this section shall be liable:

  (a) on summary conviction, to imprisonment for a term not exceeding six months or a fine not exceeding the statutory maximum or to both; or

  (b) on conviction on indictment, to imprisonment for a term not exceeding five years or a fine or to both.

3–191 (10) No constable or other person shall be guilty of an offence under this section in respect of anything done by him in the course of acting in connection with the enforcement, or intended enforcement, of any provision of this Act or of any other enactment relating to an offence to which this Part of this Act applies."

3–192 Section 93F states:

"(1) Proceedings for an offence to which this section applies ('a specified offence') may be instituted by order of the Commissioners.

(2) Any proceedings for a specified offence which are so instituted shall be commenced in the name of an officer.

(3) In the case of the death, removal, discharge or absence of the officer in whose name any proceedings for a specified offence were commenced, those proceedings may be continued by another officer.

(4) Where the Commissioners investigate, or propose to investigate, any matter with a view to determining:

  (a) whether there are grounds for believing that a specified offence has been committed; or

  (b) whether a person should be prosecuted for a specified offence; that matter shall be treated as an assigned matter within the meaning of the Customs and Excise Management Act 1979.

3–193 (5) Nothing in this section shall be taken:

  (a) to prevent any person (including the officer) who has power to arrest, detain or prosecute any person for a specified offence from doing so; or

  (b) to prevent a court from proceeding to deal with a person brought before it following his arrest by an officer for a specified offence, even though the proceedings have not been instituted by an order made under subsection (1) above.

(6) In this section: 3-194

'the Commissioners' means the Commissioner of Customs and Excise;

'officer' means a person commissioned by the Commissioners;

'proceedings', as respects Scotland, means summary proceedings; and

'specified offence' means:

(a) any offence under section s 93A to 93D above;

(b) attempting to commit, conspiracy to commit or incitement to commit any such offence; or

(c) any other offence of a kind prescribed in regulations made by the Secretary of State for the purposes of this section."

(y) Other powers

The Proceeds of Crime Act 1995 also inserted into the 1988 Act: 3-195

(i) section 93H, which enables a constable, for the purposes of an investigation into whether any person has benefited from any criminal conduct or into the extent of whereabouts of the proceeds of any criminal conduct, to apply to a Circuit judge for an order to make a person, who appears to be in possession of particular material or material of a particular description, either produce that material to the constable or to give him access to it;

(ii) section 93I which enables a constable to apply to a Circuit judge 3-196
for a search warrant for specified premises; and

(iii) Section 93J which allows the High Court on the application of a 3-197
person appearing to have the conduct of any prosecution, to order certain material in the possession of an authorised government department to be produced to the court.

So far, the courts have been reluctant to take into account the house 3-198
occupied by the defendant's wife. In *R v. Lee* (1996) 1 Cr.App.R.(S) 135, the Court of Appeal held that the sentencer should have exercised his discretion to exclude from the amount of the confiscation order the value of the appellant's share in a house which he owned jointly with his wife who had a serious illness, the court taking the view that the wife's share in the house would be insufficient to enable her to buy any other accommodation.

In *R v. Judge and Wooldridge* (13 Cr.App.R.(S) 685), where the house was owned by the wife and then transferred into joint names, the Court of Appeal held that it could not be said that the wife had benefited from the crimes in respect of which a confiscation order was made and it would be slow to make an order which would result in her home having to be sold.

However, where the defendant has deliberately tried to evade a confisca- 3-199
tion order by disposing of assets the Court of Appeal held that Parliament

had contemplated that money might continue to be realisable even though it had been the subject of gifts by the defendant.

Thus in *R v. Tighe* (1996) 1 Cr.App.R(S) 314 where the appellant had arranged for his sister to withdraw £345,000 from his bank and distribute it to relatives abroad, the court found that the sentencer had been correct in refusing to take account of the fact that the appellant might not be able to recover the money.

J. NOTIFICATION REQUIREMENTS FOR SEX OFFENDERS: SEX OFFENDERS ACT 1997

3–200   The Sex Offenders Act 1997 requires those convicted of or cautioned in respect of specified sex offences to notify the police of their names and addresses and any subsequent change.

I. THE OFFENDERS

3–201   Section 1 describes the offenders who are subject to the requirements and specifies the duration of the requirements.

"They are a person if after the commencement of this Part:

1.   (a)   he is convicted of a sexual offence to which this Part, of the Act applies;
      (b)   he is found not guilty of such an offence by reason of insanity, or to be under a disability and to have done the act charged against him in respect of such an offence; or
      (c)   in England and Wales or Northern Ireland, he is cautioned by a constable in respect of such an offence which, at the time when the caution is given, he has admitted.

2.   A person becomes subject to those requirements if, at that commencement:
      (a)   he has been convicted of a sexual offence to which this Part applies but has not been dealt with in respect of the offence; or
      (b)   he has been found not guilty of such an offence by reason of insanity, or to be under a disability and to have done the act charged against him in respect of such an offence, but has not been dealt with in respect of the finding.

3–202   3.   A person becomes subject to these requirements if, at that commencement.
      (a)   he is serving a sentence of imprisonment or a term of service detention, or is subject to a community order, in respect of a sexual offence to which this Part applies;
      (b)   he is subject to supervision, having been released from prison after serving the whole or part of a sentence of imprisonment in respect of such an offence;

(c)   he is detained in a hospital, or is subject to a guardianship order, having been convicted of such an offence; or

(d)   he is detained in a hospital, having been found not guilty of such an offence by reason of insanity, or to be under a disability and to have done the act charged against him in respect of such an offence."

A person is included in the requirement within paragraph (a), (c), or (d) if he is unlawfully at large or absent without leave on temporary release or leave of absence, or on bail pending appeal at the commencement.   3–203

Consideration must be given to the implications of this Act when a lawyer advises a client with regard to a possible caution for a sexual offence.   3–204

II. The Duration Of The Requirement

The duration of the requirement is as follows: 3–205

Person	Period
A person who, in respect of the offence, is or has been sentenced to imprisonment for life or a term of 30 months or more	An indefinite period
A person who, in respect of the offence or finding, is or has been admitted to a hospital subject to a restriction order	An indefinite period
A person who, in respect of the offence is or has been sentenced to imprisonment for a term more than six months but less than 30 months	10 years beginning with the relevant date
A person who, in respect of the offence is or has been sentenced to imprisonment for a term of six months or less	Seven years
A person who, in respect of the offence or finding has been admitted to a hospital without being subject to a restriction order	Seven years
A person of any other description	5 years

The relevant beginning date is the date of the conviction finding or caution (s.1(8)).

Where a person is sentenced in respect of two or more sexual offences which are either (a) consecutive terms of imprisonment, or (b) terms of   3–206 imprisonment which are purely concurrent, the effect is as if that person was sentenced to a term of imprisonment:

    (a)   in the case of consecutive terms, equal to the aggregate of these terms;

    (b)   in the case of concurrent terms, equal to the aggregate of those terms after making such deduction as may be necessary to secure that no period of time is counted more than once.

3–207　　If a person is found to be under a disability and to have done the act charged against him, and is then subsequently tried for the offence, the finding shall be disregarded (s. 1(7)).

III. THE REQUIREMENT

3–208　　Section 2 provides: "a person who is subject to the notification requirement shall, before the end of the period of 14 days beginning with the relevant date notify to the police the following information:

    (a)   his name and, where he also uses one or more other names, each of those names; and

    (b)   his home address".

"Home address" in relation to any person, means the address of his home, that is to say, his sole or main residence in the United Kingdom, or where he has no such residence, premises in the United Kingdom which he regularly visits (s. 2(7)). There is no provision requiring the agreement of the owner or occupier of the premises.

3–209　　The person shall also before the end of the 14–day period beginning with:

    (a)   his using a name which has not been notified to the police under this section; or

    (b)   any change of his home address;

    (c)   his having resided or stayed for a qualifying period in the United Kingdom, the address of which has not been notified to the police under this section,

notify that name, or as the case may be, the address of those premises to the police.

"Qualifying period" means:

    (a)   a period of 14 days; or

    (b)   two or more periods, in any period of 12 months, which (taken together) amount to 14 days (s. 2(7)).

3–210　　For the purpose of determining any period for the purposes of the subsection (*i.e.* the 14–day period) there shall be disregarded any time when he:

    (a)   is remanded in or committed to custody by an order of a court; or

    (b)   is serving a sentence of imprisonment or a term of service detention; or

(c) is detained in hospital; or

(d) is outside the United Kingdom.

IV. How The Notification Is To Be Given

The notification may be given: 3–211

(a) by attending at *any* police station and giving an oral notification to any police officer or to any person authorised for that purpose by the officer in charge of the station. It does not need to be the local police station for the address given.

(b) by sending a written notification to *any* police station. Any notification under this section shall be acknowledged. An acknowledgment under this section shall be in writing and in such form as the Secretary of State may direct. A notification is presumably to be sent to the premises notified as one regularly visited by a person who has no sole or main residence. There appears to be no obligation upon the person if he fails to receive the acknowledgment.

A notification given to the police by any person shall not be regarded as complying with subsections (1) or (2) above unless it also states:

(a) his date of birth;

(b) his name on the relevant date, and where he uses one or more other names on that date, each of those other names; and

(c) his home address on that date (s. 2(3)).

V. The Offence

If a person: 3–212

(a) fails, without reasonable excuse, to comply with section 2 (to notify); or

(b) notifies to the police, in purported compliance with section 2 above any information which he knows to be false,

he shall be liable on summary conviction to a fine not exceeding level 5, or to imprisonment for a term not exceeding six months or to both.

Proceedings for an offence may be commenced in any court having   3–213
jurisdiction in any place where the person charged with the offence resides or is found.

The offence is made a continuing offence throughout any period during   3–214
which the failure continues by section 3(2).

VI. Young Sex Offenders

Section 4 states that various periods of detention and custodial orders for   3–215
young persons shall be regarded as equivalent to sentences of imprisonment.

In the case of a person who is under 18 on the relevant date for the references to periods of ten, seven and five years there are substituted a reference to one half of that period.

Where a person is under the age of 18 a court may direct that until he attains that age, when he is convicted of a sexual offence, or is found not guilty of such an offence by reason of insanity, or to be under a disability and to have done the act charged against him, that an individual having parental responsibility

(a) be authorised to comply on his behalf with the provisions in section 2 (notification); and

(b) be liable in his stead for any failure to comply with these provisions.

There is no similar provision in the case of juvenile cautions. A person under the age of 18 can not be sent to prison for failing to comply with the requirements. He can only be fined.

VII. Proof By Certificate

3–216   By section 5, "where, on any date after the commencement of this Part of the Act, a person:

(a) is convicted of a sexual offence; or

(b) is found not guilty of such an offence by reason of insanity; or

(c) is found to be under a disability and to have done the act charged against him in respect of such an offence, the court by or before which the person is so convicted or so found:

    (a) states in open court:

       (i) that on that date he has been convicted, found not guilty by reason of insanity or found to be under a disability and to have done the act charged against him; and

       (ii) that the offence in question is a sexual offence to which this Part applies; and

    (b) certifies those facts (whether at the time or subsequently) the certificate shall, for the purposes of this Part be sufficient evidence of those facts."

Obviously the facts cannot be proved by certificate where, for example the defendant was serving a term of imprisonment for a sexual offence at the commencement of the Act because subsection (a) will not have been complied with.

3–217   Where, after the commencement of the Act, a person is cautioned by a constable in respect of a sexual offence which he has admitted, if the constable:

(a) informs the person that he has been cautioned on that date and that the offence in question is a sexual offence to which this Part of the Act applies; and

(b) certifies those facts (whether at the time or subsequently) in such form as the Secretary of State may by order prescribe, the certificate shall, for the purposes of the Act be evidence of those facts.

VIII. Definitions

Many of the terms used in the Act are defined in section 6 of the Act. A **3–218** person's age is his age at the time of the offence.

IX. Sexual Offences

The following are sexual offences for the purposes of this Part of the Act, set **3–219** out in Schedule 1:

(a) Sexual Offences Act 1956:

(i)   section 1: rape;
(ii)   section 5: intercourse with a girl under 13;
(iii) section 6: intercourse with a girl between 13 and 16
(iv) section 10: incest by a man;
(v)   section 12: buggery;
(vi) section 13: indecency between men;
(vii) section 14: indecent assault on a woman;
(viii) section 15: indecent assault on a man;
(ix) section 16: assault with intent to commit buggery;
(x)   section 28: causing or encouraging prostitution of, intercourse with, or indecent assault on, a girl under 16.

(b) Indecency with Children Act 1960:

• section 1(1): indecent conduct towards children.

(c) Criminal Law Act 1977:

• section 54: inciting a girl under 16 to have incestuous sexual intercourse.

(d) Protection of Children Act 1978

• section 1: indecent photographs of children.

(e) Customs and Excise Management Act 1976:

• section 170: in relation to goods prohibited from being imported by section 42 of the Customs Consolidation Act 1876.

(f) Criminal Justice Act 1988:

• section 160: possessing indecent photographs of children.

Paragraphs (a) (iii), (v) and (vi) do not apply where the offender was under 20.

Paragraphs(a) (iv) to (ix) do not apply where the victim of, or as the case may be, the other party was 18 or over, except the paragraphs do apply in (vii) indecent assault on a woman and (viii) indecent assault on a man if the offender is, or has been sentenced to imprisonment for a term of 30 months or more, or is or has been admitted to hospital subject to a restriction order.

3–220   The Act also applies to:

(a)   Army Act 1955, s. 70;
(b)   Air Force Act 1955, s. 70;
(c)   Naval Discipline Act 1957, s. 42, of which the corresponding civil offence (within the meaning of that Act) is a sexual offence to which this Part of this Act applies.

References to offences include:

(a)   a reference to any attempt, conspiracy or incitement to commit that offence and
(b)   a reference to aiding and abetting, counselling or procuring the commission of that offence.

K. SUPERVISION AFTER RELEASE

3–221   The provisions for release supervision orders contained within section 16 of the Crime (Sentences) Act 1997 are applied to sexual offenders by section 20. The provisions apply to any term of imprisonment. The court shall give a direction under the section unless it is of the opinion that there are exceptional circumstances which justify its not doing so. Where the court does not give a direction it shall state in open court that it is of that opinion and what the exceptional circumstances are. The direction shall be that the offender shall be subject to a release supervision order for a period equal to 50 per cent of the offenders term of imprisonment (rounded up to the nearest whole day) or a period of twelve months, whichever is the longer or if the court considers a longer period necessary for the purpose of preventing the commission by the offender of further offences and the securing his rehabilitation, such longer period, not exceeding 10 years as it may determine. Where the offender is released early because there exist exceptional circumstances on compassionate grounds under section 10 the period shall be equal to the aggregate of the period mentioned above and a period equal to so much of his term as he would have been liable to serve but for his release under section 10 (s. 20(2)). The term "sexual offence" has the same meaning as in the Criminal Justice Act 1991.

Part II
ASSAULTS

Chapter 4
Rape

Rape can now be committed against a woman *per vaginum*, or against a man 4–01
or a woman *per anum*. This has not affected the question of consent as
discussed in the case of *R v. Olugboja* (1981) 73 Cr.App.R.344.

Cases which predate *Olugboja* have been referred to where they are
considered to be relevant but such cases must be reviewed in the light of that
decision. Comparisons with offences akin to rape, but where consent has
been given, such as the procurement of intercourse by threats or by fraud will
be considered.

A number of other offences exist, often associated with violent rape, or the
unlawful holding of a victim, which will also be covered in this chapter.

A. DEFINITION OF "RAPE" AND "RAPE OFFENCE"

Section 1 of the Sexual Offences Act 1956 as amended by section 142 of the 4–02
Criminal Justice and Public Order Act 1994 defines the offence of rape:

"(1) It is an offence for a man to rape a woman or another man.
(2) A man commits rape if:
     (a) he has sexual intercourse with a person (whether vaginal or anal)
          who at the time of the intercourse does not consent to it; or
     (b) at the time he knows that the person does not consent to the
          intercourse or is reckless as to whether that person consents to
          it.
(3) A person also commits rape if he induces a married woman to have
     sexual intercourse with him by impersonating her husband."

Section 2 the Sexual Offences (Amendment) Act 1976, as amended by the 4–03
Criminal Justice and Public Order Act 1994, Scheds 10 and 11, adds:

"It is hereby declared that if at a trial for a rape offence the jury has to
consider whether a man believed that a woman or man was consenting to
sexual intercourse, the presence or absence of reasonable grounds for such

a belief is a matter to which the jury is to have regard, in connection with any other relevant matter, in considering whether he is to be believed."

A "relevant matter" does not include self induced intoxication (*R. v. Woods* [1982] Crim.L.R. 42).

4–04   A "rape offence" is defined by section 7 of the 1976 Act as any of the following: rape; attempted rape; aiding, abetting, counselling or procuring rape or attempted rape; incitement to rape; conspiracy to rape and burglary with intent to rape.

I. SEXUAL INTERCOURSE

4–05   Penetration of the vagina or anus is required but minimal penetration will suffice (*R v. Hill* [1781] 1 East P.C. 434; *R v. M'Rue* [1938] 8 C. & P. 641; *R v. Allen* [1839] 9 C. & P. 31; *R v. Nicholls* [1847] 2 Cox C.C. 182; *R v. Reekspear* [1832] 1 Mood C.C. 342).

A victim of rape may still therefore be *virgo intacta* as rupture of the hymen is not essential (*R v. Hughes* [1841] 2 Mood 190; *R v. Killride* [1981] 23 Cr.App.R. 12). It is sufficient if any part of the defendant's penis enters within the labia of the pudendum of the girl. This description is contained in *R v. Lines* [1844] 1 C. & K. 393.

4–06   Ejaculation is not required. Section 44 of the 1956 Act specifically states that for any offences under the Act where "it is necessary to prove sexual intercourse (whether natural or unnatural), it shall not be necessary to prove completion of the intercourse by the emission of seed, but the intercourse shall be deemed to be complete upon proof of penetration only".

4–07   Intercourse is a continuing act and if consent is withdrawn after penetration, a continuation of intercourse would, provided all other necessary ingredients were present, constitute rape (*R v. Cooper and Schaub* [1994] Crim L.R. 531, C.A; *Kaitamaki v. R.* [1985] A.C. 147, P.C.).

4–08   Any form of intercourse that is not vaginal or anal cannot be the subject of rape. Oral intercourse is not included in the definition, but constitutes indecent assault.

4–09   The Act originally specified the offence as referring to "unlawful" sexual intercourse. The term would now be inappropriate since the decision in *R v. R* [1991] 1 A.C. 599) which held that intercourse without consent within marriage is rape. The word "unlawful" was merely surplusage.

II. "MAN"

4–10   Section 46 of the Sexual Offences Act 1956 states that the word "man" without its addition of the word "boy", or vice versa, shall not prevent the provision applying to any person to whom it would have applied if both words had been used. The same applies to the words "woman" and "girl".

Originally, at common law, it was assumed that a boy under 14 was incapable of procuration. This soon became extended to an assumption, proved demonstrably incorrect on rare occasions, that a boy under 14 was incapable of achieving sexual intercourse, either natural or unnatural. The presumption was removed by section 1 of the Sexual Offences Act 1993. A boy over the age of 10 can now be convicted of rape, and attempted rape.

A woman's husband can be convicted of her rape even during the con-   **4–11** tinuance of the marriage (*R v. R (Rape: Marital exemption)* [1992] 1 A.C. 599). The rule laid down by Sir Matthew Hale in 1736 which stated that a wife gives a general consent to all future intercourse with her husband was an anachronism and offensive in modern society. The abandonment of the unacceptable idea of a husband being immune against prosecution for rape of his wife is in conformity not only with a civilised concept of marriage, but also and above all with the fundamental objectives of the European Convention of Human Rights, the very essence of which was respect for human dignity and human freedom: *SW v. U.K.*; *CR v. U.K.*, *The Times*, December 5, 1995.

A woman can be convicted of aiding and abetting rape (*R. v. Ram* (1893)   **4–12** 17 Cox 609, where the woman forces a 13 year old girl to drink whisky and then takes her to the man by force so that he can have sex with the girl) and in circumstances where for example she assists in restraining the victim, with the rape itself. In such a case the law is set out in *DPP v. Merriman* [1973] A.C. 584. See, however, paragraph 4.17 on joint offences, below.

An aider and abetter cannot take advantage of a personal defence available   **4–13** to the principal. Thus, if an aider or abetter knows a woman is not consenting but deceives the principal into genuinely believing that she is consenting, he can be convicted of this offence even though the principal is entitled to be acquitted (*R v. Cogan and Leak* (1975) 61 Crim.App.R. 217, C.A.). If a person is forced to have intercourse with a man without consent, a rape has been committed, even if the active party is not guilty of the offence himself. In *R v. Cogan and Leak*, Cogan was charged with the rape of Mrs Leak. He was ultimately found not guilty as the jury found that he believed, incorrectly that she was consenting. However, the conviction of Mr Leak of aiding and abetting was upheld. It was said:

> "The wife had been raped. The fact that Cogan was innocent of rape because he believed that she was consenting does not affect the position that she was raped. Her ravishment had come about because Leak had wanted it to happen and had taken action to see that it did by persuading Cogan to use his body as the instrument for the necessary physical act."

There had been the *actus reus*. Leak also had the necessary *mens rea* and so had committed the offence.

This case was followed in *DPP v. K and C* (unreported, Q.B.D, June 25, 1996). K and C were two girls aged 14 and 11 who assaulted, imprisoned and robbed W, another 14 year old girl. A boy who was never indentified but was between 10 and 14 years old was induced to have intercourse with W without her consent. K and C were charged with procuring the rape of W. The Magistrate dismissed the case on the basis that the prosecution had not rebutted the necessary *doli incapax* on the part of the boy. On appeal, he was directed to convict the two girls. W had been raped and they had the requisite *mens rea*, namely, the desire that rape should take place and the procuring of it.

III. ATTEMPTED RAPE

4–14   Where penetration is proved the defendant cannot be guilty of attempted rape (*R v. Nicholls* (1847) 2 Cox C.C. 182), but where it is not, he can be (Criminal Law Act 1967, ss. 6(3) and (4)).

If A is charged with rape and B with aiding and abetting, upon A being convicted of attempted rape, B can be convicted of aiding and abetting that attempt (*R v. Hapgood and Wyatt* (1870) 11 Cox C.C. 471; *R. v. Wyatt* (1968) 39 L.J.M.C. 83).

4–15   Intent and attempt must be carefully distinguished (*R. v. Robertson* [1915] 2 K.B. 342; *R v. Punch* (1927) 20 Cr.App.R. 18, C.A.) and an endeavour to commit an act may not amount to an attempt as not being sufficiently proximate (*R v. Lean* (1927) 20 Cr.App.R. 74).

4–16   However, in a charge of attempted rape it is not necessary to prove that the defendant had got as far as physically attempting to penetrate the woman's vagina (*Attorney-General's Reference (No. 1 of 1992)* [1993] 2 All E.R. 190, applying *R v. Gullefer* [1990] 3 All E.R. 882). The defendant attacked a young woman of 17 having agreed to walk her home. He dragged her behind a hedge and threatened to kill her if she did not stop screaming. The police found her lying on the ground with her breasts exposed, without her knickers and her skirt pulled up to her waist. The defendant was kneeling near by (the distance was disputed), he had his trousers around his ankles, and his penis was flaccid. It was his intention to have intercourse without her consent but claimed that he was unable to achieve an erection due to drunkenness. The court held that the intention could be inferred and that his acts had been more than merely preparatory to the commission of the offence. He had embarked on committing the offence itself and that constituted the offence of attempted rape.

IV. JOINT OFFENCES

4–17   It was stated in *DPP v. Merriman* [1973] A.C. 584 that where a woman has been raped by more than one person on one occasion all concerned should be included in one charge of rape and no mention made of aiders and abetters. The contrary advice laid down in *R v. Holley* (1969) 53 Cr.App.R. 519, C.A., should no longer be followed.

Whether the defendant committed the act himself or assisted or encouraged someone else to, does not matter.

Where an application is made under section 74 of the Police and Criminal Evidence Act 1984 to admit a co-accused's plea of guilty to rape, it is essential, before granting the application to know the basis upon which the plea was entered so as to enable the trial judge to identify the issue to which the plea is said to be relevant: *R v. Manzur*; *R v. Malhmood, The Times,* December 6, 1996.

B. CONSENT

The prosecution must prove lack of consent (*R v. Bradley* [1910] 4 Cr.App.R   4–18
225) and the defendant can in principle raise consent as a defence without
putting character into issue: *R v. Sheehan* [1908] Cox C.C. 56. Lack of
consent is an essential ingredient in proving the offence of rape and a ruling
that challenges that aspect and puts the defendant's character in issue, would
effectively limit the defendant's right to defend himself. Nonetheless, there
may be some circumstances where the cross-examination of the victim as to
her alleged consent may become dangerously close to raising character as a
live issue.

The correct proof required of the prosecution is not to prove that the   4–19
intercourse was against the victim's will, but that she was not a consenting
participant and did not consent (*R v. Camplin* [1845] 1 Den. 89; *R v.
Fletcher* [1859] Bell C.C. 63; *R v. Olugboja* (1981) 73 Cr.App.R. 344 at
349).

Any attempt to introduce a different criterion to an absence of consent is
mistaken and also contrary to law. Reference should no longer be made to
any cases which did not take into account *R v. Larter and Castleton* [1995]
Crim.L.R. 75. In that case, a 14 year old girl was raped by two men whilst
asleep. The defence submitted that the prosecution must prove that the girl
resisted or that her understanding and knowledge were such that she was not
in a position to decide whether to consent or resist. It was held that such a test
was both mistaken and contrary to law. The only test in rape is the absence
of consent. "Consent" is to be given its ordinary meaning and if need be by
way of example, the jury may be directed that there is a difference between
consent and submission.

Reference to force, fear and fraud may be misleading and text books   4–20
indicating that these terms describe the basis of rape are criticised by the
courts. Such terms when used (as they will be below) must be understood to
refer now only to examples of lack of consent, and are not of themselves
requirements for the offence of rape. Hence the words of Lord Parker C.J. in
R. v. Howard (1966) 50 Cr.App.R. 56, dealing with cases where for example
a girl is drunk, must be seen in the light of *Larter and Castleton*. He asked:
"did she at the material time understand her situation and was she then
capable of exercising a rational judgement?"—put more simply—did she
consent? His comments that the prosecution must prove either that she
physically resisted, or if she did not, she was not in a position to decide
whether to consent or to resist, are now dangerously misleading. Lack of
resistance does not equate to consent.

Since the mid-1600's it had been said that in rape, the consent must be
negatived by force, threats of force or fraud. However, non-resistance did
not necessarily imply consent if it was clear that submission was induced by
fear (*R v. Hallett* (1841) 9 C.&P. 748).

R v. Olugboja   The whole question of consent was considered in detail in   4–21
R v. Olugboja (1981) 73 Cr.App.R 344, which now sums up the present law
relating to the question of consent in rape cases. O and his friend L met the

victim J and her friend K at a discotheque and offered to run them home. Instead, L raped J in the car and later at a bungalow L raped K. Whilst that was happening, O told J that he "was going to fuck her". He told her to remove her trousers which she did. O then had intercourse with J. She did not struggle, made no resistance, did not scream or cry for help but was crying and asked O to leave her alone. It was submitted by O that there had been no force used, nor any threats made and that to be rape, the submission must be induced by fear of violence. The court held that consent or lack of consent must be given its ordinary meaning. There is a distinction between consent and submission. The correct question is simply, "at the time of sexual intercourse, did the woman consent to it?". It is not necessary for the prosecution to prove force, fear or fraud, although one, or more of these will be present in the majority of cases. It may be therefore still helpful to consider each of these terms.

4-22   If the woman is unable to consent because she is unconscious through illness, drunkenness or because she is asleep (*R v. Mayers* (1872) 12 Cox 311; *R v. Young* (1878) 14 Cox 114; *R v. Larter and Castleton,*) the offence will be rape. This is especially true if her drunkenness was induced by the defendant (*R v. Camplin,* above). It is however not rape to encourage a woman to drink in the expectation that she will lower her resistance and consent, although an offence of indecent assault may take place (*H.M. Advocate v. Logan* [1936] S.C. 100). Where however, the woman is so insensible through drink the offence is rape even if the defendant's intention in supplying her with drink was only to get her excited (*R v. Camplin,* above). Where the complainant has become voluntarily drunk it is a question for the jury to decide if she is still capable of giving consent, *i.e.* if she has the capacity for rational judgement (*R v. Lang* (1975) 62 Cr.App.R 50; *R v. Ryan* (1846) 2 Cox C.C. 115)

Likewise, because an ability to give consent is required, a woman who is asleep cannot give consent (*R v. Mayers* (1872) 12 Cox C.C. 311).

Intercourse with a woman who is mentally disadvantaged is discussed in Chapter 11 at paragraph 11.1.

4-23   A girl under the age of consent can give a valid consent to intercourse even though the act will be an offence of unlawful sexual intercourse provided she is old enough to understand the nature of the act. Where however the girl is of such tender age as to be incapable of realising the significance of the act and does not know what is happening, that is not an informed consent and the act will be rape (*R v. Allen* (1872) L.R. 1 C.C.R. 367; *R v. Harling* (1938) 26 Cr.App.R. 127 C.A.)

Consent is valid even though it is given as the result of a bigamous marriage: *R v. Clarence* (1888) 22 Q.B.D. 23; *R v. Papadimitropoulos* (1957) 98 C.L.R 249. However, in some circumstances an offence under section 3 may be committed: *R v. Williams* (1898) 62 J.P. 310.

4-24   Consent, if it exists in fact, cannot be conditional. For example, intercourse consented to is not rape even though the woman did not know the man had a venereal disease and would not have consented had she been aware of this fact, nor where payment is promised but subsequently not honoured (*R v. Clarence* (1888) 22 Q.B.D. 23; *R v. Papadimitropoulis*

(1957) 98 C.L.R. 249; *R v. Linekar* (1994) 138 S.J. 227; *The Times*, October 26, 1994).

If a prostitute would consent to intercourse with protection but the man has intercourse by force without protection the offence of rape is committed. A prostitute is as much entitled to the protection of the law as is anyone else. It has been held that it is rape for a client to insist on sexual intercourse without protection to which the prostitute did not if fact consent: *R v. Shaw, Attorney-General's Reference (1996 No.28)*, *The Times*, January 27, 1997.

The offence of rape requires *mens rea* and if the defendant genuinely   4-25
believes the woman was consenting, he can not be guilty whether or not his belief was based on reasonable grounds. In *R v. Morgan* [1975] 2 All E.R. 347, M met three other men who were strangers to him and invited them home to have intercourse with his wife. They claimed that he told them that his wife would consent although to add to her own pleasure she would probably simulate reluctance. At the house they found Mrs M asleep in bed. They awakened her and took her forcibly to another bedroom where each had intercourse with her whilst the others held her down. All three men claimed that they thought she was consenting. It was held that even an unreasonable belief would suffice to disprove rape. However, it was also held that under the circumstances, no reasonable jury could fail to convict. The men could not on the facts of this particular case have believed that the wife was consenting (see also "recklessness").

It is clearly an act of rape where the victim is overcome by physical force or   4-26
by threats of immediate violence (1 Hawk c 41. s 7; *R v. Jones* (1861) 4 L.T.; *R v. Hallett* (1841) 9 C. & P. 748).

The offence remains rape even if she initially consented but the act was   4-27
activated by force, or if she consents *post facto* (1 Hawk c 41. s.7).

Force is used where the victim, because of the obvious strength of her   4-28
attacker or the number of persons attacking her, considers resistance dangerous and absolutely useless. Such an attack will also constitute rape (it is submitted that the exception referred to in the case of R v. Hallett, above —that if she subsequently consents the offence is assault and not rape, is in the light of subsequent decisions, no longer good law).

In *R v. Jones* (1861) 4 L.T. 154, a father established a reign of terror over   4-29
his family and as a result, his daughter remained passive while he had intercourse with her. Her submission was induced by dread and terror of her father. In the circumstances, he can be convicted of rape.

C. PROCUREMENT OF INTERCOURSE BY THE USE OF THREATS

Threats of personal physical violence, or violence to another person such as   4-30
a close relative will negative consent.

However, there is an unclear dividing line between rape by threats and an offence of procurement by threats contrary to section 2 of the Sexual Offences Act 1956 which states: "It is an offence for a person to procure a woman by threats or intimidation to have sexual intercourse in any part of the world."

This offence is triable on indictment and carries a maximum sentence of two years' imprisonment. It was first enacted in the Criminal Law (Amendment) Act 1885, s.3.

The procurement can be either for intercourse with another person or with himself (*R v. Williams* (1898) 62 J.P. 310; *R v. Jones* [1896] 1 Q.B. 4).

4–31   The grey area between the two offences is easy to illustrate but difficult to resolve and was discussed in *R v. Olugboja* (73 Cr.App.R. 344). Here, it was submitted that a charge of rape could never be based upon anything other than a threat of violence and that moral or economic pressure or even blackmail could never be the foundation of a rape charge. The court disagreed. Examples were given of a film producer persuading an actress to intercourse by telling her she would not obtain a role in his new film if she did not, or a man to obtain intercourse, threatening to tell a woman's fiancée that she had previously been a prostitute.

The case also made reference to an unnamed prosecution where a police officer had a case of rape withdrawn from the jury. He had threatened to report the victim for an offence unless she had intercourse with him.

4–32   However, in a case also referred to in *R v. Wellard* (1978) 67 Cr.App.R. 368, a man pretending to be a security guard had been convicted of rape by inducing a girl to have intercourse by threatening to tell her parents and the police she had been observed having intercourse with another person in a public place.

4–33   In *R v. Harold* (1984) 6 Cr.App.R. 30, H threatened a woman that he would disclose to her employers the fact that she had once been a prostitute unless she had intercourse with him. He was convicted under section 2.

4–34   In *Olugboja*, the court stated, *obiter*, that in the case of the film producer, and the friend of the fiancée, those threats could constitute a basis for rape. The jury must concentrate on the state of mind of the victim immediately before the act of intercourse, having regard to all the relevant circumstances, in particular, the events leading up to the act and her reaction to them showing the impact on her mind. The dividing line in such circumstances between real consent on the one hand and mere submission on the other is indeed not easy to draw.

4–35   The jury must apply their combined good sense, experience and knowledge of human nature and modern behaviour to all the relevant facts of the case. Nonetheless, the example of the film producer more closely resembles procuring by fraud if it is indeed any offence at all.

D. PROCUREMENT OF INTERCOURSE BY USE OF FRAUD

4–36   Fraud can only be the basis for a rape allegation in two distinct cases. Consent is not valid when the fraud is as to the nature of the act itself, or to the identity of the other party (*R. v. Clarence* (1888) 22 Q.B.D. 23).

Thus, if an innocent woman is induced to submit to intercourse on the basis that it is a necessary medical operation (*R v. Case [1850] 1 Den. 580; R v. Flattery* [1877] 2 Q.B.D. 410), or that it is a cure for haemorrhoids (*R v. Stanton* (1844) 1 Cor. & Ker. 415), rape is committed. Consent obtained under the pretence that it will improve the girl's singing voice can be a foundation for rape.

Section 1(3) of the Sexual Offences Act 1956 states that: "A man also   **4–37**
commits rape if he induces a married woman to have sexual intercourse with him by impersonating her husband". This is merely clarification and not exclusive. It dates back, of course, to the time when a woman was obliged to submit to intercourse with her husband by the marriage vows and was unable to revoke or withdraw that consent. If the act was not rape, it would be adultery and the woman could be divorced.

The Criminal Law Amendment Act 1885 first enacted the provision. It was declared and enacted that henceforth it should be deemed to be rape because prior to that Act, there had been a conflict of authority on that particular situation between *Barrow* (1868) 11 Cox 191, and *Dee* (1884) 15 Cox 579.

It is clear now that the law is that any impersonation of another man will   **4–38**
negate consent and there is no difference between the impersonation of a husband and the impersonation of a fiancée or boyfriend. The principle is set out in its historical perspective *obiter* in *R v. Linekar* (1994) 138 S. J. L.B. 227; *The Times*, October 26, 1994, and specifically in *R v. Elbekkay* [1995] Crim.L.R. 163. It was stated that: "the vital point about rape was that it involved the absence of consent. The absence was equally crucial whether the woman believed that the man with whom she was having intercourse was her husband or another. There is no authority or statute which obliges the court to hold otherwise. To find that it is rape to impersonate a husband, but not if the person impersonated was merely, say a long term, live in partner, or in even more modern idiom, the 'partner' of the woman would be extraordinary. The vital point about rape is that it involves the absence of consent." In sexual intercourse the issue of consent goes not only to the act but to the identity of the other party. Indeed, the law may always have been so. In *R v. Clarence* (1888) 22 Q.B.D. 23, the point was discussed. It was held that the judgment in the case of *R v. Dee* (1884) 14 L.R. 1r 468, justified

> "the observation that the only sorts of fraud which so far destroy the effect of a woman's consent as to convert a connection consented to in fact into a rape are frauds as to the nature of the act itself, or as to the identity of the person who does the act".

Any other fraud-induced consent will be valid and prevent the act being   **4–39**
rape. Hence, not revealing a venereal disease, pretending to be unmarried, either as a fiancee or in a bigamous marriage or pretending to be able to provide specific employment or accommodation will not negative consent.

A false promise to pay for the sexual intercourse will certainly not negative   **4–40**
consent (*R v. Clarence*, above; *R v. Papadimitropoulos* [1957] 98 C.L.R. 249; *R v. Linekar*, above).

Certain frauds may constitute an offence contrary to section 3 of the   **4–41**
Sexual Offences Act 1956 which states: "It is an offence for a person to procure a woman by false pretences or false representations, to have sexual

intercourse in any part of the world". It also is triable on indictment and carries a sentence of two years.

4–42   The false representation must be stated on the indictment (*R v. Field* (1892) 116 C.C.Ct Cas 757).

It has been held that a pretence that the defendant was unmarried and therefore free to marry the woman was an offence under this section (*R v. Williams* (1898) 62 J.P. 310; *R v. Jones* [1896] 1 Q.B. 4)

4–43   A promise as to a future act can never be a false representation under this section. Therefore, a promise to give the woman a fur coat if she agrees to sexual intercourse will not be an offence. However, if it can be coupled to a false representation of an existing fact the offence may be made out. Therefore a false representation that the defendant has the ready means to pay now, may be the basis for a prosecution under this section (*R v. Dent* [1955] 2 All E.R. 806, C.A.).

The offer made by the film producer (described in para. 4–35) is therefore most probably not an offence if it is an inducement based on a future promise.

E. BEING RECKLESS

4–44   The *mens rea* of the offence is made out if the defendant has an intention to have sexual intercourse together with an awareness that the victim may not be consenting (*R v. Khan* [1990] 1 W.L.R. 813).

4–45   The test is subjective: did the defendant act recklessly?, not objective: what would a reasonable man have done?. If there is evidence of the defendant's reasonable belief in the woman's consent it should be put to the jury even if the defendant does not claim this belief (*R v. Baskir* [1982] Crim.L.R. 687). It is not a *Caldwell* [1982] A.C.341, recklessness, *i.e.* that he had not given any thought to the possibility, or had recognised some risk but had nevertheless gone ahead (see for further discussion Archbold 1994, Vol.2, 17–69). For all practical purposes it is a case of the defendant "carrying on regardless": *R v. Gardiner* (unreported, December 16, 1993).

4–46   A direction as to mistaken belief is however not required in every case (*R v. Taylor* (1984) 80 Cr.App.R. 327), and especially not if the facts give no grounds for a mistaken belief (*R v. Haughian*; *R v. Pearson* (1984) 80 Cr.App.R. 334).

4–47   To prove the man was reckless as to consent it must be proved either: (a) that he was indifferent and gave no thought to the possibility that she might not be consenting where, if any thought had been given to the matter, it would have been obvious that there was a risk that she was not consenting or (b) that he was aware of the possibility that she might not be consenting but persisted regardless (*R v. Pigg* [1982] 2 All E.R. 591).

F. ALTERNATIVE VERDICTS

4–48   Attempted rape is not an alternative verdict where penetration has been proved, but is if penetration is in issue (*R v. Touhey* [1960] Cr.App.R. 23,

C.C.A; *R v. Garland* [1962] Crim.L.R. 318, C.C.A.). Sections 2 and 3 of the Sexual Offences Act are alternative verdicts, as is section 4 (administering drugs to facilitate sexual intercourse).

Indecent assault is an alternative verdict. If the victim is under 16 these are   4–49
the only alternatives. Unlawful sexual intercourse is not (Criminal Law Act 1967, Sched. 3).

G. SENTENCING GUIDELINES

The maximum penalty for both rape and attempted rape is life imprison-   4–50
ment. The maximum penalty for section 2 and section 3 offences is two years. Burglary with intent to rape is a "rape offence" for the purposes of the Sexual Offences (Amendment) Act 1976 (see para 4.4). An immediate custodial sentence is called for in all but the most exceptional circumstances (*R v. Roberts and Roberts* (1982) 74 Cr.App.R. 242 C.A.). The fact that the victim acted imprudently such as by accepting a lift in a stranger's car is not a mitigating factor but actions calculated to lead the defendant to believe she would consent may be. Previous good character is of only minor significance.

Aggravating features set out in *R v. Roberts and Roberts* (above)   4–51
include:

(i)   where a gun or knife or some other weapon has been used to frighten or injure the victim;

(ii) where violence is used over and above the violence necessarily involved in the act itself;

(iii) where the victim sustains serious injury (whether that is mental or physical);

(iv) where there are threats of a brutal kind;

(v)   where the victim has been subjected to further sexual indignities or perversions;

(vi) where the offender is in a position of trust;

(vii) where the offender has intruded into the victim's home;

(viii) where the victim has been deprived of her liberty for a period of time;

(ix) where the rape or series of rapes is carried out by a group of men; and

(x)   where the offender has committed a series of rapes on different women or indeed on the same woman.

The principles for sentencing heterosexual rape were set out in *R v. Billam*   4–52
[1986] 1 W.L.R. 349, at 350–352. Aggravating features include a rape committed by two or more men acting together; rape by a man who has broken into or otherwise gained access to a place where the victim lives; or by a person who is in a position of responsibility towards the victim; or by a person who abducts the victim and holds her captive. In those cases the starting point should be eight years.

All the following are aggravating factors set out in *R v. Billam*:

(i) violence used over and above the force necessary to commit the rape;

(ii) use of a weapon to frighten the victim or wound her;

(iii) repeated rape;

(iv) carefully planned rape;

(v) the defendant's previous convictions for rape or other serious offences of a violent or sexual kind;

(vi) the victim is subjected to further sexual indignities or perversions: where the victim is forced to suck the defendant's penis the sentence will be increased. Ten years is not inappropriate (*R v. Shields*, February 11, 1994, unreported). Forceable buggery of a woman may be worse than normal vaginal rape (*R v. Mendez* (1992) 13 Cr.App.R.(S) 94). *Mendez* was followed in *Attorney-General's Reference (No.25 of 1995) (R v. B)* (1994) 16 Cr.App.R.(S) which stated that forceable buggery of a woman is worse than vaginal rape;

(vii) the victim is either very old or very young; and

(viii) the effect upon the victim, whether physical or mental is of special seriousness.

4–53 A sentence of seven years imprisonment is appropriate where an uncle rapes his 11 year old niece on two occasions and the girl suffers stress (*R v. Newton: Attorney-General's Reference (No.32 of 1992)* (1994) 98 Cr.App.R. 206).

4–54 A general fear of pregnancy or venereal disease are factors making the offence serious but a fear of AIDS is only an aggravating factor where there is a valid reason for believing she had contracted it or where it actually had occurred (*R v. Malcolm* (1987) 9 Cr.App.R.(S) 487)).

4–55 The fact that the defendant and victim had previously lived together can be taken into account but does not give the defendant a licence to have sexual intercourse with the ex-partner willy nilly. A sentence in the region of five years can be appropriate: *Attorney-General's Reference (No.7 of 1989)* (1990) 12 Cr.App.R.(S) 1; *R v. Berry* 10 Cr.App.R.(S) 329; *R v. Craft*, February 2, 1994, unreported. The victim's forgiveness is also a matter which can and should be taken into account but like previous co-habitation, it is not the be-all and end-all (*R v. Hensall*, July 28, 1994, unreported: 3 years).

4–56 In *R v. Harvey* (1987) 9 Cr.App.R.(S) 124, the defendant and victim were known to each other, there was no weapon used and no unnecessarily excessive violence, and no injuries. The correct sentence was six years' imprisonment.

4–57 Although a prostitute is entitled to refuse intercourse, it has been said that the hurt to a woman who, in the nature of her trade is prepared to have intercourse with any man who pays her is to some extent different from that of another woman who would only be prepared to have sexual intercourse with a man whom she knows and respects. A sentence of nine years' imprisonment was reduced to seven (*R v. Cole and Barik* (1993) 14 Cr.App.R.(S) 764).

Sentencing a defendant convicted of the rape of prostitutes was also discussed in *R v. Shaw, Attorney-General's Reference* (1996, No.28) *The Times*, January 27, 1997. The defendant was convicted after trial of five rapes of prostitutes aged between 14 and 21 over a period of six years. Although the trauma to a prostitute of sexual intercourse with a strange man was less than for most victims there were aggravating factors. Prostitutes were in need of the law's protection, they were particularly vulnerable to infection and had been forced to have intercourse without protection. The court was mindful of the number of offences, the consistent course of conduct involving a number of women over a period of years, the threat of force (one victim had been threatened she would be raped by two other people and then killed) and the absence of any plea of guilty. Sentences of four years concurrent were unduly lenient and the minimum sentence the trial judge could properly have imposed was eight years. (See also *R. v. Masood*, December 13, 1996.)

H. BURGLARY WITH INTENT TO RAPE

The Theft Act 1968, s.9, as amended by the Criminal Justice Act 1991, s.26 and the Criminal Justice and Public Order Act 1994, s.10 states: **4-58**

"9(1) A person is guilty of burglary if:
(a) he enters any building or part of a building and with the intent to commit any such offence as is mentioned in subsection 2 below.
(2) The offences referred to in subsection 1(a) above are offences of stealing anything in the building or part of a building in question, of inflicting on any person therein grievous bodily harm or raping any person therein, and of doing unlawful damage to the building or anything therein."

Section 9(3) of the Theft Act 1968 as amended by section 26 of the Criminal Justice Act 1991 states that:

"a person guilty of burglary shall on conviction on indictment be liable to imprisonment for a term not exceeding:
(a) where the offence was committed in respect of a building or part of a building which is a dwelling, fourteen years;
(b) in any other case, ten years."

Hence the maximum penalty for an offence of burglary with intent to rape depends upon the type of building the intended victim happened to be in. In the case of a youth the former offence (*i.e.* in a dwelling) may be a grave crime, but not in the latter.

The intent must be proved prior to entry and an intention to rape a victim formed after entry is insufficient. In *R v. Collins* [1973] Q.B. 100, C discovered that P was asleep and lying naked on her bed. He stripped off his own clothes and climbed onto her window sill. P awoke and seeing the naked   **4-59** man at her window assumed, wrongly, that it was her boyfriend and invited him in. They had intercourse with her consent and only afterwards did she realise her mistake. C's conviction for burglary with intent to rape was quashed because the judge applied the civil test for trespass. The position of C at the time P invited him in was vital. If he was inside the room, he had entered as a trespasser and would be guilty. If on the other hand he was still outside the window he would not have entered as a trespasser but as an invitee. However, he would still be guilty even though outside the window if he realised that her invitation was intended not for him, but intended to be limited to her boyfriend.

4–60   Section 10 of the Theft Act 1968 states that:

"10(1) A person is guilty of aggravated burglary if he commits any burglary and at the time has with him any firearm or imitation firearm, any weapon of offence or any explosive: and for this purpose:

   (a) 'firearm' includes an airgun or airpistol and 'imitation firearm' means anything which has the appearance of being a firearm, whether capable of being discharged or not.

   (b) 'weapon of offence' means any article made or adapted for use for causing injury or incapacitating a person, or intended by the person having it with him for such use.

   (c) 'explosive' means any article manufactured for the purpose of producing a practical effect by explosion, or intended by the person having it with him for that purpose.

(2) A person guilty of aggravated burglary shall on conviction on indictment be liable to imprisonment for life."

4–61   The term "weapon of offence" has a wider meaning than that of "weapon" under the Prevention of Crime Act 1953 in that it includes articles designed to incapacitate or restrain but not injure, *e.g.* handcuffs or a rope.

I. FIREARMS ACT 1968 AND FIREARMS (AMENDMENT) ACT 1994

4–62   Section 16A makes it:

"an offence for a person to have in his possession any firearm or imitation firearm with the intent:

   (a) by means thereof to cause, or

   (b) to enable another person by means thereof to cause, any person to believe that unlawful violence will be used against him or another person."

This indictable offence carries a fine, or 10 years' imprisonment or both.

4–63   Section 17(2) states that:

"if a person, at the time of his committing, or being arrested for an offence specified in Schedule 1 to this Act has in his possession a firearm or imitation firearm, he shall be guilty of an offence under this subsection unless he shows that he had it in his possession for a lawful object".

Offences contrary to sections 1, 17, 18 or 20 of the Sexual Offences Act 1956 are included in the Schedule.

J. OFFENCES AGAINST THE PERSON ACT 1861, S.21

Section 21 states: 4–64

"Whosoever shall, by any means whatsoever attempt to choke, suffocate, or strangle any other person, or shall, by any means calculated to choke, suffocate or strangle, attempt to render that other person insensible, unconscious or incapable of resistance with intent in any of such cases thereby to enable himself or any other person to commit, or with intent in any of such cases thereby to assist any other person in committing any indictable offence, shall be guilty of an offence, and being convicted shall be liable to imprisonment for life (as amended by the Statute Law Revision Act 1892, Criminal Justice Act 1948, s.1(1) and the Criminal Law Act 1967, s.12(5)(a))."

K. ADMINISTERING DRUGS

The Sexual Offences Act 1956, s.4 states: 4–65

"It is an offence for a person to apply or administer to or cause to be taken by a woman any drug, matter or thing with intent to stupefy or overpower her so as to enable any man to have unlawful sexual intercourse with her."

The offence consists of the applying or administering etc. and does not require a rape or attempted rape to take place. Only one offence is committed even though the intention is for several men to have intercourse (*R v. Shillingford* [1968] 2 All E.R. 200). Unlawful sexual intercourse included all intercourse outside marriage (*R v. Chapman* [1959] 1 Q.B. 100). Intercourse by a husband with his wife who is insensible can now be rape and may perhaps also now be "unlawful" sexual intercourse. Intercourse with a girl over thirteen but under sixteen by her husband is lawful even though the marriage is not recognised by British law (*H.M. Advocate v. Watson* [1885] S.C.J 6) (see also Sexual Offences Act 1956, s.6). It is generally accepted that alcohol is included in the term "drug matter or thing" although normal social drinking will, it is submitted not fall within the section (see consent).

The maximum penalty is two years' imprisonment.

The Offences Against the Person Act 1861, s.22 makes it an offence 4–66 that:

"whosoever shall unlawfully apply or administer to, or cause to be taken by, or attempt to apply or administer to, or attempt to cause to be administered to or taken by any person any chloroform, laudenum or other stupefying or overpowering drug matter or thing, or with intent in any of such cases thereby to enable himself or any other person to commit, or with intent in any of such cases thereby to assist any other person in committing, any indictable offence, shall be guilty of an offence, and being convicted thereof shall be liable to imprisonment for life."

It is submitted that the term "administer" is the same for both offences. It includes direct contact but is not limited to directed physical contact. In *R v. Gillard* (1988) 87 Cr.App.R. 189, C.A., it included the spraying of C.S. gas into a victim's face from a canister.

L. ABDUCTION

4–67   There are a number of offence concerning the abduction of women under the Sexual Offences Act 1956.
       Section 17 states:

"(1) It is [an offence] for a person to take away or detain a woman against her will with the intention that she shall marry or have unlawful sexual intercourse with that or any other person, if she is so taken away or detained either by force or for the sake of her property or expectations of property.

(2) In the foregoing subsection, the reference to a woman's expectations of property relates only to property of a person to whom she is next of kin or one of the next of kin, and 'property' includes any interest in property."

4–68   Section 19 states:

"(1) It is an offence, subject to the exception mentioned in this section, for a person to take an unmarried girl under the age of eighteen out of the possession of her parent or guardian against his will, if she is so taken with the intention that she shall have unlawful sexual intercourse with men or with a particular man.

(2) A person is not guilty of an offence under this section because he takes such a girl out of the possession of her parent or guardian as mentioned above if he believes her to be of the age of eighteen or over and has reasonable cause for the belief.

(3) In this section 'guardian' means any person having parental responsibility for or care of the girl."

4–69   Section 20 states:

"(1) It is an offence for a person acting without lawful authority or excuse to take an unmarried girl under the age of sixteen out of the possession of her parent or guardian against his will.

(2) In the foregoing subsection 'guardian' means any person having parental responsibility for or care of the girl."

4–70   Section 21 states:

"(1) It is an offence, subject to the exception mentioned in this section, for a person to take a woman who is a defective out of the possession of her parent or guardian against his will, if she is so taken with the intention that she shall have unlawful sexual intercourse with men or with a particular man.

(2) A person is not guilty of an offence under this section because he takes such a woman out of the possession of her parent or guardian as mentioned above, if he does not know and has no reason to suspect her to be a defective.

(3) In this section 'guardian' means any person having parental responsibility for or care of the woman."

Unlawful intercourse is discussed at paragraphs 4–9 and 4–89: an intention to rape is not required.

I. "To Take"

The taking need not be forceful and may even be with the consent of the   4–71
woman (*R v. Manktelow* (1853) 6 Cox 143). Indeed, where the girl planned an elopement via a ladder to her bedroom window in traditional style the man was convicted (*R v. Robbins* (1844) 1 C. & K. 456).

There must be some form of persuasion, inducement or blandishment on   4–72
the part of the defendant to constitute a taking (*R v. Kauffman* (1904) 68 J.P. 189; *R v. Olifer* (1866) 10 Cox C.C. 402; *R v. Jarvis* (1903) 20 Cox 240). So where the girl comes to the man of her own volition and he allows her to stay, and even takes her to places of entertainment and has intercourse with her, the offence is not made out. In *Jarvis* (above) a girl of 14 left home willingly to live with the defendant as man and wife. He, however, had used no persuasion and was not guilty of abduction.

Section 17 of the Sexual Offences Act is against the will of the woman. The   4–73
other offences are committed against the parent or guardian and can be committed with the agreement of the woman. However, where a servant girl under 16 went home for the weekend then left with the defendant with whom she spent several nights she was not in the possession of her father but her master and the defendant could not be convicted (*R v. Miller* (1876) 13 Cox 179).

The defendant must know that the girl is in the lawful charge of a parent   4–74
or guardian. If he meets two girls in the street and persuades them to go to another town where he seduces one, with no reason to know if she was living with her father, he is not guilty (*R v. Hibbert* (1869) L.R. 1 C.C.R. 184).

II. Consent

The consent of the parent or guardian induced by fraud will not constitute   4–75
genuine consent and abduction will still be made out (*R v. Hopkins* (1842) C. & Mar. 254). A parent who allowed his daughter a lax way of life allowing her to go out alone at night to public houses may be not exercising a control from which the girl can be taken (*R v. Premelt* (1858) 1 F. & E. 50). A parent

may not be considered so today. The willingness of the parent may be assumed from the circumstances (*R v. Handley* (1859) VF & E 648).

III. MOTIVE

4–76   There does not need to be any evil intent on the part of the man, a lover who persuades his girlfriend to elope is guilty of the offence (*R v. Booth* (1872) 12 Cox 231; *R v. Twistleton* (1668) 1 Lev. 257).

However, where a lawful authority or excuse is referred to, in section 20, giving shelter to a girl in need in good faith will be a lawful excuse. The excuse must be lawful (*R v. Tegerdine* (1982) 75 Cr.App.R. 298). A religious or philanthropic motive is no excuse for abducting a girl under 16 (*R v. Booth*, above).

IV. KNOWLEDGE OF AGE

4–77   Where the girl is under 16 a lack of knowledge of her age is no excuse. It was said in *R v. Olifier* (1866) 10 Cox C.C. 402 that "anyone dealing with an unmarried girl does so at his peril and if she turns out to he under 16 he may be guilty" (under s.55 of the Offences Against the Person Act of 1861). In *R v. Mycock* (1871) 12 Cox C.C. 28 (see also *R v. Robins* (1871) 12 Cox C.C. 28), it was confirmed that "it is not necessary to prove the prisoner knew the girl was under 16". However, where the age is under 18 a reasonable belief that the girl was 19, the age the girl claimed, could be a defence (*R v. Packer* (1886) 16 Cox C.C. 57).

4–78   The taking need not be permanent. In *R v. Timmins* (1860) 8 Cox C.C. 401, the defendant slept with the girl for three nights and in *R v. Baillie* (1859) 8 Cox C.C. 238 it was only for a number of hours although the defendant had taken the girl to a chapel and married her in that time. The marriage however had not been consummated.

4–79   Section 17 carries life imprisonment, the other offences two years.

4–80   Translating the above into modern life, the offence will not be committed where a boyfriend, even though he intends to indulge in indecent acts with her, takes his girlfriend for an evening walk. In *R v. Jones* [1973] Crim.L.R. 621, an attempt to take 10 year old girls for a walk intending to indecently assault them was held not be constitute an attempt to commit these offences. The defendant met the two girls at a local swimming baths. He rode on the same bus paying their bus fares for them. Jones then told them to go home and get changed and arranged to meet them later to take them for a walk during which he had intended to indecently assault them. Fortunately, the mother of one of the children became suspicious. The court held that "taking out of the possession and against the will of the parent" are to be taken as meaning some conduct by the accused amounting to a substantial interference with the possessary relationship of parent and child. The word "possession" in section 20 shows that it is this possessary relationship that the section sets out to preserve. The modern approach seems therefore to be that the offence occurs where the defendant challenges the parent's authority, for example by marrying her or by taking her away and living with her for several days. Jones did not challenge the parent's authority even though he intended to abuse the girls. The commentary upon *Jones* speculates about the success of a charge of attempting to commit an indecent assault. In *Jones*, however, the act could only be considered preparatory and not an attempt and can be distinguished from *Maskell* [1954] 1 All E.R. 137 where that defendant had reached the next stage after *Jones*. The serious gap in law recognised in the commentary existed.

This gap has now been addressed by section 2 of the Child Abduction Act 1984: **4–81**

"2(1) Subject to subsection (3) below, a person, other than one mentioned in subsection (2) below commits an offence if, without lawful authority or reasonable excuse, he takes or detains a child under the age of sixteen:
(a) so as to remove him from the lawful control of any person having lawful control of the child; or
(b) so as to keep him out of the lawful control of any person entitled to lawful control of the child.

(2) The persons are:
(a) where the father and mother of the child in question were married to each other at the time of his birth, the child' father and mother;
(b) where the father and mother of the child in question were not married to each other at the time of his birth, the child's mother; and
(c) any other person mentioned in section 1(2)(c) to (e) above [*i.e.* (c) a guardian of the child, or(d) a person in whose favour a residence order is in force with respect to the child, or(e) he has custody of the child.

(3) In proceedings against any person for an offence under this section, it shall be a defence for that person to prove:
(a) where the father and mother of the child in question were not married to each other at the time of his birth
(i) that he is the child's father; or
(ii) that, at the time of the alleged offence, he believed, on reasonable grounds that he was the child's father; or
(b) that, at the time of the alleged offence, he believed that the child had attained the age of sixteen."

This section will apply where for example a defendant takes a baby from a pram (*R v. Cooper* (1994) 15 Cr.App.R. (S) 470). The question of "lawful control" was considered in *R v. Leather* (1994) 98 Cr.App.R. 179. It can be distinguished from "possession". Leather induced a number of young children to go with him on the pretence of requiring help to find a bicycle. It was held that there was no necessary spatial element. The test is whether the children were deflected by some action of the defendant from that which they would with parental consent have otherwise been doing. It is a question of fact for the jury whether the defendant rather than the children's parents were effectively in control of them at the time they were together.

4-82 The charge does not require the consent of the D.P.P. to prosecute (unlike s. 1).

4-83 The average sentence appears higher than that under the Sexual Offences Act 1956. In *Whitlock* (1994) 15 Cr.App.R. (S) 146, a sentence of two years was deemed correct where a defendant induced a 13 year old boy to leave a school bus and spend the morning with him. That was of course the maximum under the earlier legislation.

M. KIDNAPPING AND FALSE IMPRISONMENT

4-84 Both are common law offences and not necessarily sexually motivated. The difference was discussed in *R v. Hutchins* [1988] Crim.L.R. 379. Both offences overlap but kidnapping involves a taking away by force or fraud, whilst false imprisonment involves only a detaining. In *R v. Rahman* (1985) 81 Cr.App.R. 349, false imprisonment was defined as "the unlawful and intentional or reckless restraint of a victim's freedom of movement from a particular place".

If there remains an alternative route for departure it would appear probable that there has been no imprisonment (*Bird v. Jones* [1845] 7 Q.B. 742).

4-85 Violence is not an essential ingredient and false imprisonment may be achieved without an assault occurring (*Hunter v. Johnson* (1884) 13 Q.B.D. 225; *R v. Linsberg and Leies* (1905) 69 J.P. 102.)

4-86 Kidnapping was considered in detail in *R v. D* [1984] 2 All E.R. 449. There are six factors:

    (i)   the nature of the offence consists of an attack on, and infringement of, the personal liberty of an individual;

    (ii) there are four ingredients:

        (a)   the taking or carrying away of one person by another;

        (b)   by force or fraud—force is not restricted to physical violent force or threat of violence. A mental or moral power or influence to compel or force another to do something against her will, will suffice. This is clear from the words "force or fraud" (*R v. Singh and Southward*, unreported, March 23, 1995, C.A.; 94/5160/75; Archbold News, Issue 8, October 4, 1995).

        (c)   without the consent of the person so taken or carried away; and

        (d)   without lawful excuse.

    (iii) At common law since the seventeenth century the offence was a misdemeanour;

    (iv) nonetheless kidnapping was always regarded by reason of its nature, as a grave and heinous offence;

    (v) originally the offence required the victim's removal from within the jurisdiction to a place outside it. This requirement is now obsolete and no longer part of the offence;

(vi) furthermore, the offence once required not only taking someone but also, or alternatively hiding them away. This requirement is also obsolete and no longer required.

The lack of consent is a requirement. A child may well have sufficient understanding and intelligence to give consent. In other cases the child may be too young to be able to give a properly informed consent (*R v. D*, above). 4–87

The taking need not be very far. In *R v. Wellard* [1978] 1 W.L.R. 921, a 17 year old girl was induced by fraud to go to the defendant's car which was a distance of some 100 yards. The defendant pretended to be a police officer. She was put in the car but the car remained stationary. She was rescued by a friend a short time later. All the necessary ingredients of kidnapping existed. 4–88

I. Detention Of A Woman In A Brothel

(See also paragraph 12–56.) 4–89
Section 24 of the Sexual Offences Act 1956 states:

"(1) It is an offence for a person to detain a woman against her will on any premises with the intention that she shall have unlawful sexual intercourse with men or with a particular man, or to detain a woman against her will in a brothel.

(2) Where a woman is on any premises for the purpose of having unlawful sexual intercourse or is in a brothel, a person shall be deemed for the purpose of the foregoing subsection to detain her there if, with the intention of compelling or inducing her to remain there, he either withholds from her her clothes or any other property belonging to her or threatens her with legal proceedings in the event of her taking away clothes provided for her by him or on his direction.

(3) A woman shall not be liable to any legal proceedings, whether civil or criminal, for taking away or being found in possession of any clothes she needed to enable her to leave premises on which she was for the purpose of having unlawful sexual intercourse or to leave a brothel."

Unlawful sexual intercourse means outside marriage (*R v. Chapman* [1959] 1 Q.B. 100).

II. Powers To Search For A Woman Detained For Immoral Purposes

(See also paragraph 12–58.) 4–90
Section 43 of the Sexual Offences Act 1956 states:

"(1) Where it is made to appear by information on oath laid before a

151

justice of the peace by a woman's parent, relative or guardian, or by any other person who in the opinion of the justice is acting in the woman's interests, that there is reasonable cause to suspect:

(a) that the woman is detained in any place within the justice's jurisdiction in order that she may have unlawful sexual intercourse with men or with a particular man; and

(b) that either she is so detained against her will, or she is under the age of sixteen or is a defective, or she is under the age of eighteen and is so detained against the will of her parent or guardian;

then the justice may issue a warrant authorising a constable to search for her and to take her and detain her in a place of safety until she can be brought before a justice of the peace.

4–91   (2) A justice before whom a woman is brought in pursuance of the foregoing subsection may cause her to be delivered up to her parent or guardian, or otherwise dealt with as circumstances may permit and require.

(3) A constable authorised by a warrant under this section to search for a woman may enter (if need be, by force) any premises specified in the warrant, and remove the woman from the premises.

(4) A constable executing a warrant issued under this section shall be accompanied by the person applying for the warrant, if that person so desires, unless the justice issuing it otherwise directs.

(5) In this section 'guardian' means any person having parental responsibility for or care of the woman.

(6) The powers conferred by this section shall be in addition to and not in derogation of those conferred by Part V of the Children Act 1989."

4–92   If the information was given in good faith, and without maliciousness or a desire to injure the person proceeded against and was not made in an attempt to mislead the justices, no civil action will lie against the woman's parent, relative, guardian or other person acting in the woman's interests (*Hope v. Evered* (1886) 17 Q.B.D. 338).

Chapter 5
Serious Assaults

The Crown Prosecution Service will review files in accordance with the Code   5–01
for Crown Prosecutors issued under section 10 of the Prosecution of Offences Act 1985.

Certain factors will influence the decision to prosecute. One of the factors
which may make an offence more serious and therefore make a prosecution
more likely as being in the public interest, is listed in the 1994 issue of the
Code at paragraph 6.4(i): "the offence was motivated by any form of
discrimination against a victim's ethnic or national origins, sex, religious
beliefs, political views or sexual preference."

A. HOMICIDE

Death may occur from sexual encounters in one of three ways. First, it may   5–02
be accidental; secondly, the perpetrator may kill the victim during or after
rape or other assault to silence the victim, and thirdly, the killing may be
deliberate for sexual satisfaction in what has been termed "lust-murder" (R.
von Krafft-Ebing, *Psychopathia Sexualis*). A "lust-murder" need not be
sadistic in nature.

The difference is important. In the later two cases the correct charge is   5–03
obviously murder. However, in the first instance the correct finding could be
manslaughter if an offence at all, even in the case of death resulting from
rape. Traditionally, rape has not been considered a serious injury and
therefore non-deliberate death caused as a result cannot constitute murder.

B. NECROPHILIA

The police are occasionally asked to investigate allegations of sexual inter-   5–04
ference including intercourse with dead bodies. The allegations are usually
made against mortuary attendants but have been made against those respon-

sible for the transportation of a corpse such as sailors. For an assault to take place the victim must be an individual known to the law and therefore alive. The act of necrophilia is therefore not an offence.

5–05 However, it is submitted it is not an act warranted by law and therefore if two or more people agree to a series of acts which facilitate an act of necrophilia there will be a conspiracy to commit a public nuisance.

Exposing a naked corpse in public is a public nuisance (*R v. Clark* (1883) 15 Cox 171).

C. SADO-MASOCHISTIC ASSAULT

5–06 Sado-masochistic relationships are by no means rare. Masochism is a term created by R. von Krafft-Ebing in *Psychopathia Sexualis*. It is, however, not sanctioned by the criminal law which states that no one can consent to an assault inflicted upon them and therefore consent is no defence (with certain limited exceptions the extent of which remain unclear).

5–07 The situation was examined in *R v. Donovan* ([1934] 2 K.B. 498. D was charged with indecent assault and common assault upon a 17 year old girl, Miss Harrison. He had taken her to a garage and beaten her with a cane "in circumstances of indecency". The arrangement had been made in advance by telephone and it is clear that she was a willing participant. She suffered what is described as a "fairly severe beating". It was held that "if an act is unlawful in the sense of being itself a criminal act, it is plain that it cannot be rendered lawful because the person consents to it. No person can licence another to commit a crime". The situation has to be distinguished from rough but innocent horseplay. The exceptions are those cases where:

(i) bodily harm is not the motive on either side and
(ii) that they are "manly diversions intended to give strength, skill and activity and may fit people for defence in times of need".

5–08 The decision in *R v. Donovan* was supported in *Attorney-General's Reference (No.6 of 1980)* [1981] 2 All E.R. 1057, although the reasoning supporting the decision was questioned as being tautologous. It was held that "it is not in the public interest that people should try to cause or should cause each other actual bodily harm for no good reason".

5–09 In *McCoy* [1953(2)] S.A. 4[S.R.] the manager of an airline company was convicted of assault when he caned an air hostess with her consent, as a punishment for a breach of airline rules. The courts have accepted that consent is a defence to the infliction of bodily harm in the course of some lawful activities which are discussed at length. Consent is a defence to common assault.

5–10 The giving and receiving of pain was again addressed in *R v. Brown and others* [1993] 2 W.L.R. 556, H.L.). A group of sado-masochistic homosexuals participated willingly and enthusiastically in acts of violence against each other. They derived sexual pleasure from the giving and receiving of pain. Consent, it was held, was no defence to charges of assault and wounding under the Offences Against the Person Act 1861. There was no permanent injury, no infection and no evidence of the need for medical attention although the activities ranged from beating on the genitals and buttocks with stinging nettles to the nailing of a man's penis to a bench. It was held that "what might be good reason was unnecessary for their Lordships to decide. It was sufficient to say, as far as the instant case was concerned, that they agreed with the trial judge that the satisfying of sado-masochistic libido did not come within the category of good reason nor can the injuries be described as merely transient or trifling. The case held that consent is not a defence to a charge of the *intentional* infliction of bodily harm under the Act. Sado-masochistic homosexual activity cannot be regarded as conducive to the enhancement or enjoyment of family life or conducive to the welfare of society. As Lord Templeman said: 'Pleasure derived from the infliction of pain is an evil thing'.

The decision was confirmed by the European Court of Human Rights as *Laskey, Jaggard and Brown v. United Kingdom (The Times*, February 20, 1997) where it was observed that the State was unquestionably entitled to regulate the infliction of physical harm through the criminal law. The determination of the tolerable level of harm where the victim consented was primarily a matter for the state authorities.

In *R v. Goodwin* (unreported, May 19, 1994) G and a married woman C 5-11 discovered they had an interest in sado-masochism. They had intercourse on a number of occasions accompanied by beating and bondage. The defendant with the woman's consent pierced her nipples and inserted hoop earrings. He was convicted of assault occasioning actual bodily harm. In *R v. Brown and others*, above, Lord Templeman said ((1993) 97 Cr.App.R. at 47) that ritual circumcision, tattooing, ear-piercing and violent sports including boxing are lawful activities. (Tattooing is subject to the Tattooing of Minors Act 1969. Ear-piercing premises must be registered with the local authority. This supervision does not extend to other forms of body piercing. The Local Government (Miscellaneous Provisions) Act 1982, s.15 specifies tattooing, ear-piercing and electrolysis as requiring registration for businesses. The Act pre-dates the modern trend of other forms of piercing.)

Brown was distinguished in *R v. Wilson (The Times*, March 5, 1996): the 5-12 defendant's wife was found to have the defendant's initials "A.W." scarred onto her buttocks. She had wanted to be tattooed but instead at her suggestion and instigation, he had burnt his initials on her with a hot knife. The injuries were not transient or trifling. The trial judge had found himself bound by *Donovan* and *Brown* and the defendant had been convicted of assault occasioning actual bodily harm. The Court of Appeal however held that *Brown* was not authority for the proposition that consent was no defence to a charge under section 47 of the Offences Against the Person Act 1861 in all circumstances where actual bodily harm was deliberately inflicted. It related only to a sado-masochistic encounter and recognised that necessarily there had to be exceptions to what was no more than a general proposition. One of these exceptions was tattooing. There did not appear to their Lordships any logical difference between what Wilson had done here and what he might have done in the way of tattoos. They did not think this was in principal any more dangerous. They asked, "Did public policy and the public interest demand that the appellant's activity should be restricted by the sanctions of the criminal law?" They felt that it did not. "In this field the law should develop upon a case-by-case basis rather than upon general propositions to which in those changing times exceptions might arise not expressly covered by authority". They felt that the proceedings served no useful purpose.

5–13 In *Brown*, a further exception was suggested for religious mortification and flagellation. There is however no logic outside public policy which seriously distinguishes religious flagellation and masochistic sexual pleasure. In *Bravery v. Bravery* [1954] 3 All E.R. 59, the court did not agree whether an operation performed without just cause but with consent was an assault or not.

5–14 The Law Commission has sent out proposals for principals clarifying the law relating to individual freedom and the criminal law "Consent in the Criminal Law, A Consultation Paper" (Law Commission Paper No.139, 1995, HMSO). In the paper the Law Commission proposes that the intentional or reckless causing of seriously disabling injury should remain criminal, even if the injured person consents to the injury or to the risk of injury. The Commission defines a seriously disabling injury as one which "causes serious distress and involves the loss of a bodily member or organ, or permanent bodily injury or permanent functional impairment, or severe or prolonged pain, or serious impairment of health, or prolonged unconsciousness". Any injury falling outside this definition would be insufficient to found a prosecution for assault, assuming that valid consent was given. The Commission proposes that a person should be regarded as having given valid consent if he, or she, believes that the act or omission is intended to cause injury or risk of injury to him or her. There would of course be safeguards for persons not having the capacity to consent.

5–15 Body piercing and other operations which might be described as mutilations will be lawful if performed for religious, socio-ethnic or even ornamental reasons and will be assaults if the object is primarily the enjoyment of pain. In other circumstances, specific enactment would be required to make the acts unlawful.

D. FEMALE CIRCUMCISION

5–16 The Prohibition of Female Circumcision Act 1985 was intended to prevent acts of mutilation against girls by some ethnic minorities. It was not intended to affect general body piercing although it does refer to "otherwise mutilate". The verb "to infibulate" means "the fastening of the sexual organs with a fibula or clasp".

Section 1 of the Prohibition of Female Circumcision Act 1985 states:

"(1) Subject to section 2 below, it shall be an offence for any person:
    (a) to excise, infibulate or otherwise mutilate the whole or any part

of the *labia majora* or *labia minora* or clitoris of another person; or

(b) to aid, abet, counsel or procure the performance by another person of any of those acts on that other person's own body.

(2) A person guilty of an offence under this section shall be liable:

(a) on conviction on indictment, to a fine or to imprisonment for a term not exceeding five years or to both; or

(b) on summary conviction, to a fine not exceeding the statutory maximum (as defined in section 74 of the Criminal Justice Act 1982) or to imprisonment for a term not exceeding six months, or to both."

Section 2 states:

"(1) Subsection (1)(a) of section 1 shall not render unlawful the perform-   5–17
ance of a surgical operation if that operation;

(a) is necessary for the physical or mental health of the person on whom it is performed and is performed by a registered medical practitioner; or

(b) is performed on a person who is in any stage of labour or has just given birth and is so performed for purposes connected with that labour or birth by:

(i) a registered medical practitioner or a registered midwife; or

(ii) a person undergoing a course of training with a view to becoming a registered medical practitioner or a registered midwife.

(2) In determining for the purposes of this section whether an operation   5–18
is necessary for the mental health of a person, no account shall be taken of the effect on that person of any belief on the part of that or any other person that the operation is required as a matter of custom or ritual".

E. NON SADO-MASOCHISTIC ASSAULT

Other activities not motivated by the desire to inflict or enjoy pain may need   5–19
to be considered. If the injuries are "more than merely transient and trifling", as described in *Donovan* and *Brown* there may be an assault, to which consent is not a defence.

Where the serious harm is unintentional the case of Brown is less clear, it specifically addresses intentional harm. The violence it was said was injurious to the participant and *unpredictably* dangerous (*per* Lord Jauncey of Tullichettle).

R v. Coney ((1882) 8 Q.B.D. 534) was referred to in *R v. Brown*, above.   5–20
That case said: "there is however abundant authority for saying that no consent can render that innocent which is in fact dangerous" and also said that "in cases where life and limb are exposed to no serious danger in the

common course of things, I think that consent is a defence to a charge of assault, even when considerable force is used".

5-21   In the case of *Boyea* [1992] Crim.L.R. 54, a woman's body showed clear signs of violence. The defence was one of consent. The court held that consent was irrelevant if the defendant's actions were likely or intended to cause bodily harm. Following the previous cases it was ruled that "an assault intended or which is likely to cause bodily harm, accompanied by indecency is an offence irrespective of consent, provided that the injury is not 'transient or trifling' ". However not all injury constitutes an offence. The court went on to say: 'the court must take into account that social attitudes have changed over the years, particularly in the field of sexual relations between adults. As a generality the level of vigour in sexual congress which is acceptable and the voluntarily accepted risk of incurring some injury is probably higher now than it was in 1934 (*Donovan*). It follows that 'transient or trifling' must be understood in the conditions of 1992. (See also para. 5–25, below, where the particular activity of fisting is considered in greater detail.) The court also confirmed that the test is objective not subjective (see para. 5–26 below).

5-22   In the case of *R v. Sharmpal Singh* [1962] A.C. 188, the defendant was convicted of manslaughter of his wife. It was alleged that he had squeezed his wife's throat too hard during a "sexual embrace". It was not alleged that he had intended that she become unconscious as it was not a case of sexual asphyxiation. In upholding his conviction their Lordships asked themselves:

> "whether they were satisfied that the degree of force used was unlawful. The question is whether what was done was within the limits permitted by the wife's submission to intercourse and its normal accompaniments or whether it went beyond those limits so as to constitute an assault upon her. Here there was extensive pressure. Since an expert (in strangling) can cause death by using very little force, it is conceivable that a husband might accidentally hit upon the same means. But deaths caused accidentally during intercourse when the wife has ordinary health must be very rare indeed. The natural inference from the medical evidence is that the accused pressed much too hard."

5-23   Two particular activities may be addressed as serious injuries and even fatalities have occurred. One of these is sexual asphyxiation. Some people enjoy the sensation of passing out during sex. This seems to apply to some women during intercourse. With men it is of course usually associated with masturbation. Death occurs accidentally on a regular basis.

5-24   Lack of consciousness cannot be considered to be transient or trifling even by 1992 standards if more than fleeting. The Law Commission would prohibit "prolonged unconsciousness", but any unconsciousness if caused by manual pressure is very close to death. Such behaviour, it is submitted, must be unlawful and death would be at the least manslaughter (*R v. Williamson* 15 Cr.App.R.(S) 364).

5-25   "Fisting" involves the insertion of the whole hand, sometimes up to the forearm either into the vagina or the anus. It is understood to be not uncommon in homosexual relations and occurs in heterosexual encounters.

Lord Mustill stated in *Brown* (at 83):

"of course things may go wrong and really serious injury or death may ensue. If this happened, those responsible would be punished according to the ordinary law in the same way as those who kill or injure in the more ordinary sexual activities are regularly punished."

R v. Boyea [1992] Crim.L.R. 54, involved "fisting". B was convicted of 5–26 indecent assault. He inserted his fist into the complainant's vagina and twisted it causing injuries consistent with force. Both *Donovan* [1934] 2 K.B. 498 and *Savage* [1991] 3 W.L.R. 914, were considered. Having discussed the relative levels of vigour in sexual congress in 1934 and 1992, the court concluded that there was no doubt that the extent of the violence inflicted upon the complainant went far beyond the risk of minor injury to which, if she did consent, her consent would have been a defence. Moreover, it was inconceivable that she would have consented to the injuries which were in fact inflicted upon her. The learned commentary points out that recklessness in this offence means the conscious taking of a risk, that is Cunningham as distinct from Caldwell/Lawrence recklessness. Taking the risk, with consent of some degree of injury in sexual congress is lawful and the court's view is that a risk of greater injury is more permissible now than 60 years ago. The degree of permissible risk is a matter for the jury to decide. The test still appears to be, subject to the reservations expressed in *R v. Wilson*, above, was there risk of an injury which was "transient or trifling". Boyea was charged with indecent assault. In cases where the aspect complained of is the injury it is submitted that a charge under the Offences Against the Person Act 1861 would be more appropriate than one under the Sexual Offences Act 1956.

Fisting was also the activity addressed at first instance in *R v. Slingsby* 5–27 [1995] Crim.L.R. 570. A different view from *Boyea* was taken. In *Boyea* the defendant had been charged with indecent assault. In *Slingsby*, the woman had died of septicaemia resulting from cuts in her rectum caused by a signet ring on S's hand when he fisted her. The court of first instance, Nottingham Crown Court heard legal arguments at the opening of the case. The Crown submitted that there had been violence for the sake of sexual gratification and that it was not lawful if a party suffered harm (*Brown* (1992), *Donovan* (1934), *Boyea* (1992)). The fisting therefore constituted an unlawful act and that the death was properly charged as manslaughter. The court held however that the question of consent to injury did not arise because neither party anticipated or considered it. All they were considering was vigorous sexual activity. Had it not been for the co-incidence of the signet ring, no injury at all would have been caused or could have been contemplated. There had therefore been no unlawful act. The case did not come within the area of sexual activity which notwithstanding the consent of the parties is prohibited by the criminal law. The Crown therefore offered no evidence and a not guilty verdict was entered. In his commentary on *Slingsby*, Professor Smith expresses the opinion that *Boyea* is based upon a misunderstanding of *R v.*

Savage ([1992] A.C.699; commentary found at [1992] Crim.L.R. 575) and that the principles set out in *Slingsby* are correct. The position would appear to be that if the parties agree to the infliction of harm, or perhaps were reckless as set out in *Cunningham, e.g.* were aware that injury might be caused and took an unjustified risk then the act is unlawful, but if they never contemplated the possibility of injury, then no offence takes place and questions of consent to the injury are irrelevant.

F. DISEASES

5-28　　In *R v. Bennett* (1866) 4 F & F 1105, the defendant had intercourse with a girl of 13 and thereby infected her with a venereal disease. He was held to be guilty of indecent assault. Her ignorance of his medical condition negatived her consent.

5-29　　The case was followed in *R v. Sinclair* (1867) 13 Cox C.C. 28. The defendant infected a girl over 12 with gonorrhoea. He was not guilty of rape (the court looked for evidence of resistance and therefore the case is no authority for that aspect any longer) but he was guilty of an assault. Shee J. said:

> "if he knew that he had such a disease and that the probable consequences would be its communication to the girl, and she, in ignorance of it, consented to connection, and you are satisfied that she would not have consented if she had known the fact then her consent is vitiated by the deceit practised upon her and the prisoner would be guilty of an assault and if he thus communicated the disease, of inflicting upon her actual bodily harm."

5-30　　However, in *R v. Clarence* (1888) 22 Q.B.D.23, a husband who also knew he had gonorrhoea infected his wife. Had she known she would not have consented. It was held that he could not be convicted of inflicting grievous bodily harm nor of an assault occasioning actual bodily harm because there was no assault committed. The infection of another person in this way was not, it was held, an assault. If a man by a grasp of the hand infects another with small-pox, it is impossible to trace out in detail the connection between the act and the disease and it would be an unnatural use of language to say that a man by such an act "inflicted" small-pox upon the other. The husband would not be guilty of rape so why should the act be any other class of assault? The woman's consent here was as full and conscious as consent could be. It was not obtained by any fraud either as to the nature of the act or as to the identity of the agent. The injury was done by a suppression of the truth. It appeared to the court to be an abuse of language to describe such an act as an assault.

　　Bennett and *Sinclair* were both referred to in *Clarence* and were specifically not overruled, as they were considered undoubtedly important and useful in the administration of the criminal law (*per* Pollock B.).

5-31　　More serious diseases especially the HIV virus may raise important questions, especially in cases alleging deliberate or reckless transmission. Offences contrary to section 23 and 24 of the Offences Against the Person Act 1861 (administering a poison, or other destructive or noxious thing so as to endanger life, or inflict grievous bodily harm, or with intent to injure, aggrieve or annoy) may be considered. Indeed, *R v. Clarence*, above, seems to be good authority that the infection of a disease is more akin to the administration of a poison than to an assault under either section 20 or section 47 of the Offences Against the Person Act 1861. Stephens J. said: "the administration of poison is dealt with by section 24. Infection is a kind of poisoning. It is the application of an animal poison, and poisoning, as already shown, is not an assault."

The transmission of AIDS or HIV virus as it related to the 1861 Act was also considered in *R v. Brown*, above. Lord Lowry said: 5–32

"when considering the danger of infection, with its inevitable threat of AIDS, I am not impressed by the argument that this threat can be discounted on the ground that, as long ago as 1967 Parliament, subject to conditions, legalised buggery, now a well-known vehicle for the transmission of AIDS. . . . If in the course of buggery, as authorised by the 1967 Act one participant, either with the other participant's consent or not, deliberately causes actual bodily harm to the other, the offence against section 47 has been committed. The 1967 Act provides no shield."

It is also referred to by Lord Jauncey of Tullichettle ((1993) 97 Cr.App.R. at 59) and Lord Templeman (at 51) but draws no conclusion. Lord Mustill believed (at 88), in a dissenting opinion, that legislation would be required to bring this activity within the 1861 Act. He said:

"I would give the same answer to the suggestion that these activities involved a risk of accelerating the spread of auto-immune deficiency syndrome (*sic*), and that they should be brought within the Act of 1861 in the interests of public health. The consequence would be strange, since what is currently the principle cause for the transmission of this scourge, namely consenting buggery between males is now legal. Nevertheless, I would be compelled to give this proposition the more anxious consideration if there had been any evidence to support it."

G. STALKING

Severe depression with marked features of anxiety may be regarded as   5–33
grievous harm of a psychiatric nature. In the case of *R v. Burstow* (*The Times*, July 30, 1996) this had been caused by a male stalker on a woman with whom he had previously had a relationship, by telephone calls, letters, photographs and frequent visits to her home. One note was menacing. It was held, following *R v. Chan-Fook* [1994] 1 W.L.R. 689, that grievous bodily harm has been inflicted by the conduct contrary to section 20 of the Offences Against the Person Act 1861. As "causing" is wider, or a least not narrower that "inflicting" (*R v. Mandair* [1995] 1 A.C. 208) it follows that grievous

bodily harm could also be caused contrary to section 18 where the necessary intent can also be proved.

(See also para. 7–51)

5-34   It is sufficient for the prosecution to prove a fear of violence at some time not excluding the immediate future for an assault to be committed and where there has been no physical action against a complainant an assault can be committed by words alone (*R v. Constanza, The Times*, March 31, 1997).

5-35   Psychiatric reports will usually be required before sentencing. The judge is however not bound by any recommendations. In *R v. Smith* (June 9, 1997, unreported) the appellant had stalked a woman for four years. He pleaded not guilty to assault occasioning actual bodily harm. After conviction psychiatric reports opined that he would not present a continuing threat to the woman. The trial judge disagreed and sentenced him to two and a half years. On appeal it was held that whilst a judge was unlikely to disagree on technical questions involving medical expertise in these circumstances the trial judge was much better placed than the doctors to decide if the appellant at liberty continued to pose a threat to the victim. A significant custodial sentence was called for but since this was the appellants first experience of custody it was hoped it would bring him to his senses. A sentence of twenty one months was substituted.

H. THE PROTECTION FROM HARASSMENT ACT 1997

5-36   This Act is primarily intended to address the problem of stalking and sexual harassment. However there is no defintion of harassment and the Act may therefore also be able to address neighbour problems, racial harassment, and possibly some examples of intrusive journalism subject to the statutory defence. The Act creates a new civil tort of harassment (s. 3) and creates four new criminal offences.

I. COMMENCEMENT

5-37   The offences of harassment (s. 2), causing fear of violence (s. 4) and breach of a restraining order (s. 5) and sections 1 and 7–12 commenced on June 16, 1997 (Protection from Harassment Act 1997 (Commencement) (No. 1) Order 1997). Sections 3(1), 3(2) and 6 (the new civil tort of harassment) also commenced on June 16, 1997 (Protection from Harassment Act 1997 (Commencement) (No. 2) Order 1997). The Act is not retrospective and all incidents which are alleged to form a course of conduct must post-date commencement. The offence of breach of a civil injunction under section 3(6) was not commenced on that date.

However a restraining order made under the Act is a protection against future offending and not a punishment. It is therefore arguable that it may take into account pre-commencement actions.

Section 2 offences are subject to the normal six months summary time limit (s. 127 of the Magistrates Courts Act 1980). It is submitted that it will suffice if part of the course of conduct occurs within the six months period. The intention of the Act would be frustrated by a defendant who only harassed his victim at greater intervals. The opposite view, that evidence of conduct over six months prior to charge is inadmissible may however be entertained by the courts.

Section 6 amends the Limitations Act 1980. The special limit for actions for personal injuries of three years does not apply to an action brought under section 3. The limit is therefore six years.

II. HARASSMENT

Section 1 prohibits a person from pursuing a course of conduct which 5-38 amounts to harassment. Section 2 creates an offence of a course of conduct which amounts to harassment of another which the defendant knows, or ought to have known amounts to harassment of another. The defendant ought to know if his course of conduct amounts to harassment if a reasonable person in possession of the same information would think the course of conduct amounted to harassment of the other. The test is therefore objective. A course of conduct involves conduct on at least two occasions (s. 7). No time limitation is imposed. Two incidents even a year apart for example on the victim's birthday may constitute a course of conduct. Two incidents separated only by a few minutes may on the other hand be in reality one continuing incident. Harassment is not defined but must include alarm or distress. Conduct is defined as including speech.

There are three defences under section 2.

(i)   That the course of conduct was pursued for the purpose of preventing or detecting crime. This obviously applies to the police, Customs and Excise and Post Office. It will presumably also apply to Neighbourhood Watch schemes and to investigative journalists.

(ii) That it was pursued under any enactment of rule of law or to comply with any condition or requirement imposed by any person under any enactment. This will apply to lawful recovery of debts or repossession of property.

(iii) That in the particular circumstances the pursuit of the course of conduct was reasonable. This may apply to private investigators who are not covered by (i) above. It may also bring into dispute public interest arguments raised by other press photographers and reporters.

The offence carries on summary conviction six months' imprisonment and/ or a level 5 fine.

III. FEAR OF VIOLENCE

Section 4 creates an offence of a course of conduct which causes another to 5-39 fear that violence will be used against him which the defendant knows or ought to know will cause another to fear that violence will be used against him.

The definitions are the same as section 2.

There are three defences. Defences (i) and (ii) are the same as for section 2. The third defence states that the pursuit of the conduct was reasonable for the protection of himself or another or for the protection of property. The offence is triable either way and carries five years' imprisonment and/or a fine on conviction on indictment. On summary conviction the penalty is the same as under section 2.

IV. BREACH OFFENCES

5–40   Sections 3(6) and 5(5) make it an offence for a person to do anything which he is prohibited from doing under an injunction under section 3, or a restraining order under section 5. Both offences are triable either way and the penalties are the same as the section 4 offence. There is one statutory defence to a breach of a criminal or civil order, to show that the defendant had a reasonable excuse. As with the defences to the other offences the onus of proof lies with the defendant to the normal standard. Whereas the offences created by sections 2 and 4 require a course of conduct, *i.e.* at least two incidents, these offences require only a single incident.

5–41   All the offences are arrestable. Section 2(3) amends section 24(2) of the Police and Criminal Evidence Act 1984, to provide a power of arrest for a section 2 offence. The other offences carry a maximum five year sentence.

5–42   Under section 12, the Secretary of State may issue a cerificate to the effect that the acts complained of were done in relation to:

    (i)   national security;
    (ii)   the economic well-being of the United Kingdom; or
    (iii)   The prevention of serious crime.

The certificate is conclusive evidence that the Act does not apply to the conduct in question. The Act does not apply to the Crown in any event. It is anticipated that the section will not be used often. Therre is a specific statutory defence that the conduct was pursued for the purpose of preventing or detecting crime. Section 12 will however prevent private prosecutions taken on behalf of surveillance targets in order to expose those keeping surveillance. It is not envisaged that it will be used to protect ordinary police activities but will apply to the Security Service.

V. RESTRAINING ORDERS

5–43   Both the Crown Court and the Magistrates Court may make a restraining order under section 5. The intention of the order is to protect the victim, or any other person named in the order from further conduct which amounts either to harassment or causing fear of violence. It is not intended as part of the punishment. It is arguable that the order may therefore reflect conduct prior to the commencement of the Act or which is not admissible in evidence in the criminal trial because, *e.g.* it occurred more than six months prior to charge. The length of the order should reflect the need for future protection and not the seriousness of the previous conduct. An indefinite order may therefore be appropriate. Applications to vary the order can be made under section 5(4) by the prosecutor, the defendant or any other party mentioned in the order for variation or discharge. A variation can include an application by the prosecution to extend the order. A custodial sentence does not preclude an order being made. It may be of a greater length than the sentence, and as many victims are aware it is possible to continue to harass a victim for custody.

Applications to vary should not be granted without good cause. All interested parties should be able to make representations. A victim may make an application to vary. The court has a residual power to prevent an abuse of process and may exercise this power to prevent a defendant using applications to vary an order as a means of further harassing a victim.

Although the court may make an order of its own volition it is appropriate for the prosecution to seek an order. The contents of the order are at the court's discretion provided that the general principal of protection not punishment is complied with. Orders should contain a written statement of the consequences of a breach of the order.

An action by a defendant may constitute an offence itself (*e.g.* a breach of   **5–44** the peace, an assault, etc.). It may also form part of a course of conduct. It is unclear whether a prosecution or a caution will prevent the prosecution from presenting that evidence before a court to show a course of conduct. It is submitted that it would be improper to allow evidence which had been presented to a court in prosecution to be used again to support a second prosecution as part of a course of conduct. Even to use evidence upon which a caution had been given may be an abuse of process. Such evidence could however it is submitted be presented to assist the court in making a restraining order.

Where the prosecution proceed on a charge alleging a course of conduct and a specific charge at the same time it is submitted there must be evidence to support both charges.

Chapter 6
Indecent Assault

6-01 Indecent assaults cover a multitude of sins from minor equivocal touchings and assaults where no contact takes place to the most serious of attacks. Some indecent assaults, such as forcing the victim by threats of violence to perform oral sex and other acts considered by the victim to be deeply degrading may well be more traumatic than rape would have been. Nonetheless the sentencing range of options for indecent assault remains less than that for rape.

A. DEFINITIONS

Section 14 of the Sexual Offences Act 1956 makes it an offence to indecently assault a woman:

"(1) It is an offence, subject to the exception mentioned in subsection (3) of this section, for a person to make an indecent assault on a woman.

(2) A girl under the age of sixteen cannot in law give any consent which would prevent an act being an assault for the purposes of this section.

(3) Where a marriage is invalid under section two of the Marriage Act 1949, or section one of the Age of Marriage Act 1929 (the wife being a girl under the age of sixteen), the invalidity does not make the husband guilty of any offence under this section by reason of her incapacity to consent while under that age, if he believes her to be his wife and has reasonable cause for the belief.

(4) A woman who is a defective cannot in law give any consent which would prevent an act being an assault for the purposes of this section, but a person is only to be treated as guilty of an indecent assault on a defective by reason of that incapacity to consent, if that person knew or had reason to suspect her to be a defective."

6-02 Section 15 of the Sexual Offences Act 1956 makes it an offence to indecently assault a man:

"(1) It is an offence for a person to make an indecent assault on a man.

(2) A boy under the age of sixteen cannot in law give any consent which would prevent an act being an assault for the purposes of this section.

(3) A man who is a defective cannot in law give any consent which would prevent an act being an assault for the purposes of this section, but a person is only to be treated as guilty of an indecent assault on a defective by reason of that incapacity to consent, if that person knew or had reason to suspect him to be a defective".

Consent by a mental defective is discussed in Chapter 11. See particularly the case of *R v. Hall* (1987) 86 Cr.App.R. 159, discussed at 11.2.

B. SENTENCING GUIDELINES

Both offences carry the same penalties: upon conviction upon indictment, the **6–03** maximum penalty is 10 years; upon summary conviction, six months or the prescribed sum or both. In the unreported case of *R v. Blair* (August 7, 1995, C.A.) it was pointed out that sexual intercourse with a defective (contrary to s. 7 of the Sexual Offences Act 1956) carries a maximum sentence of 2 years. An indecent assault upon a mental defective who is technically unable to give consent even though she may not be an unwilling participant under section 14(4) carries 10 years' imprisonment. The Sexual Offences Act 1985 increased the maximum sentence for indecent assault from 2 years but did not change the penalty for intercourse with a defective. The court should have regard to this anomaly and limit the penalty for indecent assault where it is appropriate to do so.

The Mode of Trial Guidelines set out in *Practice Note (Mode of Trial* **6–04** *Guidelines)* [1990] 1 W.L.R. 1439, state that indecent assaults should in general be tried summarily unless the court considers that one or more of the following features is present and that its sentencing powers are insufficient:

(i)   substantial disparity in age between the victim and the defendant;

(ii)   violence or threats of violence;

(iii) relationship of trust or responsibility between defendant and victim;

(iv) several similar offences and assaults more than trivial;

(v)   the victim is particularly vulnerable; and

(vi) serious nature of the assault.

It was stated in *R v. Bibi* [1980] 1 W.L.R. 1193 that: **6–05**

"many offenders can be dealt with equally justly and effectively by a sentence of six or nine months' imprisonment as by one of 18 months or three years. We have in mind the minor cases of sexual indecency."

Substantially longer periods of imprisonment will be appropriate where the assault in committed upon a child by a person in a position of authority over them. (See also R. v. Clarke, November 11, 1996.)

6–06   *R v. Bibi* was illustrated in the case of *R v. Freeman* (1982) 2 Cr.App.R (S) 194: a man indecently assaulted young girls between eight and 13 years of age by kissing them on the lips and momentarily touching their private parts. A sentence of 12 months was considered appropriate.

6–07   Rubbing against a young woman for example on an underground train does not normally require a custodial sentence: *R v. Neem* (1993) 14 Cr.App.R. (S) 18; *R v. Chagan* (1994) 16 Cr.App.R. (S) 15; although in some circumstances such a sentence, albeit short, may be appropriate: *R v. Townsend* (1994) 16 Cr.App.R. (S) 553.

6–08   A youth court can only commit a youth to stand trial at the Crown Court if it finds that the allegation constitutes a grave crime. Normally, this will require a maximum sentence of 14 years imprisonment being available (Children and Young Persons Act 1933, s. 53). However, the youth court may find an allegation of indecent assault upon a woman contrary to section 14 to be a grave crime even though the maximum penalty is 10 years (s. 64 of the Criminal Justice Act 1991). The same provision does not extend to an indecent assault upon a man. The section applies to a person who has attained the age of 16.

In the situation where a man indecently assaults an older consenting adolescent girl the range of appropriate sentences varies according to the circumstances: where the man is himself young and the victim is his long-standing girlfriend in a loving relation the young man only needs to be advised to mend his way.

6–09   In *R v. Hessey* (1987) 9 Cr.App.R. (S) 268, where a step-father fingered the 12 year step-daughter's vagina on a number of occasions over the period of a year, a sentence of 15 months' imprisonment was appropriate. In *R v. Gibbons* (1987) 9 Cr.App. R (S) 391, where a man fingered the vagina of a 13 year old girl in a house where he had earlier been baby-sitting, a sentence of nine months was considered appropriate.

6–10   Women going about their business in a public street have the right to be protected from indecent assaults. In *R v. Goodway* (1996) 1 Cr.App.R.(S) 16, a traffic warden was indecently assaulted by being handled in the region of the lower part of her bottom over her clothing. A sentence of two months' imprisonment was upheld on appeal although an order to pay costs of £200 was quashed because the appellant had lost his job.

6–11   In the case of *R v. Allen* [1996] Crim.L.R. 208, a young woman aged 18 became involved in a lesbian relationship with a 13 year old girl which involved mutual masturbation. The 13 year old was a willing participant, although she could not in law consent. On appeal, a two year sentence was reduced to 21 months. Had the offence been unlawful sexual intercourse (which here was physically impossible) two years' imprisonment would have been the maximum sentence possible. Had the defendant been male it is submitted a lesser sentence, non-custodial, would have been appropriate.

6–12   Indecent assault does not carry life imprisonment and a sentencing court should not try to achieve an equivalent sentence using consecutive terms of imprisonment. If appropriate the provisions of the Criminal Justice Act 1991, s. 2(2)(b) should be invoked. In *R v. Hodgson* [1996] Crim.L.R. 915, H pleaded guilty to six counts of indecent assault, four of indecency with a child, five of taking indecent photographs and one of escaping from lawful custody. He had committed indecency of the grossest kind with eighteen children aged between six and 11. He was sentenced to terms of imprisonment totalling 27 years with an order under the Criminal Justice Act 1991, s. 44 extending his licence period. Upon appeal, the sentence was reduced to one totalling 18 years for the sexual offences. The appellant had been likely to serve longer in custody than most life sentence prisoners and "it was wrong to seek to achieve the same result as a life sentence when a life sentence was not legally available."

C. AN ASSAULT

I. Elements Of The Offence

An indecent assault is an assault which is committed in circumstances of   6–13
indecency. The offences may be committed by a woman: *R v. Hare* [1934] 1 K.B. 354 is often quoted. It merely confirmed that indecent assault under the Offences Against the Person Act was not limited to buggery and could be committed by a woman: the boy involved was 12 years old.

A detailed analysis of the basics of indecent assault was set forth in *R v.*   6–14
Court [1989] A.C. 28:

   (a)   there must be an assault or a battery;

   (b)   most but not all indecent assaults will be clearly of a sexual nature. Some may only have sexual undertones. It is for the jury to decide whether "right-minded persons would consider the conduct indecent or not". The jury must decide if what occurred was so offensive to contemporary standards of modesty and privacy as to be indecent;

   (c)   if the circumstances of the assault are incapable of being regarded as indecent then the undisclosed intention of the accused could not make the assault an indecent one: *R v. George* [1956] Crim.L.R. 52. The taking of a shoe was not an indecent assault even though motivated by a shoe fetish. The indecency was directed to the shoe, not the woman;

   (d)   it is not necessary for the prosecution to prove that the victim was aware of the circumstances of indecency;

   (e)   cases which ordinarily present no problem are those in which the   6–15
facts devoid of explanation, will give rise to the irresistible inference that the defendant intended to assault his victim in a manner which right-minded persons would clearly think was indecent. However, where the circumstances were such as only to be capable of constituting an indecent assault, in order to determine whether or not right-minded persons might think that the assault was indecent, the following factors are relevant:

      (i)   the relationship of the defendant to the victim (relative, friend or stranger);

(ii) how had the defendant come to embark on this conduct and why was he so behaving? Are the jury sure that the defendant not only intended to commit an assault but an assault which was indecent? Is there any evidence which tends to explain the reason for the defendant's conduct? Such evidence is relevant to establish whether or not he intended to commit not only an assault but an indecent one.

(f) on a charge of indecent assault the Crown must prove:

(i) that the defendant intentionally assaulted his victim;

(ii) that the assault, or the assault and the accompanying circumstances, are capable of being considered by right-minded persons as being indecent;

(iii) that the defendant intended to commit that assault;

(g) evidence of the accused's explanation for assaulting the victim, whether or not it reveals an indecent motive, is admissible both to support or negative that the assault was indecent, and that it was so intended by the defendant.

6–16　　The normal legal rules concerning assaults apply with the exception that by virtue of the Act, a person under 16 years cannot consent to the assault. The rule however is more complex than at first appears. It is better practice where the victim is under 16 to include the age in the indictment (*R v. Stephenson* [1912] 3 K.B. 341). Where the victim is under 13 the age should be referred to in the indictment.

6–17　　There must be an assault or a battery if only a technical one. Where a man approaches a woman with his trousers open and makes indecent suggestions to the woman there is no assault even though she arms herself with a knife and runs away. It is assumed she did not fear immediate violence: *Finington v. Hutchinson* (1866) 15 L.T. 390. Where in a more recent case however, he indecently exposes his penis to her and approaches her inviting her to have intercourse, an indecent assault can take place: *R v. Rolfe* (1952) 36 Cr.App.R. 4. The assault need not involve contact between the parties: there need not be an indecent touching. For example, if the defendant compels a boy aged 16 to commit an indecent act in a public place, an indecent assault may have occurred: *R v. Sargeant, The Times*, October 15, 1996.

6–18　　The act must still constitute at the least a technical assault. Therefore passively allowing a person under 16 to touch a man in the area of his penis, which caused him to have an erection for a period of some minutes, is not an indecent assault on the child: *Fairclough v. Whipp* [1951] 2 All E.R. 834. The act would now be an offence of gross indecency with a child if under 14.

6–19　　Where a woman allows a boy under 16 to have intercourse with her, she commits no offence of indecent assault upon him unless she performs some act such as pulling him down upon her, or guiding his penis with her fingers into her vagina.

6–20　　The earlier case of *R v. Mason* (1969) 53 Cr.App.R. 21 involved a married woman who had intercourse with a number of young boys between 14 and 16. Despite feeling that "she. . . . behaved in a wholly disgraceful way and in a way of which I imagine many harlots would be ashamed", the Court took the pragmatic view that: "acts of touching readily submitted to and enjoyed during or preliminary to intercourse in such circumstances should be regarded as part of the intercourse and are equally not an assault by the woman on the boys."

However, that approach, sensible as it may appear, was disapproved in **6–21** *Faulkner v. Talbot* [1981] 1 Crim.L.R. 705. This case confirmed that intercourse by a woman with a boy between 14 and 16 was not an offence if she remains passive. However, the defendant put her hand on the boy's penis, pulled him on top of her and guided his penis into her vagina. It was held that holding the boy's penis was plainly an indecent touching, the provisions of section 15(2) of the 1956 Act prevent a boy under 16 consenting to an act which would otherwise be an assault, therefore he could not consent to this indecent touching, and there was an indecent assault. The commentary to the case properly points out that there are no savings for a woman who believes that the boy is lawfully her husband. The draughtsmen presumably accepted that intercourse with a boy over 14 was lawful. More seriously though, the situation is that the lesser action, touching the boy's penis is a serious crime whereas the full intercourse is not of itself unlawful. The practical effect is that a woman can be convicted of an action which may well be an attempt to commit a lawful act.

An assault will have occurred if the defendant remains passive if the **6–22** activity was induced by threats. So a threat to injure a woman unless she performs fellatio on the man will be an indecent assault (*R v. Kowalski* (1987) 86 Cr.App.R. 339 C.A.). The assault will be even more obvious if for example, he holds her by the hair.

Submission to a person of authority may be an assault, so that where a **6–23** schoolmaster places his hands indecently on the body of a girl pupil of 13 who makes no actual resistance, there is an assault against her will considering her tender age: *R v. M'Gavaran* (1853) 6 Cox CC 64. The submission does not amount to consent.

II. CONSENT

Although a person over 16 may consent to the assault, no person may **6–24** consent to an assault upon themselves which will result in injury to them other than injuries which are transient or trifling (see *R v. Donovan* [1934] 2 K.B. 498; *Attorney-General's Reference* (No.6 of 1980) [1981] 2 All E.R. 1057; *R v. Brown* [1993] 2 All E.R. 75, and compare *R v. Boyen*, unreported January 28, 1992 and R v. Wilson (above Chap. 5, para. 12)).

Although a person under 16 cannot consent to an indecent assault it is the **6–25** aspect of indecency to which their consent is invalid. If the act is one which is in itself indecent, *e.g.* the inserting of a finger into a vagina, mutual masturbation, or oral sex then no valid consent can be given. If on the other hand the act is one which is not on the face of it indecent but has undertones of indecency, then a valid consent may be given even by someone under 16. In *DPP v. Rogers* [1953] 2 All E.R. 644, a father took his daughter upstairs, placing his arm around her shoulders, and asked her to masturbate him which she did apparently willingly. It was held that there must be some compulsion, hostile act, threat or threatening gesture to constitute an assault.

6–26   The act in these circumstances must therefore be one which is:

       (a)   inherently indecent *or*
       (b)   is hostile, threatening or an act to which the child is demonstrably reluctant to accept (*DPP v. Rogers*, above; *Williams v. Gibbs* [1958] Crim.L.R. 127).

In *R v. Sutton* [1977] Cr.App.R. 21 C.A. a photographer touched partially clothed and unclothed boys on the hands, legs or torso to pose them for photographs, he was not guilty of an indecent assault as no assault had taken place, the acts not being inherently indecent.

D. INDECENCY

6–27   The indecency need not be appreciated by the victim, who may for example be unconscious, but must in those cases where specific intent is required, *i.e.* as in *R v. Court* [1989] A.C. 28, be appreciated by the defendant. So in *R v. Court* it was suggested by the court that where the defendant uses words, perhaps in a foreign language the meaning of which he is unaware, he cannot be guilty of an indecent assault (see below).

6–28   In most cases, the indecency will arise from the defendant's circumstances. So in *Beal v. Kelley* (1951) 35 Cr.App.R. 1238 a defendant asked a boy to handle his penis, the boy refused and the defendant pulled the boy towards himself. Although the act itself was not indecent, an indecent assault had occurred evidenced by the defendant's clear motive. On the other hand in *R v. Thomas* (1985) 81 Cr.App.R.331 the defendant took hold of the bottom of the skirt of an 11 year old girl. It was held that this could be an assault, but the circumstances were not themselves indecent, nor capable of permitting an inference of indecency.

6–29   Kissing a girl on the face and shoulders against her will together with suggestions of sexual intercourse may be an indecent assault: *R v. Leeson* (1968) 52 Crim.App.R. 185.

6–30   As to indecent motives not directed towards the victim but arising from other circumstances, see paragraph 6–38, below.

E. INTENT

6–31   In *R v. Court*, above, a distinction was made between cases where the indecency was an obvious part of the assault and cases where the action was capable of being indecent. It was held in *R v. Culyer* (*The Times*, April 14, 1992) that where an assault was indecent in itself the basic intent was sufficient to establish assault. It is not necessary to establish a specific indecent intent. In *R v. C* [1992] Crim.L.R. 642 the defendant inserted one of his fingers into a child's vagina. He was drunk at the time. His intent was irrelevant: the act was of itself indecent whether the defendant had an indecent intent or not. His drunkenness was therefore also irrelevant.

The law before *Court* remained the law and indecent assault remained an offence of basic intent. The issue was simply whether the appellant did what was alleged. The case distinguished the case of *Court* where whether what had happened amounted to an indecent assault or not turned on the motive, and therefore a specific intent had been necessary to the verdict. 6–32

A drunken intention is no defence to a charge of indecent assault where basic intent is required. The drunken intent was considered in *R v. Kingston* [1993] Crim.L.R. 781. K was a known paedophile, P hoped to blackmail K. P drugged a young boy who became unconscious and offered the unconscious youth to K. There was some evidence that K also consumed the same drugs prior to abusing the boy. In quashing his conviction, the court held that if drink or a drug surreptitiously administered causes a person to lose his self-control that intent may not be a criminal intent. If the offence is not one of specific intent self-induced intoxication is not a defence. Involuntary intoxication may be used by the defence to negative *mens rea*. 6–33

Nonetheless, the wording used in *Kingston* must be read with care. If there is an intent to commit a crime the defendant can be convicted. The intoxication may amount to no more than mitigation even though involuntary.

A genuine belief that the victim is consenting is a valid defence: *R v. Kimber* (1983) 77 Cr.App.R. 225 (subject to what is said in para. 6–32, above); but a genuine belief that a victim under 16 was over 16 and consenting is not a defence: *R v. Maughan* (1935) 24 Cr.App.R. 130. 6–34

If the question of consent may be reasonably inferred by the jury then the judge should direct them upon the onus on the prosecution to negative consent and as to the bearing on the particular case that consent has. However, if the defence is such, or the facts proved show that consent is not a primary issue then no such direction need be given: *R v. May* [1912] 3 All E.R. 572.

The law remains vague as to the position where the indecent motive is secret. A direction to the jury that an indecent assault constitutes a deliberate touching of another persons' body with an indecent intention is too wide: *R v. Kilbourne* [1972] 3 All E.R. 545. It is submitted that the victim need not be aware of the intention, or for that matter the assault, for an indecent assault upon an unconscious victim is an offence. 6–35

In *Beal v. Kelley,* above the defendant, prior to touching the boy's arm and pulling him forward, had already indicated he wished the boy to touch his penis, so indicating his indecent intention. 6–36

In *R v. Court* (discussed above) the defendant was a 26 year old shop assistant who pulled a 12 year old girl into his shop and smacked her 12 times with his hand on her buttocks over her shorts. He admitted to the police a secret buttock fetish. The trial court, Court of Appeal and House of Lords (Lord Goff dissenting) had no difficulty finding him guilty and allowing his admission of his fetish to be admitted to prove the indecency. 6–37

On the other hand, in *R v. George* [1956] Crim.L.R. 52, the defendant stole a woman's shoe because of a secret shoe fetish. It was held that the motive for the assault did not make the act indecent. 6–38

173

6–39 It may be viewed that the act in *Court* was in any event ambiguous and the secret motive was admitted to confirm the indecency. In *George,* the act could not have the appearance of being sexually motivated and the motivation was not directed towards the person of the woman, but towards the shoe itself. The two cases may therefore be reconciled.

F. DEFENDANT UNDER TWENTY-FOUR

6–40 If a man under 24 and not previously charged with a like offence has intercourse with a girl under 16 he is not guilty of unlawful sexual intercourse (see Chap. 9). He may be guilty however of indecent assault in identical circumstances as that defence is not open to him for the latter offence. In the case of *R v. Laws* (1928) 21 Cr.App.R. 45, it was opined that: "it is indeed a grotesque state of affairs that the law offers a defence upon a major charge but excludes that defence if the minor charge is preferred". Nonetheless, the Sexual Offences Act 1956 continued to deprive defendants of this defence.

G. ENCOURAGING

6–41 (See also paragraph 12–59.)

Encouraging another to commit an indecent assault is an offence. Section 28 of the Sexual Offences Act 1956 states:

"(1) It is an offence for a person to cause or encourage the prostitution of, or the commission of unlawful sexual intercourse with, or of an indecent assault on, a girl under the age of sixteen for whom he is responsible.

(2) Where a girl has become a prostitute, or has had unlawful sexual intercourse, or has been indecently assaulted, a person shall be deemed for the purposes of this section to have caused or encouraged it, if he knowingly allowed her to consort with, or to enter or continue in the employment of, any prostitute or person of known immoral character.

(3) The persons who are to be treated for the purposes of this section as responsible for a girl are (subject to subsection (4) of this section):
   (a) her parents;
   (b) any person who is not a parent of hers but who has parental responsibility for her; and
   (c) any person who has care of her.

(4) An individual falling within subsection (3)(a) or (b) of this section is not to be treated as responsible for a girl if:
   (a) a residence order under the Children Act 1989 is in force with respect to her and he is not named in the order as the person with whom she is to live; or

(b)   a care order under that Act is in force with respect to her.
(5)   If, on a charge of an offence against a girl under this section, the girl
appears to the court to have been under the age of sixteen at the time
of the offence charged, she shall be presumed for the purposes of this
section to have been so, unless the contrary is proved".

Although primarily intended to prevent prostitution, the section has a   6–42
wide application covering both indecent assault and unlawful sexual intercourse with a girl under 16.

"Encouraging" means more than merely not preventing. Hence in *R v.*   6–43
Moon [1910] 1 K.B. 818 where the girl's parents, the girl and the man all
slept in the same barn, the parents had not encouraged his behaviour towards
their 15 year old daughter. They had however been prepared to allow the
intercourse to occur. The case against them was dismissed purely because of
the definition of the word "seduce" in previous legislation. It was held that
the word's meaning was to take the girl away from chastity. This could only
happen once and had occurred previously. In *R v. Chainey* [1914] 1 K.B. 137
a lack of proper supervision by a father who regularly worked nights and a
step-mother addicted to drunkenness was held not to be encouragement.

Moon was distinguished in *R v. Ralphs* (1913) 9 Cr.App.R. 86, where a   6–44
father allowed his eldest daughter's lover to share a bed with his girlfriend
and a younger daughter, Rose aged 11. The boy had intercourse with Rose.
In the previous case it had been ruled that encouraging means doing something more than merely not preventing. Encouraging means actively doing
something. Allowing the man to share a bed with the two daughters was
sufficient an act to justify his conviction. The court held: "to put the two
persons to sleep in the one bed when there is power to prevent it is, in the
opinion of the Court, ample evidence of encouraging".

There must be both encouragement and an intention to encourage. Allow-   6–45
ing a 14 year old girl to consume drink and to permit a male friend to indulge
in indiscreet activity, embracing the girl and kissing her face and breast will
also suffice: *R v. Drury* (1974) 60 Cr.App.R. 195.

Drury also discussed when a man is responsible for the girl, *i.e.* when he   6–46
has charge or care of her. In that case, D, aged 27 had three children for
whom the girl aged 14 acted as baby-sitter. D returned home from work with
a male friend L who indecently assaulted the girl probably with her consent
after she had consumed drink. When asked if he had any responsibility for
her, D replied: "No, I don't think so, she agreed to what was happening to
her and that's her affair." It was accepted that if a five year old child had
come round to play with the defendant's children he would have care of, and
responsibility for her. The court was unable to see as a matter of principle
any difference between the two situations (although the dangers to a five year
old and a 14 year old were different). It was a question of fact and degree for
a jury to find, but there was no reason in law why a jury could not find the
accused had care of the girl.

However, it was important to distinguish between a moral duty and a legal
duty. The jury were correctly directed that a man might be guilty of a most
serious moral offence but not guilty of any offence under our law (at 198).

Chapter 7
Insults and Nuisances

This chapter discusses a number of lesser offences which often have sexual implications: the Vagrancy Act 1824; the Town Police Clauses Act 1847; the Common Law offences of outraging public decency; the Public Order Act 1986; bind overs; and offences committed using the telephone.

7–01   There are a number of offences created to prevent offence being caused to other people in public places.

A. VAGRANCY ACT 1824

7–02   Any person committing one of a number of offences may be found by a justice of the peace to be a rogue and a vagabond and may be sentenced to a level 3 fine or to a period of imprisonment not exceeding three calendar months (Vagrancy Act 1824, s.4; Magistrates Court Act 1980, s.34(3)). The offences under section 4 do not need to be committed in a public place but can be in a private room: *Ford v. Falcone* [1971] 2 All E.R. 1138.

7–03   The offences referred to in the Vagrancy Act 1824 include a person who wilfully, openly, lewdly and obscenely exposes his person with intent to insult any female.

7–04   The term "person" means his genital organ, *i.e.* penis: *Evans v. Ewels* [1972] 2 All E.R. 22. The offence is not committed by exposing the buttocks or any other parts of the body. The offence is limited to exposure by a man to a woman.

There need not be direct evidence before the justices that the defendant's penis was actually seen by a female, if there is sufficient evidence that his penis was in fact exposed: *Hunt v. DPP* [1990] Crim.L.R. 812. A man who could be seen at a window by passers-by had his trousers around his thighs. He held a curtain open with his left hand and was masturbating himself with his right hand. Although his penis was held in his hand the justices rightly held that it was exposed.

7–05   In certain circumstances, the complainant may be led on evidence of other occasions when this behaviour occurred and the defendant may be cross-examined on such instances. The evidence is relevant to prove identity and also to rebut a defence that the exposure was accidental to show that it was to the contrary wilful and intended to insult her. Where the defence put forward is one of accident or mistake, evidence that there has been exposure to other women is also relevant.

Exposure to other women may also be relevant where it is sufficiently proximate to show a systematic course of conduct.   7–06

B. TOWN POLICE CLAUSES ACT 1847

This Act creates a number of offences. Section 28 states that "every person who in any street to the obstruction, annoyance or danger of the residents or passengers commits one of the listed offences shall be liable to a level 3 fine or imprisonment for a period not exceeding 14 days".   7–07

The Act applies to any street in England and Wales outside Greater London (Public Health Act 1875, s.171; Local Government Act 1972, s.180, Sched. 14, paras 23 and 26).   7–08

One of the prohibited acts is to wilfully and indecently expose his person. The offence must be committed in a street. The definition of street is made wide by the Public Health Acts Amendment Act 1907, s.81.   7–09

Public places and streets

A place of public resort or recreation ground belonging to, or under the control of the local authority and any unfenced ground adjoining or abutting upon any street in an urban district shall, for the purposes of the Vagrancy Act 1824 be deemed to be an open and public place (this applies to s. 3, not s. 4) and shall be deemed to be a street for the purposes of the section 29 of the Town Police Clauses Act 1847 and also for section 28 of that Act as it applies to every person who wilfully and indecently exposes his person.   7–10

It is not necessary to prove an intention to insult but the action must be to the annoyance of passengers or residents. It is not necessary to call a complainant who was annoyed. Evidence may show that unidentified passengers appeared to be annoyed (*Woolley v. Corbishly* (1860) 24 J.P. 773; *Cheeseman v. DPP* (1991) 93 Cr.App.R. 145). If the actions are deliberate and wilful the court will usually infer that annoyance resulted (*Cheeseman v. DPP*, above. Where the acts are not witnessed by ordinary members of the public, problems of proof may arise.   7–11

In *Cheeseman v. D.P.P.*, police officers from a vice squad were sent on surveillance of public lavatories where there had been complaints of men performing acts of masturbation. The defendant was arrested after masturbating at a urinal for some ten minutes and was convicted under the Town Police Clauses Act. No other members of the public were present. Upon appeal, it was held that the police officers on surveillance were not pas-   7–12 sengers, although an officer on patrol who called at the lavatory in pursuance of its normal use would be. The court did not decide whether the officers could be annoyed. Vice Squad officers in these circumstances would not inevitably be annoyed by "witnessing squalid acts of self-abuse", especially when that was the very purpose of their visit. There could be no inference of annoyance.

However, it would be wrong to suggest that police officers would be incapable of being annoyed by acts of indecency such as this (compare with *Parker v. Norman* [1985] Q.B. 92, discussed below at paras 7–32, 7–42 & 7–43).

7-13   The Town Police Clauses Act, s. 28 also makes it an offence to sing any profane or obscene song or ballad, or use any profane or obscene language.

C. COMMON LAW

7-14   It is an offence at common law to outrage public decency. The essentials of the offence are an act committed in public, which is of a lewd, obscene or disgusting nature as amounts to an outrage to public decency. The purpose of the law to ensure that "reasonable people may venture out in public without the risk of outrage to certain minimum accepted standards of decency" (*per* Lord Simon of Glaisdale in *R v. Knuller (Publishing, Printing and Promotions) Ltd* [1973] 2 A.C. 435). The offence is triable upon indictment.

I. "IN PUBLIC"

7-15   There must be two or more people present. However it will suffice if only one person actually saw the lewd, obscene or disgusting act provided other people might have also seen it: *R v. Farrell* (1862) 9 Cox 446: *R v. Mayling* (1963) 47 Cr.App.R, 162.

7-16   If two or more people can see the defendant it is in public. He need not be in a public place. The people seeing him need not be there as of right, *e.g.* in a field (*R v. Wellard* (1884) 15 Cox 559) or a roof-top (*R v. Thallman* (1863) 9 Cox C.C. 388). An indecent exhibition in a booth at a race meeting, the public being admitted upon payment, may be prosecuted (*R v. Saunders* [1875] 1 Q.B.D. 15).

7-17   However the offence requires more than just two witnesses. There must be a real possibility that members of the public might witness the outrageous act. So, a man exposing himself to two young girls in the security of his own sitting-room does not commit this offence (*R v. Walker*, The Times, April 14, 1995).

The defendant cannot set up a defence of customary right for example, of regular nude bathing although local by-law can create such lawful right. In *R v. Reed* ([1871] 12 Cox C.C. 1) it was held unlawful for men to bathe naked near inhabited houses, or a public way.

II. "LEWD, OBSCENE OR DISGUSTING"

The act must itself be lewd, obscene or disgusting. If it is not, a secret motive or intent will not suffice to satisfy this requirement (*R. v. Rowley* (1992) 94 Cr.App.R. 95). Leaving notes offering to give preserves to young boys is not of itself disgusting. The act complained of may also constitute an offence under the Vagrancy Act 1824, the Town Police Clauses Act 1847, or the Indecency with Children Act 1960, s.1. (*R v. May* (1989) 91 Cr.App.R. 157), or some other statute. This does not prevent the activity also constituting the common law offence (*R v. May*, above). There is one statutory exception—no prosecution for the common law offence may be brought with regard to the performance of a play (Theatres Act 1968, s.8). **7–18**

The offence of conspiracy to outrage public decency is discussed in Chapter 13. **7–19**

It is not necessary to prove that the acts actually disgusted or outraged any member of the public. The test is objective, not subjective. Where evidence is called that members of the public were disgusted or outraged this evidence may be given by a police officer. Men masturbating in a public toilet and smiling at each other are outraging public decency and such evidence can be given by police officers. There is no further requirement to show that the officers, any other passengers or any other members of the public were actually outraged or disgusted. **7–20**

It is not necessary for the Crown to prove an intent to outrage, nor recklessness. The only *mens rea* required is to commit the act in question or where appropriate publish the object (*R v. Gibson and Sylveire* (1990) 91 Cr.App.R. 341). **7–21**

Where the complaint is of the public display of an article which is obscene the test of obscenity is not that contained in the Obscene Publications Act 1959 (see Chap. 13). The affront is to public decency not a corruption of public morals. There is no defence of public good and therefore expert evidence of public good should not be admitted (*R v. Gibson and Sylveire*, above). **7–22**

The common law offence can be committed by a woman. *Evans v. Ewels* [1972] 2 All E.R. 22 distinguished the offence under the Vagrancy Act 1824 about which Ashworth J. said "unlike the common law offence this crime is limited to exposure by a male to a female". **7–23**

The "lewd, obscene or disgusting" behaviour must be of an extreme nature so that public decency is outraged. Outrage is a strong word and should be interpreted according to its normal usage. Public decency will for example, not be outraged by matters seen constantly in magazines and daily newspapers.

A public omnibus is a public place (*R v. Holmes* (1853) 3 Car. & Kir. 360) as is a public urinal (*R v. Harris and Cocks* (1871) L.R. 1 C.C.R. 282, distinguishing *R v. Orchard and Thirtle* (1848) 13 J.P. 269). **7–24**

7–25   If a man indecently exposes himself in a locked room, but can be seen by two people through a window the offence may be committed *R v. Bunyan and Morgan* [1844] 3 L.T.O.S. 453.

D. PUBLIC ORDER ACT 1986

7–26   Although not specifically designed to deal with sexual offences, the Public Order Act 1986 has sections which may be applicable to some types of minor sexual abuse.

Section 4 states:

"(1)   A person is guilty of an offence if he:

     (a)   uses towards another person threatening, abusive or insulting words or behaviour, or

     (b)   distributes or displays to another person any writing, sign or other visible representation which is threatening, abusive or insulting,

    with intent to cause that person to believe that immediate unlawful violence will be used against him or another by any person, or to provoke the immediate use of unlawful violence by that person or another, or whereby that person is likely to believe that such violence will be used or it is likely that such violence will be provoked.

(2)   An offence under this section may be committed in a public or a private place, except that no offence is committed where the words or behaviour are used, or the writing, sign or other visible representation is distributed or displayed, by a person inside a dwelling and the other person is also inside that or another dwelling.

(3)   A constable may arrest without warrant anyone he reasonably suspects is committing an offence under this section.

(4)   A person guilty of an offence under this section is liable on summary conviction to imprisonment for a term not exceeding 6 months or a fine not exceeding level 5 on the standard scale or both."

Section 4(A)(1) States:

"(1)   A person is guilty of an offence if, with intent to cause a person harrassment, alarm or distress, he:

     (a)   uses threatening, abusive or insulting words or behaviour, or disorderly behaviour; or

     (b)   displays any writing, sign, or other visible representation which is threatening, abusive or insulting, thereby causing that or another person harrassment alarm or distress.

(2)   (As (2) above.)

(3)   It is a defence for the accused person to prove:

     (a)   that he was inside a dwelling and had no reason to believe that the words or behaviour used, or the writing, sign or other visible representation displayed, would be heard or seen by a person outside or in any other dwelling; or

(b)   that his conduct was reasonable.
(4)   (As (3) above.)
(5)   (As (4) above.)"

Section 5 states: 7-27

"(1) a person is guilty of an offence if he:
  (a)   uses threatening, abusive or insulting words or behaviour, or
        disorderly behaviour, or
  (b)   displays any writing, sign or other visible representation which is
        threatening, abusive or insulting,
        within the hearing or sight of a person likely to be caused
        harassment, alarm or distress thereby.
(2)   An offence under this section may be committed in a public or a
      private place, except that no offence is committed where the words or
      behaviour are used, or the writing, sign or other visible representa-
      tion is displayed, by a person inside a dwelling and the other person
      is also inside that or another dwelling.
(3)   It is a defence for the accused to prove:
  (a)   that he had no reason to believe that there was any person within
        hearing or sight who was likely to be caused harassment, alarm
        or distress, or
  (b)   that he was inside a dwelling and had no reason to believe that
        the words or behaviour used, or the writing, sign or other visible
        representation displayed, would be heard or seen by a person
        outside that or any other dwelling, or
  (c)   that his conduct was reasonable.
(4)   A constable may arrest a person without warrant if:
  (a)   he engages in offensive conduct which the constable warns him
        to stop, and
  (b)   he engages in further offensive conduct immediately or shortly
        after the warning.
(5)   In subsection (4) 'offensive conduct' means conduct the constable
      reasonably suspects to constitute an offence under this section, and
      the conduct mentioned in paragraph (a) and the further conduct need
      not be of the same nature.
(6)   A person guilty of an offence under this section is liable on summary
      conviction to fine not exceeding level 3 on the standard scale."

The offences may be committed from a house towards someone in a road,   7-28
or from the road to someone in a house, but not from one house to someone
in either that or some other house.
The words or actions must be threatening, abusive or insulting and not   7-29
merely rude (*R v. Ambrose* (1973) 57 Cr.App.R. 538). It was held in *Simcox
v. Rhodes* [1977] Crim.L.R. 75 that telling a police officer to "fuck off" was
an insult and that if third parties were likely to cause a breach of the peace as
a result it was also an offence. The police officer was not likely to cause a
breach of the peace himself.

7-30   Although in the late 1970s successful prosecutions under section 5 of the
Public Order Act 1936 were brought against women who exposed their
breasts in public, it is submitted that only in the most unusual circumstances
could a woman wearing a transparent blouse or exposing her nipples be
described as threatening, abusive or even insulting. It is submitted that such
behaviour is not, of itself an offence under this section. In medieval times it
was not unusual for a woman to lift her skirts towards a man as a form of
insult and such an action may well be so interpreted today.

7-31   It is a question of fact whether a police officer may be caused harassment,
alarm or distress (*DPP v. Orum* [1988] 3 All E.R. 449).

7-32   The behaviour must be viewed objectively and facts hidden from the
defendant and unknown to him should not, it is submitted, be taken into
account. Where a defendant masturbates himself towards a plain clothed
officer on surveillance in a public toilet was discussed in the cases of *Parkin
v. Norman; Valentine v. Lilley* [1982] 2 All E.R. 583. The wording of the
Public Order Act 1936, s. 5 was of course different. Nonetheless, the cases
are of interest. In both cases the fact that the other man to whom the
defendant masturbated was a police officer was unknown to him.

7-33   The Public Order Act 1936 required a likelihood of a breach of the peace
and it is submitted that the arguments put forward in *Parkin v. Norman;
Valentine v. Lilley*, above, are now relevant to the test to be applied to bind
overs after the decision in *Percy v. DPP*, below.

E. BIND OVERS

7-34   The practical use of bind overs has been severely limited by the Queen's
Bench Division in the case of *Percy v. DPP* [1995] Crim.L.R. 714.

7-35   In Saxon England, crimes were addressed by private vengeance which
often led to a blood-feud. To help secure stability, Ethelbert, King of Kent
introduced the concept that a crime, including some more violent crimes,
such as theft constituted a breach of the King's peace and gave the King a
right to interfere in what had previously been a private matter. Cnut, King of
all England and the Danes (1016–35) extended the concept which included
all crimes as being a breach of the King's special peace. Long before 1361,
breaches of the criminal law were considered to be breaches of the peace.

The Justice of the Peace Act 1361 introduced a new bind over. In addition
to the common law breach of the peace (*i.e.* criminal matters) the justice had
a power to bind over to be of good behaviour. This power was to deal with
bad behaviour which could not be considered to amount to criminal acts.
The Act is commonly referred to as "The Peeping Tom Act" which reflects
this approach. The Act also gives the justices power to bind over witnesses
who appear before them.

7-36   Prior to *Percy v. DPP*, the situation was as follows: There was a power to
bind over to keep the peace at Common Law. It was always accepted that
under this particular power to bind over all that needed to be proved was that
the Queen's peace had been broken, *i.e.* a criminal offence, no matter how

minor, had been committed. The definition of breach of peace was clearly totally different from modern statutory definitions of breach of the peace.

There was a distinct and separate power to bind over to be of good 7-37 behaviour under the provisions of the Justice of the Peace Act 1361. Traditionally such a bind over should be made in the terms that the individual should agree to be bound over to be of good behaviour to all the Queen's subjects but especially towards a named individual. It had always been accepted that for a bind over to be of good behaviour all that was required was proof that the individual had conducted himself in a way which was not acceptable to current moral and social standards. There should also be a fear of future re-occurrence. This was also the power to bind over witnesses. The Act applied to breaches of moral standards such as being a peeping tom, *i.e.* looking in windows to watch women undress.

There are clear differences between bind overs at common law and under 7-38 the 1361 Act. In *Goodlad v. Chief Constable of South Yorkshire* [1979] Crim.L.R.51, it was confirmed that conditions can be attached to a common law bind over but cannot be annexed to a bind over under the Justice of the Peace Act 1361, confirming the observations of Parker C.J. in *R v. Ayu* [1958] 3 All E.R. 636 that "he knew of no case where a condition can be inserted in a bind over under the Justice of the Peace Act 1361". (The case appears to contradict *Lister v. Morgan* [1978] Crim.L.R. 292 although the commentary to *Lister v. Morgan* does conform to the proposition.)

Section 115 of the Magistrates Courts Act 1980 contains no power to bind 7-39 over. The 1361 Act authorised a pursuit and arrest but no power to issue a complaint. Section 115 subsection (1) gives the power to issue complaint and subsection 2 creates the power to commit an individual to custody if he does not agree to the bind over. The bind over was a civil matter and the standard of proof was therefore civil, *i.e.* on a balance of probabilities (*R v. Aubrey-Fletcher, ex p. Thompson* [1969] 1 W.L.R. 872).

All the above submissions were approved in *R v. Sandbach, ex p. Williams* 7-40 (1935) 99 J.P. 251 and supported by Blackstone. The case held that it was far too late in 1935 to attempt to show that Blackstone was wrong (see also, "Binding over kerb crawlers" (1993) 147 J.P. 771).

Percy v. DPP [1995] Crim.L.R. 714, took a totally different view. It held 7-41 that a breach of the peace is limited to violence or threats of violence as set out in *R v. Howell* [1982] 1 Q.B. 416. Although an example of the working of common law, it is our view that the decision in *R v. Percy* is so contrary to the historical context explained above, and such an unnecessary and undesirable limitation upon the use of the bind over as to be wrongly decided. To establish a breach of the peace the conduct in question does not itself have to be disorderly or a breach of the criminal law. It is sufficient if its natural consequences would, if persisted in, be to provoke others to violence, and so some actual danger to the peace is established. Harm to property will constitute a breach of the peace only if done or threatened in the owners presence and the natural consequences of such harm is likely to be a violent retaliation. (Compare para. 7-45.)

In *Parkin v. Noman; Valentine v. Lilley* [1982] 2 All E.R. 583, both 7-42 involving masturbation towards a police officer in a public toilet, the appeal was allowed because the case of *R v. Howell* [1981] 3 All E.R. 743 had specified the breach of the peace to be considered. (*R v. Howell* was reported after the magistrates had heard *Valentine* and they did not have the benefit of that case being argued before them).

7-43   The appeal of *Parkin* was allowed because the Court believed that although a breach of the peace was liable (*i.e.* a possible result), it had not been shown to their satisfaction that it was a likely result. It was expressed in the course of that case that the likely result of such behaviour was for the other man in the toilet to feel disgust turn around and leave. The appeal was allowed not because the plain clothed officer would not cause a breach of the peace but because the court could not be sure that any man was likely to cause a breach of the peace in those circumstances. It was said (at 587) that "insulting behaviour does not lose its insulting character simply because no one who witnessed it was insulted, any more than it would lose its liability (*sic*) to provoke a breach of the peace merely because no one who witnessed it broke the peace". Reference was made to an unreported case of *Ballard v. Blythe* (November 3, 1980) in which a youth was ejected from a school dance. He insulted, abused threatened and spat at a man. Unknown to him the man was the headmaster of the school who reacted with an unusual degree of self-restraint. The correct question for the court is, "is this conduct such as is inherently likely to cause a breach of the peace? What is the natural and probable result of the conduct?".

7-44   The standard of proof is the higher criminal standard: proof beyond all reasonable doubt. This is required because a failure to comply with the order can result in imprisonment.

7-45   It is the person being bound over who must be acting unreasonably rather than some other person. The complaint will not be found proved if the defendant's conduct was not merely lawful but was such as in no material way interfered with the other's rights, *a fortiori*, if the defendant was properly excercising his own basic rights (*Nicol and another v. DPP, The Times*, November 22, 1995).

F. OFFENSIVE COMMUNICATIONS

7-46   There are occasions when the indecency or obscenity arises as a result of non face-to-face verbal communications for example, by telephone or letter. Two Acts specifically cover this situation, the Telecommunications Act 1984 and the Malicious Communications Act 1988, although there are circumstances in which the court has found that the Offences Against the Person Act 1861 may also apply.

I. THE TELECOMMUNICATIONS ACT 1984

7-47   By virtue of section 43 of the 1984 Act:

"(1)   a person who:

(a) sends, by means of a public telecommunication system, a message or other matter that is grossly offensive or of an indecent, obscene or menacing character; or

(b) sends by those means, for the purpose of causing annoyance, inconvenience or needless anxiety to another, a message that he knows to be false or persistently makes use for that purpose of a public telecommunication system, shall be guilty of an offence."

For offences committed before February 3, 1995 the penalty on summary conviction is a fine not exceeding level 3 on the standard scale, for offences committed on or after that date, the penalty is a maximum six months' imprisonment and/or a fine not exceeding level 5 on the standard scale (Criminal Justice and Public Order Act 1994, s.92). By section 103, proceedings for any offence under the Act which is punishable on summary conviction may be commenced at any time within twelve months next after the commission of the offence.   **7–48**

Subsection (1) does not apply to anything done in the course of providing a programme service within the meaning of the Broadcasting Act 1990 (Telecommunications Act, s. 43(2)). An offence contrary to section 43 of the 1984 Act is a recordable offence (National Police Records (Recordable Offences) Regulations 1985 (S.I. 1985 No. 1941)) and therefore fingerprints may be taken in accordance with the Police and Criminal Evidence Act 1984, s.27.   **7–49**

II. The Malicious Communications Act 1988

Section 1 states: **7–50**

"(1) Any person who sends to another person:
  (a) a letter or other article which conveys:
    (i) a message which is indecent or grossly offensive;
    (ii) a threat; or
    (iii) information which is false and known or believed to be false by the sender; or
  (b) any other article which is, in whole or part, of an indecent or grossly offensive nature,
is guilty of an offence if his purpose, or one of his purposes, in sending it is that it should, so far as falling within paragraph (a) or (b) above, cause distress or anxiety to the recipient or to any other person to whom he intends that it or its contents or nature should be communicated.

(Subsection (2) not printed.)

(3) In this section references to sending include references to delivering and to causing to be sent or delivered and 'sender' shall be construed accordingly.

(4) A person guilty of an offence under this section shall be liable on summary conviction to a fine not exceeding level 4 on the standard scale."

III. OTHER OFFENCES

7–51   In *R v. Johnson (Anthony Thomas), The Times*, May 22, 1996, it was held that making obscene telephone calls on many occasions to numerous women was conduct capable of constituting a public nuisance since it materially affected the reasonable comfort and convenience of a section of the public. Consequently, where the appellant over a period of five and a half years had made obscene telephone calls on hundreds of occasions to at least 13 different women, his appeal against conviction for public nuisance would be dismissed.

7–52   In *R v. Ireland, The Times*, May 22, 1996 it was held that a telephone call or a series of telephone calls followed by silence could constitute an assault occasioning actual bodily harm. The appellant had made a large number of unwanted silent telephone calls to three women. Each of the complainants was examined by a psychiatrist who said that the result of the repeated telephone calls was that each of them suffered significant psychological symptoms which included palpitations, difficulty in breathing, cold sweats, anxiety, inability to sleep, dizziness and stress. The Court of Appeal held that the making of the telephone call was a relevant act for the purposes of section 47 of the Offences against the Person Act 1861 irrespective of whether that call was followed by silence or speech. The fact that the violence was inflicted indirectly causing psychological harm did not render the act to be any less an act of violence.

    The Court of Appeal decision was upheld by the House of Lords (*R. v. Ireland, The Times*, July 25, 1997). The House of Lords also upheld the Court of Appeal decision in *R. v. Burstow, The Times*, July 30, 1996 (C.A.) and July 25, 1997 (H.L.), holding that an offence of inflicting grievous bodily harm (contrary to s. 20 of the Offences Against the Person Act 1861) could be committed where no physical evidence was applied directly or indirectly to the body of the victim.

Part III
PROHIBITED RELATIONSHIPS

Chapter 8
Unnatural Acts

Buggery covers both bestiality and intercourse *per anum* with a man or a woman. If there is no consent this latter act now constitutes rape. Other offences, such as gross indecency are similar in that they prevent some consensual sexual activity and are therefore included in this chapter.

A. UNNATURAL OFFENCES OF BUGGERY

1   Buggery is defined as carnal copulation against nature by human beings with each other or with a beast (1 East P.C 480). It involves intercourse by a man *per anum* with a woman or another man, or any intercourse *per anum* or *per vaginum* between either a man or a woman with an animal.

Other forms of sexual encounter such as fellatio are not unnatural and not the act of buggery *R v. Jacobs* [1817] Russ. & Ry. 331 C.C.R.

2   The criminal offence of buggery is set out in section 12 of the Sexual Offences Act 1956 as amended by the Police and Criminal Evidence Act 1984, s.7(f) and the Criminal Justice and Public Order Act 1994, s.143:

> "It is [an offence] for a person to commit buggery with another person otherwise than in the circumstances described in subsection (1A) below (see para. 8.13) or with an animal."

I. BESTIALITY

3   Kinsey reported that approximately eight per cent of men and four per cent of women had sexual contact with an animal at some point in their life.

In the case of bestiality by women, the animal involved is almost always a dog, although more exotic animals may in very rare cases feature: in one example (Coke Institutes Vol. 3, 59) "a very good lady" committed buggery with a baboon.

4   Bestiality consists purely of sexual intercourse with an animal. Other acts of indecency with animal do not constitute bestiality. Oral sex with an animal or masturbation do not constitute bestiality. Such acts however

constitute an act outraging public decency against common law and acts involving animals, such as horses, have been prosecuted under that provision.

8–05   Bestiality committed by men is normally a rural activity and a wide range of animals have been involved including dogs, sheep, mares, cows, rabbits and birds. Domestic fowls are animals within the Act (s.6 of the Offences Against the Person Act 1861) and therefore the offence can be committed against a duck (*R v. Brown* (1889) 16 Cox C.C. 715 C.C.R., overruling *R v. Dodd* [1877] unreported).

8–06   As with other forms of intercourse where a man penetrates an animal, penetration itself suffices and there is no need to prove ejaculation. In *R v. Cozens* (1834) 6 C & P 35, the defendant was interrupted having intercourse with a ewe, prior to ejaculation but was nonetheless convicted.

8–07   Occasionally, displays or films may involve bestiality. Bestiality features in some pornographic films.

8–08   Where a woman is forced to submit to an act of bestiality, or to attempt to, she will have a defence of duress. In *R v. Bourne* (1952) 36 Cr.App.R. 125, a wife was compelled to have intercourse with a dog by her husband who had just sexually excited the dog. She was not charged with the offence as it was felt she would have a defence of duress but her husband was charged with aiding and abetting. His somewhat audacious defence was that as there was no principal he could not be convicted of aiding and abetting. It was held that the offence of buggery does not depend upon consent and that duress indicates not that the offence has not been committed but that an individual has a personal excuse for committing the act, of which a third party should not be permitted to take advantage.

Sentencing guidelines

8–09   The more serious cases are those where a man persuades or forces his wife to indulge in such practices for his own satisfaction. In such cases a short custodial sentence is entirely appropriate. In *R v. Tierney* (1990) 12 Cr.App.R.(S) 216 the defendant took photographs of his wife having intercourse with his Alsatian dog for his own continuing satisfaction. Three months' imprisonment was held to be appropriate. Where a man performs buggery with an animal help is often required. This is best afforded by a probation order: *R v. Higson* ((1984) 6 Cr.App.R(S) 20). Where a man persuades his wife to commit buggery with a dog while he takes photographs: a sentence of three months' imprisonment was appropriate for him: *R v. Tierney* ((1990) 12 Cr.App.R.(S) 216) but not for the woman where she consented to perform the act in desperation to retain his affections and where she regrets her actions: *R v. P* (1991) 13 Cr.App.R (S) 369.

II. SODOMY

(a) Anal intercourse without consent

8–10   If a man has anal intercourse with either a woman or another man without their consent the offence is rape (Sexual Offences Act 1956 as amended by s. 142 of the Criminal Justice and Public Order Act 1994).

Consent to vaginal intercourse does not imply consent to anal inter- **8-11**
course.

Section 16 of the Sexual Offences Act 1956 makes it "an offence for a **8-12**
person to assault another person with intent to commit buggery."

Where intent is a necessary ingredient of an offence, as in this case, the
onus of proof is upon the prosecution: *R v. Steane* [1947] 32 Cr.App.R. 61:
[1947] 1 All E.R. 813). Where it may be relevant to sentence, the age of the
victim should be included in the indictment.

(b) Anal intercourse with consent

Section 12 of the Sexual Offences Act 1956 (as amended by s. 143 of the **8-13**
Criminal Justice and Public Order Act 1994):

"It is an offence for a person to commit buggery with another person
otherwise than in the circumstances described below:
(1A) The act of buggery takes place in private and both parties have
attained the age of eighteen.
(1B) An act of buggery by one man with another shall not be treated as
taking place in private if it takes place;
(a) when more than two persons take part or are present; or
(b) in a lavatory to which the public have or are permitted to have
access, whether on payment or otherwise.
(1C) In any proceedings against a person for buggery with another person
it shall be for the prosecutor to prove that the act of buggery took
place otherwise than in private or that one of the parties to it had not
attained the age of eighteen."

Such acts are also dealt with by the Sexual Offences Act 1967 ss. 1, 4, 7
and 8:

Section 1 (as amended by s.145 of the Criminal Justice and Public Order
Act 1994) states:
"(1) Notwithstanding any statutory or common law provision, but subject to the provisions of the next following section, a homosexual act
in private shall not be an offence provided that the parties consent
thereto and have attained the age of eighteen.
(2) An act which would otherwise be treated for the purposes of this Act **8-14**
as being done in private shall not be so treated if done:
(a) when more than two persons take part or are present; or
(b) in a lavatory to which the public have or are permitted to have
access, whether on payment or otherwise.
(3) A man who is suffering from severe mental handicap cannot in law
give any consent which, by virtue of subsection (1) of this section,
would prevent a homosexual act from being an offence, but a person
shall not be convicted, on account of the incapacity of such a man to
consent, of an offence consisting of such an act if he proves that he
did not know and had no reason to suspect that man to be suffering
from severe mental handicap.
(3A) In subsection (3) of this section 'severe mental handicap' means a

191

state of arrested or incomplete development of mind which includes severe impairment of intelligence and social functioning.

(4) Section 128 of the Mental Health Act 1959 (prohibition on men on the staff of a hospital, or otherwise having responsibility for mental patients, having sexual intercourse with women patients) shall have effect as if any reference therein to having unlawful sexual intercourse with a woman included a reference to committing buggery or an act of gross indecency with another man."

Subsection 5 has been repealed.

8–15 "(6) It is hereby declared that where in any proceedings it is charged that a homosexual act is an offence the prosecutor shall have the burden of proving that the act was done otherwise than in private or otherwise than with the consent of the parties or that any of the parties had not attained the age of eighteen.

(7) For the purposes of this section a man shall be treated as doing a homosexual act if, and only if, he commits buggery with another man or commits an act of gross indecency with another man or is a party to the commission by a man of such an act."

8–16 Section 4 states:

"(1) A man who procures another man to commit with a third man an act of buggery which by reason of section 1 of this Act is not an offence shall be liable on conviction on indictment to imprisonment for a term not exceeding two years."

Subsection (2) has been repealed.

"(3) It shall not be an offence under section 13 of the Act of 1956 for a man to procure the commission by another man of an act of gross indecency with the first-mentioned man which by reason of section 1 of this Act is not an offence under the said section 13."

Section 7 states:

"(1) No proceedings for an offence to which this section applies shall be commenced after the expiration of twelve months from the date on which that offence was committed.

(2) This section applies to:
    (a) any offence under section 13 of the Act of 1956 (gross indecency between men);
    (b) repealed
    (c) any offence of buggery by a man with another man not amounting to an assault on that other man and not being an offence by a man with a boy under the age of sixteen."

8–17 Section 8 states:

"No proceedings shall be instituted except by or with the consent of the Director of Public Prosecutions against any man for the offence of buggery with, or gross indecency with, another man or for aiding, abetting, counselling, procuring or commanding its commission where either of

those men was at the time of its commission under the age of twenty-one."
(See, however, paragraph 8–37.)

(c) Limitations on prosecutions

A prosecution of a man for buggery with another man where either is under   8–18
21 but not with a woman, can only be instituted by or with the consent of the
Director of Public Prosecutions. Where the consent has not been obtained the
proceedings are a nullity: *R v. Angel* [1968] 2 All E.R. 607. A prosecution of
a man for buggery with another man over 16 must be commenced within 12
months of the commission of the offence. If the date of the offence is unclear
and could have been more than 12 months before, the conviction must be
quashed: *R v, Lewis T.S.* (1979) 68 Cr.App.R 310.

The consent is no defence to the offence, lack of consent would constitute   8–19
rape. Both parties, the active and the passive are guilty of the offence. So
where the active partner is under 14 and the passive partner is an adult, the
adult can be convicted of buggery: *R v. Allen* (1849) 1 Den 364.

The term "man" indicates a biological man. It does not include a person   8-20
who has undergone a sex change operation: *R v. Tan* [1983] Q.B. 1053 (see
also para. 8.48).

The question of age is subject to strict proof and mistakes as to age by the   8–21
defendant, even if held to be reasonable, will not afford a defence: *R v. Prince*
(1875) L.R. 2 C.C.R. 154.

(d) Public place

There is no definition of a public place for the purposes of the Sexual   8–22
Offences Acts. In *R v. Reakes* [1974] Crim.L.R. 614, the buggery took place
in an unlit, enclosed private yard in the middle of the night. However, the
yard was used as a lavatory by people visiting two neighbouring restaurants
and employees of a taxi firm and there was a gate from a public road into the
yard. The following direction was given by the Court of Appeal:

> "You look at all the surrounding circumstances, the time of night, the
> nature of the place including such matters as lighting and you consider
> further the likelihood of a third person coming upon the scene."

Subsection 1B of section 12 of the Sexual offences Act 1967 as amended,   8–23
applies only to acts of buggery taking place by one man against another, *i.e.*
another second man. The section therefore does not apply to buggery of a
woman. However, subsection 1A does apply to buggery of a woman. It is
submitted therefore that it is a question for the jury if buggery of a woman
took place in public when more than two persons take part or are present, or
in a lavatory. The section mirrors section 1 of the Sexual Offences Act 1967
relating to homosexual acts. However, the wording in section 12 must be
significant. Section 1 refers to a person committing buggery with another
person whereas section 1B deliberately refers to one man with another
(one).

III. Buggery Of A Woman

8–24 Buggery of a woman is not an offence if both parties are over 18 and the act took place in private. If the act took place in public, or one party was under 18, the offence is committed contrary to section 12 of the 1956 Act.

Where the victim is under 18 it is submitted that the principle set out in *R v. Tyrrell* [1894] 1 Q.B.710, that the young person intended by the Act to be protected should not be protected, does not apply because the legislation was enacted to prevent unnatural acts and not to protect young people. The girl can be prosecuted as a principal offender as both parties commit the offence.

Sentencing guidelines

8–25 Buggery or attempted buggery with a person under 16 carries a sentence of life imprisonment. Buggery or attempted buggery with a person under 18 by a man over 21 carries a sentence of five years' imprisonment. For any other buggery the maximum sentence is two years.

Because of the different penalties, it is essential to include a specific averment as to the age of the victim in the particulars of the offence where the victim is under 16 or 18: *R v. D* (1993) 14 Cr.App.R.(S) 776.

8–26 The guideline case is *R v. Willis* [1975] 1 W.L.R. 292. This case addresses sentencing of cases of buggery by an adult with a person under 16, in this case the judges should always regard buggery with boys under 16 as a serious offence: the younger the boy, the more serious the offence. In the absence of strong mitigating factors, there should be an immediate custodial sentence. If there are no mitigating or aggravating factors, the offence should attract a sentence of three to five years.

8–27 Aggravating factors include:

(i) physical injury to the boy, whether by the penetration itself or by the use of force to overcome his resistance. Offenders who use violence should be discouraged from repetition by severe sentences. Such cases would now be correctly charged as rape;

(ii) emotional and psychological damage to the victim. Judges should not assume that either of these forms of damage is a probable result for a boy who has been the victim of buggery or that being buggered when young causes homosexuality to develop in later life;

(iii) moral corruption such as the case of gifts of money and clothes and the provision of attractive outings and material comforts to corrupt boys; and

(iv) the abuse of authority or trust. Offences by social workers, scout masters and others in such positions of trust are particularly serious.

8–28 Mitigating factors include:

(i) the offender being in a state of emotional stress; or

(ii) his suffering from mental illness. In this case the defendant was described as being "dull witted". Lawton L.J. recommended that where the defendant is suffering from a personality disorder which falls short of justifying a hospital order, a probation order with a condition of psychiatric treatment may be appropriate: "However, if the offender represents a danger to boys (or girls) if at liberty, a lengthy custodial sentence may be necessary to protect other victims." Where the parties are both consenting adults but the act committed constitutes a criminal offence because, for example it occurred in a public lavatory a custodial sentence would not be appropriate: *R v. Tosland* (1981) 3 Cr.App.R.(S) 364.

B. GROSS INDECENCY

Section 13 of the Sexual Offences Act 1956 states: 8–29

"it is an offence for a man to commit an act of gross indecency with another man, whether in public or in private, or to be a party to the commission by a man of an act of gross indecency with another man, or to procure the commission by a man of an act of gross indecency with another man."

Homosexuality was classified as a psychiatric disorder until 1973.

It is now however no longer an offence if committed by consenting men   8–30
over the age of 18, and performed in private: Sexual Offences Act 1967, ss. 1 and 4(3).

The offence is triable either way.

I. LIMITATIONS UPON PROSECUTIONS

There is a time limit of twelve months from the commission of the offence to   8–31
the commencement of the prosecution.

Where one of the parties is under the age of 21 the proceedings may only be commenced by or with the consent of the Director of Public Prosecutions. In *R v. Angel* [1968] 2 All E.R. 607 a conviction following a guilty plea was quashed, the procedure being a nullity because consent had not been obtained. The consent may be given by a member of the Crown Prosecution Service and need not be in writing.

In *R v. Jackson* (unreported, November 19, 1996) a defendant appealed against his conviction for buggery on the ground that consent had not been given. The Court dismissed the appeal accepting that although there was no written form of consent, the prosecutor had been aware prior to committal that consent was required and had given consent. Unless the statute requires it, the consent does not have to be in writing but as a matter of good practice and commonsense, it is desirable for it to be in writing to avoid doubt and uncertainty.

Gross indecency defines only acts between two men. Actions undertaken between a man and a woman, or between two women are not acts of gross indecency.

II. The Act

8–32   One man acting alone does not commit this offence although in some circumstances the act may be an offence of Indecency with Children (see para.9–28).

8–33   The two men must be acting in concert therefore and there must be some participation between them: a degree of co-operation or a sense of acting in concert: *R v. Hornby and People* [1946] 2 All E.R. 487.

8–34   It is however not necessary for there to be direct physical contact between the two men. It will suffice if the two men have placed themselves in such a position that a grossly indecent exhibition is going on: *R v. Hornby* [1946] 2 All E.R. 370. In *R v. Hunt and Badsey* (1950) 43 Cr.App.R. 135, the two men were indulging in a grossly indecent exhibition in a shed although there was no physical contact. It was held that actual contact was not a necessary ingredient.

8–35   In *R v. Preece*; *R v. Howells* [1976] 2 All E.R. 696, the two defendants were in separate cubicles in a public lavatory. There was a hole in the connecting wall so each would have been able to see the other. P admitted watching H masturbate. He admitted also that he hoped that he, in turn, was being watched by H. H only admitted masturbating and denied he had watched P. There was no evidence of any prior agreement or consent between them. It was held that the offence requires the participation and co-operation of the two men. "With" implied the participation of two men. However, on the evidence in this case the jury could conclude that there was tacit consent by each to participate.

8–36   It is not essential that both men be charged: *R v. Jones and Bowerbank* [1846] 1 Q.B. 4, and there is no reason in law why one man should not be convicted and the other acquitted: *R v. Pearce* [1951] 2 All E.R. 493. It may be that one man confessed and the other man did not. As to the admissibility of the confession of one man see *R v. Mattison* [1990] Crim.L.R. 117 C.A.

8–37   However where the issues against both men are identical, and the requirement is that they had been acting in concert, the Court of Appeal has overturned the conviction of one man when the other was acquitted: *R v. Batten, The Times*, March 16, 1990.

III. To Procure The Commission

8–38   One man can procure the commission of the act with himself: *R v. Jones and Bowerbank* [1896] 1 Q.B. 4.

8–39   It is not essential that the identity of the other man be established: *R v. Bentley* [1923] 1 K.B. 403. In that case, the defendant telephoned W asking him if he could have two boys for immoral purposes, saying "Can I have two boys at 10/- each? I want them at eight o'clock or soon after". No particular boys were identified. It was held that the defendant had incited W to commit what, if he had done the acts, would have been a criminal offence. It did not matter that the identities of the two boys had not been ascertained, or that W may have been incited to incite another person to commit a criminal offence.

An invitation to meet followed by an actual meeting has been held to be an attempt to procure a boy: *R v. Miskell* [1954] 1 All E.R. 137. The defendant's conduct and conversation were such as to convey his desire that the two act indecently together. 8–40

The attempt, or the incitement can be by letter. In *R v. Cope* (1921) 16 Cr.App.R. 77, the defendant wrote to another man, known to have committed acts of indecency in the past. The letters suggested a meeting. One letter contained the sentence, "I am jealous of the boy you picked out". It was held: 8–41

(a) a man can procure the commission of the act towards himself—following *R v. Jones and Bowerbank* [1896] 1 Q.B. 4;

(b) it is not necessary that the letter which constitutes the attempt, should reach and be read by the addressee. It was intercepted by his mother: following *R v. Ransford* (1874) 13 Cox C.C 9 and *R v. Banks* (1873) 12 Cox 393; and

(c) an invitation in writing, itself prima facie innocent may be shown by other evidence to be an attempt to procure: following *R v. Robert* (1855) Dean C.C.39.

In *R v. Woods* (1930) 46 T.L.R. 401, letters couched in lecherous terms but purporting to be written by a woman sent to a man the defendant did not know and did not meet was too remote to be an attempt. The letters were written from Dorset to London to a man who advertised for a position as a hairdresser. They invited him to travel to Dorset for immoral purposes. The addressee believed that they were from a woman. 8–42

Items found in the possession of the defendant are not admissible in evidence if they merely go to show bad character.

However, they may be admissible to prove identity if this is in dispute, for example where an alibi is given. In *Thompson v. R* [1918] A.C. 22; *Thompson v. DPP* (1918) 13 Cr.App.R. 61, evidence that the defendant had powder-puffs with him and indecent photographs of boys in his room was admissible to prove identity. It has also been admitted to show inclination. In *R v. Twiss* [1918] 2 K.B. 853, indecent photographs were admitted to show the practice of the defendant. It is probable that evidence would be excluded to-day, as being prejudicial.

In *R v. Gillingham* (1939) 27 Cr.App.R. 143 indecent photographs which were not homosexual in nature were admitted in evidence on the basis that they could be used by someone guilty of the offence to inflame the passions of his victim, or to arouse his own passions. 8–43

IV. SENTENCING GUIDELINES

The maximum penalty upon conviction of a man over 21, committing the offence with a man under 18 is five years. 8–44

For other offences it is two years on indictment and six months and/or a fine on summary conviction.

The guideline case is *R v. Morgan* [1978] C.S.P.B4–9.2(3). The defendants who were 61 and 39 had committed the offence in a public lavatory. It was 8–45 held that such circumstances did not warrant a custodial sentence. A fine is generally all that is required. Occasionally, they may be put on probation or some other non-custodial order is made. Only for those who persist in this kind of behaviour is a prison sentence appropriate.

C. HOMOSEXUAL ACTIVITIES IN THE ARMED SERVICES AND ON SHIPS

8–46   Section 146 of the Criminal Justice and Public Order Act 1994 finally repealed those provisions of the Sexual Offences Act 1967 which related to members of the armed services and the merchant navy. Accordingly, acts committed by armed service personnel, and by merchant seamen on board a United Kingdom ship will not in themselves be offences which are not offences under the civilian criminal law. However, section 146(4) makes it clear that these repeals do not prevent a homosexual act from constituting a ground for discharging a member of HM armed forces from the service, or dismissing a member of the crew of a United Kingdom merchant ship from his ship. In the case of a member of the forces, where the act occurs in conjunction with other acts or circumstances, from constituting an offence under the Service Discipline Acts i.e. the Army Act 1955, the Air Force Act 1955 or the Navy Discipline Act 1957, that offence is still committed.

8–47   The dismissal of a member of the Armed forces for homosexual orientation was challenged in the case of R v. Secretary of State of Defence, ex p. Smith, ex p. Grady; R v. Admiralty Board of the Defence Council, ex p. Lustig-Prean, ex p. Beckett, The Times, November 6, 1995. The Court of Appeal however did not find the policy to be irrational. The Court "could not interfere with the exercise of an administrative decision on substantive grounds save where it was satisfied that the decision was unreasonable in the sense that it was beyond the range of responses open to a reasonable decision maker". The human rights question was unimportant. However, "the greater the policy content of a decision and the more remote the subject matter from ordinary judicial experience, the more hesitant the court had necessarily to be in holding a decision to be irrational". The policy was supported by both Houses of Parliament and was made after professional advice. The Court held that, "the threshold of irrationality was a high one. It was not crossed here."

D. THE STATUS OF THE TRANSSEXUAL

8–48   A transsexual is a man, or woman who has the feelings and inclinations of the opposite sex. With the use of hormones and reconstructive surgery, they can be made to resemble or match their sexual identity, often known as a "sex change". Transsexuality is not the same as homosexuality.

8–49   In law, however, a person retains the sex they were born, and a man will therefore remain biologically a man despite medical or surgical alteration or natural development of organs of the opposite sex.

The following description of a transsexual was given in *Rees v. United Kingdom, The Times,* October 21, 1986 and confirmed in *P v. S, The Times,* May 7, 1996:

> "the term 'transsexual' is usually applied to those who, while belonging physically to one sex, feel convinced that they belong to the other; they often seek to achieve a more integrated, unambiguous identity by undergoing medical treatment and surgical operations to adapt their physical characteristics to their psychological nature. Transsexuals who have been operated upon thus form a fairly well defined and identifiable group".

The description implies that the physical sex is constant although physical characteristics may be adapted by surgery.

This was first held in *Corbett v. Corbett (orse. Ashley)* [1970] 2 W.L.R.   8–50
1306. The only cases where the term "change of sex" is appropriate is where a mistake as to sex is made at birth which is subsequently revealed by medical investigation. In the case of *R v. Registrar General for England and Wales, ex p. P,* and *R v. Registrar General for England and Wales, The Times,* March 27, 1996, it was stated that a birth certificate was an historical record not a statement of current sexual status. Section 29(3) of the Births and Deaths Registration Act 1953 allows for errors of fact or substance in a birth certificate to be corrected by an entry in the margin. However, the Registrar is entitled to apply the tests approved of in *Corbett v. Corbett* and *R v. Tan.*

The test in *Corbett v. Corbett* was extended to the criminal law by *R v. Tan*   8–51
and others [1983] 1 Q.B. 1053. It was held that:

> "Gloria Greaves was born a man, and remained biologically a man albeit he had undergone both hormone and surgical treatment, consisting in what are called 'sex change operations' consisting essentially in the removal of the external male organs and the creation of an artificial vaginal pocket."

Such a male transsexual can therefore be a male prostitute, but not a   8–52
female prostitute and is male for the purposes of gross indecency.

An anomaly remains. In *Corbett v. Corbett*, the surgical reconstruction   8–53
was described as "an artificial cavity which opened onto the percineum". It is therefore presumably not a vagina which can only logically be defined as a female organ. Rape is the offence of having sexual intercourse with a person (whether vaginal or anal) who at the time of the intercourse does not consent to it (Sexual Offences Act 1956, s.1 as amended by s.142 of the Criminal Justice and Public Order Act 1994). Anal rape of a trans-sexual creates no problem, but vaginal rape would appear to be impossible. The relevant offences would be gross indecency with a man, indecent assault, or possibly attempted rape.

Chapter 9
Unlawful Sexual Acts With Children

9-01   Paedophilia is, understandably, a practice which causes much public con-
        cern. Offences of rape and indecent assault may have children as their victims
        but there is also a number of specific offences which have grown piecemeal to
        protect children from those who would use them for their own sexual
        gratification.

A. SEX WITH A CHILD UNDER THE AGE OF CONSENT

9-02   The Sexual Offences Act 1993 came into force on September 20, 1993. It
        removed the previous irrefutable presumptions in criminal law that a boy
        under the age of 14 is incapable of sexual intercourse (either natural or
        unnatural)(s. 1). A boy between 10 and 14 can therefore be charged with
        offences of rape, assault with intent to commit rape, buggery, unlawful
        sexual intercourse with a girl under 16 or under 13 and sexual intercourse
        with a mental defective (see *Home Office Circular* 41/1993).

I. CONSENT

9-03   A table of ages of consent is set out in Appendix 9.

        (a) Rape

        A child under the age of 16 may give valid consent to sexual intercourse if she
        is aware of the nature of that consent. In such circumstances rape would be
        negatived by consent. However, in the case of a very young girl she may not
        properly understand the seriousness and significance of the act and would
        not therefore be able to give a valid consent. In such cases, rape would be the
        appropriate charge: *R. v. Harling* (1938) 26 Cr.App.R. 127.

(b) Unlawful sexual intercourse

It is inaccurate to refer to 16 as an age of consent. If the girl does not consent   9–04
the offence is rape. 16 is an age below which it is unlawful to have intercourse
with a girl.

II. GIRLS UNDER 13

It is an offence contrary to section 5 of the Sexual Offences Act 1956 to have   9–05
unlawful sexual intercourse with a girl under 13. The offence is triable only
on indictment and carries life imprisonment.

Consent is no defence. If however, there was not consent rape is the   9–06
alternative and preferable charge: *R. v. Ratcliffe* (1882) 10 Q.B.D. 74: *R v.
Howard* [1966] 1 W.L.R. 13, *R. v. Dicken* (1877) 14 Cox 8.

The offence is one of strict liability as far as age is concerned: *R v. Prince*   9–07
(1875) L.R. 2 C.C.R. 154, and therefore must be proved by the prosecution.
The girl's age at the date of the offence requires formal proof either by
evidence from a parent or by production of a certified birth certificate
coupled with proof of identity: *R. v. Weaver* (1873) L.R. 2 C.C.R. 85; *R. v.
Cox* [1898] 1 Q.B. 179; *R. v. Bellis* (1911) 6 Cr.App.R. 283. The age of an
adopted child may be proved by a certified copy of an entry in the Adopted
Children Register under the Adoption Act 1976, s. 50(2). In *Cox*, proof of
the girl's age could be given by someone who knew the girl.

Section 99 of the Children and Young Persons Act 1933 which deals with   9–08
presumptions or declarations made by a court as to a persons age, and which
states that: "an order or judgement of the court shall not be invalidated by
any subsequent proof that the age of that person has not been correctly stated
to the court", does not apply to either section 5 or section 6.

III. GIRLS UNDER 16

Section 6 of the Sexual Offences Act 1956 states: 9–09

"(1)   It is an offence, subject to the exceptions mentioned in this section,
       for a man to have unlawful sexual intercourse with a girl under the
       age of sixteen.
(2)   Where a marriage is invalid under section two of the Marriage Act
       1949, or section one of the Age of Marriage Act 1929 (the wife being
       a girl under the age of sixteen), the invalidity does not make the
       husband guilty of an offence under this section because he has sexual
       intercourse with her, if he believes her to be his wife and has
       reasonable cause for the belief.
(3)   A man is not guilty of an offence under this section because he has
       unlawful sexual intercourse with a girl under the age of sixteen, if he
       is under the age of twenty-four and has not previously been charged
       with a like offence, and he believes her to be of the age of sixteen or
       over and has reasonable cause for the belief."

In this subsection "a like offence" means an offence under this section or   9–10

201

an attempt to commit one, or an offence under paragraph (1) of section 5 of the Criminal Law Amendment Act 1885 (the provision replaced for England and Wales by this section).

Sentencing guidelines

9–11   The offence is triable either way. Tried summarily the offence carries six months' imprisonment, and/or the statutory maximum fine; tried upon indictment it carries two years' imprisonment. The offence should be tried summarily unless one or more of the following features is present and also the court feels that its sentencing powers are insufficient:

  (i)   wide disparity of age;
  (ii)   breach of position of trust;
  (iii) the victim is particularly vulnerable (*National Mode of Trial Guidelines*, 1995; see also *Practice Note (Mode of Trial Guidelines)* [1990] 1 W.L.R. 1439).

9–12   The sentencing guidelines are laid down by Lawton L.J. in *R v. Taylor* [1977] 1 W.L.R. 612, subject to *Practice Statement (Crime: Sentencing)* [1992] 1 W.L.R. 948:

> "It is clear from what the learned trial Judge said that there is doubt among many at the present time as to the proper way of dealing with these cases. What does not seem to have been appreciated by the public is the wide spectrum of guilt which is covered by the offence known as having unlawful sexual intercourse with a girl under the age of 16. At one end of the spectrum is the youth who stands in the dock, maybe 16, 17 or 18 who has had what started off, as a virtuous friendship with a girl under the age of 16. That virtuous friendship has ended with them having sexual intercourse with each other. At the other end of the spectrum is the man in the supervisory capacity, a school-master or social worker, who sets out deliberately to seduce a girl under the age of 16 who is in his charge. The penalties appropriate for the two types of case to which I have just referred are very different. When an older man in his twenties or older goes off to dances and picks up a young girl, he can expect to get a much stiffer fine, and if the girl is under 15 he can expect to go to prison for a short time. A young man who deliberately sets out to seduce a girl under the age of 16 can expect to go to detention. The older man who deliberately so sets out can expect to go to prison. Such is the wide variety of penalties which can be applied in this class of case."

9–13   The purpose of the section is to protect young women. It is not appropriate therefore to prosecute those intended to be protected for aiding and abetting the offence committed against them: *R v. Tyrrell* [1894] 1 Q.B. 710.

9–14   Subject only to the exceptions set out in the section, consent is not a defence. The onus of proof lies with the defendant to prove the statutory defence (Sexual Offences Act 1956 s.47).

The defendant must not only have reasonable cause to believe the girl was   9–15
over 16 to have the benefit of the statutory defence at section 6(3) but must
actually believe it: *R v. Banks* [1916] 2 K.B. 621; *R v. Harrison* (1938) 26
Cr.App.R. 2 168. The question of a reasonable cause to believe should be left
to the jury: *R v. Forde* [1923] 2 K.B. 400.

The defendant must not have been charged with a similar offence. A   9–16
defendant is charged with an offence at committal if the magistrates discharge the allegation upon a submission of no case to answer, but if he is
committed he is not charged until he appears before the Crown Court and
the indictment is put: *R v. Rider* [1954] 1 W.L.R. 463. If there are two
committals but the charges appear on one indictment, the defence is available
for both allegations.

The defence is available for an attempt to commit the offence (*R v. Collier*
[1960] Crim. L.R. 204) but not to an allegation of indecent assault.

The defence under section 6(2) will apply to foreign marriages where the   9–17
wife is 13 or over but under 16. Such a marriage would not be valid under
British law but will be recognised by the British courts. In *Mohammed v.
Knott* [1968] 2 All E.R. 563, a Nigerian marriage where the wife was 13 was
recognised. The girl was not necessarily exposed to moral danger. Although
a "fit person order" under the Children and Young Persons Act 1933 could
be made the Sexual Offences Act 1956 did not make it essential.

IV. LIMITATIONS TO PROSECUTIONS

A prosecution may not be commenced more than twelve months after the   9–18
offence charged (Sexual Offences Act 1956, s. 37 and Sched. 2, Pt. 2).

V. ALTERNATIVE VERDICTS

A defendant can be found guilty of attempting to commit the full offence: *R*   9–19
v. Beale (1865) L.R. 1 C.C.R. 10; *R v. Ryland* (1868) 11 Cox 11.

If sexual intercourse is not proved the defendant may be convicted of
indecent assault: *R v. Taylor* (1869) L.R. 1 C.C.R. 194; *R v. Catherall* (1875)
13 Cox 109; R v. O'Brien (1911) 6 Cr.App.R. 108. The statutory defence
under section 6(3) does not apply to indecent assault.

B. PERMITTING GIRLS TO USE PREMISES FOR UNLAWFUL SEXUAL INTERCOURSE

The Sexual Offences Act 1956, sections 25 and 26 create two similar   9–20
offences:

Section 25 states: 9–21

"It is an offence for a person who is the owner or occupier of any premises,
or who has, or acts or assists in, the management or control of any

premises, to induce or knowingly suffer a girl under the age of thirteen to resort to or be on those premises for the purpose of having unlawful sexual intercourse with men or with a particular man."

9–22   Section 26 states:

It is an offence for a person who is the owner or occupier of any premises, or who has, or acts or assists in, the management or control of any premises, to induce or knowingly suffer a girl under the age of sixteen, to resort to or be on those premises for the purpose of having unlawful sexual intercourse with men or with a particular man."

9–23   Section 25 is triable only on indictment, section 26 is either way.

9–24   The offence is committed even though the premises are the girl's normal residence where she lives with the defendant: *R v. Webster* (1885) 16 Q.B.D. 134. However in *R v. Merthyr Tydfil Justices* (1894) 10 T.L.R. 375, a mother was held to have a valid defence where she allowed her daughter to have intercourse with a man at her house in order to obtain evidence against him.

9–25   Encouraging unlawful sexual intercourse with a girl under sixteen: section 28 of the 1956 Act is discussed elsewhere (see Chapter 12, para.59).

C. THE POSITION OF DOCTORS

9–26   Doctors who prescribe contraceptives for girls under 16 were discussed at length in *Gillick v. West Norfolk A.M.A* [1986] A.C. 112, H.L. An offence may be committed by a doctor who acts to encourage the girl to have unlawful sexual intercourse. Lord Scarman, at 190 said:

"Clearly a doctor who gives a girl contraceptive advice or treatment not because in his clinical judgment the treatment is medically intended for the maintenance or restoration of her health but with the intention of facilitating her having unlawful sexual intercourse may well be guilty of criminal offences. He may prescribe only if she has the capacity to consent or if exceptional circumstances exist which justify him in exercising his clinical judgment without parental consent, The adjective 'clinical' emphasises that it must be a medical judgment based upon what he honestly believes to be necessary for the physical, mental and emotional health of his patient, The bona fides exercise by a doctor of his clinical judgment must be a complete negation of the guilty mind which is an essential ingredient of the criminal offence of aiding and abetting the commission of unlawful sexual intercourse."

D. INDECENCY WITH CHILDREN

9–27   Section 1 of the Indecency with Children Act 1960 states:

"(1) Any person who commits an act of gross indecency with or towards a child under the age of fourteen, or who incites a child under that age to such an act with him or another, shall be liable on conviction on indictment to imprisonment for a term not exceeding two years, or on summary conviction to imprisonment for a term not exceeding six months, to a fine not exceeding the statutory maximum or to both."

The Act was passed to remedy the gap in the law created by *Fairclough v. Whipp* [1951] 2 All E.R. 834, which held that there was no indecent assault where the defendant invited the child to touch him in an indecent manner (see Chapter 6).   **9–28**

As a result, in certain circumstances, remaining passive may constitute an incitement. In *R v. Speck* [1977] 2 All E.R. 859, the defendant allowed the child's hand to remain on his erect penis outside his trousers for about five minutes, the defendant remained inactive throughout and did not remove the girl's hand.   **9–29**

In *R v. Morley* [1989] Crim.L.R. 566, a four-year-old child had been present when a number of sexual activities occurred between the defendant and his wife and some involving the defendant alone: some activities were in a bath and some in a bed. The court distinguished between occasions where there was no evidence that the defendant had either invited the child to do what she did, invited her to continue or in any form co-operated with her, and occasions where he had in fact invited or co-operated with her in the sexual activity described.   **9–30**

In *R.v. Frances* (1988) 88 Cr.App.R. 127, the defendant masturbated in the presence of children under 14 knowing that they were watching and derived pleasure from that act. He had committed an act of gross indecency towards them whether or not he had deliberately attracted their attention. If he had believed that they were unaware of his actions however, no offence would have been committed under this Act.   **9–31**

The correct wording of a charge is either "with or towards a child", or alternatively "did incite A, a child under the age of 14, namely—, to an act of gross indecency with" (*DPP v. Burgess* [1971] 1 Q.B. 432). The first alternative is not duplicitous.   **9–32**

The child's age should be stated in the indictment (*R.v. Goss and Goss* (1990) 90 Cr.App.R. 400; *R.v. Radcliffe* [1990] Crim.L.R. 524).   **9–33**

Although the allegation of incitement involves a reference to "gross indecency" the requirement under section 8 of the Sexual Offences Act 1967 requiring the consent of the DPP for a prosecution of a man for gross indecency does not extend to an offence of incitement under the Indecency with Children Act 1960 (Criminal Justice Act 1971, s.48): *R.v. Assistant Recorder of Kingston-upon-Hull, ex p. Morgan* [1969] 1 All E.R. 416.   **9–34**

E. INDECENT PHOTOGRAPHS OF CHILDREN

See Chapter 13.   **9–35**

F. MARRIAGE ACT 1949, s. 2

9–36   The Marriages Act 1949, s. 2 states: "a marriage solemnised between parties either of whom is under the age of sixteen shall be void."

G. ALLOWING PERSONS UNDER 16 TO BE IN BROTHELS

9–37   Section 3 of the Children and Young Persons Act 1933 as amended (by the Sexual Offences Act 1956, Sched. 4; the Children and Young Persons Act 1963, Sched. 5; the Criminal Law Act 1977, Sched. 1; the Criminal Justice Act 1982, s.46; and the Children Act 1989, Sched. 13) states:

> "if any person having the responsibility for a child or young person who has attained the age of four years and is under the age of 16 years, allows that child or young person to reside in, or to frequent a brothel, he shall be liable on summary conviction to a fine not exceeding level 2 and/or imprisonment for any term not exceeding six months."

H. SEXUAL OFFENCES (CONSPIRACY AND INCITEMENT) ACT 1996

9–38   Section 1 deals with conspiracies to commit certain sexual acts outside the United Kingdom against children. When a number of conditions have been satisfied in the case of any agreement, Part 1 of the Criminal Law Act 1977 (conspiracy) has effect in relation to the agreement as it has effect in relation to an agreement falling within section 1(1) of that Act.

9–39   The first condition is that the pursuit of the agreed course of conduct would at some stage involve:

     (i)   an act by one or more of the parties, or

     (ii)   the happening of some other event, intended to take place in a country or territory outside the United Kingdom. It is not necessary that one or more of the conspirators actually commit the act themselves (s.1(2)).

9–40   The second condition is that that act or other event constitutes an offence under the law in force in that country or territory.

9–41   The third condition is that the agreement would fall within section 1(1) of that Act as an agreement relating to the commission of a listed sexual offence but for the fact that the offence would not be an offence triable in England and Wales if committed in accordance with the parties' intentions.

9–42   The fourth condition is that:

     (i)   a party to the agreement, or a party's agent, did anything in England and Wales in relation to the agreement before its formation, or

(ii)   a party to the agreement became a party in England and Wales (by joining it either in person or through an agent), or

(iii) a party to the agreement, or a party's agent, did or omitted anything in England and Wales in pursuance of the agreement (s.1(5)).

In the application of Part 1 of the 1977 Act to such an agreement, any reference to an offence is to be read as a reference to what would be the listed sexual offence in question, but for the fact that it is not an offence triable in England and Wales.   9–43

Section 2 deals with incitement to commit certain sexual acts against children outside the United Kingdom and applies where: 9–44

"(a)   any act done by a person in England and Wales would amount to the offence of incitement to commit a listed sexual offence but for the fact that what he had in view would not be an offence triable in England and Wales,

(b)   the whole or part of what he had in view was intended to take place in a country or territory outside the United Kingdom, and

(c)   what he had in view would involve the commission of an offence under the law in force in that country or territory."

"Where the section applies—   9–45

(a)   what he had in view is to be treated as that listed sexual offence for the purposes of any charge of incitement brought in respect of that act, and

(b)   any such charge is accordingly triable in England and Wales."

Any act of incitement by means of a message (however communicated) is to be treated as done in England and Wales if the message is sent or received in England and Wales.   9–46

Conduct punishable under the law in force in any country or territory is an offence under that law for the purposes of section 1 (conspiracy) and section 2 (incitement), however it is described in that law.   9–47

There was at committee stage debate as to whether the act should be an offence in the other state or territory. It was said, however, that "removing that feature would make it more difficult to persuade overseas countries to assist us in the provision of evidence for prosecutions here in Britain under extra-territorial provisions, if the offences being prosecuted were—for whatever reason—not offences in the overseas country concerned."

I. PROOF OF FOREIGN LAW

"Subject to subsection (3), a condition in section 1(3) or 2(1)(c), *i.e.* that the act must consititute an offence in the other jurisdiction, is to be taken to be satisfied unless, not later than the rules of court may provide the defence serve on the prosecution a notice—   9–48

(a)   stating that, on the facts as alleged with respecet to the relevant conduct, the condition is not in their opinion satisfied;

(b)   showing their grounds for that opinion; and

(c)   requiring the prosecution to show that it is satisfied."

9–49   "Relevant conduct" means either the agreed course of conduct in a conspiracy, or what the accused had in view in an incitement (s.3(3)).

9–50   If the court thinks fit it may permit the defence to require the prosecution
to show that the condition is satisfied without prior service of notice.

9–51   In the Crown Court the question whether the condition is satisfied is to be
decided by the judge alone.

9–52   It is immaterial to guilt whether or not the accused was a British citizen at
the time of any act or other event, proof of which is required for conviction
of the offence (s.3(6)).

II. LISTED SEXUAL OFFENCES

9–53   In England and Wales the listed offences are:

  (a)   Under the Sexual Offences Act 1956:
        I.   section 1—rape
        II.   section 5—intercourse with a girl under 13
        III. section 6—intercourse with a girl under 16
        IV.   section 12—buggery
        V.   section 14—indecent assault on a girl
        VI.   section 15—indecent assault on a boy
  (b)   section 1 of the Indecency with Children Act 1960—indecent
        conduct towards a young child.

However, I, IV, V and VI do not apply where the victim of the offence has
attained the age of 16 years.

Commencement

9–54   The Act received Royal Assent on July 4, 1996 and its provisions came into
force on October 1, 1996 by virtue of the Sexual Offences (Conspiracy and
Incitement) (Commencement) Order 1996.

I. SEX OFFENDERS ACT 1997

9–55   Part II of this Act makes it an offence for British citizens or residents to
commit certain sexual acts abroad against children. Section 7(1) states:

  "(1) subject to subsection (2), any act done by a person in a country or
        territory outside the United Kingdom which
        (a)   constituted an offence under the law in force in that country or
              territory; and
        (b)   would constitute a sexual offence to which this section applies if
              it had been done in England and Wales, or in Northern Ireland,
              shall constitute that sexual offence under the law of that part of
              the United Kingdom.
  (2)   No proceedings shall by virtue of this section be brought against any

person unless he was at the commencement of this section, or has subsequently become, a British citizen or resident in the United Kingdom.

(3) An act punishable under the law in force in any country or territory constitutes an offence under that law for the purposes of this section, however it is described in that law."

I. Proof That The Act Is An Offence

Subsection (4) states: **9–56**

"subject to subsection (5) below, the condition in subsection (1)(a) above shall be taken to be satisfied unless, not later than the rules of court may provide, the defence serve on the prosecution a notice—
  (a) stating that, on the facts as alleged with respect to the act in question the condition is not, in their opinion satisfied;
  (b) showing their grounds for that opinion; and
  (c) requiring the prosecution to show that it is satisfied.

(5) The court, if it thinks fit, may permit the defence to require the prosecution to show that the condition is satisfied without prior service of the notice under subsection (4) above.

(6) In the Crown Court the question whether the condition is satisfied is to be decided by the judge alone."

II. The Sexual Offence

Section 7(7) and Schedule 2 apply the section to the following offences: **9–57**

  (a) Sexual Offences Act 1956
      I.   section 1—rape *
      II.   section 5—intercourse with a girl under 13
      III. section 6—intercourse with a girl under 16
      IV.   section 12—buggery *
      V.   section 14—indecent assault on a girl *
      VI.   section 15—indecent assault on a boy *
      VII. section 16—assault with intent to commit buggery
      * sub-paragraphs I, IV, V and VI do not apply where the victim of the offence was 16 or over at the time of the offence.
  (b) Indecency with Children Act 1960, s. 1—indecent conduct towards a young child.
  (c) Protection of Children Act 1978, s.1—indecent photographs of children.

References to an offence include:

  (a) a reference to any attempt, conspiracy or incitement to commit that offence; and
  (b) a reference to aiding and abetting, counselling or procuring the commission of the offence (para. 3).

Chapter 10
Incest

A. INTRODUCTION

10–01   The prohibited relationships of incest are not the same as the prohibited relationships for marriage. In the latter case, marriage is prohibited either by a relationship of consanguinity to the third degree or by affinity. A husband is of affinity to his wife's kin, and she to his kin, but beyond that his kin are not of affinity to her kin. Therefore, a man may not marry his wife's daughter's daughter although he may legally be able to have sex with her.

10–02   Nor can he marry his adopted daughter. He cannot marry his son's wife. The laws of consanguinity and affinity in marriage date back to 1536 (28 Hen. 8 c. 7 1536, and Ecclesiastical Licences Act 1536). They were tabulated in 1563 and are annexed to the Book of Common Prayer. They are now specified by the Marriage Act 1949, s.1(1). Affinity does not extend to deceased or divorced spouses' siblings or the divorced spouses of siblings or to nephews or nieces by marriage: Marriage (Enabling) Act 1960, s.14.

10–03   The most common form of incest is brother/sister intercourse, which is also one of the least likely to be reported, or prosecuted. Father/daughter incest is the most frequently prosecuted. Mother/son incest is also rare before the courts but may be more common than that would indicate.

10–04   Sections 10 and 11 of the Sexual Offences Act 1956 address the offences of incest.

I. INCEST BY A MAN—SECTION 10

10–05   "(1) It is an offence for a man to have sexual intercourse with a woman he knows to be his granddaughter, daughter, sister or mother.

(2) In the foregoing subsection 'sister' includes half-sister, and for the purposes of that subsection any expression importing a relationship between two people shall be taken to apply notwithstanding that the relationship is not traced through lawful wedlock."

210

II. Incest By A Woman—Section 11

"(1) It is an offence for a woman of the age of sixteen or over to permit a man whom she knows to be her grandfather, father, brother or son to have sexual intercourse with her by her consent.

(2) In the foregoing subsection 'brother' includes half-brother, and for the purposes of that subsection any expression importing a relationship between two people shall be taken to apply notwithstanding that the relationship is not traced through lawful wedlock."

B. SENTENCING GUIDELINES

Both offences are triable upon indictment only and both require the consent   **10–06**
of the DPP. The maximum penalties are as follows:

- Incest by a man with a girl under 13—life imprisonment
- Incest by a man with a girl over 13—seven years
- Attempted incest by a man with a girl under 13—two years
- Attempted incest by a man with a girl over 13—two years
- Incest by a woman—seven years
- Attempted incest by a woman—two years

The age of the girl should therefore be referred to in the indictment when the incest is by or attempted by a man.

The guidelines for sentencing are contained in *Attorney–General's Refer-*   **10–07**
ence (No.1 of 1989) [1989] W.L.R. 1117. These guidelines apply to incest by a father with a daughter and do not normally include a discount for guilty pleas:"The gravity of the offence varies greatly according, primarily to the age of the victim and ... the degree of coercion or corruption."

Incest between a father and a daughter in her late teens or older where the   **10–08**
daughter has been a willing participant or even an instigator will require little, if anything in the way of punishment.

Where on the other hand, the father is convicted of rape of his daughter,   **10–09**
the guidelines set out in *Billam* [1986] 1 W.L.R. 349 are to be followed rather than the incest guidelines *R v. Richard Stephen C* (1990) 12 Cr.App.R.(S.) 292.

I. Where The Girl Is Over 16

Generally speaking a range from three years' imprisonment down to a   **10–10**
nominal penalty will be appropriate depending on the one hand, whether force was used and upon the degree of harm, if any, to the girl, and on the other, the desirability where it exists of keeping family disruption to a minimum. The older the girl the greater the probability that she may have been willing or even the instigating party to the liaison, a factor which will be reflected in the sentence. In other words, the lower the degree of corruption, the lower the penalty.

II. Where The Girl Is Aged From 13 To 16

10–11   Here a sentence between about five years and three years seems on the authorities to be appropriate. Much the same principles will apply as in the case of a girl over 16, though the likelihood of corruption increases in inverse proportion to the age of the girl. Nearly all the cases in this category have involved pleas of guilty and the sentences in this category seem to range between about two years and four years, credit having been given for the plea.

III. Where The Girl Is Under 13

10–12   It is here that the widest range of sentence is likely to be found. If one can properly describe any case of incest as the "ordinary" type of case, it will be one where the sexual relationship between husband and wife has broken down; the father has probably resorted to excessive drinking and the eldest daughter is gradually, by way of familiarities, indecent acts and suggestions, made the object of the father's frustrated sexual inclinations. If the girl is not far short of her thirteenth birthday and there are no particularly adverse or favourable features on a not guilty plea, a term of about six years on the authorities would seem to be appropriate. It scarcely needs to be stated that the younger the girl when the sexual approach is started, the more likely it will be that the girl's will was overborne and accordingly, the more serious would be the crime.

10–13   Other aggravating factors, whatever the age of the girl may be, are, *inter alia*, as follows:

  (a)   if there is evidence that the girl has suffered physically or psychologically from the incest;

  (b)   if the incest has continued at frequent intervals over a long period of time;

  (c)   if the girl has been threatened or treated violently by, or was terrified of the father;

  (d)   if the incest has been accompanied by perversions abhorrent to the girl, *e.g.* buggery or fellatio;

  (e)   if the girl has become pregnant by reason of the father failing to take contraceptive measures; and

  (f)   the defendant has committed similar offences against more than one girl.

10–14   Possible mitigating features are, *inter alia*, the following:

  (a)   a plea of guilty (it is seldom that such a plea is not entered, and it should be met by an appropriate discount, depending on the usual considerations, that is to say, how promptly the defendant confessed and the degree of contrition and so on;

  (b)   if it seems that there was genuine affection on the part of the defendant rather than the intention to use the girl simply as an outlet for his sexual inclinations;

(c)   where the girl has had previous experience;

(d)   where the girl has made deliberate attempts at seduction; and

(e)   where, as very occasionally is the case, a shorter term of imprison-
ment for the father may be of benefit to the victim and the family.
Such a situation was discussed in *Attorney-General's Reference
(No.4 of 1989)* (1989) 11 Cr.App.R.(S.) 517.

It should be noted that these guidelines may also apply to cases where the
victim's relationship to the defendant is outside that covered by incest.'
Attorney-General's Reference (No.4 of 1991) (1992) 13 Cr.App.R. (S.)
182.

A custodial sentence may not be appropriate in cases of incest between   **10–15**
brother and sister: *R. v. Veek* (1984) 6 Cr.App.R. (S.) 171; and where there
is only one instance a conditional discharge may be a more appropriate
sentence: *R. v. P* (1993) 15 Cr.App.R. (S) 116.

In *R. v. F* (1991) 13 Cr.App.R. (S.), a mother who had masturbated her   **10–16**
son when he was 10 years old and subsequently committed incest with him
on a number of occasions when he was 13 and 14, was sentenced to 18
months' imprisonment. The sentence was upheld on appeal, with Lord Lane
C.J. commenting that the sentence was certainly not excessive and indeed
could be considered lenient.

C. INCITEMENT TO COMMIT INCEST

Section 11 is worded to prevent girls under 16 being prosecuted. However,   **10–17**
the result was that a father could not be convicted of inciting his daughter
under 16 to commit incest unless she was also under 14 when the offence
would be addressed by section 1 of the Indecency with Children Act 1960.

This gap was identified in the case of *R. v. Whitehouse* (1977) 65   **10–18**
Cr.App.R. 33 and was resolved by section 54 of the Criminal Law Act
1977:

"(1)   It is an offence for a man to incite to have sexual intercourse with him
a girl under the age of sixteen whom he knows to be his grand-
daughter, daughter or sister.

(2)   In the preceding subsection 'man' includes boy, 'sister' includes half-
sister, and for the purposes of that subsection any expression
importing a relationship between two people shall be taken to apply
notwithstanding that the relationship is not traced through lawful
wedlock."

(3)   The following provisions of section 1 of the Indecency with Children
Act 1960, namely—
"subsection (3) (references in Children and Young Persons Act 1933
to the offences mentioned in Schedule 1 to that Act to include
offences under that section); subsection (4) (offences under that
section to be deemed offences against the person for the purpose of

213

section 3 of the Visiting Forces Act 1952), shall apply in relation to offences under this section.

(4) A person guilty of a offence under this section shall be liable—
(a) on summary conviction, to imprisonment for a term not exceeding six months or to a fine not exceeding the statutory maximum, or both;
(b) on conviction on indictment, to imprisonment for a term not exceeding two years."

10–19 Section 11 is designed to prevent acts of incest. The rule in *R. v. Tyrrell* [1984] 1 Q.B. 710 does therefore not apply to girls over 16, but clearly does to girls under 16 otherwise the intention of the Act would be defeated. It was held in *R. v. Draper* (1929) 21 Cr.App.R. 147 that a girl over the age of 16 may be an accomplice.

10–20 In *R. v. Pickford* [1995] 1 Cr.App.R. 420 both *Whitehouse* and *Tyrrell* were considered. A father incited a 14-year-old boy to have intercourse with his, the boy's, mother. At the time a boy under 14 was presumed to be incapable of intercourse. The boy became 14 during the period covered by the indictment. It was held that a girl under 16 could not aid and abet an offence of incest against her. Therefore, neither she nor the 14-year-old boy in the instant case could be unlawfully incited to commit the offence as no offence would be committed. The defendant could, however, be convicted of aiding and abetting the mother to commit the offence even though she was an unwilling participant (and would have been able to plead duress if charged: *cf. R. v. Bourne* (1952) 36 Cr. App. R. 125) An indictment alleging incest on divers days between two dates is duplicitous in that it alleges more than one offence. Section 4(1) of the Criminal Appeal Act 1907 was applied: *R. v. Thompson* (1914) 24 Cox C.C. 43.

D. RELATIONSHIPS

10–21 It is evident that incest between a grandson and grandmother is not within the Act. The relationship is consanguine. Adopted parents and children do not have the necessary relationship but it still exists between an adopted child and its natural family: Adoption Act 1976, s.47(1).

10–22 The relationship includes half blood and brother and sister include half-brother and -sister but excludes step-parent: *R. v. Geddeson* (1906) 25 N.Z.L.R. 323.

10–23 Illegitimate children are included and the relationship need not be traced through marriage.

10–24 The relationship must be proved by the prosecution. This is usually by oral evidence from the mother or by certificate of marriage and birth, and evidence of identification. There must also be evidence that the defendant knew of the relationship.

10–25 In *R. v. Jones* (1933) 24 Cr.App.R. 55, the prosecution's evidence of the relationship was based upon the defendant's admission that the girl was his daughter. In *Jones*, the admissions were, "G is my daughter and I am sorry to say that I have had connection with her and I am responsible for the condition she is now in. ... I never looked on G as my daughter, more like a sister to me. ... We (G's mother and I) did not get married until five years after G was born."

In *R. v. Carmichael* [1940] 2 All E.R. 165 the defendant had made   **10–26** statements on occasion acknowledging that the girl was his daughter. However, at trial, he should have been entitled to give evidence that he had been told by his former wife, the girl's mother, that he was not the father and that he believed that to be true; that he had told his second wife that he was not the father, and to explain his other seeming acknowledgements.

E. INTERCOURSE

Sexual intercourse is required to be proved in a prosecution for incest. Other   **10–27** sexual acts including mutual masturbation, oral sex or buggery are insufficient, and do not constitute this offence. Any penetration will suffice and the hymen need not be ruptured but in such cases the summing up should contain a direction as to the differences between incest, attempted incest and indecent assault: *R. v. Killride* (1931) 23 Cr.App.R. 12.

Lack of consent by a woman will constitute rape. It was held that where a   **10–28** defendant is charged with both rape and incest but is convicted of incest only that decision does not necessarily indicate that the girl was fully consenting: *R. v. Dimes* (1911) 7 Cr.App.R. 43. However, since *R. v. Olugboja* (1981) 73 Cr.App.R. 344, rape should be made out.

If, on separate counts of incest against a brother and sister, the brother is   **10–29** convicted and the sister discharged the verdict is good as she may be innocent on the ground that she did not know the man was her brother: *R. v. Gordon* (1925) 19 Cr.App.R. 20.

F. PROOF

On an indictment for incest evidence of previous relations is admissible to   **10–30** prove both "guilty passion" and to rebut a defence of innocent association: *R. v. Ball* [1911] A.C. 47: *R. v. Bloodworth* [1913] Cr.App.R. 50.

Evidence of a previous offence by the defendant with the same person may constitute corroboration: *R. v. Hartley* (1941) 28 Cr.App.R. 14.

G. ORDERS DIVESTING DEFENDANT OF AUTHORITY OVER A VICTIM

Section 38 of the Sexual Offences Act 1956 as amended by the Guardianship   **10–31** Act 1973, s.17(8) states:

215

"(1)   On a person's conviction of an offence under section 10 of this Act against a girl under the age of eighteen, or of an offence under section 11 of this Act against a boy under that age, or of attempting to commit such an offence, the court may by order divest that person of all authority over the girl or boy.

(2)   An order divesting a person of authority over a girl or boy under the foregoing subsection may, if that person is the guardian of the girl or boy, remove that person from the guardianship.

(3)   An order under this section may appoint a person to be the guardian of the girl or boy during his or her minority or any less period.

(4)   An order under this section may be varied from time to time or rescinded by the High Court and, if made on conviction of an offence against a girl or boy who is a defective, may, so far as it has effect for any of the purposes of the Mental Health Act 1983, be rescinded either before or after the girl or boy has attained the age of eighteen."

H. CRIMINAL INJURIES

10–32 Congenital characteristics such as a permanent severe mental handicap resulting from an incestuous conception are not personal injuries within the meaning of the Criminal Injuries Compensation Scheme 1969. In *A's Curator Bonis v. Criminal Injuries Compensation Board, The Times*, January 24, 1997, a petition was made to the Court of Session on behalf of A who suffered such a mental handicap being conceived and born as the result of incestuous sexual intercourse. Her state was not an "injury" which term presupposed a pre-injury state which she had never enjoyed.

Chapter 11
The Mentally Disadvantaged

The mentally disadvantaged may be physically adult people with all the emotional needs and desires enjoyed by the rest of the adult population. They may also be particularly suggestible, easily manipulated and be very vulnerable. A small body of law exists which attempts to address this problem. Public concern has been expressed, however, at the limited sentencing powers available for offences which fall short of rape. Sexual intercourse with a defective carries only a two-year maximum sentence. A defective cannot give consent under sections 14(4) or 15(3) of the Sexual Offences Act 1956 to other sexual activity.

A. INTERCOURSE WITH A WOMAN WHO IS MENTALLY DISADVANTAGED

I. LAW

The Sexual Offences Act 1956, s.7 states: 11–01

"(1) It is an offence, subject to the exception mentioned in this section, for a man to have unlawful sexual intercourse with a woman who is a defective.
(2)   A man is not guilty of an offence under this section because he has unlawful sexual intercourse with a woman if he does not know and has no reason to suspect her to be a defective."

Section 45 defines the term "defective" as "a person suffering from a state   11–02
of arrested or incomplete development of mind which includes severe impairment of intelligence and social functioning within the meaning of the Mental Health Act 1959 (Sexual Offences Act 1956, s.45 as amended by the Mental

Health Act 1959, s.127(1) and the Mental Health (Amendment) Act 1982, s.3).

The test of severe impairment is measured against the standards of normal people: *R. v. Hall* (1987) 86 Cr.App.R. 159. The defendant H was the principal of a residential college for the education of profoundly mentally handicapped young people. The victim, A, was a young woman who had been a student at the college. She had a mental age of nine or 10, and an I.Q. of 53. The defendant had, behind locked doors, taught her how to masturbate, had assisted her to masturbate and on many occassions had himself masturbated her. He claimed the defence of consent to indecent assault. The defence submitted that in relation to other mentally handicapped people she suffered from a moderate impairment. It was held that the correct comparison was with normally developed people. The words severely impaired carried their ordinary meaning. Expert evidence, it is clear, is admissible to establish the extent of the victim's intelligence. The jury are, however, entitled to form their own conclusion. In this case there was disagreement between doctors called for the prosecution and for the defence as to the degree of A's impairment.

(a) Defence

11-03 There is a defence set out in subsection (2). It is submitted that it is for the defendant to prove the defence on a balance of probabilities. The test must be subjective and the defendant must show that he did not know, and had no reason to suspect that the woman was a defective: *R. v. Hudson* [1966] 1 Q.B. 448.

11-04 Women who are defectives are also protected by sections 9, 21, 27 and 29 of the Sexual Offences Act 1956:

(b) Procurement of defectives—section 9

"(1) It is an offence, subject to the exception mentioned in this section, for a person to procure a woman who is a defective to have unlawful sexual intercourse in any part of the world.

(2) A person is not guilty of an offence under this section because he procures a defective to have unlawful sexual intercourse, if he does not know and has no reason to suspect her to be a defective."

11-05 **(c) Abduction of a defective from parent or guardian—section 21 (as amended by section 108(4) and Sched. 12 of the Children Act 1989)**

"(1) It is an offence, subject to the exception mentioned in this section, for a person to take a woman who is a defective out of the possession of her parent or guardian against his will, if she is so taken with the intention that she shall have unlawful sexual intercourse with men or with a particular man.

(2) A person is not guilty of an offence under this section because he takes such a woman out of the possession of her parent or guardian

as mentioned above, if he does not know and has no reason to suspect her to be a defective.

(3) In this section "guardian" means "any person having parental responsibility for or care of the woman."

The use of the word "possession" is discussed in Chapter 4.

(d) Permitting a defective to use premises for intercourse—section 27   11–06

"(1) It is an offence, subject to the exception mentioned in this section, for a person who is the owner or occupier of any premises, or who has, or acts or assists in, the management or control of any premises, to induce or knowingly suffer a woman who is a defective to resort to or be on those premises for the purpose of having unlawful sexual intercourse with men or with a particular man.

(2) A person is not guilty of an offence under this section because he induces or knowingly suffers a defective to resort to or be on any premises for the purposes mentioned, if he does not know and has no reason to suspect her to be a defective."

(e) Causing or encouraging prostitution of a defective—section 29   11–07

"(1) It is an offence subject to the exception mentioned in this section, for a person to cause or encourage the prostitution in any part of the world of a woman who is a defective.

(2) A person is not guilty of an offence under this section because he causes or encourages the prostitution of such a woman, if he does not know and has no reason to suspect her to be a defective." (See also para. 12–64.)

II. CONSENT

Whether a woman who is mentally disadvantaged has sufficient under-   11–08
standing to give a valid consent to intercourse is a question of degree in every case.

If the woman is incapable of distinguishing between right and wrong or of exercising any judgment in the matter her consent to the intercourse is invalid and the correct charge will be rape: *R. v. Fletcher* (1859) Bell 63. In *R. v. Barratt* (1873) L.R. 2 C.C.R. 81, the complainant was found to be hardly capable of understanding anything said to her but would passively obey instructions. The defendant was convicted of rape.

Carrying out instructions in a docile way is not consent even when the woman is capable of distinguishing between right and wrong: *R. v. Pressy* (1876) 10 Cox C.C. 635.

The situation must, however, be distinguished from that where the woman   11–09
is an adult with strong but basic instincts. Although, in the terms used in the nineteenth century, she was "an idiot girl", she was quite capable of

recognising the defendant and of giving a valid consent to intercourse in *R. v. Fletcher* (1866) L.R. 1 C.C.R. 39.

B. SEXUAL INTERCOURSE WITH A PATIENT

11–10   An offence of having intercourse with a mental patient is created by section 128 of the Mental Health Act 1959 as amended by the Mental Health Act 1983 and the Registered Homes Act 1984:

11–11   "(1) Without prejudice to s.7 of the Sexual Offences Act 1956, it shall be an offence, subject to the exception mentioned in this section—
   (a) for a man who is an officer on the staff of or is otherwise employed in, or is one of the managers of, a hospital or mental nursing home to have unlawful sexual intercourse with a woman who is for the time being receiving treatment for mental disorder in that hospital or home, or to have such intercourse on the premises of which the hospital or home forms part, with a woman who is for the time being receiving such treatment there as an out-patient;
   (b) for a man to have unlawful sexual intercourse with a woman who is a mentally disordered patient and who is subject to his guardianship under the Mental Health Act 1983 or is otherwise in his custody or care under the Mental Health Act 1983 or in pursuance of arrangements under Part III of the National Assistance Act 1948, or the National Health Service Act 1977, or as a resident in a residential care home within the meaning of Part I of the Registered Homes Act 1984.
  (2) It shall not be an offence under this section for a man to have sexual intercourse with a woman if he does not know and has no reason to suspect her to be a mentally disordered patient.
  (3) Any person guilty of an offence under this section shall be liable on conviction on indictment to imprisonment for a term not exceeding two years.
  (4) No proceedings shall be instituted for an offence under this section except by or with the consent of the Director of Public Prosecutions.
  (5) This section shall be construed as one with the Sexual Offences Act 1956; and s.47 of that Act (which relates to the proof of exceptions) shall apply to the exception mentioned in this section."

11–12   The reference to unlawful sexual intercourse with a woman, is now extended by section 1(4) of the Sexual Offences Act 1967 to include a reference to committing buggery or an act of gross indecency with another man.

11–13   Section 131 of the 1959 Act states that a local social services authority may institute proceedings for the offences, but without prejudice to any provisions in that part of the Act requiring the consent of the DPP for the institution of such proceedings contained in section 128(4).

Sentencing guidelines

In *R. v. Goodwin* (unreported, May 19, 1994), D, a state enrolled psychiatric   **11–14** nurse discovered that he and C, a inpatient, had a mutual interest in sadomasochistic relationships. They went out on a number of occasions and had intercourse accompanied by bondage and beatings. The relationship continued when she became an outpatient. *Held*: this was as gross, deliberate and wicked breach of trust as one might regret to see. A maximum penalty of two years' imprisonment was not too excessive.

Part IV
COMMERCIALISATION OF SEX

Chapter 12
Prostitution

Although being a prostitute is not illegal there are a number of statutory   **12–01**
offences concerning prostitution, relating not only to the prostitute herself or
himself, but also to people who encourage the continuance of the industry
and who profit from it.

A. OFFENCES RELATING TO THE PROSTITUTE

I. STREET OFFENCES ACT 1959

Section 1: loitering or soliciting for purposes of prostitution: "(1) It shall be   **12–02**
an offence for a common prostitute to loiter or solicit in a street or public
place for the purpose of prostitution."

Sentencing guidelines

A person guilty of an offence contrary to section 1(1) of the Street Offences   **12–03**
Act 1959 is liable on summary conviction to a fine of an amount not
exceeding level 2 on the standard scale (as defined in s. 75 of the Criminal
Justice Act 1982) or, for an offence committed after a previous conviction, to
a fine of an amount not exceeding level 3 on that scale (s.1(2)). Since the
offence is not imprisonable, the courts are restricted in their sentencing
options to a fine, discharge or probation order.

(a) Prostitute

A prostitute is defined as a woman who offers her body for acts of lewdness   **12–04**
for reward. There need be no act or offer of an act of ordinary sexual
intercourse (*R. v. De Munck* [1918] 1 K.B. 635), any form of lewdness will
be sufficient and includes active forms of indecency, such as masturbation of
a male client (*R. v. Webb* [1964] 1 Q.B. 357), as well as passive. It seems that
proof of payment for these acts is not necessary (*Winter v. Woolfe* [1931] 1
K.B. 549), nor does the act have to take place (*R. v. Eric McFarlane* (1994)

99 Cr.App.R. 8, C.A. where it was held that a "clipper", *i.e.* one who offered the sexual service but pocketed the reward without providing or even intending to provide the service, was a prostitute nonetheless, albeit a dishonest one).

The elements which constitute a prostitute are the offering, for lewdness, for reward.

12–05 Men cannot be prostitutes for the purposes of the Street Offences Act. In *DPP v. Bull* [1995] 1 Cr.App.R. 413, QBD, it was held that notwithstanding the use of the words "a person" and "anyone" in section 1(2) and (3) of the Act, section 1(1) of that Act was confined to women since it "seems improbable that Parliament intended to create a new male offence which was but subtly different from the extant section 32 of the Sexual Offences Act 1956" (*per* Mann L.J. at 415).

12–06 A common prostitute is a woman who offers herself to men generally for acts of lewdness and not merely to one or two: *R. v. Morris-Lowe* (1984) 80 Cr.App.R. 114, C.A. This aspect of the offence is usually proved by showing that the woman has continued with conduct for which she has previously been cautioned (see section 2, below).

(b) Loitering

12–07 Loitering has no legal definition, but more than the dictionary definition of "standing or acting aimlessly" must be intended since the Act requires that the loitering is for the purpose of prostitution. Without an admission from the prostitute herself, the *actus reus* is normally proved with evidence of the woman's behaviour, such as the standing by the road side or on a street corner and staring into passing vehicles, especially those containing lone males, combined with exaggerated body movements. Her manner of dress and possession of condoms can also assist the prosecution case.

(c) Soliciting

12–08 Soliciting can involve both active and passive conduct on the part of the prostitute. In *Behrendt v. Burridge* (1976) 63 Cr.App.R. 202, D.C., the respondent was seen for some 50 minutes by police officers sitting motionless on a stool in a downstairs bay window of a house. She was wearing a low-cut top and a mini-skirt and the window was lit by a red light. Her purpose was to advertise to passers-by in the street that she was available for sexual services in those premises. During the time that she was under observation, two men entered the premises and one paid money for sexual intercourse. At no time was she seen to communicate actively with anyone in the street. The Justices upheld a submission of no case and dismissed the information, holding that her conduct could only be regarded as an explicit form of advertising and not soliciting within section 1. On a successful appeal by the prosecution, it was held that although the respondent had not actively approached prospective clients, her presence at the window in those circumstances was sufficient to constitute soliciting in the sense of tempting or alluring such clients to enter for the purposes of prostitution.

The prostitute must, however, be physically present in order to solicit: in **12–09** *Weisz v. Monahan* [1962] 1 All E.R. 664 it was held that a prostitute who only displays an advertisement indicating that she is available as a prostitute is not soliciting.

Given the case law on soliciting, especially *Behrendt v. Burridge* (above), **12–10** there appears to be an overlap between actions which constitute loitering and those which fall within soliciting. A common prostitute stood on a street, dressed or posing in a certain way for example, is no different from the prostitute sat in a bay window and is therefore guilty of soliciting, albeit that it is more usual for the police to charge her with loitering and only charge the girl with soliciting when she makes a verbal offer.

(d) Street or public place

The final element of the section 1(1) offence is that the loitering or soliciting **12–11** must be in a street or public place. "Street" by virtue of section 1(4) includes any bridge, road, lane, footway, subway, square, court, alley or passage, whether a thoroughfare or not, which is for the time being open to the public; and the doorways and entrances of premises abutting on a street, and any ground adjoining and open to a street. *Behrendt v. Burridge* (above) and *Smith v. Hughes* [1960] 2 All E.R. 859 further extend section 1(4) by holding that a prostitute who is on a balcony or in a window of a house adjoining the street or public place comes within section 1(1).

"Public place" is not specifically defined but should, it is submitted, be **12–12** given a definition in accordance with that commonly found in statue and case law, namely "any place to which the public have access (whether on payment or otherwise)" (*cf.* the Licensing Act 1902, s. 8; the Indecent Displays (Control) Act 1981, s. 1(3); the Prevention of Crime Act 1953, s. 4; *R. v. Collinson* (1931) 23 Cr.App.R. 49, in which a field to which the public were admitted for one day was held to be a public place; *Elkins v. Cartlidge* [1947] 1 All E.R. 829, where an enclosure at the rear of an inn, entered through a open gateway, and in which cars were parked was held to be a public place; and *Glynn v. Simmonds* [1952] 2 All E.R. 47, in which it was held that Tattersall's enclosure at a racecourse was a "place of public resort" notwithstanding a charge for admission and a right to exclude any person).

(e) Power of arrest

Section 1(3) gives a constable the power to arrest without warrant anyone he **12–13** finds in a street or public place and suspects, with reasonable cause to be committing a section 1(1) offence. An offence under section 1 of the 1959 Act is, by virtue of the National Police Records (Recordable Offences) Regulations 1985, (S.I. 1985 No. 1941, amended by S.I. 1989 No. 694), a recordable offence.

(f) Cautioning policy

Section 2 of the Street Offences Act 1959 enables a woman who has been **12–14** cautioned to apply to the court for the entry to be deleted from any record.

This follows the introduction by the Commissioner of Police of the Metropolis of a system of cautioning (which requires the co-operation of the women: *Collins v. Wilcox* [1984] 3 All E.R. 374), whereby a woman who has not previously been convicted of loitering or soliciting for the purpose of prostitution will not be charged with a section 1(1) offence unless she has two recorded police cautions.

12-15   By virtue of section 2(1), where a woman has been cautioned by a constable in respect of her conduct in a street or public place, that if she persists in such conduct it may result in her being charged with an offence under section 1 of the 1959 Act, she may not later than 14 clear days (*i.e.* 14 complete intervening days) afterwards apply to a magistrates' court for an order directing that there is to be no entry made in respect of that caution in any record maintained by the police of those so cautioned and that any such entry already made is to be expunged; the court shall make the order unless satisfied that on the occasion when she was cautioned she was loitering or soliciting in a street or public place for the purpose of prostitution.

12-16   The application must be by way of complaint against the chief officer of police for the area in which the woman is cautioned or against such officer of police as he may designate for the purpose in relation to that area or any part of it (s. 2(2)). Unless rules are made to the contrary under the Magistrates' Court Act 1980, s. 144, on the hearing of the complaint, the procedure is as if it were the complaint of the police officer against the woman so that the officer must establish his case before the woman is called upon to reply. Sections 55 to 57 of the 1980 Act which relates to the non–attendance of the parties to a complaint, does not apply.

12-17   The proceedings will be heard and determined *in camera*, unless the woman requests otherwise (s. 2(3)) and it is suggested that unless the woman is represented that she should be informed of her rights in this respect.

II. Sexual Offences Act 1956

(a) Solicitation by men

12-18   Section 32 states: "It is an offence for a man persistently to solicit or importune in a public place for immoral purposes."

Sentencing guidelines

12-19   This offence can be tried either on indictment, in which case it carries a maximum of two years' imprisonment, or summarily where the penalty is a maximum of six months' imprisonment and/or a fine not exceeding level five (Sexual Offences Act 1956, Sched. 2, Pt II and Criminal Justice Act 1982, s. 37).

(b) Power of arrest

12-20   Section 41 of the 1956 Act gives anyone the power of arrest without warrant in respect of a person found committing a section 32 offence and a constable the power of arrest without warrant in accordance with section 25 of the

Police and Criminal Evidence Act 1984 (where the general arrest conditions apply).

(c) Extent of section 32

Section 32 clearly relates only to men and, as stated previously, it is the   12–21
existence of this section which persuaded the Queen's Bench Division in *DPP v. Bull* [1995] 1 Cr. App.R. 413 to hold that section 1 of the Street Offences Act 1959 is exclusively for female prostitutes. The main differences between the law relating to female prostitutes and that which applies to their male counterparts is that section 32 does not require the man to be a prostitute or the purpose to be prostitution; it does not encompass loitering; and "street" is excluded. However, it introduces the requirement that the soliciting must be persistent and the purpose immoral.

(d) Persistence

Persistence is a pre-requisite for the soliciting or importuning and means a   12–22
degree of repetition of either more than one invitation to one person, or a series of invitations to different people. It has been held in *Dale v. Smith* [1967] 1 W.L.R. 700 that two separate acts of importuning within the period named in the information or indictment are sufficient to render the importuning persistent.

The case law relating to soliciting applies equally to section 32 of the 1956   12–23
Act as it does to section 1 of the 1959 Act. It must involve physical presence (*Burge v.DPP* [1962] 1 All E.R. 666; *Weiss v.Monahan* [1962] 1 All E.R. 664), but it may be by action unaccompanied by words (see *Behrendt v.Burridge*, above). It is suggested therefore that although section 32 specifically excludes loitering, behaviour commonly associated with female prostitutes loitering, such as standing on street corners, can in fact be applied to a male soliciting, provided it is readily apparent that his presence on the street is to advertise his availability for a immoral purpose. His continued presence, it is submitted can amount to persistence especially if, as is often common with the female prostitute, a specific movement or action is made whenever a potential customer approaches.

"Importune" has not been given a legal definition and therefore the   12–24
dictionary definition of persistently request or harass with persistent demands, must be relied upon. In *Dale v. Smith* (above) it was found by the Divisional Court that an invitation to look at sexy photographs was an act of importuning. The Queen's Bench Division in *Field v. Chapman, The Times*, October 9,1953 decided that there is no real distinction to be drawn between importuning and soliciting and that has continued to be good law.

(e) Public place

"Public place" in section 32, as in section 1 of the Street Offences Act 1959,   12–25
does not benefit from interpretation but, it is submitted, the same interpretation should apply for both, there being no reason to do otherwise.

(f) Immoral purpose

12-26   The final requirement of section 32 is that the importuning or soliciting must be for an immoral purpose. There is no statutory use of the phrase "for immoral purposes" elsewhere than in section 32 of the Sexual Offences Act 1956 and its predecessor, the Vagrancy Act of 1898.

12-27   In *Crook v.Edmondson* [1966] Q.B.D. 81, Winn L.J. held at page 90 that:

> "the words 'immoral purposes' in their ordinary meaning connote in a wide and general sense all purposes involving conduct which has the property of being wrong rather than right in the judgment of the majority of contemporary fellow-citizens. ... However, ... Parliament cannot be supposed to have used those words in their general sense, as comprising all wrong conduct, in a statute relating solely to sexual offences: soliciting persons to commit non-sexual crime is dealt with by the law relating to accessories before the fact or specifically by statute. ... It seems to me to follow that the 'immoral purposes' here in question must be immoral in respect of sexual conduct."

In *Crook v. Edmondson*, the defendant had been soliciting female prostitutes and the point of law raised by case stated was whether the persistent importuning by a man of a woman for the purpose of having sexual intercourse with him was an offence under section 32 of the 1956 Act. Winn L.J. and Lord Parker C.J. considered that it was not, Winn L.J. holding (at 91) that "in their context in the [Vagrancy] Act of 1898 the words 'soliciting for immoral purposes' may well .... have been intended to relate not merely to soliciting for homosexual intimacies but also to the soliciting of customers for prostitutes. ... In my judgment, such a context of subject—matter of trading in or exploiting prostitution even more plainly displayed by sections 22–31 and 33–36 of the Sexual Offences Act 1956 must ... produce a controlling effect on section 32" and that the justices were correct to limit the section to homosexual activity. Sachs L.J. dissented on the grounds that while he agreed that the immoral purposes should be limited to sexual purposes there was no basis for further restricting it to homosexual practices.

(g) Later cases

12-28   Subsequent cases, while never going so far as overruling *Crook v. Edmunson* have nevertheless undermined the reasoning of the majority and tended to agree with the dissenting judgment. In 1977, the Court of Appeal held in *R.v.Dodd* (1978) 66 Cr.App.R. 87, in which the appellant had solicited 14-year-old girls, that *Crook v. Edmundson* could be distinguished on the grounds that Winn L.J. was clearly "seeking to draw some distinction between what is immoral and what is criminal and not very surprisingly came to the conclusion that not all things which are immoral are to be regarded as criminal". Since the appellant was soliciting for the purpose of sexual intercourse with girls of the age of 14, then if the argument is advanced that in order for there to be a conviction under section 32 what is done must not only be immoral but also a criminal offence, on the facts, the requirements of section 32 are satisfied.

In *R v. Ford* [1978] 1 All E.R. 1129 the applicant had stood outside a   **12–29**
public lavatory and persistently suggested to another man (who happened to be a police officer) that he should go to the applicant's flat to take part in homosexual practices. Following conviction, he sought leave to appeal on the ground that section 1(1) of the Sexual Offences Act 1967 had legalised homosexual acts in private between consenting adults and therefore his actions could not be regarded as importuning for immoral purposes. The Court of Appeal held that while it was correct to apply Winn L.J.'s test in *Crook v. Edmondson* in so far as immoral purposes must be restricted to immoral sexual purposes, the phrases "immoral purposes" and "offence against the law" cover entirely different areas. It may be that the areas overlap, but they are different and the fact that the conduct contemplated by the applicant had now ceased to have the stamp of criminality does not make the slightest difference.

This was further reinforced in *R v. Gray* (1982) 74 Cr.App.R. 324, where   **12–30**
the appellant having importuned others then approached the witness (again a police officer) and invited him back to the appellant's flat to stay the night. The Court of Appeal held that had Parliament intended to exempt homo-sexual activity between consenting adults over 21 from the ambit of section 32 of the 1956 Act, then it would have made the appropriate amendment in 1967 when it passed the Sexual Offences Act. The Lord Chief Justice said (at 328) that:

> "these provisions are aimed at the importuning, rather than at the contem-plated acts, and that importuning for acts which are to take place in private may be as offensive to the public at large as importuning for acts which are to take place in public. .... It cannot be that from 1967 onwards it was the intention of Parliament (or even within its contemplation) that, whereas soliciting in public for the purposes of heterosexual prostitution was to remain unlawful (under section 1 of the Street Offences Act 1959), it would (or might) henceforth be lawful for some homosexuals, even for some homosexual prostitutes, to solicit in public."

The courts in both *R v. Ford* and *R v. Gray* also agreed that the proper approach in a case of this nature was for the judge to rule on whether the act complained of could amount to an offence and having so ruled for the jury to decide whether the conduct involved immoral purposes.

In *R v. Goddard* (1991) 92 Cr.App. R. 185 the dicta of Sachs L.J. (who   **12–31**
gave the dissenting judgment in *Crook v. Edmondson*) was approved. In this case the appellant had importuned first Miss B (aged 28) and then some 15 minutes later Miss R (aged 14) for sexual intercourse. The appellant argued that importuning Miss B for consensual sexual intercourse was not immoral and, although clearly importuning Miss R was immoral, due to her age, remove the conduct towards Miss B from the equation and there has not been any persistence. The Court of Appeal dismissing the appeal, approved the direction of the trial judge to the jury namely that "in deciding whether it was for sexually immoral purposes, as a matter of law you should apply the

standards of ordinary right—thinking men and women living in England in 1989 and 1990, considering all the circumstances in which the overtures were made and the nature of those overtures".

12–32   Finally, in *R.v.Kirkup* (1993) 96 Cr.App.R. 352, a case of importuning in a public lavatory, the judge at first instance had directed the jury that any form of sexual contact, sexual activity or sexual congress was an immoral purpose. The Court of Appeal held that that was a misdirection by the judge and fully endorsed the Court's decisions in *Gray* and *Ford*. However, Staughton L.J. said that the court did not find it altogether satisfactory that it should be for the jury to decide whether or not a purpose is immoral since different juries and different magistrates may arrive at differing conclusions in cases which basically involve similar sets of facts.

III. Sexual Offences Act 1985

12–33   Section 1(1) states that:

"a man commits an offence if he solicits a woman (or different women) for the purpose of prostitution—
(a)   from a motor vehicle while it is in a street or public place; or
(b)   in a street or public place while in the immediate vicinity of a motor vehicle that he has just got out of or off, persistently or in such manner or in such circumstances as to be likely to cause annoyance to the woman (or any of the women) solicited, or nuisance to other persons in the neighbourhood."

Sentencing guidelines

12–34   The offence is summary only and punishable on conviction with a fine not exceeding level 3 on the standard scale (s.1(2)).

(a) Soliciting

12–35   Soliciting for the purpose of prostitution refers to soliciting the woman for the purpose of obtaining her services as a prostitute (s.4(1)).

(b) Nuisance

12–36   The prosecution need only prove that there was a likelihood of nuisance to other persons—it is not necessary for evidence to be called that a specific individual was in fact caused nuisance or annoyance. Justices may also use their local knowledge concerning the presence of prostitutes in a particular neighbourhood and the fact that the area is heavily populated and residential: *Paul v. DPP* (1989) 90 Cr.App.R. 173 and *Cheeseman v. DPP* (1991 93 Cr.App.R. 145).

(c) Persistence

12–37   For persistent soliciting the prosecution must prove that there was more than one act of soliciting, although it can be for example two invitations to the same person *R.v. Goddard* (1991) 92 Cr.App.R. 185) or one invitation to different people (*R. v. Tuck* [1994] Crim.L.R. 375). There must be some positive indication by physical act or words that the defendant required the services of the prostitute—driving a car round and round late at night down a street frequented by prostitutes was held not to constitute soliciting: *Darroch v. DPP* [1990] Crim.L.R. 814.

Where the prosecution allege that the conduct complained of was beckoning, evidence that the defendant had earlier been seen in the company of a prostitute in that area may be relevant to rebut innocent explanation: *Darroch v. DPP*, above. **12–38**

In *Ollerenshaw v. DPP, The Independent*, January 6, 1992, the woman whom the appellant had allegedly solicited had called out to him, offering her services as a prostitute. He had accepted and invited her to his car. His conviction was quashed by the Divisional Court on the ground that "soliciting" implies begging a favour, an element of importuning or asking and that given the existing agreement between them for sexual intercourse, the appellant's act of inviting the woman to his car was not soliciting. However, the court said that its decision did not mean that if the prostitute makes the first approach that the man cannot be guilty of soliciting thereafter, provided that there is some importuning or asking on his part. **12–39**

(d) Motor vehicle and street

"Motor vehicle" has the same meaning as in the Road Traffic Act 1988 (s.3). **12–40**

"Street" includes any bridge, road, lane, footway, subway, square, court, alley or passage, whether a thoroughfare or not, which is for the time being open to the public; and the doorways and entrances of premises abutting on a street, and any ground adjoining and open to a street, shall be treated as forming part of a street (s.4(4)).

Section 2 of the Act is in similar terms to section 1 but without the vehicular requirement: "A man commits an offence if in a street or public place he persistently solicits a woman (or different women) for the purpose of prostitution" (s.2(1)). **12–41**

The offence is summary only and punishable on conviction with a fine not exceeding level 3 on the standard scale (s.2(2)).

Section 4(2) states that "man" also encompasses "boy" and equally, "woman" encompasses "girl", in other words, the sections do not limit the commission of the offences to adults. The masculine gender, where used, does not, however, include the feminine and vice versa, so that the offences can only be committed by males soliciting females (s.4(4)). **12–42**

B. OFFENCES RELATING TO PROSTITUTION

Offences of this nature are found within the Sexual Offences Act 1956 and the Sexual Offences Act 1967 and cover persons causing the prostitution of women/girls and profiting from their (and male) prostitution. **12–43**

I. Causing And Procuring Prostitution — Sexual Offences Act 1956

12-44 The sections which cover this aspect are sections 22, 23, 24, 28, and 29. All the offences under these sections are triable only on indictment.

(a) Section 22

12-45 Section 22(1) states:

"It is an offence for a person—
(a) to procure a woman to become, in any part of the world, a common prostitute; or
(b) to procure a woman to leave the United Kingdom, intending her to become an inmate of or frequent a brothel elsewhere; or
(c) to procure a woman to leave her usual place of abode in the United Kingdom intending her to become an inmate of or frequent a brothel in any part of the world for the purposes of prostitution."

(i) Sentencing guidelines

12-46 Offences contrary to section 22 of the 1956 Act are on conviction punishable by a term of imprisonment not exceeding two years (s.37 and Sched.2).

(ii) Procure

12-47 Procure has been defined as "to produce by endeavour" (*Att.-Gen.'s Reference (No.1 of 1975)* [1975] Q.B. 773), and "to obtain by care and effort" (*re Royal Victoria Pavilion, Ramsgate* [1961] Ch.581). *In R. v. Broadfoot* (1977) 64 Cr.App.R. 71, it was suggested that procuring could be regarded as bringing about a course of conduct which the woman in question would not have embarked upon spontaneously or of her own volition. In this case, the appellant was concerned in the running of massage parlours and advertised for girls to work in them. Amongst applicants for the job were two women journalists whose only interest was in the carrying out an investigation into massage parlours. Each woman, when interviewed was told by the appellant that if she provided "extra services" she would be well paid for them, the "extra services" being acts of prostitution. Neither woman was prepared to do this. The appellant was charged with two counts of attempting to procure a woman to become a common prostitute and was convicted. On appeal, the appellant contended that the judge had wrongly directed the jury by saying: (i) that "procure" meant to "recruit" and (ii) that the mention of possible earnings to the women without pressure of persuasion was incapable of amounting to an attempt to procure. It was held, dismissing the appeal: (i) that "procure" was a word in common usage and had no special meaning in the context of section 22. A jury had to use their common sense when interpreting the word and there was nothing wrong in the judge using the expression "recruit" when directing them on the issue of whether there had been a procurement or attempted procurement; (ii) that an offer of a large sum of money for undertaking tasks could, in the absence of any other pressure, amount to persuasion and therefore an attempt to procure; whether there had been such persuasion was a matter for the jury to decide on the evidence before them.

It is necessary that the woman be persuaded, since procuration could be **12–48** negatived by evidence showing that she acted of her own free will.

If the woman is already a common prostitute, then she cannot become one and be procured for the purposes of this section. The defendant's belief that, as to whether the woman is or is not a prostitute, is relevant since if he genuinely believes that she is a prostitute, and has reasonable grounds for that belief, he cannot be guilty of procuring or attempting to procure her to become one. The question of whether the belief is genuine is a matter for the jury: *R. v. Brown* [1984] 3 All E.R. 1013. Conversely, if the woman is in fact a common prostitute, but the defendant believes that she is not, he can be convicted of attempt even though commission of the full offence is impossible.

The intention necessary for an offence of attempting to procure is the same **12–49** as that necessary for an offence under section 22(1)(a). An expression of intention or mere idle threat does not constitute an attempt: *R v. Landow* (1913) 77 J.P. 364; *R. v. Woods* (1930) 46 T.L.R 401.

The term "common prostitute" has been considered in paragraph 12.06, **12–50** above. As to what constitutes a brothel, see paragraph 12.94, below.

(iii) Jurisdiction

An offence under this section is a continuing offence which the English courts **12–51** have jurisdiction to try if any part of it takes place within their jurisdiction: *R. v. Mackenzie and Higginson* (1910) 75 J.P. 159.

(b) Section 23

Section 23(1) states: **12–52**

"It is an offence for a person to procure a girl under the age of twenty-one to have unlawful sexual intercourse in any part of the world with a third person."

(i) Sentencing guidelines

Offences contrary to section 23 of the 1956 Act are on conviction punishable **12–53** by a term of imprisonment not exceeding two years (s.37 and Sched.2).

(ii) Unlawful sexual intercourse

Unlawful sexual intercourse means illicit sexual intercourse, *i.e.* outside the **12–54** bond of marriage: *R. v. Chapman* [1959] 1 Q.B. 100.

Before the defendant can be convicted of this offence, it must be proved **12–55** that the sexual intercourse occurred. If intercourse is not proved to have taken place, then the defendant can be guilty of attempt procurement if it is proved that he procured her with the intention that it should: *R. v. Johnson* [1964] 2 Q.B. 404.

(c) Section 24

12–56   Section 24(1) states:

> "It is an offence for a person to detain a woman against her will on
> any premises with the intention that she shall have unlawful sexual
> intercourse with men or with a particular man, or to detain a woman
> against her will in a brothel.
>
> (2)   Where a woman is on any premises for the purpose of having
> unlawful sexual intercourse or is in a brothel, a person shall be
> deemed for the purpose of the foregoing subsection to detain her
> there if, with the intention of compelling or inducing her to remain
> there, he either withholds from her her clothes or any other property
> belonging to her or threatens her with legal proceedings in the event
> of her taking away clothes provided for her by him or on his
> directions.
>
> (3)   A woman shall not be liable to any legal proceedings, whether civil or
> criminal, for taking away or being found in possession of any clothes
> she needed to enable her to leave premises on which she was for the
> purpose of having unlawful sexual intercourse or to leave a
> brothel."

Sentencing guidelines

12–57   Offences contrary to section 24 of the 1956 Act are on conviction punishable
by a term of imprisonment not exceeding two years (s.37 and Sched.2).

(d) Section 43

12–58   Section 24 is supported by section 43 of the Act which gives a power to
search for and remove a woman detained. Section 43(1) states:

> "Where it is made to appear by information on oath laid before a justice of
> the peace by a woman's parent, relative or guardian, or by any other
> person who in the opinion of the justice is acting in the woman's interests,
> that there is reasonable cause to suspect—
>
> (a)   that the woman is detained in any place within the justice's
> jurisdiction in order that she may have unlawful sexual inter-
> course with men or with a particular man; and
>
> (b)   that either she is so detained against her will, or she is under the
> age of sixteen or is a defective, or she is under the age of eighteen
> and is so detained against the will of her parent or guardian;
>
> then the justice may issue a warrant authorising a constable to search for
> her and to take her and detain her in a place of safety until she can be
> brought before a justice of the peace.
>
> (2)   A justice before whom a woman is brought in pursuance of the
> foregoing subsection may cause her to be delivered up to her parent
> or guardian, or otherwise dealt with as circumstances may permit
> and require.
>
> (3)   A constable authorised by a warrant under this section to search for

a woman may enter (if need be, by force) any premises specified in the warrant, and remove the woman from the premises.

(4) A constable executing a warrant issued under this section shall be accompanied by the person applying for the warrant, if that person so desires, unless the justice issuing it otherwise directs.

(5) In this section 'guardian' means any person having parental responsibility for or care of the woman."

No action will lie for inducing a justice to issue a search warrant, if the information was given bona fide, without malicious desire to injure the person proceeded against, and was not based upon false statements intended to mislead the justice: *Hope v. Evered* (1886) 17 Q.B.D. 338.

(e) Section 28

Section 28(1) states: **12–59**

"It is an offence for a person to cause or encourage the prostitution of, or the commission of unlawful sexual intercourse with, or of an indecent assault on a girl under the age of sixteen for whom he is responsible.

(2) Where a girl has become a prostitute, or has had unlawful sexual intercourse, or has been indecently assaulted, a person shall be deemed for the purposes of this section to have caused or encouraged it, if he knowingly allowed her to consort with, or to enter or continue in the employment of, any prostitute or person of known immoral character.

(3) The persons who are to be treated for the purposes of this section as responsible for a girl are (subject to subsection (4) of this section)—
  (a) her parents;
  (b) any person who is not a parent of hers but who has parental responsibility for her; and
  (c) any person who has care of her.

(4) An individual falling within subsection (3)(a) or (b) of this section is not to be treated as responsible for a girl if—
  (a) a residence order under the Children Act 1989 is in force with respect to her and he is not named in the order as the person with whom she is to live; or
  (b) a care order under that Act is in force with respect to her.

(5) If, on a charge of an offence against a girl under this section, the girl appears to the court to have been under the age of sixteen at the time of the offence charged, she shall be presumed for the purposes of this section to have been so, unless the contrary is proved."

Note that there is no requirement under the section for the girl to become a "common" prostitute.

(i) Sentencing guidelines

Offences contrary to section 28 of the 1956 Act are on conviction punishable   **12–60**
by a term of imprisonment not exceeding two years (s.37 and Sched.2).

(ii) Encouragement

12–61　If a person is present and knows that his acts are encouraging indecency, and is in control of the situation and knows that indecency is likely to occur, then that has been held to be capable of being encouragement: *R. v. Ralphs* (1913) 9 Cr.App R. 86. Where, as in *R. v. Drury* (1974) 60 Cr.App.R. 195, a man plies a girl with alcohol, knowing that it will enable another to engage in familiarities with her, he can be held to encourage the resulting indecent assault. However, "knowingly allowing" must be such a permission as would be deemed to be "causing or encouraging"—mere negligence is not sufficient: *R. v. Chainey* [1914] 1 K.B. 137.

(iii) Extent of offence

12–62　The offence can only be committed by a person who falls within subsections (3) and (4) and whether a person has such custody, charge or care is a question of fact for the jury: *R. v. Drury*, above.

12–63　In *Gillick v. West Norfolk and Wisbech Area Health Authority* [1986] A.C. 112, the court had to consider whether a doctor who prescribes contraceptive advice or treatment to a girl under 16 is guilty of an offence contrary to section 28. It was held that he is not guilty because: (a) the girl is not in the ad hoc care of the doctor; (b) the bona fide exercise of clinical judgment is inconsistent with the requisite *mens rea* for the offence; and (c) the doctor will not have the particularity of knowledge required to make him a party to the offence.

(f) Section 29

12–64　Section 29(1) states:

> "It is an offence subject to the exception mentioned in this section, for a person to cause or encourage the prostitution in any part of the world of a woman who is a defective.
>
> (2)　A person is not guilty of an offence under this section because he causes or encourages the prostitution of such a woman, if he does not know and has no reason to suspect her to be a defective."

(i) Sentencing guidelines

12–65　Offences contrary to section 29 of the 1956 Act are on conviction punishable by a term of imprisonment not exceeding two years (s.37 and Sched.2).

(ii) Defective

12–66　A "defective" is defined in section 45 to mean a person suffering from a state of arrested or incomplete development of mind which includes severe impairment of intelligence and social functioning within the meaning of the Mental Health Act 1959. "Severe mental impairment" means a state of arrested or incomplete development of mind which includes severe impairment of intelligence and social functioning and is associated with abnormally aggressive or seriously irresponsible conduct on the part of the person concerned: Mental

Health Act 1983, s.1. Severe impairment is measured against the standard of normal persons: *R. v. Hall* (1987) 86 Cr.App.R. 159.

(iii) Statutory defence

The burden of proving the exception in subsection (2) lies with the defendant   **12–67**
(s.47) and can be discharged on the balance of probabilities: *R. v. Carr-Briant* [1943] K.B. 607.

II. PROFITING FROM PROSTITUTION

Section 30 of the Sexual Offences Act 1956 and section 5 of the Sexual   **12–68**
Offences Act 1967 deal with living off the earnings of prostitution—both
female prostitutes (s.30) and male prostitutes (s.5). The section 30 offence
can only be committed by men, the female equivalent is section 31 of the
1956 Act—a woman exercising control over a prostitute for gain. An offence
under section 5 of the 1967 Act can be committed by either sex. In *R. v. Tan
and others* [1983] Q.B. 1053, it was held that a person's gender is that at
birth irrespective of a subsequent sex-change operation.

Offences under the three sections are triable either way.

(a) Section 30

The Sexual Offences Act 1956, s.30(1) states: **12–69**

"It is an offence for a man knowingly to live wholly or in part on the
earnings of prostitution.

(2)   For the purposes of this section a man who lives with or is habitually
in the company of a prostitute, or who exercised control, direction or
influence over a prostitute's movements in a way which shows he is
aiding, abetting or compelling her prostitution with others, shall be
presumed to be knowingly living on the earnings of prostitution,
unless he proves the contrary."

(i) Sentencing guidelines

Offences contrary to section 30 of the 1956 Act are punishable, on summary   **12–70**
conviction with a term of imprisonment not exceeding six months and/or a
fine not exceeding the statutory maximum; and on conviction on indictment
with a term of imprisonment not exceeding seven years: s.37 of and Sched.2
to the 1956 Act.

The guideline case for sentencing is *R. v. Farrugia* (1979) 69 Cr.App.R.
108, where it was said that the crucial factor is whether there is any evidence
of coercion, either physical or mental, of the prostitute involved, or corruption. Where there is evidence of coercion or corruption, Lawton L.J. said that
a sentence exceeding two years was appropriate. *Farrugia* was followed in *R.
v. Hall* (1987) 9 Cr.App.R.(S.) 121, where the defendant, the landlord of
premises used by prostitutes, had a three-year sentence reduced to 18
months, in the absence of coercion or corruption. In *R. v. Smyle* (1990) 12
Cr.App.R.(S.) 258, the defendant had received £10,000 during 14 months

from an established prostitute, using the money to support his drug habit; there was no evidence of physical oppression or corruption and two years' imprisonment was reduced to 15 months. In *R. v. Smith* (1995) 16 Cr.App.R.(S.) the appellant had his sentence of 15 months reduced to 10 months since he had only lived with the prostitute for two-and-a-half months and the woman had been a prostitute for some time. In *R. v. Thomas* (1983) 5 Cr.App.R.(S.) 138 the Court of Appeal upheld a three-year sentence since the offender had a history of similar offending.

For a defendant who operated an escort agency, 12 months was considered appropriate: *R. v. Gazzar* (1986) 8 Cr.App.R.(S.) 182. In *R. v. Luke* (1980) 2 Cr.App.R.(S.) 232 the defendant received a reduction in sentence from six months to three months for managing two massage parlours which offered masturbation and oral sex. However, in *R. v. Smith* (1993) 14 Cr.App.R.(S.) 708 the defendant's sentence of two years' imprisonment was upheld—Beldham L.J. accepted that there was no violence or coercion used and that the defendant was of good character, but held that he was a mature man who deliberately set up a brothel and a call–girl service involving some 44 prostitutes and that the sentence was not therefore excessive.

(ii) Evidential burden for the prosecution

12–71   The prosecution must prove that at the relevant time the woman was acting as a prostitute: *R. v. Wilson* (1984) 78 Cr.App.R. 247; *R. v. Grizzle* [1991] Crim.L.R. 553. The definition of a prostitute is dealt with in paragraph 12.04, above.

(iii) Evidential guidelines

12–72   The wording of section 30(1) and in particular, that a man need knowingly to live only in part on the earnings of a prostitute, is such that a number of people could be caught by the section since a prostitute needs the same goods and services as any other member of society, *i.e.* that of a grocer, doctor or landlord. Clearly, the legislature could not have intended that everyone who supplied a prostitute with anything should be prosecuted, although it has been left to the courts to set the parameters.

12–73   From the leading cases have emerged certain guidelines, the presence or absence of which may assist a jury in determining guilt or innocence:

Trading in prostitution. In *Calvert v. Mayes* [1954] 1 All E.R. 41 the respondent visited from October 1952 to April 1953 certain public houses known to be frequented by prostitutes. He allowed his car to be used for the purposes of prostitution, sometimes while it was parked outside the public house and sometimes while he was driving American service men back to their camp. Occasionally, he would drive American servicemen and prostitutes into the neighbouring countryside and either wait while intercourse took place or return and collect them later. There were standard charges for the hire of the car which the men paid to him, the prostitutes getting their reward in the form of food, drink and clothing. From January to April 1953, the respondent permitted his house to be used by prostitutes and service men and during March 1953 one of the prostitutes stayed at the respondent's house on the terms that she would pay for her board and lodging by prostituting herself with men whom she either brought herself to, or were brought to her, at the house. On all these occasions, the respondent received money from the men and the prostitutes received food, drink and clothing. An information was preferred against the respondent charging that he, for a period of six months, knowingly lived in part on the earnings of prostitution. Appealing against conviction, it was held: (a) although all the money was paid direct to the respondent, he was in the same position as if it had been paid to the prostitutes and they had passed it on to him—it was being earned by prostitution and so he was guilty. He was trading in prostitution; (b) in any event his behaviour had brought him within the presumption (now s.30(2)).

Earnings derived from prostitution as opposed to the normal earnings of the defendant in his lawful business. In *R. v. Silver* [1956] 1 All E.R. 716, eight of the nine defendants were charged with living wholly or in part on the earnings of prostitution (contrary to s.1 of the Vagrancy Act 1898, as amended). The ninth defendant was a woman who was charged with aiding and abetting. The defendants, as either landlords or estate agents, had let or been concerned in letting flats to individual prostitutes knowing that the tenants intended to use the premises for prostitution, and charging rents higher than they would otherwise have done. It was held that the defendants were not guilty of the offence charged, because, although the defendants by receiving moneys from the tenants in the circumstances either as rent or in consideration of granting tenancies or of work as estate agents, were receiving moneys which wholly or in part had been derived from prostitution, the moneys so received were the earnings of defendants who were not, therefore living on the earnings of prostitution.   **12-74**

The receipt of inflated rent because the tenant is a prostitute. In *R. v. Thomas* [1957] 2 All E.R. 181, it was alleged that the accused, knowing that a woman was a convicted prostitute agreed to let her have the use of a room between 9pm and 2am at £3 a night. It was held that where as in the present case, there was evidence that the accused had let a room at a grossly inflated rent to a prostitute for the express purpose of letting her ply her immoral trade, it was for the jury to determine whether the accused was in fact knowingly living wholly or in part on the earnings of prostitution.   **12-75**

In *R. v. Calderhead* and *R. v. Bidney* (1978) 68 Cr.App.R. 37, it was held on appeal that a landlord who knew his tenant was a prostitute and took advantage of her difficulty in getting accommodation by letting the property at an exorbitant rent, could be guilty of living wholly or in part on the earnings of prostitution because he was not then acting merely as a landlord but making his tenant engage in a joint venture, bringing him a part of her immoral earnings over and above the normal rent.

The defendant is supplying goods and services which he would not have supplied but for the fact that they are prostitutes. In *Shaw v. DPP* [1962] A.C. 220, Shaw published a "Ladies Directory" which gave details of prostitutes and their specialties and was prosecuted for conspiracy to corrupt   **12-76**

public morals. Lord Reid when considering living off immoral earnings characterised the essence of the mischief as that of men who live parasitically on prostitutes and their earnings, who would not have an occupation without them. Viscount Simonds held that a person may be said to be living in whole or in part on the earnings of prostitution if he is paid by prostitutes for goods and services that he would not have supplied if they were not prostitutes.

Similarly, in *R. v. Howard* (1992) 94 Cr.App.R. 89, the appellant had produced cards and adhesive stickers to be used by prostitutes to advertise their services and their telephone numbers. He knew that his products were to be used by the prostitutes to obtain clients and that the payment he received came from the earnings of prostitution. That profitable business provided his sole source of income at the relevant time.

12-77   **The defendant is exercising some influence, direction or control over the prostitute** In *R. v. Ansell* [1974] 3 All E.R. 568, the accused knew a number of prostitutes who were interested in certain types of sexual activity. He placed advertisements in a magazine offering to supply the names, addresses and telephone numbers of those prostitutes to men who were interested in those activities. A number of men responded to the advertisements and the accused sold them the information. The prostitutes whom the men contacted as a consequence, did not know that it was the defendant who had effected the introduction. In each case, the defendant received his fee before the identity of the prostitute was made known to the man concerned. It was not certain that the introduction would lead to sexual intercourse between the men and the prostitute. In each case the man was left to pay the prostitute for the services she rendered. The accused appealed against his conviction for living on the earnings of prostitution. Held allowing the appeal: although the fact that the money paid to the accused came from the men and not from the prostitute did not in law prevent that money from being the earnings of prostitution, in order to establish that it was, its receipt had to be shown to be so closely connected with the exercise by the accused of direction, influence and control over the movements of prostitutes that it could clearly and fairly be said to be the earnings of prostitution. There was no evidence to support the conclusion that the accused has exercised any form of control over the prostitutes concerned.

12-78   **The defendant and the prostitute are engaged in the business of prostitution together.** In *R. v. Stewart* (1986) 83 Cr.App.R. 327, the Court of Appeal considered the elements of the offence contrary to section 30 of the 1956 Act and was referred to the above outlined cases. It was held that a good working test, in assessing whether a defendant has "knowingly lived wholly or in part on the earnings of prostitution" is whether the fact of supply by the defendant of goods or services to a prostitute means that the supplier and the prostitute was engaged in the business of prostitution together. The "fact of supply" will include the scale of supply, the price charged and the nature of the goods or services. In a case, such as the instant case where a defendant lets premises to a prostitute, the fact that the rent charged is or is not exorbitant is not conclusive, nor is the question whether the premises are occupied or capable of occupation as residential premises. The trial judge in such a case must not allow the jury to believe that knowledge of the use to which the premises are put is sufficient to found a conviction, but must draw the attention of the jury to whatever factors are material to the individual case. These might include the nature and location of the premises, the involvement of the lessor in adapting or furnishing the premises for prostitution, the duration of the letting, the hours during which the premises are let, the rent at which they are let, the method of payment of rent, whether the prostitute lives as well as works there, the presence or absence of a personal relationship between the lessor and the lessee and the steps taken by the lessor to disguise his relationship with the premises and the persons working there.

The case law provides some guidance, although in what circumstances a **12-79** defendant can be held to be living wholly or in part on the earnings of prostitution where he is the provider of goods or services to the prostitute, will still turn largely on the facts of each individual case—it cannot be said in advance that certain services will be within or outside the section.

(iv) The presumption

Subsection (2) provides that if one or more of three grounds are present, a **12-80** presumption is raised that the accused is living on the earnings of prostitution, and doing so knowingly; *R. v. Clarke* [1976] 2 All E.R. 696. The grounds are that the accused:

(a)   was living with a prostitute;
(b)   was habitually in the company of a prostitute; or
(c)   exercised control, direction or influence over a prostitute's movements in a way which showed that he was aiding, abetting or compelling her prostitution.

This subsection is of great benefit to the prosecution since it means that to **12-81** support an allegation of living on the earnings of prostitution, direct evidence is not required from the prostitute herself (who may well be a reluctant or hostile witness) but can be supplied by circumstantial evidence, for example, police officers who have been keeping surveillance on the prostitute and noting her movements and associations; or documents found in the prostitute's home showing that she is living with the accused.

As far as (a) and (b) are concerned, it is not necessary to prove that the defendant was living with or habitually in the company of a prostitute in a way which showed that he was aiding, abetting or compelling her prostitution—that is only required for (c): *R. v. Lawrence* (1963) 47 Cr.App.R. 72.

Whether sufficient proof has been adduced to raise the presumption is a **12-82** question of fact for the jury. Once evidence giving rise to the presumption has been led, the onus then shifts to the defendant to prove on the balance of probabilities that he was not living wholly or in part on the earnings of a woman he knew to be a prostitute: *R.v. Ptohopoulos* (1967) 52 Cr.App.R. 47.

(v) Warrant to enter and search

12–83 Section 42 of the 1956 Act gives a justice of the peace the power to issue a warrant authorising a constable to enter and search a house used by a woman for the purposes of prostitution and to arrest a man residing in or frequenting the house. It must be made to appear to the justice by information on oath that there is reasonable cause to suspect that any house or part of a house is used by the woman for the purposes of prostitution and that the man residing in or frequenting it, is living wholly or in part on her earnings.

(b) Male prostitution

12–84 The Sexual Offences Act 1967, s.5(1) states: "A man or woman who knowingly lives wholly or in part on the earnings of prostitution of another man shall be liable. ... "

(i) Sentencing guidelines

12–85 Offences contrary to section 5 of the 1967 Act are punishable, on summary conviction with a term of imprisonment not exceeding six months and/or a fine not exceeding the statutory maximum; and on conviction on indictment with a term of imprisonment not exceeding seven years (s.5(1)).

In *R.v. Puckerin* (1990) 12 Cr.App.R. (S) 602 the appellant was seen by police officers on a number of occasions introducing male prostitutes to clients, taking money and using his car to transport them. He appealed against the sentence of two years' imprisonment. It was held that such cases must be compared for sentencing purposes with cases involving living off the earnings of female prostitution. That being so, taking into account the fact that there was no evidence of coercion or force or that the defendant had made much money out of the enterprise (although he must have made some); and that the defendant had not being doing it for a protracted period of time just a matter of weeks, a sentence of nine months' imprisonment was appropriate.

(ii) Power of arrest

12–86 By virtue of subsection (3) anyone may arrest without a warrant a person found committing an offence under this section. However, section 5 is an arrestable offence within section 24 of the Police and Criminal Evidence Act 1984 which carries more extensive powers of arrest than subsection (3).

Unlike section 30 of the 1956 Act, section 5 does not contain a presumption similar to that found in subsection 30(2).

(c) Section 31

12–87 The Sexual Offences Act 1956, s.31 states: "It is an offence for a woman for purposes of gain to exercise control, direction or influence over a prostitute's movements in a way which shows she is aiding, abetting or compelling her prostitution."

The *actus reus* of this offence is the same as for a section 30 1956 Act offence.

Sentencing guidelines

Offences contrary to section 31 of the 1956 Act are punishable, on summary   **12-88**
conviction with a term of imprisonment not exceeding six months and/or a
fine not exceeding the statutory maximum; and on conviction on indictment
with a term of imprisonment not exceeding seven years (s.37 of and Sched.2
to the 1956 Act).

The criteria to be considered in sentencing an offence under section 5(1)
are similar to that for an offence under section 30(1). In R. *v. Brown*
(unreported, May 16, 1994) the defendant was convicted of four offences
contrary to section 31 which covered different prostitutes over a period of
eight years. There was no evidence of any corruption, procurement or
coercion. She was fined £5,000 for each offence and ordered to complete 60
hours' community service. On appeal against the fine, it was held that given
the information before the court as to the defendant's assets, the fine was not
manifestly excessive.

C. BROTHELS AND DISORDERLY HOUSES

I. BROTHELS

Offences relating to brothels are contrary to statute, whereas keeping a   **12-89**
disorderly house is still an offence contrary to common law. The main
difference between a brothel and a disorderly house is that a brothel is a place
where people of the opposite sex are allowed to resort for illicit intercourse
(*Winter v. Woolfe* [1931] 1 K.B. 549) or people of the same sex resort to for
lewd homosexual practices (Sexual Offences Act 1967, s.6), while a house
may, but need not have, a sexual connection to be disorderly.

(a) Section 33

The Sexual Offences Act 1956, s.33 states: "It is an offence for a person to   **12-90**
keep a brothel, or to manage or act or assist in the management of, a
brothel."

(i) Homosexual brothels

The Sexual Offences Act 1967, s.6 states: "Premises shall be treated for   **12-91**
purposes of sections 33 to 35 of the Act of 1956 as a brothel if people resort
to it for the purpose of lewd homosexual practices in circumstances in which
resort thereto for lewd heterosexual practices would have led to its being
treated as a brothel for the purposes of those sections."

(ii) Sentencing guidelines

The offence can only be tried summarily and punishment on conviction for a   **12-92**
first offence is a term of imprisonment not exceeding three months and/or a

fine not exceeding level three on the standard scale. Where the defendant has a previous conviction for an offence contrary to sections 33, 34, 35 or 36 of the 1956 Act, the offence is punishable with a term of imprisonment not exceeding six months and/or a fine not exceeding level four on the standard scale (s.37 and Sched.2).

It is unusual for a defendant to be charged with the sole offence of keeping a brothel. Normally there will be an additional charge of living off immoral earnings, the penalty for which will be in accordance with *R. v. Farrugia* (see para. 12.70, above).

(iii) Charging practice

12–93 Keeping a brothel can be regarded as a single continuing transaction and an information charging the offence over a period of time is not bad for duplicity (Anderton v. Cooper (1980) 72 Cr.App.R. 232).

(iv) Definition of brothel

12–94 Whether premises constitute a brothel is a question of fact for the jury. *Winter v. Woolfe* (above) defined a brothel as being a place where people of opposite sexes were permitted to have unlawful sexual intercourse. It does not have to be used for the purposes of prostitution (which involves the provision of sexual services for reward) or be frequented by known prostitutes. However, the fact that women visiting the premises were prostitutes can be relevant and probative on the question of whether the premises were a brothel, and such evidence is admissible since its probative value outweighs its prejudice to the defendant: *R.v. Korie* [1966] 1 All E.R. 50.

12–95 In *Kelly v. Purvis* [1983] 1 All E.R. 525, the justice had found that the defendant (who was an assistant manageress in a massage parlour) and other women were common prostitutes, but was not satisfied that a prima facie case had been established that the premises were a brothel within the meaning of the Act. There was evidence that masturbation, but not full sexual intercourse was offered at the premises. It was held on appeal by way of case stated that it was not essential to have evidence of normal sexual intercourse to prove a charge under section 33. It was only necessary to prove that the premises were kept to allow people to have illicit connection there, and that more than one woman offered to participate in physical acts of indecency for the sexual gratification of men.

12–96 Where premises are used by a number of prostitutes, but never by more than one at any one time, the premises could properly be called a brothel: *Stevens and Stevens v. Christy* (1987) 151 J.P. 366. Conversely, if the premises are used by only one woman for prostitution, it is not a brothel: *Singleton v. Ellison* (1895) 1 Q.B. 607; *Stevens and Stevens v. Christy* above; *Gorman v. Standen; Palace-Clark v. Standen* [1963] 3 All E.R. 627.

In *Gorman v. Standen; Palace-Clark v. Standen*, Palace-Clark was tenant of premises where she lived with her step-daughter Gorman. On eight days in October 1962, the police kept observation on the premises and found that at least 19 different men, some on more than one occasion, resorted to the premises, in company with either of the women. In the early hours of October 26, 1962, police officers under the authority of a warrant, entered the premises and found both women, unclothed, in bed, each with a man. When taken to the police station and shown a statement made by Palace-Clark, Gorman said "It's my fault—she is frightened of me. If I told her to go upstairs and sleep with a man she would do it". Palace-Clark was convicted of keeping a brothel and Gorman was convicted of assisting in the management of that brothel. On appeal it was held that: (i) Palace-Clark had been rightly convicted because, if there were two women bringing men to premises for the purposes of fornication, the fact that one woman was tenant and occupier of the premises did not prevent the premises from being a brothel; (ii) although the words "assisting in the management of a brothel" contemplated ordinarily the position where a man ran the brothel with the assistance of a woman on the premises who helped in the management, yet in the present case, Gorman had some say in what went on in the house and her conviction should stand.

A brothel may be a house, a room or a set of rooms or it may be that sets **12-97** of rooms let separately within one building render the whole building a brothel, especially if the separate lettings are a subterfuge.

In *Strath v. Foxon* [1955] 3 All E.R. 398, the respondent, as agent of the **12-98** lessor of premises which comprised three floors, let the first and second floors and the third floors respectively to two women whom she knew to be prostitutes. Access to the premises was obtained by the same street door and there was a common staircase on which a substantial door fitted with a Yale lock divided the whole of the third floor from the lower floors, thus making it completely self-contained. A kitchen on the second floor was used by both the women. The respondent was charged with letting the premises with the knowledge that they were to be used as a brothel. The magistrate, having found that there were separate lettings of the two flats and no common use other than a joint user of the kitchen, dismissed the charge. On appeal it was held that the premises did not constitute a brothel since premises used by only one woman could not be regarded as a brothel and, there being evidence to justify the magistrate's findings, the court would not interfere with them.

An opposing view was held in *Abbott v. Smith* [1964] 3 All E.R. 762, **12-99** where the upper floors of the premises, a large terrace house going to seed, were let off in single room apartments, though not structurally converted for the purpose. Each occupant had a right of exclusive occupation of his or her room, the staircase and the toilet and washing facilities being used in common. The premises were used by two of the occupants, who were known prostitutes, and by three other women, including a known prostitute, who were not known to be living there, for the purposes of prostitution. There was no evidence that any room was used by more than one woman, whether simultaneously or successively for these purposes. The first appellant lived with three sons and a daughter then aged 16 (the second appellant), in one room on the ground floor. The first appellant had no authority from the landlord to evict undesirable tenants, did not collect the rents and received no remuneration from him or any rake-off from the tenants. There was evidence that on one occasion she opened the front door to one of the known prostitutes late at night, who addressed her by her Christian name. There was also evidence that the second appellant, who was not a prostitute, was on intimate terms with the two known prostitute occupants and had assisted someone on the premises by telling a man outside when he could go in. On appeal by the first appellant against her conviction for managing and by the second appellant against her conviction for assisting in the management of a brothel it was held, allowing the appeal for want of evidence of management or assisting in the management, that the premises constituted a brothel because, although they were occupied by many persons with separate rights as regards individual rooms, the premises were a single entity and that single entity was used by more than one woman for the purposes of sexual lewdness with more than one man.

12–100   In *Durose v. Wilson* (1907) 96 L.T. 645 the appellant was employed by the owner as the porter in charge of a block of 18 flats, among the tenants of which were 12 women who were in the habit of bringing men to the flats for the purposes of prostitution. The appellant knew the purpose for which the women used the premises, and was convicted of wilfully being a party to the continued use of the premises or part thereof as a brothel contrary to section 13(3) of the Criminal Law Amendment Act 1885. It was held that as it was open to the magistrate upon the evidence to find that it was not a case of each single flat being used for prostitution by the woman who was the tenant of it, but of the building as a whole being used as a brothel, the appellant had been rightly convicted.

12–101   In *Donovan v. Gavin* [1965] 2 All E.R. 611, the defendant owned a house in which he occupied himself a self-contained ground floor flat. There were other rooms on the ground floor of which three were let separately on separate occasions to three women, M, C and Y, who were common prostitutes. These lettings were continuing in June 1964. Two of those three rooms, occupied by M and C were on either side of the street door and had windows facing on to the street. The third room (Y's) was across the corridor from M's. Each of the three rooms had a separate Yale lock and each woman had a key to the front door. The tenancies were made genuinely and not as a subterfuge to avoid the provisions of the Sexual Offences Act. There were also in the house other separate rooms on the ground, first and second floors, each with its own Yale lock and each let separately. Between June 15 and June 19,1964, 38 different men were seen to enter the house, either with or after being admitted by one or more of the three prostitutes for the purposes of prostitution. M and Y had regularly joined together to solicit men in the nearby streets; moreover on four different days of the five, they had together solicited men from the bay window of M's room and on one occasion from the doorway of the house. Men used to knock on the bay window of M's room and were then admitted at the front door for prostitution by M or Y or both. On one occasion, Y used M's room for business. C did not solicit in the company of either M or Y and only used her own room for her own purposes. Some time before the information charging Donovan, he had learnt that M, C and Y were prostitutes. He was charged under section 34 of the 1956 Act as landlord of the premises, with being wilfully a party to the use of part of the premises as a brothel continuing on the days in June 1964.

On appeal by the prosecutor from the allowance by quarter sessions of Donovan's appeal it was held: (i) where, as in the present case, the premises concerned were being used by more than one prostitute for the purposes of her trade, the question whether those premises or part thereof were being used as a brothel was a question of fact in each case to be deduced from the circumstances as a whole; and the mere fact individual rooms in the house or the relevant part of it were originally let under separate tenancies did not preclude the whole or part of the house being a brothel; (ii) further where, as in the present case, the offence was charged under the second part of the Sexual Offences Act, s.34 (namely being wilfully a party to the use continuing) and separate rooms in the house concerned were occupied and used by common prostitutes for their trade in sufficient proximity to constitute what might be described as a "nest" of prostitutes, the fact that the rooms were the subject of independent lettings for exclusive occupation might be of no weight and regard should be had to the user of the rooms; the present case was of that class, and accordingly quarter session, by attaching weight to the original independence of the lettings, had misdirected themselves.

(b) Section 33 offences

An offence under section 33 can be committed in three ways, namely: **12–102**

    (i)   to keep a brothel;
    (ii) to manage a brothel; or
    (iii) to act or assist in the management of a brothel.

(i) Keeping a brothel

A woman who uses premises exclusively for her own prostitution does not keep a brothel: *Stevens and Stevens v. Christy* above. A landlord who lets flats to tenants, but does not retain a part of the house in which the flats are located and has no control over it does not keep a disorderly house: (*R. v. Stannard* (1863) 9 Cox C.C. 405), nor does he become liable if, having notice of the nature of the occupation, he does not give the tenants notice to quit (*R. v. Barrett* (1862) 9 Cox C.C. 255) although such a person may fall foul of other sections of the Sexual Offences Act.

(ii) Managing a brothel

This requires the taking of an active part in the running of the business as a business, and in order to establish that, the evidence must show something suggesting control, not purely menial or routine duties; *Abbott v. Smith* (above).

(iii) Acting or assisting in the management of a brothel

A distinction must be drawn between assisting in the management of, and assisting the management of a brothel, the former being an offence whereas the latter is not. It is a matter of fact and degree where the one ends and the other begins.

In *Gorman v. Standen; Palace-Clark v. Standen* (above) it was held that **12–103** since Gorman lived on the premises and had some say in what went on, then she was assisting in the management. A person who keeps an appointments system, answers the telephone, decides to a large extent on the price of the services, pays the rent and opens and locks the premises can also be said to assist in the management: (DPP v. Curley and Farrelly [1991] C.O.D. 186.

12–104　　In *Jones and Wood v. DPP* (1993) 96 Cr.App.R. 130 it was held that it is not a necessary condition for the offence of assisting in the management of a brothel that a defendant has actually exercised some control over the brothel or carried out some specific act of management. In that case, in support of a conviction, the Crown Court found that: (i) there was a close personal relationship between the two appellants and the male prostitute who operated the brothel; (ii) both appellants had placed numerous advertisements in local shops advertising the availability of both male and female sexual services at the premises; and (iii) both appellants frequently visited the premises and carried out jobs for the male prostitute, often when customers were also in the building. In *Elliot v. DPP; Dublides v. DPP, The Times,* January 19, 1989, the Divisional Court found that where women in a massage parlour not only performed lewd acts but, *inter alia*, discussed the nature of the acts to be performed and negotiated the terms of payment for their services, they were assisting in the management of a brothel.

12–105　　Where there is a specific act of management, then the defendant can be said to be acting in the management of a brothel.

(c) Section 34

12–106　　The Sexual Offences Act 1956, s.34 states: "It is an offence for the lessor or landlord of any premises or his agent to let the whole or part of the premises with the knowledge that it is to be used, in whole or in part, as a brothel, or where the whole or part of the premises is used as a brothel, to be wilfully a party to that use continuing."

(i) Sentencing guidelines

12–107　　The offence can only be tried summarily and punishment on conviction for a first offence is a term of imprisonment not exceeding three months and/or a fine not exceeding level three on the standard scale. Where the defendant has a previous conviction for an offence contrary to sections 33, 34, 35 or 36 of the 1956 Act, the offence is punishable with a term of imprisonment not exceeding six months and/or a fine not exceeding level four on the standard scale (s.37 and Sched. 2).

(ii) Wilful

12–108　　"Wilful" requires knowledge of the intended use or continued use of the premises.

(d) Section 35

12–109　　The Sexual Offences Act 1956, s.35(1) states

"It is an offence for the tenant or occupier, or person in charge, of any premises knowingly to permit the whole or part of the premises to be used as a brothel.

(2) Where the tenant or occupier of any premises is convicted (whether under this section or, for an offence committed before the commencement of this Act, under section thirteen of the Criminal Law Amendment Act 1885) of knowingly permitting the whole or part of the premises to be used as a brothel, the First Schedule to this Act shall apply to enlarge the rights of the lessor or landlord with respect to the assignment or determination of the lease or other contract under which the premises are held by the person convicted.

(3) Where the tenant or occupier of any premises is so convicted, or was so convicted under the said section thirteen before the commencement of this Act, and either —

(a) the lessor or landlord, after having the conviction brought to his notice, fails or failed to exercise his statutory rights in relation to the lease or contract under which the premises are or were held by the person convicted; or

(b) the lessor or landlord, after exercising his statutory rights so as to determine that lease or contract, grants or granted a new lease or enters or entered into a new contract of tenancy of the premises to, with or for the benefit of the same person, without having all reasonable provisions to prevent the recurrence of the offence inserted in the new lease or contract; then, if subsequently an offence under this section is committed in respect of the premises during the subsistence of the lease or contract referred to in paragraph (a) of this subsection or (where paragraph (b) applies) during the subsistence of the new lease or contract, the lessor or landlord shall be deemed to be a party to that offence unless he shows that he took all reasonable steps to prevent the recurrence of the offence."

References in this subsection to the statutory rights of a lessor or landlord refer to his rights under Schedule 1 to this Act or under subsection (1) of section 5 of the Criminal Law Amendment Act 1912 (the provisions replaced for England and Wales by that Schedule).   **12-110**

Schedule 1 states: **12-111**

"1. Upon the conviction of the tenant or occupier (in this Schedule referred to as 'the tenant'), the lessor or landlord may require the tenant to assign the lease or other contract under which the premises are held by him to some person approved by the lessor or landlord.

2. If the tenant fails to do so within three months, the lessor or landlord may determine the lease or contract (but without prejudice to the rights or remedies of any party thereto accrued before the date of the determination).

3. Where the lease or contract is determined under this Schedule, the court by which the tenant was convicted may make a summary order for delivery of possession of the premises to the lessor or landlord.

4. The approval of the lessor or landlord for the purposes of paragraph 1 of this Schedule shall not be unreasonably withheld.

5. This Schedule shall have effect subject to the Rent and Mortgage

Interest Restrictions Acts 1920 to 1939, the Furnished Houses (Rent Control) Act 1946, Part II of the Reserve and Auxiliary Forces (Protection of Civil Interests) Act 1951, Part I of the Landlord and Tenant Act 1954, Part I of the Housing Act 1988 and Schedule 10 to the Local Government and Housing Act 1989."

(i) Sentencing guidelines

12–112 The offence can only be tried summarily and punishment on conviction for a first offence is a term of imprisonment not exceeding three months and/or a fine not exceeding level three on the standard scale. Where the defendant has a previous conviction for an offence contrary to section 33, 34, 35 or 36 of the 1956 Act, the offence is punishable with a term of imprisonment not exceeding six months and/or a fine not exceeding level four on the standard scale (s.37 and Sched. 2).

(ii) Charging practice

12–113 It is a continuing offence and may be charged as having been committed "on or between" specified dates: *Anderton v Cooper* (above).

(iii) Lessee

12–114 In *Siviour v Napolitano* [1931] 1 K.B. 636, the defendant was and had been for about seven years lessee of premises consisting of four floors and a basement. He used the ground floor and basement as a shop in which he carried on the business of a tailor. He sub-let unfurnished the first and second floors respectively as flats to two women. These flats were approached not through the shop but by a separate entrance, and apart from his position as landlord, the defendant had no right to enter them and did not occupy them. It was stated by the police that the women were known to them as prostitutes, each of whom took men to her own flat. The defendant was charged for that he being lessee of the premises unlawfully and knowingly permitted part of them, namely, the first and second floors, to be used for the purposes of habitual prostitution contrary to the Criminal Law Amendment Act 1885, s.13(2). It was held on appeal that the defendant was not the "lessee" of the flats within the subsection and the charge should be dismissed.

(e) Section 36

12–115 The Sexual Offences Act 1956, s.36 states "It is an offence for the tenant or occupier of any premises knowingly to permit the whole or part of the premises to be used for the purposes of habitual prostitution."

(i) Sentencing guidelines

12–116 The offence, while not falling within the category of a "brothel" can only be tried summarily and punishment on conviction for a first offence is a term of imprisonment not exceeding three months and/or a fine not exceeding level three on the standard scale. Where the defendant has a previous conviction for an offence contrary to sections 33, 34, 35 or 36 of the 1956 Act, the offence is punishable with a term of imprisonment not exceeding six months and/or a fine not exceeding level four on the standard scale (s.37 and Sched.2).

(ii) Occupation

It is sufficient for the purposes of this section if the premises are used by a   12–117
single prostitute, there is no requirement for the premises to be used as a brothel.

The wording of the section suggests that the tenant or occupier must give permission to another to use the premises for the purposes of habitual prostitution. A prostitute who is the sole occupant of a house, and used the house for that purpose could not be convicted for permitting the premises to be used for the purposes of habitual prostitution: *Mattison v. Johnson* [1916–1917] All E.R. 727.

II. Keeping A Disorderly House

The offence of keeping a disorderly house is an indictable offence. The   12–118
Disorderly Houses Act 1751, s.8 states:

> "Any person who shall at any time hereafter appear, act or behave him or herself as master or mistress, or as the person having the care, government or management of any bawdy-house, or other disorderly house, shall be deemed and taken to be the keeper thereof, and shall be liable to be prosecuted as such, notwithstanding he or she shall not in fact be the real owner or keeper thereof."

Sentencing guidelines

The common law offence is punishable by imprisonment at large and a fine.   12–119
An offence under section 8 is triable either way, punishable by a fine and/or imprisonment. However, since *R. v. Payne* (1980) 2 Cr.App.R. (S.) 161, the courts have in effect limited the term of imprisonment for these offences to a maximum of six months.

In *R. v. Payne* (above) the appellant pleaded guilty to, *inter alia* keeping a disorderly house. The disorderly house was a brothel in a suburban house. The appellant had four previous convictions for brothel keeping and was sentenced to 18 months' imprisonment (and fines for the other offences). On appeal, the court reduced the sentence to six months' imprisonment because of the policy of the Sexual Offences Act 1956: "If the maximum sentence permitted by Parliament for keeping or managing a brothel is six months, we find it difficult to see why in this case it should be more than six months" (*per* Lawton L.J.).

The sentencing rationale in *Payne* was followed in *R. v. Martin* (1988) 10 Cr.App.R. (S.) 339. In this case the appellant was convicted of keeping a disorderly house. She, working alone, had offered various sexual activities at premises in London. Her original sentence of nine months' imprisonment was reduced to three months, the court finding that if Mrs Payne (whose offending was far worse) had her sentence reduced from 18 months' imprisonment to six months' imprisonment, then it was appropriate that Martin's sentence should be reduced.

(a) Evidential requirements

12–120   In order to establish the offence of keeping a disorderly house at common law, the prosecution must show that the defendant habitually or persistently kept such a house since the mischief at which the common law was aimed was the continuity of keeping a house to which members of the public resorted for the purposes of disorderly recreation which was available there. Knowledge of the use to which the premises were being put is also a prerequisite to a defendant's conviction: *Moores v. DPP* [1991] 4 All E.R. 521.

(b) Disorderly house

12–121   A disorderly house is one which is not regulated by the restraints of morality and which is so conducted as to violate law and good order: *R. V. Berg and others* (1928) 20 Cr.App.R. 38.

12–122   In *R. v. Quinn; R. v. Bloom* [1961] 3 All E.R. 88, two club proprietors were indicted, each for keeping a disorderly house, the substance of the charge in each case arising out of matters alleged to have occurred in the course of "strip-tease" performances at the club before members of the club. There was evidence of police officers, who saw the acts at both premises, which showed that the indecency involved was serious and, in some respects, revolting. It was sought on behalf of the defence in one case to put in evidence a film showing what certain of the performers actually did in the course of their acts, and to support this by evidence that the performances in the film were identical with the performances on the occasions complained of. This film was taken three months after the events complained of and the evidence was not admissible at trial. In the summing-up at one trial the jury were directed to consider whether what has been portrayed was, among other adjectives, "obscene" without reference to the definition in the Obscene Publications Act 1959, s.1(1). The accused were convicted.

On appeal, it was held that a disorderly house, for the purposes of a charge of the common law offence of keeping a disorderly house in a case where the essence of the charge is the taking place of indecent performances or exhibitions, may be defined as follows: a house conducted contrary to law and good order in that matters are performed or exhibited of such a character that their performance or exhibition in a place of common resort (a) amounts to an outrage of public decency or (b) tends to corrupt or deprave, or (c) is otherwise calculated to injure the public interest so as to call for condemnation and punishment. The alternatives (a), (b) and (c) in this definition are not mutually exclusive.

A jury should be warned that in applying the definition they should approach the matter as ordinary reasonable citizens, putting aside as far as possible any prejudices that they may have, but each juror's decision is his own subjective decision, so that in effect the morality of the jury determines the guilt or innocence of the accused. The fact that persons resorting to the premises were mere spectators and committed no acts of indecency did not prevent the premises constituting in law a disorderly house. While a disorderly house might in some instances amount to a common nuisance the latter element was not a necessary ingredient of the offence in question. The film was an alleged reconstruction of the alleged crimes and evidence by its exhibition was properly rejected as inadmissible, for it was not the best evidence. *Per curiam*: if a direction in a summing-up uses the adjective "obscene" it is in general desirable to mention the definition of "obscene" contained in the Obscene Publications Act 1959, s.1(1), and there is danger in multiplying offensive adjectives.

Many forms of conduct may fall within the scope of keeping a disorderly **12-123** house and need not be limited to matters of a sexual nature so that it can include for example, gaming houses, betting houses and disorderly places of entertainment. In *R. v. Tan and others* [1983] Q.B. 1053, the court summed up the elements of the offence as:

(i) there must be some element of keeping open house;
(ii) the house must not be regulated by the restraints of morality, or must be unchaste or of bad repute; and
(iii) it must be so conducted as to violate law and good order. Although there must be some element of keeping open house, the house need not be open to the public at large: *R. v. Berg* (above), nor need any indecent or disorderly conduct be perceptible from outside the house: *R. v. Rice and Wilton* [1866] L.R. 1 C.C.R. 21.

The prosecution are entitled to call evidence to show that what happened **12-124** during the period covered by the indictment was merely a continuation of a prior user, the evidence being relevant to the issue of persistence and to rebut any suggestion of unintentional or casual excess: *R. v. Brady and Ram* (1963) 47 Cr.App.R 196.

III. BAWDY-HOUSES

A common bawdy-house is a house or room, or set of rooms in any house **12-125** kept for the purposes of prostitution. A "brothel" is the same thing as a "bawdy-house" and is a term which in its legal acceptance applies to a place resorted to by persons of both sexes for the purposes of prostitution; it does not apply to a place where one woman receives a number of men: *Singleton v. Ellison* [1895] 1 Q.B. 607.

IV. ALLOWING PROSTITUTES ON PREMISES

(a) Town Police Clauses Act 1847

Section 35 states that: **12-126**

"Every person keeping any house, shop, room, or other place of public resort for the sale or consumption of refreshments of any kind, who knowingly suffers common prostitutes or reputed thieves to assemble and continue in his premises shall, for every such offence, be liable to a penalty not exceeding level 1 on the standard scale."

A public house is a place of public resort: *Cole v. Coulton* (1860) 24 J.P. 596.

(b) Licensing Act 1964

12-127 Section 175(1) states:

"The holder of a justices' licence shall not knowingly allow the licensed premises to be the habitual resort or place of meeting of reputed prostitutes, whether the object of their so resorting or meeting is or is not prostitution; but this section does not prohibit his allowing any such persons to remain in the premises for the purposes of obtaining reasonable refreshment for such time as is necessary for that purposes.

(2) If the holder of a justices' licence contravenes this section he shall be liable, to a fine not exceeding level 2 on the standard scale."

"Knowingly" means that the character of the persons resorting to the house was known to the licence holder: *Somerset v. Wade* [1894] 1 Q.B. 574.

The licence holder may not allow prostitutes to remain in his house except for the purpose of obtaining refreshment. If prostitutes frequent the house to pursue their calling, or for ulterior purposes known to the licence holder, there may be a conviction, but not if the women go there merely for refreshment. For a conviction to follow, it must be proved that the premises are being used as the habitual resort of prostitutes to the knowledge of the licence holder and that they are allowed to remain longer than necessary for reasonable refreshment.

12-128 Section 176(1) states:

"If the holder of a justices' licence permits the licensed premises to be a brothel, he shall be liable to a fine not exceeding level 2 on the standard scale.

(2) If the holder of a justices' licence is convicted, whether under this section or under any other enactment, of permitting his premises to be a brothel, he shall forfeit the licence."

This section creates a distinct summary offence and does not supersede the remedy by indictment or under the Sexual Offences Act 1956. However, if proceedings are taken under this section the defendant cannot be convicted in any other proceedings.

Chapter 13
Obscene Publications

A. INTRODUCTION

The law relating to obscene material whether in the form of text, video film   **13-01**
or photographs is mainly found in the Obscene Publications Acts of 1959
and 1964, although there has been subsequent legislation which imposes
greater restriction on matters such as photographs of children (Protection of
Children Act 1978 and Criminal Justice Act 1988) and indecent displays
(Indecent Displays (Control) Act 1981).

The intention of the 1959 Act was to provide for the protection of   **13-02**
literature and to strengthen the law concerning pornography and it may be
thought that the success of the first objective was achieved in 1960 with the
decision in *R. v. Penguin Books Ltd* [1961] Crim. L.R.176 (*Lady Chatter-
ley's Lover*). However, since whether an article is obscene or not, is a matter
of fact for the jury, and the members of a jury could either be in favour of the
permissive and liberal attitudes of the 1960s and 1970s or react against them,
the verdicts that emerged over the course of years following the passing of the
1959 and 1964 Acts often resulted in anomalies, upheld in the higher courts,
which are difficult to reconcile.

Advances in technology and the advent of both the video and more   **13-03**
especially the computer have given rise to problems with the law. Case law
has been able to resolve the difficulties encountered with the video. It will
require legislation to address the computer and until then, Acts which were
passed before the Internet for example was created are being employed to
cope with behaviour for which they were never intended.

B. OBSCENE PUBLICATIONS

The Obscene Publications Act 1959 (as amended by the Obscene Publica-   **13-04**
tions Act 1964), s. 2(1) states:

"Subject as hereinafter provided, any person who, whether for gain or not, publishes an obscene article or who has an obscene article for publication for gain (whether gain to himself or gain to another) shall be liable."

Offences under section 2 of the 1959 Act are serious arrestable offences (s.85 of the Criminal Justice and Public Order Act 1994).

(i) Sentencing guidelines

13–05   Offences under this section are triable either way and carry a maximum of six months' imprisonment or the statutory maximum fine on summary conviction, and a maximum of three years' imprisonment or a fine on indictment. By virtue of section 2(3) a prosecution under section 2 may not be commenced more than two years after the commission of the offence.

13–06   The guideline cases are *R. v. Emmerson* (1977) 65 Cr.App.R.154 and *R. v. Holloway* (1982) 4 Cr.App.R. (S.) 128. In the former, the appellant was convicted of conspiring to publish obscene articles for gain and conspiring to send postal packets containing indecent or obscene articles. He was sentenced to 12 months' imprisonment and fined £4,000. The court upheld the sentence, Roskill L.J. stating that:

> "If people engage in this type of trade, taking the profits that it is notorious come from it, it is quite wrong when they are convicted after a long trial, for them to expect to escape a long prison sentence which is entirely proper both as a punishment for the offence and as a warning to others. No member of this court sees the slightest reason for interfering with the 12 months' sentence. Indeed, had it been longer this court would have been most unlikely to reduce it. ... we see no reason at all why a substantial financial penalty should not be imposed in addition to a prison sentence, in order to take the profit out of this filthy trade."

13–07   In *R. v. Holloway* (above) the appellant had been engaged in selling pornographic books, films and video tapes on a commercial scale from a shop in London. He was convicted of six offences of having obscene articles for publication for gain and sentenced to a total of six months' imprisonment. The court, dismissing the appeal held that:

> "the only way of stamping out this filthy trade is by imposing sentences of imprisonment on the first offenders and all connected with the commercial exploitation of pornography. ... salesmen, projectionists, owners and suppliers behind the owners should on conviction lose their liberty. For first offenders sentences need only be comparatively short, but persistent offenders should get the full rigour of the law. In addition courts should take the profit out of this illegal filthy trade by imposing very substantial fines." *(Per* Lawton L.J.)

The court continued by emphasising that the guidelines apply to those who commercially exploit pornography. Others such as the newsagent who through carelessness has the odd pornographic magazine, or the person who takes an obscene video to the rugby club to amuse his friends can be deterred by a fine.

13–08   Later cases include *R. v. Doorgashurn* (1988) 10 Cr.App.R. (S.) 195, where the appellant who ran a small store pleaded guilty to 14 counts of possessing obscene articles for publication for gain. His sentence of 12 months' imprisonment was reduced to six months' on each concurrent, the court taking into account the fact that the defendant operated on a small scale and it was a first offence. Also *R. v. Xenofhontos and Mace* (1992) 13 Cr.App.R. (S.) 580, where X pleaded guilty to a joint offence of publishing an obscene article and to five offences of having an obscene article for publication for gain and M pleaded guilty to the joint offence, to five different offences of having an obscene article for publication for gain and to possessing six further cassettes on a later date. A total of 214 cassettes were recovered from them and the appellants admitted that they bought 100 cassettes every weekend with a view to resale. The tapes were not the worst kind and did not involve children or animals. X was sentenced to 12 months' imprisonment and M to 18 months. On appeal X's sentence was reduced to eight months and M's to 12 months.

(ii) Sentencing guidelines for cinema clubs

Sentences in this category have varied from 28 days' imprisonment to 12 months: in *R. v. Sharman* (unreported, January 30, 1981) the appellant owned a small cinema club where obscene films were shown to adults. He received a sentence of 28 days, the court considering him to be at the lower end of the scale; *R. v. Decozar* (1984) 6 Cr.App.R. (S.) 266, the appellant was the manager of an unlicensed cinema where pornographic homosexual films were shown. He pleaded guilty to eight offence of having an obscene article for publication for gain. His sentence of 12 months' imprisonment was reduced to six on each count concurrent; and *R. v. Calleja* (1985) 7 Cr.App.R. (S.) 13, where the appellant was convicted of having an obscene article for publication for gain. He was concerned with a cinema club operating in premises of which he was part owner. A film was found by the police depicting explicit acts of buggery, but animals or children were not involved. The appellant had received a nine months' prison sentence in 1981 for an offence of publishing an obscene article and this offence was committed within 10 months of his release. He was sentenced to 12 months' imprisonment and a fine of £10,000 with 12 months' imprisonment, consecutive, in default. On appeal, the court found that "the sentence of 12 months' imprisonment was not in any sense excessive nor wrong in principle", although the fine was reduced to £5,000.

13–09

I. CONSENT OF THE DPP REQUIRED

Section 2(3A) of the 1959 Act states that:

13–10

"where the article in question is a moving picture film of a width of at least sixteen millimetres and the relevant publication or the only other publication which followed or could reasonably have been expected to follow from the relevant publication took place or (as the case may be) was to take place in the course of a film exhibition, the consent by, or of; the Director of Public Prosecutions is required before proceedings can be instituted."

13–11   "Relevant publication" means

> "(a) in the case of any proceedings under section 2 for publishing an obscene article, the publication in respect of which the defendant would be charged in the proceedings were brought; and
>
> (b) in the case of any proceedings under section 2 for having an obscene article for publication for gain, the publication which, if the proceedings were brought, the defendant would be alleged to have had in contemplation."

13–12   "Film exhibition" means any exhibition of moving pictures which is produced otherwise then by the simultaneous reception and exhibition of programmes included in a programme service Cinemas Act 1985 s.21 (1959 Act s.2(7)) (see para. 13–45 for definition of "programme service").

II. RESTRICTION ON PROCEEDING AT COMMON LAW

13–13   Section 2(4) states:

> "A person publishing an article shall not be proceeded against for an offence at common law consisting of the publication of any matter contained or embodied in the article where it is of the essence of the offence that the matter is obscene."

Section 2(4A) states:

> "Without prejudice to subsection (4) above, a person shall not be proceeded against for an offence at common law:
>
> (a) in respect of a film exhibition or anything said or done in the course of a film exhibition, where it is of the essence of the common law offence that the exhibition or, as the case may be, what was said or done was obscene, indecent, offensive, disgusting or injurious to morality; or
>
> (b) in respect of an agreement to give a film exhibition or to cause anything to be said or done in the course of such an exhibition where the common law offence consists of conspiring to corrupt public morals or to do any act contrary to public morals or decency."

13–14   The purpose of sections 2(4) and 2(4A) was to prevent the prosecution from charging the common-law offence and thus depriving the defence of the defences available under the 1959 Act.

III. DISCLOSURE

13–15   A magistrates' court has not power under the Magistrates' Courts (Advance Information) Rules (S.I. 1985 No. 601) to order that the prosecution provide the defence with copies of the allegedly pornographic material but may adjourn the case if disclosure is considered to be inadequate: *R. v. Dunmow Justices, ex p. Nash, The Times*, May 17, 1993.

IV. "OBSCENE"

The test of obscenity to be applied is that laid down in section 1(1) of the 1959 Act, namely that: 13–16

> "an article shall be deemed to be obscene if its effect or (where the article comprises two or more distinct items) the effect of any one of its items is, if taken as a whole, such as to tend to deprave and corrupt persons who are likely, having regard to all the relevant circumstances, to read, see or hear the matter contained or embodied in it."

Section 1(1) as far as it relates to publishing an obscene article, must be read in conjunction with section 2(6) of the 1959 Act, which states that: " . . . the question whether an article is obscene shall be determined without regard to any publication by another person unless it could reasonably have been expected that the publication by the other person would follow from publication by the person charged"; and, in relation to having an obscene article for publication for gain, must be read in conjunction with section 1(3)(b) of the 1964 Act, which states that: 13–17

> " . . . the question whether the article is obscene shall be determined by reference to such publication for gain of the article as in the circumstances may reasonably be inferred he had in contemplation and to any further publication that could reasonably be expected to follow from it, but not to any other publication."

In section 1(3)(b), the jury need to decide: first, what publication it may be reasonably inferred that the defendant contemplated; and secondly, what further publication could reasonably be expected to follow from it (*i.e.* not what the defendant contemplated might follow from it).

(a) Intention of the author

The purpose or intention of the author or publisher is irrelevant: *R. v. Hicklin* [1868] L.R. 3 Q.B. 360 the appellant had a pamphlet consisting of extracts from the writings of theologians on the doctrine and discipline of the Romish Church and of which the second half was grossly obscene. He argued that he kept and sold the pamphlet for the purpose of exposing what he thought were the errors of the Church of Rome and the immorality of the confessional. It was held that the publication of such an obscene pamphlet was not justified or excused by the appellant's innocent motives or object— he must be taken to have intended the natural consequences of his act: *Shaw*   13–18 *v. DPP* [1962] A.C. 220. Shaw had compiled a *Ladies' Directory* advertising the services and specialties of prostitutes. *R. v. Calder and Boyars Ltd* [1968] 3 All E.R. 644 concerned the book *Last Exit to Brooklyn* which gave a graphic description of the depravity and degradation of life in Brooklyn. The appellants had contended that the tendency of the book was to shock the reader into a rejection of the evils described.

(b) Non-sexual matters

13-19 Although the Obscene Publications Acts are most commonly used to address articles relating to sexual matters, there is in fact no such limitation. In *John Calder (Publications) Ltd v. Powell* [1965] 1 All E.R. 159, the appellants were the publishers of a book—*Cain's Book*—which concerned the life of a drug addict in New York and, according to the prosecution, highlighted the favourable effects of drug taking. The book was seized under a warrant issued under section 3(1) of the 1959 Act and the appellants intervened to show cause why the book should not be forfeited. On appeal, it was held, *inter alia*, that there was no reason to confine obscenity and tendency to deprave or corrupt to sex and there was ample evidence on which the justices could hold that the book was obscene. This decision has never been challenged and was accepted without argument in *DPP v. A & BC Chewing Gum Ltd* [1967] 2 All E.R. 504 and *R. v. Calder and Boyars Ltd* (above) which involved violence.

(c) Evidential requirement

13-20 In *R. v. O'Sullivan* [1995] 1 Cr.App.R. 455, the Court of Appeal agreed with the summing-up of the recorder who had directed the jury that:

"it is not necessary for the prosecution to prove that anybody was depraved and corrupted by reading or seeing the article. . . . The expression 'deprave and corrupt' is directed to the effect on the minds of those who might be exposed to the material. Who those persons may be and whether the material would tend to corrupt them, or some of them, is a matter for you as the judges of the facts, having regard to all the circumstances. Those circumstances include the nature of the material, whether Mr O'Sullivan was acting as a distributor or retailer who was likely to read the article or see the video tape, whether there was any effective restrictions on distribution of the material and whether any further publication could be expected to follow from the supplier. . . . The fact that the article in question is sold in premises frequented only by persons who are already depraved and who go there for the purpose of feeding their depravity, is not in itself sufficient to negative obscenity. . . . You should bear in mind that the law is not confined to protecting only those of tender years who are not yet morally corrupted and it is sufficient if the article increases or sustains an existing state of corruption derived from exposure to material of this kind. . . . A retailer of pornographic material to a large number of customers who are not likely to be corrupted by such material does not thereby acquire a licence to expose for sale or to sell such articles to other people who are likely to be corrupted by them."

V. "Corrupt And Deprave"

The words "corrupt and deprave" have been considered in a number of cases **13–21**
and were defined by Byrne L.J. in *R. v. Penguin Books Ltd* [1961] Crim L.R.
176 to mean "to render morally unsound or rotten, to destroy the moral
purity or chastity of, to pervert or ruin a good quality, to debase, to defile" in
respect of corrupt, and, as far as deprave is concerned, "to make morally
bad, to pervert, to debase or corrupt morally". However, in *R. v. Anderson*
[1972] 1 Q.B. 304 it was held that it is the test laid down in section 1(1) alone
which is to be applied and that to refer a jury to the dictionary definition of
obscenity is a misdirection.

In *Knuller (Publishing, Printing and Promotions) Ltd v. DPP* [1973] A.C.
435, Reid L.J. found that the words "deprave" and "corrupt" were synon-
ymous and that corrupt is a strong word meaning far more than "led morally
astray".

It is the effect of pornographic articles on the mind, including the emotions **13–22**
that is relevant and it is not necessary that any physical or overt sexual
activity should result: *DPP v. Whyte* [1972] 3 All E.R. 12.

In *DPP v. Whyte* [1972] 3 All E.R. 12 the justices reached the decision that **13–23**
the books consisting of "hard pornography" which the defendants sold in
their bookstore were likely to be read by men whose morals were already in
a state of depravity or corruption and they could not therefore be satisfied
that the books would have a tendency to deprave and corrupt as required by
the Act. The House of Lords rejected the argument, holding that the
proposition that the likely readers of books, being addicts to that type of
material whose morals were already in a state of depravity, were incapable of
being further depraved or corrupted, was fallacious—the 1959 Act was
concerned not merely with the once and for all corruption of the wholly
innocent but protected equally the less innocent from further corruption and
the addict from feeding or increasing his addiction.

(a) Position of police officers

However, in *R. v. Clayton, R. v. Halsey* [1962] 3 All E.R. 500—which was **13–24**
cited in *DPP v. Whyte*—the defendants were the proprietor and assistant in
a book shop. They sold on two separate occasions obscene publications to
plain clothes police officers. At the trial the officers were cross-examined on
the basis that they could not be corrupted or depraved by the material that
they had purchased. Following conviction, the defendants successfully
appealed and it was held that the degree of inherent obscenity must be related
to the susceptibility of the viewer and, though it was theoretically possible
that a jury could take the view that even a most experienced police officer,
despite his protestations, was susceptible to the influence of the article
concerned, yet bearing in mind the onus and degree of proof in a criminal

case, it would be unsafe and therefore wrong to leave that question to the jury. Since the amendment to the 1959 Act by the 1964 Act which created the offence of having an obscene article for publication for gain, the problems encountered by the prosecution when obscene articles are purchased by police officers may seldom arise or, depending on the circumstances, may be overcome with a charge of attempt publication.

(b) Application of obscenity test

13–25   In applying the test of obscenity, the jury must decide whether the tendency of any publication is to corrupt and deprave those whose minds today are open to immoral influences and into whose hands the publication may fall at the time when it is published or in the future. It is necessary to take into account the changing attitude toward sex and the fact that what is acceptable today was not necessarily so acceptable for example in 1868: *R. v. Martin Secker Warburg Ltd* [1954] 2 All E.R. 683. However, it is inappropriate for the jury when considering whether sex videos shown in a private cinema are obscene, to be directed to have regard to what was available and permissible elsewhere in the world so that they might decide what society in 1995 considers acceptable: *R. v. Elliot* [1996] 1 Cr.App.R. 432. The Court of Appeal, applying *R. v. Reiter* [1954] 2 Q.B.16 held that evidence of other publications in circulation is inadmissible if designed to show that they are as obscene as, or not materially different from, the articles in question. The jury must be directed to decide on the effect of each video, applying the standards of ordinary decent people in today's world.

(c) Expert evidence

13–26   Generally the admission of expert evidence on the issue whether or not the article is obscene is wrong (*R. v. Anderson* [1971] 3 All E.R. 1152), since the question is entirely one for the jury. However, it has been held in *R. v. Skirving* [1985] Q.B. 819 that expert evidence is admissible if the subject matter of the obscenity (in this case cocaine and the effects of using it) was outside the knowledge of the ordinary person, but only for the purpose of informing the jury. Once they are in possession of that knowledge it is still a matter for them whether an article has a tendency to corrupt or deprave. Similarly, in *DPP v. A & BC Chewing Gum Ltd* [1968] 1 Q.B. 159 it was held that the evidence of psychiatrists was admissible to show the sort of effect bubble gum battle cards would have on the minds of children of different groups and what the cards would lead them to do.

(d) Judge to remind jury of defence case

13–27   Where the trial judge failed to remind the jury that the proposition central to the defence case was that the article was so disgusting that instead of corrupting and depraving, it would tend to cause people to revolt from activity of that kind, it was held that the omission was fatal to the conviction:

R. v. Calder and Boyars Ltd [1969] 1 Q.B. 151 and *R. v. Anderson* [1972] 1 Q.B. 304.

VI. "ITS EFFECT OR ... THE EFFECT OF ANY ONE OF ITS ITEMS ... IF TAKEN AS A WHOLE"

The section 1(1) test should, with respect to novels, be applied to the book as   13–28
a whole rather than to selected passages in isolation *R. v. Penguin Books Ltd*
[1961] Crim L.R. 176. As far as magazines are concerned, it was held in *R. v. Anderson* [1972] 1 Q.B. 304 that such a direction to a jury would be
wrong. In that case, the appellants were editors and company publishers of a
magazine, *Oz (No. 28) School Kids Issue*, which over some 48 pages
contained serious and innocuous articles as well as articles, illustrations and
advertisements which related to lesbianism, homosexuality and oral sex. At
the trial the prosecution and the judge accepted that the jury should look at
the magazine as a whole and not at the individual items in isolation.

On appeal following conviction on the Obscene Publication Act 1959
counts, it was held that it was clear from section 1 of the 1959 Act that
where, as in this case, the article comprised a number of distinct items, the
proper view of obscenity was to apply the test to the individual items in
question. If the test when so applied showed that one item was obscene that
was enough to make the whole article obscene. The case follows the decision
in *Paget Publications Ltd v Watson* [1952] 1 All E.R. 1256 where the only
obscene part of the publication was the inside of the covers. The appellant
argued that the magistrates had no power to order the destruction of the
whole publication in those circumstances. It was held however that a
publication was an obscene publication even if only a part of it was
obscene.

VII. "PERSONS WHO ARE LIKELY ... TO READ"

One of the grounds of appeal in *R. v. Calder and Boyars Ltd* [1968] 3 All   13–29
E.R. 644 was that the trial judge failed to give guidance to the jury in
summing-up on the question of what is meant by "persons who were likely to
read the book". It was held that the jury should have been directed to
consider whether the effect of the book was to tend to deprave and corrupt a
significant proportion of those persons who were likely to read it and that
what amounted to a significant proportion was a matter for the jury.

DPP v. Whyte [1972] 3 All E.R. 12 decided that in determining the   13–30
question who are the "likely" readers, it is not appropriate for the justices or
the jury to consider what is the largest category of "most likely" readers and
then to exclude persons falling within other categories from consideration,
since it does not follow that the latter are not also "likely" readers. Pearson
L.J. observed that the "significant proportion" direction had been suitable
on the facts of the case in *Calder and Boyars* but that it cannot be safely
transplanted to cases of a different character. He said that the definition of
obscenity contains no requirement as to the number of persons or as to the

proportion of its readers which the article will tend to corrupt or deprave. It was held that "persons" refers to "some persons" though if the number is really negligible then the *de minimis* rule might apply and Cross L.J. further stated that: "a significant proportion of a class means a part which is not numerically negligible but which may be much less than half."

13–31　　　By virtue of section 2(6) of the 1959 Act "in any proceedings against a person under ... [section 2] ... the question whether an article is obscene shall be determined without regard to any publication by another person unless it could reasonably have been expected that the publication by the other person would follow from publication by the person charged".

Section 1(3)(b) of the 1964 Act states: "the question whether the article is obscene shall be determined by reference to such publication for gain of the article as in the circumstances may reasonably be inferred he had in contemplation and to any further publication that could reasonably be expected to follow from it, but not to any other publication."

13–32　　　The issue of "persons who are likely ... to read" and the effect of sections 2(6) of the 1959 Act and 1(3)(b) of the 1964 Act was considered in *Att.-Gen.'s Ref. (No.2 of 1975)* (1976) 62 Cr.App.R.255, where the question referred to the Court of Appeal was:

"Whether, for the purposes of section 2(1) of the 1959 Act (as amended), in relation to offences for having an obscene article for publication for gain and publishing an obscene article, the persons who are likely, having regard to all the relevant circumstances, to read, see or hear the matter contained or embodied in an allegedly obscene article, are to be or can be defined by reference to their opportunity to read, see or hear the matter otherwise than as a result of a publication of the article within section 1(3) of the 1959 Act and whether and if so, to what extent section 2(6) of the 1959 Act and section 1(3)(b) of the 1964 Act affect either the definition of the potential audience within section 1(1) or the publication of the article within section 1(3) of the 1959 Act."

13–33　　　The court held that: (i) in determining whether an article was obscene, within section 1(1) of the 1959 Act, the jury were only entitled to take into account the effect of the article on persons who were likely to read, see or hear the matter complained of as a result of the "publication" to them of the article within section 1(3) of the 1959 Act; (ii) the word "publication" in section 2(6) of the 1959 Act and section 1(3)(b) of the 1964 Act had the meaning prescribed by section 1(3) of the 1959 Act, and accordingly the jury were only entitled to have regard to the effect of the article on persons likely to read, see or hear the matter complained of in consequence of a publication of the article by another person following the publication by the person charged, where the distribution, circulation, showing, etc., of the article by the other person amounted to "publication" of the article by that person within section 1(3)".

13–34　　　Bell J., in giving the judgment of the Court of Appeal in *R. v. O'Sullivan* [1995] 1 Cr.App.R.455, commented that it was not easy to understand the relationship of section 1(1) of the 1959 Act to section 1(3)(b) of the 1964 Act as far as the question of obscenity was concerned but that it is clear that the provisions of the two Acts must be read together, as in this case, where the appellant was not alleged to have published the articles in fact but had contrcl of the articles with a view to their publication by sale or offer for sale in sex shops.

VIII. "ARTICLE"

"Article" is defined by section 1(2) of the 1959 Act and "means any description of article containing or embodying matter to be read or looked at or both, any sound record, and any film or other record of a picture or pictures".   13–35

A video cassette is an article for the purposes of section 1(2): *Att.-Gen.'s Ref. (No.5 of 1980)* [1981] 1 W.L.R. 88.   13–36

The 1963 case of *Straker v. DPP* [1963] 1 All E.R. 697 decided that negatives did not come within the ambit of section 1(2) of the 1959 Act since they were not capable of publication. This loophole was closed by the Obscene Publications Act 1964 section 2 which states that: 13–37

"(1) The Obscene Publications Act 1959 (as amended by this Act) shall apply in relation to anything which is intended to be used, either alone or as one of a set, for the reproduction or manufacture therefrom of articles containing or embodying matter to be read, looked at or listened to as if it were an article containing or embodying that matter so far as that matter is to be derived from it or from the set.

(2) For the purposes of the Obscene Publications Act 1959 (as so amended) an article shall be deemed to be had or kept for publication if it is had or kept for the reproduction or manufacture therefrom of articles for publication; and the question whether an article so had or kept is obscene shall—

   (a) for purposes of section 2 of the Act be determined in accordance with section 1(3)(b) above as if any reference there to publication of the article were a reference to publication of articles reproduced or manufactured from it; and

   (b) for purposes of section 3 of the Act be determined on the assumption that articles reproduced or manufactured from it would be published in any manner likely having regard to the circumstances in which it was found, but in no other manner."

An article can either be one item (*e.g.* a book) in which case it must be considered as a whole for the purposes of the Act, or it may comprise a number of items (*e.g.* a magazine) in which case each item must then be considered individually and it is sufficient if the effect of any one of the items, taken as a whole, is to tend to deprave and corrupt.   13–38

In *R. v. Anderson* [1971] 3 All E.R. 1152, Lord Widgery C.J. said that:

"a novelist who writes a complete novel and who cannot cut out particular passages without destroying the theme of the novel is ent itled to have his work judged as a whole, but a magazine publisher who has a far wider

267

discretion as to what he will and will not insert by way of items is to be judged under the 1959 Act on what we call the item to item basis."

IX. PUBLICATION

13–39   "Publication" is defined by section 1 of the 1959 Act:

> "(3) For the purposes of this Act a person publishes an article who—
>   (a) distributes, circulates, sells, lets on hire, gives, or lends it, or who offers it for sale or for letting on hire; or
>   (b) in the case of an article containing or embodying matter to be looked at or a record, shows, plays or projects it, or, where the matter is data stored electronically, transmits that data.
> (4) For the purposes of this Act a person also publishes an article to the extent that any matter recorded on it is included by him in a programme included in a programme service.
> (5) Where the inclusion of any matter in a programme so included would, if that matter were recorded matter, constitute the publication of an obscene article for the purposes of this Act by virtue of subsection (4) above, this Act shall have effect in relation to the inclusion of that matter in that programme as if it were recorded matter.
> (6) In this section 'programme' and 'programme service' have the same meaning as in the Broadcasting Act 1990."

(a) Publication to be divided into groups

13–40   According to *R. v. Barker* [1962] 1 All E.R. 748, section 1(3)(a) of the 1959 Act puts the forms of publication into three distinct groups in so far as the words: "sells, lets on hire, gives, or lends" refers to publication to an individual; "distributes, circulates" is in respect of publication to a wider group, involving more than one person; and, finally, "offers for sale or for letting on hire" requires no more than a simple offer or letting to constitute publication. This case considered the issue of re-publication albeit without reference to section 2(6) of the 1959 Act. The appellant was charged with five counts of publishing obscene articles (photographs) to named individuals. There was evidence that one of these individuals kept the photographs to himself and did not show them to anyone.

It was held that where publication is to an individual the following issues are for the jury:

> (a) whether the effect of the article is such as to tend to deprave and corrupt the individual to whom it is published; on this issue the jury should take into account the article itself, and should have regard to the age and occupation of the person to whom the article is published, if these are proved in evidence, but the fact that the accused may be unaware of these details concerning the individual to whom it is published is irrelevant;

(b) whether any other person or persons were likely to see the article, *i.e.* whether re-publication could reasonably be expected. In this respect, the age and occupation of the individual to whom the article as published are relevant and evidence that the individual to whom the article was published kept it locked up is a relevant but not conclusive factor;

(c) if the answer to (b) is yes, then a further issue arises whether the article is such as to tend to deprave and corrupt the person or persons to whom re-publication could reasonably have been expected and on this issue, similar considerations as in (a) apply.

As far as publication only is concerned, *R. v. Carlile* (1845) 1 Cox C.C. **13–41** 229 found that the sale of an obscene print to a person in private, he having in the first instance requested that such prints should be shown to him, his object being to prosecute the seller, is sufficient to sustain the charge.

More recently, in *R. v. Taylor* [1994] Crim L.R. 527 the Court of Appeal **13–42** held that a photographic developer, who develops a film sent to him by customers depicting obscene acts and who makes prints as requested and sends the prints back to those customers, publishes the prints by way of selling or distributing them. The court found that the development of negatives into prints created new articles by the process of printing.

(b) Definition of programme and programme service

Section 1(4) and (5) of the 1959 Act refer to "programme" and "programme **13–43** service" which is defined in section 1(6) as having the same meaning as in the Broadcasting Act 1990.

"Programme" by virtue of the Broadcasting Act 1990, ss 202 and 203 **13–44** includes: "an advertisement and, in relation to any service, includes any item included in that service" and in relation to a programme service, "includes any item included in that service".

"Programme services" are defined in section 201 of the 1990 Act as **13–45** follows:

"(1) In this Act, 'programme Service' means any of the following services (whether or not it is, or it requires to be, licensed under this Act), namely—

(a) any television broadcasting service or other television programme service (within the meaning of Part I of this Act);

(b) any sound broadcasting service or licensable sound programme service (within the meaning of Part III of this Act);

(c) any other service which consists in the sending, by means of a telecommunication system, of sounds or visual images or both either—

(i) for reception at two or more places in the United Kingdom (whether they are so sent for simultaneous reception or at different times in response to requests made by different users of the service); or

(ii) for reception at a place in the United Kingdom for the

purpose of being presented there to members of the public
or to any group of persons.

(2)   Subsection (1)(c) does not apply to—

    (a)   a local delivery service (within the meaning of Part II of this
Act);

    (b)   a service where the running of the telecommunications system
does not require to be licensed under Part II of the Telecommunications Act 1984; or

    (c)   a two-way service (as defined by section 46(2))."

X. "WHETHER FOR GAIN OR NOT ... PUBLISHES ... OR HAS ... FOR PUBLICATION FOR GAIN"

13-46   The addition of the words "for gain" introduces a commercial element into
section 2 of the 1959 Act. However, it is only a mandatory requirement in
respect of *having* an obscene article for publication—it is immaterial for the
purposes of the offence whether a person who *publishes* an obscene article
does so for gain or not (although it may well affect sentence).

13-47   The words "has an obscene article for publication for gain" (whether gain
to the same person or another) were added to section 2 of the Obscene
Publications Act 1959 by the Obscene Publications Act 1964, s. 1(1) to deal
with the limitations on the publication form of the offence, thus closing
loopholes in the 1959 Act revealed by cases such as *Mella v. Monahan* [1961]
Crim. L.R. 175 (the displaying an obscene article in a shop window is an
invitation to treat and not an offer for sale); *R. v. Clayton; R. v. Halsey*
[1963] 1 Q.B. 163 (that supplying to a supposedly non-corruptible person
may not be publication).

13-48   Section 2(1) as amended should be read in conjunction with section 1(2) of
the 1964 Act, which states that "a person shall be deemed to have an article
for publication for gain if with a view to such publication he has the article in
his ownership, possession or control". Therefore, a person who, as in the
case of *R. v. O'Sullivan* [1995] 1 Cr.App.R.455, has obscene items in a lock-
up garage as stock-in-trade for supplying sex-shops, is rightly convicted of
having them for publication for gain even though he may not have offered
them for sale at the time they are seized.

13-49   References in section 1 of the 1964 Act to "publication for gain" apply to
any publication with a view to gain, whether the gain is to accrue by way of
consideration for the publication or in any other way (s. 1(5) of the 1964
Act).

13-50   By virtue of the 1964 Act, s. 1(4), where articles are seized under section 3
of the 1959 Act and a person is convicted under section 2 of the 1959 Act of
having them for publication for gain, the court on his conviction shall order
the forfeiture of those articles. Such an order shall not take effect until the
expiration of the ordinary time within which an appeal in the matter of the
proceedings in which the order was made may be instituted or, where such an
appeal is duly instituted, until the appeal is finally decided or abandoned. An
application for a case to be stated or for leave to appeal shall be treated as the

institution of an appeal, and where a decision on appeal is subject to a further appeal, the appeal shall not be deemed to be finally decided until the expiration of the ordinary time within which a further appeal may be instituted or, where a further appeal is duly instituted, until the further appeal is finally decided or abandoned.

C. DEFENCES

I. No Cause To Suspect

It is a defence to a 1959 Act section 2 offence (publishing an obscene article)   **13–51**
to prove (on a balance of probabilities—*R. v. Carr-Briant* [1943] K.B. 697) that the accused had not examined the article in respect of which he is charged and had no reasonable cause to suspect that it was such that his publication of it would make him liable to be convicted of the offence (1959 Act, s. 2(5)).

It is a defence also to an offence of having an obscene article for publication for gain (s. 2(1) of the 1959 Act as amended by s. 1(1) of the 1964 Act) to prove that the accused had not examined the article and had no reasonable cause to suspect that it was such that his having it would make him liable to be convicted of the offence (1964 Act, s. 1(3)(a)).

II. Public Good

The Obscene Publications Act 1959, s. 4 (as amended by the Criminal Law   **13–52**
Act 1977, s. 53(b)) states:

"(1) Subject to subsection (1A) of this section, a person shall not be convicted of an offence against section 2 of this Act, and an order for forfeiture shall not be made under the foregoing section, if it is proved that publication of the article in question is justified as being for the public good on the ground that it is in the interests of science, literature, art or learning, or of other objects of general concern.

(1A) Subsection (1) of this section shall not apply where the article in   **13–53**
question is a moving picture film or soundtrack, but—

(a) a person shall not be convicted of an offence against section 2 of this Act in relation to any such film or soundtrack, and

(b) an order for forfeiture of any such film or soundtrack shall not be made under section 3 of this Act,

if it is proved that publication of the film or soundtrack is justified as being for the public good on the ground that it is in the interests of drama, opera, ballet or any other art, or of literature or learning.

(2) It is hereby declared that the evidence of experts as to the literary, artistic, scientific or other merits of an article may be admitted in any proceedings under this Act either to establish or to negative the said ground.

(3)   In this section 'moving picture soundtrack' means any sound record designed for playing with a moving picture film, whether incorporated with the film or not."

Section 4 does not negative obscenity but enables a defendant to argue that an article should be published in spite of its obscenity because to do so is for the public good.

(a) Directions for the jury

13-54   The proper approach, when the section 4 defence is raised, is for the judge to direct the jury to determine: first whether the article is obscene; secondly, whether it was published by the defendant; and thirdly, whether the defendant has succeeded in establishing (on the balance of probabilities—R. v. Calder and Boyars Ltd [1968] 3 All E.R. 644) the defence under section 4(1) by showing that publication of the article is justified as being for the public good: DPP v. Jordan [1976] 3 All E.R. 775. In relation to the third limb, the jury must be directed to consider on the one hand the number of readers they believe would tend to be depraved and corrupted by the book, the strength of the tendency to deprave or corrupt, and the nature of the depravity or corruption; on the other hand, they should assess the strength of the literary, sociological or ethical merit which they considered the book to possess; they should then weigh up all these factors and decide whether on balance the publication was proved to be justified as being for the public good: R. v. Calder and Boyars Ltd (above).

(b) Expert evidence

13-55   Expert evidence is admissible under section 4(2) only in relation to whether the article is in the interests of science, literature, art, etc., and not in relation to whether the article is obscene in the first place. The defence witnesses should be called first, followed by the Crown's in rebuttal, since the Crown could not know in advance on what section 4 grounds the defence were relying and to call Crown witnesses first would be a potential waste of time and money: R. v. Calder and Boyars Ltd (above).

Even where the only expert evidence called supports the defence, the court is entitled to reject it, if having considered the article, they think that publication is not justified as being for the public good: John Calder (Publications) Ltd v. Powell [1965] 1 All E.R. 159.

(c) Evidence of other publications

13-56   In R. v. Penguin Books Ltd [1961] Crim. L.R. 176 it was held that where a defence of public good was raised, evidence relating to other books and their literary merits may be admitted but only to establish the "climate of literature"—it is not permissible to prove that other books as obscene as the one in issue are in circulation and have not been the subject of prosecution.

(d) Definitions

The phrase " ... other objects of general concern" in section 4(1) falls within   **13–57**
the same field or dimension as "science, literature, art or learning" and can
not fall in the totally different area of effect on sexual behaviour which is
covered in section 1(1) of the 1959 Act. Expert evidence that obscene
material is psychologically beneficial and may divert certain deviant and
perverted persons from anti-social activities is inadmissible: *D P P v. Jordan*
[1976] 3 All E.R. 775.

"Learning" in section 1(1) means a "product of scholarship" and in the   **13–58**
context of that section does not include teaching or any form of education
including sex education and consequently, expert evidence to show that an
article contains material which has merit in the field of sex education or
providing information about sexual matters is not admissible: *Att.-Gen.'s
Ref. (No. 3 of 1977)* [1978] 3 All E.R. 1166.

(e) Other defence submissions

Another argument put forward (unsuccessfully) by the defence in support of   **13–59**
"for the public good" was that it is in the interest of science, learning, or
other objects of general concern that members of society can read and that if
obscene material tempted people to read, society was benefited: *R v. Sumner*
[1977] Crim. L.R. 362.

D. POWERS OF SEARCH, SEIZURE AND FORFEITURE

By virtue of the obscene Publications Act 1959, s. 3, justices of the peace may   **13–60**
issue a search warrant empowering any constable to enter, if need be by
force, search for, seize and remove any articles found (which includes
negatives: Obscene Publications Act 1964, s.2) which the constable has
reason to believe to be obscene articles and to be kept for publication for
gain.

Before the warrant can be issued, the justice must hear the information on   **13–61**
oath and be satisfied that there are reasonable grounds for suspecting that in
any premises (including a stall or a vehicle) in the petty sessions area for
which he acts, and which is named in the information, obscene articles are, or
are from time to time, kept for publication for gain. The information must be
laid by or on behalf of the Director of Public Prosecutions or by a constable
(Criminal Justice Act 1967, s.25) and if the article is such that proceedings
under section 2 of the 1959 Act could only be instituted by or with the
consent of the Director of Public Prosecutions, forfeiture can only be ordered
if the information for a section 3 warrant was laid by or on behalf of the
Director of Public Prosecutions (1959 Act, s.3(3A)). The issue and execution
of the warrant must be in conformity with the Police and Criminal Evidence
Act 1984, ss. 15 and 16.

Where any obscene articles are seized, the warrant also empowers the   **13–62** seizure and removal of any documents found in the premises, stall or vehicle which relate to a trade or business carried on at the premises or from the stall or vehicle (s. 3(2) of the 1959 Act).

13–63   The warrant authorises only one entry, search and seizure although where the police have entered more than once on the same warrant, it is not necessarily fatal: see *R. v. Adams* (1979) 70 Cr.App.R. 149 where *R. v. Sang* [1980] A.C.402 was applied).

I. Procedure For Seized Articles

13–64   Once articles have been seized under section 3(1), they shall be brought before a justice of the peace, acting for the same petty sessions area as the justice who issued the warrant, who may issue a summons to the occupier of the premises (or user of the stall or vehicle) to appear before the magistrates' court for that petty sessions area, to show cause why the articles or any of them should not be forfeited. The summons will be issued on the information previously made on oath for the warrant and must be issued within a reasonable time after the execution of the warrant: *Cox v. Stinton* [1951] 2 K.B. 1021.

By virtue of the Prosecution of Offences Act 1985, s.3(2)(d), it is the duty of the Director of Public Prosecutions to take over the conduct of any proceedings commenced by summons under the Obscene Publications Act, s.3.

II. After Service Of The Summons

13–65   When the person summoned has either appeared, or service of the summons has been proved, the court shall make an order for forfeiture if it is satisfied as respects any of the articles, that at the time when they were seized they were obscene articles kept for publication for gain.

13–66   There is no reason why the justices who issued the summons should not comprise the court which hears and determines whether the articles should be forfeited: *Morgan v. Bowker* [1963] 1 All E.R. 691.

13–67   It is for the justices to decide whether the articles are obscene and they can only do this by reading or looking at the articles themselves. It is not for the prosecution to read particular paragraphs of books alleged to be obscene or to indicate in what respects they allege that pictures are obscene unless the justices ask them to address them or point out some particular matter: *Thomson v. Chain Libraries Ltd* [1954] 2 All E.R. 616.

13–68   However, it is not necessary for a justice to read every word of a book—it is only necessary for him to make himself fully acquainted with the book as a whole so that he is in a position to pass judgment on it. In *Olympia Press Ltd v. Hollis* [1974] 1 All E.R. 108 34 books had been seized. Although not all the justices had read all the books, having divided the books between them so that each book had been read by at least two of the six presiding, it was clear that with the material before them they had discussed and deliberated on the books as a whole so that a collective opinion could be formed and formulated into a specific decision of the bench. Nor is there an obligation on the court to examine each article individually and the judge is entitled to ask the police to divide material into classes according to their degree of obscenity and decide the issue of obscenity on the basis of samples taken from each class: *R. v. Snaresbrook Crown Court, ex p. Commissioner of Police of the Metropolis* [1984] 79 Cr.App.R. 184.

III. DETERMINATION OF OBSCENITY

The question whether an article is obscene for the purposes of section 3 shall   13–69
be determined on the assumption that copies of it would be published in any manner likely having regard to the circumstances in which it was found, but no other manner (1959 Act, s.3(7)). The correct procedure is for the court to hear evidence of the nature of the publication and what publication (as defined by s. 1(3)) was likely. Evidence as to the defendant's intention is irrelevant, although the nature of the business carried on and the methods employed in it are relevant since they are as much part of "the circumstances in which the articles were found" as is the nature of the premises. The court should then determine whether the articles would tend to deprave or corrupt persons to whom publication would be so made: *Morgan v. Bowker* [1964] 1 All E.R. 691.

IV. DEFENCE OF PUBLIC GOOD

The defence of public good under section 4(1) applies to section 3 proceed-   13–70
ings. Where such a defence is raised, it is for the justices to conduct the proceedings in a manner which they consider to be right and which will do justice to the parties. Each case depends on its own facts. The justices should first determine the issue of obscenity and then invite evidence and representations from the defence on the issue of public good.

V. JURISDICTION

Publication can include publication outside the jurisdiction: *Gold Star*   13–71
Publications v. DPP [1981] 2 All E.R. 257, where the articles seized were kept in crates in a warehouse prior to export for sale overseas.

VI. EXTENT OF THE FORFEITURE ORDER

The order for forfeiture relates to the whole article even if parts only are   13–72
obscene: *Paget Publications Ltd v. Watson* [1952] 1 All E.R. 1256, where only the illustrations on the inside covers of a book were obscene) and cannot relate to any articles which have already been returned to the occupier of the premises (s.3(3) of the Obscene Publications Act 1959).
Position of third parties
    By virtue of section 3(4) of the Obscene Publications Act 1959, in addition   13–73

to the person summoned, any other person being the owner, author or maker of any of the articles brought before the court, or any other person through whose hands they had passed before being seized, shall be entitled to appear before the court on the day specified in the summons to show cause why they should not be forfeited. There is no requirement to issue separate summons to persons so entitled although each of them is entitled to "show cause" separately—their knowledge of the proceedings will be obtained from the summons issued to the occupier of the premises or user of the stall or vehicle.

13–74 Where an order is made under section 3 for the forfeiture of any articles, any person who appears or was entitled to appear, to show cause against the making of the order may appeal to the Crown Court. The order for forfeiture shall not take effect until the expiration of the period within which notice of appeal to the Crown Court may be given against the order, or, if before the expiration thereof notice of appeal is duly given or application made for the statement of a case, until the final determination or abandonment of the proceedings on the appeal or case (Obscene Publications Act 1959, s.3(5)).

VII. Costs

13–75 If, in respect of any articles brought before the court, forfeiture is not ordered, the court may if it thinks fit, order such costs as it considers reasonable, to be paid by the person on whose information the warrant was issued, to any person who has appeared before the court to show cause why those articles should not be forfeited (Obscene Publications Act 1959, s.3(6)). The order for costs is enforceable as a civil debt.

E. APPLICATION OF THE OBSCENE PUBLICATIONS ACT 1959 TO TELEVISION AND SOUND PROGRAMMES

13–76 The Broadcasting Act 1990, Sched. 15 states:

"1.   In this Schedule—
      'the 1959 Act' means the Obscene Publications Act 1959;
      'relevant programme' means a programme included in a programme service;
      and other expressions used in this Schedule which are also used in the 1959 Act have the same meaning as in that Act.

2.   Where—
      (a)   any matter is included by any person in a relevant programme in circumstances falling within section 1(5) of the 1959 Act, and
      (b)   that matter has been provided, for inclusion in that programme, by some other person,
      the 1959 Act shall have effect as if that matter had been inclusion in that programme by that other person (as well as by the person referred to in sub-paragraph (a)).

3.   It is hereby declared that where a person has an obscene article in his ownership, possession or control with a view to the matter recorded on it being included in a relevant programme, the article shall by taken for the purposes of the 1959 Act to be an obscene article had or kept by that person for publication for gain.

4(1)   Proceedings for an offence under section 2 of the 1959 Act for   **13-77**
publishing an obscene article shall not be instituted except by or with the consent of the Director of Public Prosecutions in any case where—
(a)   the relevant publication, or
(b)   the only other publication which followed from the relevant publication,
took place in the course of the inclusion of a programme in a programme service; and in this sub-paragraph 'the relevant publication' means the publication in respect of which the defendant would be charged if the proceedings were brought.

(2)   Proceedings for an offence under section 2 of the 1959 Act for having an obscene article for publication for gain shall not be instituted except by or with the consent of the Director of Public Prosecutions in any case where—
(a)   the relevant publication, or
(b)   the only other publication which could reasonably have been expected to follow from the relevant publication,
was to take place in the course of the inclusion of a programme in a programme service; and in this sub-paragraph 'the relevant publication' means the publication which, if the proceedings were brought, the defendant would be alleged to have had in contemplation.

(3)   Without prejudice to the duty of the court to make an order for the   **13-78**
forfeiture of an article under section 1(4) of the Obscene Publications Act 1964 (orders on conviction), in a case where by virtue of sub-paragraph (2) above proceedings under section 2 of the 1959 Act for having an article for publication for gain could not be instituted except by or with the consent of the Director of Public Prosecutions, no order for the forfeiture of the article shall be made under section 3 of the 1959 Act (power of search and seizure) unless the warrant under which the article was seized was issued on an information laid by or on behalf of the Director of Public Prosecutions.

5(1)   A person shall not be convicted of an offence under section 2 of the   **13-79**
1959 Act in respect of the inclusion of any matter in a relevant programme if he proves that he did not know and had no reason to suspect that the programme would include matter rendering him liable to be convicted of such an offence.

(2)   Where the publication in issue in any proceedings under that Act consists of the inclusion of any matter in a relevant programme, section 4(1) of that Act (general defence of public good) shall not apply; but—
(a)   a person shall not be convicted of an offence under section 2 of that Act, and

(b) an order for forfeiture shall not be made under section 3 of that Act,

if it is proved that the inclusion of the matter in question in a relevant programme is justified as being for the public good on the ground that it is in the interest of—

(i)   drama, opera, ballet or any other art,

(ii) science, literature or learning, or

(iii) any other objects of general concern.

(3) Section 4(2) of that Act (admissibility of opinions of experts) shall apply for the purposes of sub-paragraph (2) above as it applies for the purposes of section 4(1) and 4(1A) of that Act.

13-80   6. Without prejudice to section 2(4) of the 1959 Act, a person shall not be proceeded against for an offence at common law—

(a) in respect of a relevant programme or anything said or done in the course of such a programme, where it is of the essence of the common law offence that the programme or (as the case may be) what was said or done was obscene, indecent, offensive, disgusting or injurious to morality; or

(b) in respect of an agreement to cause a programme to be included in a programme service or to cause anything to be said or done in the course of a programme which is to be so included, where the common law offence consists of conspiring to corrupt public morals or to do any act contrary to pubic morals or decency."

F. OBSCENE LIBEL AND CONSPIRACY TO CORRUPT PUBLIC MORALS

13-81   The publication of an obscene libel is an indictable offence punishable at common law: *R. v. Wilkes* [1770] 4 Burr. 2527: *R. v. Hicklin* [1868] L.R. 3 Q.B. 360. However, in order to prevent the prosecution from depriving the defence of the defences available under the Obscene Publications Act 1959, by charging the common law offence, section 2(4) of the Obscene Pubications Act provides:

"A person publishing an article shall not be proceeded against for an offence at common law consisting of the publication of any matter contained or embodied in the article where it is of the essence of the offence that the matter is obscene.

2(4A)Without prejudice to subsection (4) above, a person shall not be proceeded against for an offence at common law—

(a) in respect of a film exhibition or anything said or done in the course of a film exhibition, where it is of the essence of the common law offence that the exhibition or, as the case may be, what was said or done was obscene, indecent, offensive, disgusting or injurious to morality; or

(b) in respect of an agreement to give a film exhibition or to cause anything to be said or done in the course of such an exhibition where the common law offence consists of conspiring to corrupt public morals or to do any act contrary to public morals or decency."

Paragraph 6 of Schedule 15 to the Broadcasting Act 1990 extends section **13–82**
2(4) of the 1959 Act to sound and television:

"Without prejudice to section 2(4) of the 1959 Act, a person shall not be proceeded against for an offence at common law—
(a) in respect of a relevant programme or anything said or done in the course of such programme, where it is of the essence of the common law offence that the programme or (as the case may be) what was said or done was obscene, indecent, offensive, disgusting or injurious to morality; or
(b) in respect of an agreement to cause a programme to be included in a programme service or to cause anything to be said or done in the course of a programme which is to be so included, where the common law offence consists of conspiracy to corrupt public morals or to do any act contrary to public morals or decency."

Although section 2(4A) of the 1959 Act and Schedule. 15, para. 6(b) to the **13–83**
1990 Act prevent a prosecution for conspiracy to corrupt public morals in respect of an agreement to give a film exhibition or cause a programme to be included in a programme service or to cause anything to be said or done in the course of a programme, section 2(4) of the 1959 does not similarly prevent a prosecution for conspiracy to corrupt public morals in respect of an agreement to publish an article. The existence of the offence of conspiracy to corrupt public morals was tested in *Shaw v. DPP* [1962] A.C. 220, where it was held that the offence did not fall within section 2(4) since the *actus reus* is the agreement to corrupt public morals, not an agreement to publish. In 1964, law officers gave an undertaking to Parliament (*Hansard*, H.C., col. 1212, June 3, 1964) that conspiracy to corrupt public morals would not be used to circumvent the defences available under section 4 of the 1959 Act.

There have been cases of conspiracy to corrupt public morals since the **13–84**
undertaking and the House of Lords in *Knuller (Publishing, Printing and Promotions) Ltd v. DPP* [1973] A.C. 435 defined it very restrictively, only a bare majority preventing *Shaw v. DPP* (above) being overruled. In *Knuller* it was held that corrupting public morals and leading morally astray were not identical concepts, and that the latter did not necessarily involve the former. Corrupting public morals involved an undermining of the morals of society or something destructive of the very fabric of society.

The Criminal Law Act 1977, s.5 (1) states: **13–85**

"Subject to the following provisions of this section, the offence of conspiracy at common law is hereby abolished.
(2) [Not printed.]
(3) Subsection (1) above shall not affect the offence of conspiracy at

common law if and in so far as it may be committed by entering into an agreement to engage in conduct which—

(a)   tends to corrupt public morals or outrages public decency; but

(b)   would not amount to or involve the commission of an offence if carried out by a single person otherwise than in pursuance of an agreement."

(4)–(10) [Not printed.]

(11) [Repealed.]

G. OUTRAGING PUBLIC DECENCY

13–86   The offences of outraging public decency and conspiracy to do so are offences at common law. It was decided in *R. v. Gibson and Sylveire* [1990] 2 Q.B. 619 that these offences are not caught by section 2(4) of Obscene Publications Act 1959 if the articles are not obscene (*i.e.* likely to deprave and corrupt). The Criminal Law Act 1977, s.5(1) and (3) (see para. 13–85, above) applies to conspiracy to outrage public decency.

13–87   The intention required is to do an act that in fact outraged public decency, not an intention to outrage public decency. If the defendant's acts are not capable of outraging public decency, then evidence that he intended them so to be is irrelevant: *R. v. Rowley* [1991] 1 W.L.R. 1020.

13–88   In *R. v. Gibson and Sylveire* (above) the defendant had sculpted a human head and attached to each ear an earring made from a freeze-dried human foetus of three to four months gestation. He then displayed the sculpture in Sylveire's gallery.

(i) Sentencing Guidelines

13–89   The offence is punishable with a fine and/or imprisonment at large. There is no limit to the amount of either the fine or the imprisonment that may be imposed provided the sentence is not inordinate: *R. v. Morris* [1951] 1 K.B. 394.

(ii) Evidential Requirements

13–90   The prosecution must prove:

(a)   That the act complained of was committed in public which means that more than one person must at least have been able to see it: *R. v. Farrell* [1862] 9 Cox 446. It is sufficient if it is proved that one person saw the act, and there is evidence that others might have witnessed it at the time: *R. v. Mayling* [1963] 2 Q.B. 717. In *R. v. Walker* [1996] 1 Cr.App.R. 111) the defendant exposed himself to two children in his house. His conviction for outraging public decency was upheld on the ground that the law required that at least two people must have been able to witness what happened and, further, that the act had been committed in a place where there was a real possibility that members of the general public might witness it.

(b) That the act was of such a lewd, obscene or disgusting character as constitutes an outrage on public decency. It is not necessary for the prosecution to prove that the act in fact disgusted or annoyed the persons within whose purview it was committed. If evidence is called, it can be given by a police officer.

H. PLAYS

I. OBSCENITY IN PLAYS

The performance of plays in the theatre and the prohibition on obscenity is governed by the Theatres Act 1968. Section 2(1) states: **13–91**

"For the purposes of this section a performance of a play shall be deemed to be obscene if, taken as a whole, its effect was such as to tend to deprave and corrupt persons who were likely, having regard to all relevant circumstances, to attend it.

(2) Subject to section 3 and 7 of this Act, if an obscene performance of a play is given, whether in public or private, any person who (whether for gain or not) presented or directed that performance shall be liable—

(a) on summary conviction, to a fine not exceeding the prescribed sum or to imprisonment for a term not exceeding six months;

(b) on conviction on indictment, to a fine or to imprisonment for a term not exceeding three years or both.

(3) A prosecution on indictment for an offence under this section shall not be commenced more than two years after the commission of the offence.   **13–92**

(4) No persons shall be proceeded against in respect of a performance of a play or anything said or done in the course of such a performance—

(a) for an offence at common law where it is of the essence of the offence that the performance or, as the case may be, what was said or done was obscene, indecent, offensive, disgusting or injurious to morality;

(b) repealed

and no person shall be proceeded against for an offence at common law of conspiring to corrupt public morals, or to do any act contrary to public morals or decency, in respect of an agreement to present or give a performance of a play, or to cause anything to be said or done in the course of such a performance."

Section 18(1) states: **13–93**

"in this Act—'licensing authority' means—

(a) as respects premises in a London borough or the City of London,

the council of that borough or the Common Council as the case
may be;

(b) as respects premises in a district in England ... , the council of
that district;

(bb) as respects premises in a county or county borough in Wales, the
council of that area;

(c) [*Scotland.*]

13–94   'play' means—

(a) any dramatic piece, whether involving improvisation or not,
which is given wholly or in part by one or more persons actually
present and performing and in which the whole or a major
proportion of what is done by the person or persons performing,
whether by way of speech, singing or action, involves the playing
of a role; and

(b) any ballet given wholly or in part by one or more persons
actually present and performing, whether or not it falls within
paragraph (a) of this definition;

'police officer' means a member ... of a police force;

'premises' includes any place;

'public performance' includes any performance in a public place within the
meaning of the Public Order Act 1936, and any performance which the
public or any section thereof are permitted to attend, whether on payment
or otherwise;

'script' has the meaning assigned by section 9(2) of this Act.

13–95   (2) For the purposes of this Act—

(a) a person shall not be treated as presenting a performance of a
play by reason only of his taking part therein as a performer;

(b) a person taking part as a performer in a performance of a play
directed by another person shall be treated as a person who
directed the performance if without reasonable excuse, he performs otherwise than in accordance with that person's direction;
and

(c) a person shall be taken to have directed a performance of a play
given under his direction notwithstanding that he was not present during the performance;

and a person shall not be treated as aiding or abetting the
commission of an offence under section 2 ... or 6 of this Act in
respect of a performance of a play by reason only of his taking
part in that performance as a performer."

13–96   An actor does not present or direct a play unless he is responsible for an
unauthorised ad lib. This confirms the spirit of the earlier case of *Lovelace v.
DPP* [1954] 3 All E.R. 481, which concerned the causing a play to be
presented, as opposed to actual presentation under section 15 of the Theatres
Act 1843 (repealed) and reverses *Grade v. DPP* [1942] 2 All E.R. 118.

13–97   Nudity alone does not make a play obscene: *Conway v. R (1944) 2 D.L.R.
530 and Johnson v. R (1973) 40 D.L.R. 205*—both Canadian cases. It is
submitted that the same principle applies in English law.

II. Defence Of Public Good

The Theatres Act 1968, s.3 provides a similar defence to the offence as that found in Obscene Publications Act 1959, s.4 namely, the defence of public good. If this defence is successfully raised then the court has decided that the performance is obscene but that its giving is justified because it is in the public good.

13-98

The Theatres Act 1968, s. 3(1) states:

"A person shall not be convicted of an offence under section 2 of this Act if it is proved that the giving of the performance in question was justified as being for the public good on the ground that it was in the interests of drama, opera, ballet or any other art, or of literature or learning.

(2) It is hereby declared that the opinion of experts as to the artistic, literary or other merits of a performance of a play may be admitted in any proceedings for an offence under section 2 of this Act either to establish or negative the said ground."

Under the Canadian Criminal Code the test is different; however, it is submitted that the general approach in *R. v. Heller* is correct.

The Court of Appeal has held in *R. v. Hellier* (1953) 9 W.W.R. N.S. 361 that a Canadian conviction for appearing in an immoral play was correct. The magistrate had held that (a) he had to decide if the presentation of the play was [immoral, indecent or] obscene; (b) the fact that what is presented on stage is "true to life" does not justify the presentation of obscenity; and (c) the testimony of defence witnesses that they were not shocked by the play did not reflect truly the feelings of the audience as a whole.

13-99

III. Exceptions

The Theatres Act 1968 does except performances given in certain circumstances. Section 7(1) states:

13-100

"Nothing in section 2 to 4 of this Act shall apply in relation to a performance of a play given on a domestic occasion in a private dwelling.

(2) Nothing in sections 2 to 6 of this Act shall apply in relation to a performance of a play given solely or primarily for one or more of the following purposes, that is to say—
(a) rehearsal; or
(b) to enable
(i) a record or cinematograph film to be made from or by means of the performance; or
(ii) the performance to be broadcast; or
(iii) the performance to be included in a programme service (within the meaning of the Broadcasting Act 1990);
but in any proceedings for an offence under section 2 or 6 of this Act alleged to have been committed in respect of a performance of a play or an offence at common law alleged to have been committed in

England and Wales by the publication of defamatory matter in the course of a performance of a play, if it is proved that the performance was attended by persons other than persons directly connected with the giving of the performance or the doing in relation thereto of any of the things mentioned in paragraph (b) above, the performance shall be taken not to have been given solely or primarily for one or more of the said purposes unless the contrary is shown.

13–101   (3)   In this section—

'broadcast' means broadcast by wireless telegraphy (within the meaning of the Wireless Telegraphy Act 1949), whether by way of sound broadcasting or television;

'cinematograph film' means any print, negative, tape or other article on which a performance of a play or any part of such a performance is recorded for the purposes of visual reproduction; 'record' means any record or similar contrivance for reproducing sound, including the sound-track of a cinematograph film;"

13–102   Evidence

The Theatres Act 1968, s. 9(1) states that:

"Where a performance of a play was based on a script, then, in any proceedings for an offence under section 2 . . . or 6 of this Act alleged to have been committed in respect of that performance—

     (a)   an actual script on which that performance was based shall be admissible as evidence of what was performed and of the manner in which the performance or any part of it was given; and

     (b)   if such a script is given in evidence on behalf of any party to the proceedings then, except in so far as the contrary is shown, whether by evidence given on behalf of the same or any other party, the performance shall be taken to have been given in accordance with that script.

     (2)   In this Act 'script', in relation to a performance of a play, means the text of the play (whether expressed in words or in musical or other notation) together with any stage or other directions for its performance, whether contained in a single document or not."

13–103   Section 10(1) states:

"If a police officer of or above the rank of superintendent has reasonable grounds for suspecting—

     (a)   that an offence under section 2 . . . or 6 of this Act has been committed by any person in respect of a performance of a play; or

     (b)   that a performance of a play is to be given and that an offence under the said section 2 . . . or 6 is likely to be committed by any person in respect of that performance,

he may make an order in writing under this section relating to that person and that performance.

13–104   (2)   Every order made under this section shall be signed by the police officer by whom it is made, shall name the person to whom it relates, and shall describe the performance to which it relates in a manner sufficient to enable that performance to be identified.

(3) Where an order under this section had been made, any police officer, on production if so required of the order—

    (a) may require the person named in the order to produce, if such a thing exists, an actual script on which the performance was or, as the case maybe, will be based; and

    (b) if such a script is produced to him, may require the person so named to afford him an opportunity of causing a copy thereof to be made.

(4) Any person who without reasonable excuse fails to comply with a requirement under subsection (3) above shall be liable on summary conviction to a fine not exceeding level 3 on the standard scale.

(5) Where, in the case of a performance of a play based on a script a copy of an actual script on which that performance was based has beer made by or on behalf of a police officer by virtue of an order under this section relating to that performance, section 9(1) of this Act shall apply in relation to that copy as it applies in relation to an actual script on which the performance was based."

Section 16 states: **13–105**

"Where any offence under this Act committed by a body corporate is proved to have been committed with the consent or connivance of, or to be attributable to any neglect on the part of, any director, manager, secretary or other similar officer of the body corporate, or any person purporting to act in any such capacity, he as well as the body corporate shall be guilty of that offence and shall be liable to be proceeded against and punished accordingly."

According to section 8:   **13–106**

"Proceedings for an offence under section 2 or 6 of this Act or an offence at common law committed by the publication of defamatory matter in the course of a performance of a play shall not be instituted in England and Wales except by or with the consent of the Attorney-General."

I. OFFENCES RELATING TO THE IMPORTATION OF PORNOGRAPHY

I. THE CUSTOMS CONSOLIDATION ACT 1876

The importation of pornography into Britain is prohibited by the Customs   **13–107**
Consolidation Act of 1876. While that Act goes no further, because it is an enactment which imposes a prohibition or restriction, it brings into play the Customs and Excise Management Act 1979 and all the provisions in relation to not only offences, but also the powers of forfeiture, search and seizure thereunder.

Under section 42 of the Customs Consolidation Act 1876, indecent or   **13–108** obscene prints, paintings, photographs, books, cards, lithographic or other engravings, or any other indecent or obscene articles are prohibited from being imported or brought into the United Kingdom.

"Obscene" has the same definition as under the Obscene Publications Act 1959. However, in respect of obscene books, there is no requirement for the court to hear evidence as to whether publication of the books could be justified as being for the public good on the grounds specified in section 4 of the 1959 Act: *R. v. Bow Street Stipendiary Magistrate, ex p. Noncyp Ltd* [1990] 1 Q.B. 123.

Cinematographic films are included in "or any other indecent or obscene articles": *Derrick v. Customs and Excise Commissioners* [1972] 1 All E.R. 993.

13–109   Despite the fact that any law of a Member State which prohibits the importation of pornographic material constitutes a measure having the equivalent effect to a quantitive restriction and is prima facie in conflict with Article 30 of the EEC Treaty, Article 36 of the Treaty reserves to Member States the power to impose prohibitions on the importation from other Member States of articles of an indecent or obscene character on the grounds of public morality, thereby preserving section 42 of the 1876 Act; *Henn and Darby v. DPP* [1980] 2 All E.R. 166. However, a Member State may not rely on the public morality ground within the meaning of Article 36 of the Treaty in order to prohibit the importation of goods on the ground that they are indecent or obscene, if the same goods may be manufactured freely in its territory and marketed in that territory subject only to an absolute prohibition on their transmission by post, a restriction on their display or a system of licensing premises for the sale of such goods: Case 121/85: *Consgate Ltd v. Customs and Excise Commissioners* [1986] 2 All E.R. 688.

II. The Customs And Excise Management Act 1979

(a) Procedure, jurisdiction and evidence

(i) Procedure

13–110   By virtue of section 145, no proceedings for an offence under the custom and excise Acts or for condemnation under Schedule 3 may be instituted except by order of the Commissioners, and, if in the magistrates' court must be commenced in the name of an officer. However, this does not prevent the institution of proceedings for an offence under the customs and excise Acts by order and in the name of a law officer of the Crown in a case in which he thinks it proper that proceedings should be so instituted (s.145(5)). A court before which a person arrested for an offence for which he is liable to be arrested under the customs and excise Acts is not prohibited from dealing with the case even though proceedings have not been instituted by order of the Commissioners or in the name of an officer (s.145(6)).

13–111   The summons or other process issued anywhere in the United Kingdom shall be deemed to have been served (except in relation to High Court proceedings) if: delivered to the person to whom it is addressed personally; or left at his last known place of abode or business or in the case of a body corporate, at their registered or principal office; or if left on board any vessel or aircraft to which he may belong or have lately belonged (s.146).

Proceedings for an indictable offence (including an either way offence) must be commenced within 20 years of the day on which the offence was committed (s.146A(2)).

Proceedings for a summary offence shall not be commenced after the end of the period of three years beginning with the day on which the offence was committed but, subject to that, may be commenced at any time within six months from the date on which sufficient evidence to warrant the proceedings came to the knowledge of the Commissioners (s.146A(3) & (7)) and a certificate of the Commissioners as to the date on which such evidence came to their knowledge shall be conclusive evidence of that fact (s.146A(4)).

Where a magistrates' court has begun to inquire into an information as examining justices the court shall not proceed under section 25(3) of the Magistrates' Court Act 1980 to try the information summarily without the consent of the Commissioners (s.147(2)). The prosecutor has a right of appeal under section 147(3) to the Crown Court against any decision of the magistrates' court, without prejudice to any right to require a case to be stated.

(ii) Jurisdiction

Proceedings may be commenced in any court having jurisdiction in the place **13-112** where the person charged resides or is found; or if any thing was detained or seized in connection with the offence, in any court having jurisdiction in the place where that thing was detained or seized or was found or condemned as forfeited; or in any court having jurisdiction in the place where the offence was committed (s.148(1)).

(iii) Evidence

Any document purporting to be signed either by one or more of the **13-113** Commissioners, or by their order, or by any other person with their authority, shall until the contrary be proved, be deemed to have been so signed and to be made and issued by the Commissioners, and may be proved by the production of a copy thereof (s.153(1)). Without prejudice to section 153(1), the Documentary Evidence Act 1868 shall apply in relation to (a) any document issued by the Commissioners; (b) any document issued before April 1, 1909, by the Commissioners of Customs or the Commissioners of Customs and the Commissioners of Inland Revenue jointly, as it applies in relation to the documents mentioned in that Act (s.153(2)). A photograph of any document delivered to the Commissioners for any customs and excise purpose and certified by them to be such a photograph shall be admissible in any proceedings, whether civil or criminal, to the same extent as the document itself (s.153(4)).

Under section 154(1): **13-114**

"An averment in any process in proceedings under the customs and excise Acts—

(a) that those proceedings were instituted by the order of the Commissioners; or

(b) that any person is or was a Commissioner, officer or constable, or a member of Her Majesty's armed forces or coastguard; or

(c) that any person is or was appointed or authorised by the Commissioners to discharge or was engaged by the orders or with the concurrence of the Commissioners in the discharge of, any duty; or

(d) that the Commissioners have or have not been satisfied as to any matter as to which they are required by any provision of those Acts to be satisfied; or

(e) that any ship is a British ship; or

(f) that any goods thrown overboard, staved or destroyed were so dealt with in order to prevent or avoid the seizure of those goods,

shall, until the contrary is proved, be sufficient evidence of the matter in question.

13-115 (2) Where in any proceedings relating to customs or excise any question arises as to the place from which any goods have been brought or as to whether or not—

(a) any duty has been paid or secured in respect of any goods; or

(b) any goods or other things whatsoever are of the description or nature alleged in the information, writ or other process; or

(c) any goods have been lawfully imported or lawfully unloaded from any ship or aircraft; or

(d) any goods have been lawfully loaded into any ship or aircraft or lawfully exported or were lawfully water-borne; or

(e) any goods were lawfully brought to any place for the purpose of being loaded into any ship or aircraft or exported; or

(f) any goods are or were subject to any prohibition of or restriction on their importation or exportation,

then, where those proceedings are brought by or against the Commissioners, a law officer of the Crown or an officer, or against any other person in respect of anything purporting to have done in pursuance of any power or duty conferred or imposed on him by or under the customs and excise Acts, the burden of proof shall lie upon the other party to the proceedings."

(b) Offences and penalties

(i) Offences

13-116 Section 50(2) states that:

"any person who with intent to evade a prohibition, unships or lands in any port or unloads from any aircraft in the United Kingdom or from any vehicle in Northern Ireland any goods, or assists or is otherwise concerned in such unshipping, landing or unloading; or removes from their place of importation or from any approved wharf, examination station, transit shed or customs and excise station any goods or assists or is otherwise concerned in such removal is guilty of an offence and may be arrested."

(ii) Definitions

"Approved wharf" is a place for the loading or unloading of goods of any class or description approved by the Commissioners for such periods and subject to such conditions and restrictions as they think fit (ss.1(1) and 20(1)).

13–117

"Examination station" is a part of or a place at any customs and excise airport approved by the Commissioners and subject to such conditions and restrictions as they think fit for the loading and unloading of goods and the embarkation and disembarkation of passengers (ss.1(1) and 22(1)).

"Transit shed" is a place approved by the Commissioners, for such periods and subject to such conditions and restrictions they think fit for the deposit of goods imported and not yet cleared out of charge (ss.1(1) and 25(1)).

Section 50(3) states that "any person who imports or is concerned in importing any goods contrary to any prohibition, whether or not the goods are unloaded, and does so with intent to evade the prohibition shall be guilty of an offence and may be arrested."

13–118

Goods which enter the country by air or sea are imported before they are actually unloaded or landed and under section 5(2), the time of importation shall be deemed to be: (a) where the goods are brought by sea, the time when the ship carrying them comes within the limits of a port; and (b) where the goods are brought by air, the time when the aircraft carrying them lands in the United Kingdom or the time when the goods are unloaded in the United Kingdom, whichever is the earlier. Goods which are unloaded at an airport and held in a customs area awaiting trans-shipment are regarded as having been imported into the United Kingdom: *R. v. Smith (Donald)* [1973] Q.B. 924.

"Evade" in this context means no more than "get around", it does not require a person to be fraudulent or dishonest.

(iii) Section 170

Under Section 170(1):
"If any person—

13–119

    (a) knowingly acquires possession of any:
        [(i) – (ii) not printed;]
        (iii) goods with respect to the importation of which any prohibition or restriction is for the time being in force under or by virtue of any enactment; or
    (b) is in any way knowingly concerned in carrying, removing, depositing, harbouring, keeping or concealing or in any manner dealing with any such goods, and does so with intent to evade any such prohibition or restriction with respect to the goods he shall be guilty of an offence and may be arrested.
  (2) If any person is, in relation to any goods, in any way knowingly concerned in any fraudulent evasion or attempt at evasion—(b) of any prohibition or restriction for the time being in force with respect

13–120

to the goods under or by virtue of any enactment, he shall be guilty of an offence and may be arrested."

In the words of Griffiths L.J. in *R. v. Neal and others* [1983] 3 All E.R. 156, section 170(1) "is so embracing and casts the net so wide that one is left to wonder what purpose is served by subsection (2) for it is difficult to think of any behaviour aimed at defrauding the Customs and Excise that would not be caught by subsection (1)". However, section 170(2) is intended as a "sweeping up" section to deal with persons who, while not involved with the importation as such, are involved in criminal acts relating to the goods after the importation.

(iv) Evidential requirements

13-121 Under section 170(1) the prosecution must prove that: the goods were imported; they were subject to a prohibition; the accused knowingly acquired possession of them (for s. (1)(a)); that the accused was knowingly concerned in carrying, removing, etc., the goods (for s.(1)(b)); and that he intended to evade the prohibition.

Under section 170(2) the prosecution must prove that: the goods were subject to a prohibition; that a fraudulent evasion or attempt at evasion of the prohibition has taken place in relation to the goods; that the accused was in any way concerned in that evasion or attempted evasion; and that the accused was knowingly so concerned.

(v) "Proving importation"

13-122 This burden on the prosecution is not displaced by any of the presumptions in section 154 of the 1979 Act. In *R. v. Watts and Slack* (1979) 70 Cr. App R. 187, the Court of Appeal quashed the conviction on the ground that the trial judge had wrongly directed the jury that on the true construction of the subsection, it was unnecessary to prove an actual importation. However, the Court accepted that once an importation was proved, the onus of proving that it was a lawful importation is on the accused. This does not mean that the offence could only be committed by a person involved in the actual smuggling operation; it is simply intended to discourage the Crown from prosecuting under section 170 where the only evidence is of possession.

(vi) "Evading the prohibition"

13-123 Offences under section 170 are continuing offences not stopping at the moment of importation, so that persons who were not part of the original team which brought the goods into the country nevertheless fall within the section. In *R. v. Ardalan and others* [1972] 2 All E.R. 257, it was held that the offence of acquiring possession of prohibited goods may be committed at any time after their actual importation and at any place provided that the acquisition is done knowingly and with the requisite intent. The evasion does not cease merely because the goods are seized by the authorities since the *actus reus* of the offence is not confined only to successful evasions: *R. v. Green* [1976] 2 W.L.R. 57, where the customs officers removed cannabis from a crate after it was imported and replaced it with peat—the offence was complete when the defendant later stored the crate in a garage he had rented using a false name. See also *R. v. Ciaparra* (1988) 87 Cr.App.R. 316.

(vii) "Concerned"

"Concerned" should be given its ordinary meaning and implies some act of **13-124** participation in the venture: *R. v. Ciaparra* (above). For the purpose of showing the defendant had been "knowingly concerned" in the fraudulent evasion of the prohibition against the importation it was sufficient to prove that he had been a party to the importation of the goods into the United Kingdom as a staging post for its onward transmission to another country and it was unnecessary to show that he had done anything in the United Kingdom to further the transaction: *R. v. Smith (Donald)* [1973] Q.B. 924, where the argument that the goods had merely been unloaded as opposed to imported was rejected. Generally, acts committed abroad cannot be the subject of criminal proceedings in England, but steps taken abroad leading to fraudulent evasion in this country can make a defendant "knowingly concerned": *R. v. Wall* [1974] 2 All E.R. 245. For guilt to be established, the importation must result as a consequence, if only in part, of the activity of the accused: R. v. Jakeman (1983) 76 Cr. App R. 223, where it was held that an act of remorse, even if coupled with a desire not to pursue the venture, will not avoid conviction under section 170 if an importation in fact results.

(viii) "Knowingly . . . goods which are prohibited or restricted"

Offences created by section 170(1) and (2) apply not only to prohibited or **13-125** restricted goods but also goods which are dutiable; the two categories are very different. Therefore, an accused who imports a prohibited item believing it to be a dutiable commodity does not have the requisite *mens rea*: *R. v. Hussain* (1969) 53 Cr.App.R. 448. However, if the accused imports drugs believing that they are pornographic goods which he knows are subject to a prohibition, he does commit an offence because both goods are within the same category, *i.e.* prohibited goods: *R. v. Ellis* (1987) 84 Crim.App.R. 235 and *R. v. Hennessey* (1978) 68 Cr.App.R. 419. In *R. v. Taffe* [1984] 2 W.L.R. 326, *Hussain* and *Hennessey* were distinguished by the House of Lords who held that on the true construction of section 170(2), the accused was to be judged on the facts as he believed them to be and assuming that Taffe believed that he was importing currency (which was not subject to a prohibition) he had not been knowingly concerned in the fraudulent evasion of the prohibition on the importation of cannabis (which is what he had imported) and it made no difference that he thought that the importation of currency was prohibited. Subsequent decisions (*R. v. Shivpuri* [1986] 2 All E.R. 334, H.L. and *R. v. Ellis* (above)) approved the decisions in *R. v. Hussain* and *R. v. Hennessey*.

(ix) "Fraudulent"

In section 170(2) requires the prosecution to prove fraudulent conduct in the **13-126** sense of dishonest conduct deliberately intended to evade the prohibition or restriction with respect to the goods. There is no necessity for the prosecution to prove acts of deceit practised on a customs officer in his presence: *Att.-Gen.'s Reference (No. 1 of 1981)* [1982] 2 W.L.R. 875. There must be a specific intent to be knowingly concerned in a fraudulent evasion of a prohibition—recklessness is not sufficient: *R. v. Panayi (No.2)* [1989] 1 W.L.R. 187.

(x) Conspiracy—jurisdiction

13-127   A conspiracy to commit in England an offence against English law is triable in England if it has been wholly or partly performed in England: *DPP v. Doot* [1973] A.C. 807. English courts also have jurisdiction to try inchoate crimes committed abroad which are intended to result in the commission of criminal offences in England: *Liangsiriprasert v. U.S. Government* [1990] 2 All E.R. 866. Therefore, in the case of an allegation of conspiracy tried in England, the crime is complete once the agreement is made (albeit abroad) and no further overt act in England need be proved as an ingredient of the crime.

(xi) Sentencing guidelines

13-128   The penalty for offences under the above sections is: on summary conviction to a penalty of the prescribed sum (currently £5,000—Criminal Justice Act 1991, s.17(2)) or of three times the value of the goods, whichever is the greater, and/or to imprisonment for a term not exceeding six months; or on conviction on indictment to a penalty of any amount, and/or to imprisonment for a term not exceeding seven years (ss.50(4) and 170(3)).

13-129   The guideline case on sentencing for offences concerning the importation of pornography is *R. v. Nooy and Schyff* (1982) 4 Cr.App.R. (S.) 308. Here the appellants had been concerned in the importation of a large quantity of books, magazines and videotapes, with a total value of £137,655. They had been engaged by others to convey the material from the continent to a distributor in England. On a guilty plea to an offence contrary to section 170(2) of the Act, they were sentenced to nine months' imprisonment and 18 months' imprisonment respectively. The Court of Appeal uupholding the sentences, held that the case should go out as a warning as to what can happen and that in future, severer sentences may be passed in addition to substantial fines to take the profit out of the enterprise. Lawton L.J. said that: "The public interest in this realm calls for the law and the courts to do everything they reasonably can to stop this kind of filth coming into the United Kingdom with the danger that it may corrupt our young." The court was of the opinion that a sentence of three months' imprisonment was inappropriate in deterring offenders given the huge profits that are made out of importing pornography.

13-130   This was followed in 1984 with *R. v. Rolt* (1984) 6 Cr.App.R. (S.) 117, where the appellant pleaded guilty to being knowingly concerned in the importation of obscene articles. He arrived at Dover in a ferry in charge of a tractor and refrigerated trailer ostensibly carrying meat. When the trailer was searched it was found to contain 6.000 obscene magazines, 42 video cassettes and 53 films. The films included sado-masochism, children and animals. His appeal against an 18 months' sentence of imprisonment was partially successful in that it was reduced to 12 months but only because his tractor unit had been forfeited which caused him heavy financial loss. Lord Lane C.J. said that:

"The matters which have to be taken into consideration seem to be these: first of all the quantity and the value at street level of the pornographic material which has been imported; secondly, the nature of the porno-graphic material. . . . Next, the position of the defendant in the hierarchy of distribution; in other words, the closer to the centre of the organisation, the heavier must be the penalty. Next, the amount of profit which the defendant is likely to make. Then the affront to public decency must be marked and in the end a sentence has to be imposed which will be sufficient to deter others from peddling in this country, or facilitating the peddling in this country of the corruptive filth which was contained in these boxes."

More recent cases include: *R. v. Wallace* (1992) 13 Cr.App.R.(S.) **13-131** 628—the appellant's sentence of four years' imprisonment for three counts of importing obscene publications was reduced to 15 months' imprisonment on each to run concurrently since the books and magazines imported were for personal use and not on a commercial scale; *R. v. Holt* (1994) 16 Cr.App.R.(S.) 510—the appellant, a schoolteacher, was convicted on five counts of being knowingly concerned in the fraudulent evasion of the prohibition of the importation of indecent or obscene articles. He imported by post a number of magazines containing pictures of naked children, albeit not engaged in sexual activities. The sentence of two months' imprisonment was quashed on appeal and fines totalling £500 substituted. The court arrived at their decision having taken into account the nature of the photographs (there was no corruption nor likely to be any in the future) and the effect upon the appellant.

By virtue of section 86 any person concerned in the movement, carriage or **13-132** concealment of goods contrary to or for the purpose of contravening any prohibition or restriction, who while so concerned, is armed with any offensive weapon or disguised in any way, and any person so armed or disguised found in the United Kingdom in possession of any goods liable to forfeiture under any provision of the customs and excise Acts relating to imported goods or prohibited or restricted goods shall be liable on conviction on indictment to imprisonment for a term not exceeding 3 years and may be arrested. "Armed" should be given its ordinary meaning and involves either physically carrying arms or proof that the defendant knows that they are immediately available, but it is not necessary for the prosecution to prove an intent to use the weapon: *R. v. Jones* [1987] 2 All E.R. 692.

Where a person convicted is ordered by a magistrates' court to a term of **13-133** imprisonment in addition to a fine for the same offence and, further orders him to be imprisoned for non–payment of that fine, the aggregate term of imprisonment shall not exceed 15 months (s.149). Where liability for any offence is incurred by two or more persons jointly, they are jointly and severally liable for the full amount of the pecuniary penalty (s.150(1)).

(c) Power of arrest

13-134 Section 138(1) states that:

> "A person who has committed, or whom there are reasonable grounds to suspect of having committed any offence for which he is liable to be arrested under the Act may be arrested by any officer (in the context of the 1979 Act, this means a person commissioned by the Commissioners— s.l(1)) or any member of Her Majesty's armed forces or coastguard at any time within 20 years from the date of the commission of the offence."

If the arresting person is not an officer, then the arresting person shall give notice of the arrest to an officer at the nearest convenient office of customs and excise (s.138(4)). Where it was not practicable to arrest the person at the time of the commission of the offence or he was arrested but escaped, he may be arrested by any of the persons listed in subsection (1) above at any time and proceeded against in like manner as if the offence had been committed at the date when he was finally arrested (s.138(2)). Where a crew member of a ship in Her Majesty's employment or service is arrested by an officer, the commanding officer of the ship shall, if so required by the arresting officer, keep that person secured on board that ship until he can be brought before a court and shall then deliver him up to the proper officer (s.138(3)).

Section 24(1) and (2) of the Police and Criminal Evidence Act 1984 provide that the powers of summary arrest conferred by subsections 24(4) to (7) apply to offences for which a person may be arrested under the customs and excise Acts and such offences are accordingly "arrestable offences" within the meaning of the 1984 Act.

(d) Forfeiture and condemnation

13-135 Goods which are imported, landed or unloaded contrary to section 42 of the 1876 Act shall be liable to forfeiture (s.49(1)(b) of the 1979 Act) unless they are on their importation either: (a) reported as intended for exportation in the same ship, aircraft or vehicle; or (b) entered for transit or transshipment; or (c) entered to be warehoused for exportation or for use as stores, when the Commissioners may, if they see fit, permit the goods to be dealt with accordingly (s.49(2)).

13-136 Any thing liable to forfeiture may be seized or detained by any officer (definition as for s.138) or constable or any member of Her Majesty's armed forces or coastguard (s.139(1)) and if it is seized other than by an officer, it shall be delivered to the nearest convenient customs and excise office or, if that is not practicable, notice shall be given in writing (including particulars of the thing seized) of the seizure or detention to the Commissioners at the nearest convenient office (s.139(2)). If a constable seizes or detains any thing as liable to forfeiture under the customs and excise Acts and the thing is or may be required for use in connection with proceedings brought other than under those Acts, it may be retained in the custody of the police until either those proceedings are completed or it is decided that no such proceeding shall be brought (s.139(3)). Where things are retained by the police by virtue of subsection (3), notice in writing of the seizure and of the intention to retain the thing in the custody of the police, together with particulars of the thing shall be given to the Commissioners at the nearest convenient customs and excise office; and any officer shall be permitted to examine that thing and take account thereof at any time while it remains in police custody (s.139(4)). The Police Property Act 1897 does not apply to the thing seized (s.139(4)(c)). Subject to subsections (3) and (4) and Schedule 3 any thing seized or detained under the customs and excise Acts shall, pending the determination as to its forfeiture or disposal, be dealt with, and, if condemned or deemed to have been condemned or forfeited, shall be disposed of in such manner as the Commissioners may direct (s.139(5)).

The destruction of goods by the Commissioners between the date of **13–137** forfeiture of the goods and committal proceedings in respect of an alleged offence in relation to the goods did not necessarily result in prejudice to the defendant or a breach of the rules of natural justice where secondary evidence in the form of photographs was available and could be put before a jury: *R. v. Uxbridge Justices, ex p. Sofaer and another* (1987) 85 Cr.App.R.367.

Any person, not being an officer, by whom any thing is seized or detained **13–138** or who has custody thereof after its seizure or detention, who fails to comply with any requirement of section 139 or any directions of the Commissioners given thereunder, is liable on summary conviction to a penalty of level 2 on the standard scale (s.139(7)).

(i) Offence of removing goods awaiting examination

By virtue of section 159(5), "If any imported goods which an officer has **13–139** power under the Customs and Excise Acts 1979 to examine are without the authority of the proper officer removed from customs and excise charge before they have been examined, those goods shall be liable to forfeiture."

If any goods falling within section 159(5) are removed by a person with intent to evade any prohibition, that person shall be guilty of an offence and may be arrested (s.159(6)). A person guilty of an offence under section 159(6) shall be liable: on summary conviction to a penalty of the prescribed sum or of three times the value of the goods, whichever is the greater and/or to not more than six months' imprisonment; and on conviction on indictment, to a penalty of any amount and/or to imprisonment not exceeding seven years (s.159(7)).

(ii) Provisions relating to forfeiture

Schedule 3 to the 1979 Act deals with the provisions relating to forfeiture: **13–140** Paragraph 1(1) requires the Commissioners to give notice in writing of the seizure of any thing as liable to forfeiture and of the grounds therefor to any person who to their knowledge was at the time of the seizure the owner or one of the owners thereof. Notice need not be given if the seizure was made in the presence of the person whose offence or suspected offence occasioned the seizure; or the owner of the thing seized or his servant or agent; or in the case of any thing seized in any ship or aircraft, the master or commander (para.1(2)). The notice is deemed to have been served on the person if delivered to him personally; or posted to him at his usual or last known place of abode; or, where his address is unknown or outside the United Kingdom, by publication of notice of the seizure in the London, Edinburgh or Belfast *Gazette* (para.1(2)).

13–141   Where a person claims that the thing seized is not liable to forfeiture, paragraph 3 states that he may give notice of his claim in writing (specifying his name and address or that of his solicitor if the claimant is outside the United Kingdom—para.4) to the Commissioners within one month of the date of the notice of seizure, or where no notice has been served on him, within one month of the date of the seizure.

13–142   If no notice of claim is given to the Commissioners or any requirement of paragraph 4 is not complied with, the thing in question shall be deemed to have been duly condemned as forfeited (para.5). Where a notice of claim is given, the Commissioners shall take proceedings for the condemnation of that thing by the court, and if the court finds for the Commissioners, it shall condemn the thing as forfeited (para.6). Once it is established that the thing in question does come within the class of articles which are liable to forfeiture, justices are not entitled to take into consideration mitigating circumstances so as to remove the thing from that class, but are bound to condemn it: *De Keyser v. British Railway Traffic and Electric Co. Ltd* [1936] 1 K.B. 224.

Where any thing is condemned or deemed to be condemned as forfeited, the forfeiture shall have effect as from the date when the liability to forfeiture arose (para.7).

(iii) Condemnation

13–143   Proceedings for condemnation are civil and may be instituted in either the High Court or the magistrates' court, the latter having jurisdiction: in the place where any offence in connection with that thing was committed or where any proceedings for such an offence are instituted; or where the claimant resides or his solicitor has his office (if the claimant is outside the United Kingdom); or in the place where that thing was found, detained or seized or to which it is first brought after being found, seized or detained (paras 8 and 9). Unless the claimant or his solicitor make oath that the thing seized was, or was to the best of his knowledge and belief, the property of the claimant at the time of the seizure, and, in High Court proceedings the claimant give security for the costs of the proceedings, judgment shall be given for the Commissioners (para.10). Where the owner is a body corporate, the oath may be taken by the secretary or some duly authorised officer of that body; where the owners are in partnership, any one of those owners; and where the owners are any number of persons exceeding five not being in partnership, any two of those persons on behalf of themselves and their co-owners (para. 15).

13–144   Either party may appeal the decision of the magistrates' court to the Crown Court, without prejudice to any right to require a case to be stated (para.11). Pending the decision of an appeal or case stated, the thing in question shall be left with the Commissioners (para.12).

13–145   In any proceedings arising out of the seizure of any thing, the fact, form and manner of the seizure shall be taken to have been as set forth in the process without any further evidence thereof, unless the contrary is proved (para.13). In any proceedings, the condemnation of any thing as forfeited may be proved by the production either of the order or certificate of condemnation or of a certified copy thereof purporting to be signed by an officer of the court by which the order or certificate was made or granted (para.14).

(iv) Forfeiture of ships etc.:

Section 88 states: 13–146

"Where:

- (a) a ship is or has been in United Kingdom waters; or
- (b) an aircraft is or has been at any place, whether on land or on water, in the United Kingdom; or
- (c) a vehicle is or has been within the limits of any port or at any aerodrome while in Northern Ireland, within the prescribed area, while constructed, adapted, altered or fitted in any manner for the purpose of concealing goods, that ship, aircraft or vehicle shall be liable to forfeiture."

Section 89 states: 13–147

"(1) If any part of the cargo of a ship is thrown overboard or is staved or destroyed to prevent seizure:
  - (a) while the ship is in United Kingdom waters; or
  - (b) where the ship, having been properly summoned to bring to by any vessel in the service of Her Majesty, fails so to do and chase is given, at any time during the chase, the ship shall be liable to forfeiture.
(2) for the purposes of this section a ship shall be deemed to have been properly summoned to bring to:
  - (a) if the vessel making the summons did so by means of an international signal code or other recognised means and while flying her proper ensign; and
  - (b) in the case of a ship which is not a British ship, if at the time when the summons was made the ship was in United Kingdom waters."

Section 90 states: 13–148

"where a ship has been within the limits of any port in the United Kingdom or Isle of Man, or an aircraft has been in the United Kingdom or the Isle of Man, with a cargo on board and a substantial part of that cargo is afterwards found in the United Kingdom to be missing, then if the master of the ship or commander of the aircraft fails to account therefor to the satisfaction of the Commissioners, the ship or aircraft shall be liable to forfeiture."

Section 9(1) states: 13–149

"(1) If, save for just and sufficient cause any ship which is liable to forfeiture or examination under or by virtue of any provision of the

Customs and Excise Acts 1979 does not bring to when required to do so, the master of the ship shall be liable on summary conviction to a penalty of level 2 on the standard scale.

(2) where any ship liable to forfeiture or examination as aforesaid has failed to bring to when required to do so and chase has been given thereto by any vessel in the service of Her Majesty and, after the commander of that vessel has hoisted the proper ensign and caused a gun to be fired as a signal, the ship still fails to bring to, the ship may be fired upon."

13-150   Section 141 states:

"(1) without prejudice to any other provision of the Customs and Excise Acts 1979, where any thing has become liable to forfeiture under the customs and excise Acts:

(a) any ship, aircraft, vehicle, animal, container (including any article of passengers' baggage) or other thing whatsoever which has been used for the carriage, handling, deposit or concealment of the thing so liable to forfeiture, either at a time when it was so liable or for the purposes of the commission of the offence for which it later became so liable; and

(b) any other thing mixed, packed or found with the thing so liable, shall also be liable to forfeiture."

13-151   These forfeiture provisions are absolute and it is not necessary for the seizing authority to establish the state of mind or the degree of knowledge of the owner or user of the ship etc. (*Customs and Excise Comrs. v. Air Canada* [1991] 1 All E.R. 570: where the cargo from an aircraft on a scheduled international flight, unknown to the operator, was found to contain cannabis resin, it was held that the Commissioners were entitled to seize the aircraft under s.141). Where kerosene oil which was liable to forfeiture was found in the fuel tanks of vehicles, the vehicles were held liable to forfeiture since they had been used for the carriage of such oil.

Section 141 states:

"(2) where any ship, aircraft, vehicle or animal has become liable to forfeiture under the customs and excise Acts, whether by virtue of subsection (1) above or otherwise, all tackle, apparel or furniture thereof shall also be liable to forfeiture.

(3) where any ship not exceeding 100 tons or any aircraft or any hovercraft becomes liable to forfeiture under this section by reason of having been used in the importation, exportation or carriage of goods contrary to or for the purpose of contravening any prohibition or restriction for the time being in force with respect to those goods, the owner and the master or commander shall each be liable on summary conviction to a penalty equal to the value of the ship, aircraft or hovercraft or level 5 on the standard scale, whichever is the less."

13-152   Section 142 states:

"(1) Notwithstanding any other provision of the Customs and Excise Acts 1979, a ship of 250 or more tons register shall not be liable to forfeiture under or by virtue of any provision of the 1979 Acts, except under section 88, unless the offence in respect of or in connection with the forfeiture is claimed:

(a) was substantially the object of the voyage during which the offence was committed; or

(b) was committed while the ship was under chase by a vessel in the service of Her Majesty after failing to bring to when properly summoned to do so by that vessel."

All hovercraft of whatever size shall be treated as ships of less than 250 tons register (s.142(4)). This section does not affect any liability for forfeiture of the goods carried in the ships (s.142(4)). **13–153**

Under section 144, where in any proceedings for the condemnation of any thing seized as liable to forfeiture under the customs and excise Acts, judgment is given for the claimant, the court may, if it sees fit, certify that there were reasonable grounds for the seizure (s.144(1)). If in any civil or criminal proceedings against the Commissioners, a law officer of the Crown or any person authorised by or under the Customs and Excise Acts 1979 to seize or detain any thing liable to forfeiture, brought on account of the seizure or detention of any thing, judgment is given for the plaintiff or prosecutor, then if (a) a certificate relating to the seizure has been granted under s.144(1) or (b) the court is satisfied that there were reasonable grounds for seizing or detaining that thing under the customs and excise Acts, the plaintiff or prosecutor shall not be entitled to recover any damages or costs and the defendant shall not be liable to any punishment (s.144(2)). Section 144(2) does not affect the right of any person to the return of the thing seized or detained or to compensation in respect of any damage to the thing or in respect of the destruction thereof (s.144(3)). A certificate under section 144(1) may be proved by the production of either the original certificate or a certified copy thereof purporting to be signed by an officer of the court by which it was granted (s.144(4)). **13–154**

(e) Powers of search

Under section 159(1), an officer may examine and take account of any goods which are imported or which are (*inter alia*) in a warehouse and may for that purpose require any container to be opened or unpacked. **13–155**

By virtue of section 161: **13–156**

"where there are reasonable grounds to suspect that any thing liable to forfeiture is kept or concealed in any building or place, any officer having a writ of assistance may:

(a) enter that building or place at any time, whether by day or night, on any day, and search for, seize and detain or remove any such thing; and

(b) so far as is reasonably necessary for the purpose of such entry, search, seizure, detention or removal, break open any door, window or container and force and remove any other impediment or obstruction."

No officer shall exercise such a power of entry by night unless accompanied by a constable: section 161(2).

Without prejudice to section 161(1), if a justice of the peace is satisfied by information on oath given by an officer that there are reasonable grounds to suspect that any thing liable to forfeiture under the Customs and Excise Acts is kept or concealed in any building or place, he may by warrant under his hand given on any day authorise any officer and any person accompanying an officer to enter and search the building or place named in the warrant within one month from that day: section 161(3). An officer or other person so authorised shall have the like powers in relation to the building or place, named in the warrant, subject to like conditions as to entry by night, as if he were an officer having a writ of assistance and acting upon reasonable grounds of suspicion: section 161(4).

13–157   Section 164(1) gives an officer the power to search any article a person has with him and to submit to such searches of his person whether rub-down, strip or intimate as the officer may consider necessary or expedient if there are reasonable grounds to suspect that the person is carrying any article contrary to section 42 of the 1876 Act. If the person is not under arrest, he may be detained for so long as may be necessary for the search to take place. The officer may not require a search of the suspect's person without first informing him that he may require to be taken, except in the case of a rub-down search, before a justice of the peace or a superior of the officer concerned; and in the case of a rub-down, before such a superior and that the justice or superior shall consider the grounds for suspicion and direct accordingly whether the suspect is to submit to the search. This section applies to any person: (a) who is on board or has landed from any ship or aircraft; (b) entering or about to leave the United Kingdom; (c) within the dock area of a port; (d) at a customs and excise airport; (e) in, entering or leaving any approved wharf or transit shed which is not in a port; (ee) in, entering or leaving a free zone.

13–158   An intimate search is any search which involves a physical examination (which is more than visual) of a person's body orifices and shall only be carried out by a registered medical practitioner or a registered nurse.

A strip search is any search which is not an intimate search but which involves the removal of an article of clothing which is being worn (wholly or partly) on the trunk and is being so worn either next to the skin or next to an article of underwear.

A rub-down search is any search which is neither an intimate search not a strip search and neither a strip search nor a rub-down shall be carried out except by a person of the same sex as the suspect.

J. CHILDREN AND PORNOGRAPHY

13–159   Children are given especial protection under statute law. The Children and Young Persons (Harmful Publications) Act 1955 prohibits certain publications being made available to children, whilst the Protection of Children Act

1978 and the Criminal Justice Act 1988 relate to indecent photographs of children.

I. THE CHILDREN AND YOUNG PERSONS (HARMFUL PUBLICATIONS) ACT 1955

By virtue of section 1:   **13–160**

"This Act applies to any book, magazine or other like work which is of a kind likely to fall into the hands of children or young persons and consists wholly or mainly of stories told in pictures (with or without the addition of written matter) being stories portraying:
(a)   the commission of crimes; or
(b)   acts of violence or cruelty; or
(c)   incidents of a repulsive or horrible nature;
in such a way that the work as a whole would tend to corrupt a child or young person into whose hands it might fall."

A "child" is a person under the age of 14 years and a "young person" is between 14 and 18 years (Children and Young Persons Act 1933, s.107 as applied by the 1955 Act, s.5(2)).

Section 2 states: **13–161**

"(1)   a person who prints, publishes, sells or lets on hire a work to which this Act applies, or has any such work in his possession for the purpose of selling it or letting it on hire, shall be guilty of an offence and liable, on summary conviction to imprisonment for a term not exceeding four months or to a fine not exceeding level 3 on the standard scale or to both ... "

A prosecution for the offence may not be instituted except by or with the consent of the Attorney-General (s.2(2)). Instituted being the laying of an information for a summons or a warrant (*Willace's Case* [1797] 1 East P.C. 186; *Brooks v. Bagshaw* [1904] 2 K.B. 798).

Section 2 states: **13–162**

"(1)   ... in any proceedings taken under this subsection against a person in respect of selling or letting on hire a work or of having it in his possession for the purposes of selling it or letting it on hire, it shall be a defence for him to prove that he had not examined the contents of the work and had no reasonable cause to suspect that it was one to which this Act applies."

The importation of any section 1 work and any plate prepared for the   **13–163**
purpose of printing copies of any such work and any photographic film prepared for that purpose is prohibited (s.4) and such importation will be an offence under the Customs and Excise Management Act 1979. "Plate" includes a block, mould matrix and stencil and "photographic film" includes photographic plate (s.5(2)).

(a) Justices' warrants

13-164 Where a justice of the peace has issued a summons or warrant of arrest, being satisfied upon an information being laid that a person has or is suspected of having committed an offence under section 2, that justice or another may issue a search warrant authorising any constable to enter, if need be by force, premises specified in the warrant and any vehicle or stall used by the said person for the purposes of trade or business and to search for and seize: (a) any copies of section 1 work and any copies of any other work which the constable has reasonable cause to believe to be one to which this Act applies; and (b) any plate which the constable has reasonable cause to believe to have been prepared for the purposes of printing copies of any such work and any photographic film which he has reasonable cause to believe to have been prepared for that purpose (s.3).

Such a search warrant can only be issued if the justice is satisfied by written information (note, that it must be submitted at the same time or after a prosecution has been instituted) substantiated on oath that there is reasonable ground for suspecting that the said person has in his possession or under his control (a) any copies of the work or any other section 1 work; or (b) any plate prepared for the purpose of printing copies of the work or any other section 1 work or any photographic film prepared for that purpose.

(b) Forfeiture

13-165 Following conviction for an offence under section 2, the court may order the forfeiture of any copies of that work and any plate prepared for the purpose of printing copies of that work or photographic film prepared for that purpose, being copies which have, or a plate or film which has, been found in his possession or under his control (s.3(2)). Such a forfeiture order shall not take effect until the expiration of the ordinary time within which an appeal in the matter of the proceedings in which the order was made may be lodged (whether by giving notice of appeal or applying for a case to be stated) or, where such an appeal is duly lodged, until the appeal is finally decided or abandoned (s.3(2)).

II. THE PROTECTION OF CHILDREN ACT 1978

13-166 This act was subject to amendment by the Criminal Justice and Public Order Act 1994 (CJPOA) insofar as it inserted pseudo-photographs into section 1 and made a section 1 offence a serious arrestable offence under the Police and Criminal Evidence Act 1984.

13-167   By virtue of section 1:

"(1) It is an offence for a person:

    (a) to take, or permit to be taken or to make, any indecent photograph or pseudo-photograph of a child; or

    (b) to distribute or show such indecent photographs or pseudo-photographs; or

(c) to have in his possession such indecent photographs or pseudo-photographs, with a view to their being distributed or shown by himself or others; or

(d) to publish or cause to be published any advertisement likely to be understood as conveying that the advertiser distributes or shows such indecent photographs or pseudo-photographs, or intends to do so."

Proceedings for an offence must be instituted by or with the consent of the Director of Public Prosecutions (s.1(3)).   **13–168**

Sentencing guidelines

The offences are punishable either way and carry a term of up to three years' imprisonment and/or a fine on indictment; and a term of up to six months' imprisonment and/or a fine not exceeding the statutory maximum on summary conviction (s.6).   **13–169**

In *R v. Russell* (1986) 8 Cr.App.R.(S) 367, the appellant pleaded guilty to six counts of distributing indecent photographs of children and one of possessing indecent photographs of children with a view to distribution. He was found in possession of a large quantity of indecent photographs of children and admitted distributing them to others. His sentence of two years' imprisonment was reduced on appeal to 18 months' purely because he had pleaded guilty. Otherwise the court held that sentences of such length were required to discourage such activity.

In *R v. Dash* (1993) 15 Cr.App.R.(S) 76, the appellant pleaded guilty to eight counts of possessing indecent photographs of children with a view to their being distributed or shown. Of the video tapes seized, 730 contained material of a sexually explicit nature, and nine of these involved children. Each count of the indictment related to a particular video; they showed children estimated to be aged between 11 and 14 years, involved in various sexual acts with other children or an adult. The appellant unsuccessfully appealed against a sentence of nine months' imprisonment. The Court referred to the case of Russell (above) and the judgment of the Lord Chief Justice who said:

"We take the view that the distribution, whether for profit or not, of this type of photograph is to be sharply discouraged particularly at times such as these when the prevalence of indecent acts perpetrated upon children seems to be increasing."

(a) Recent cases

In *R v. McGuigan* [1996] 2 Cr.App.R.(S) 253, the appellant pleaded guilty to six counts of possessing indecent photographs of a child with a view to distribution and two counts of having an obscene article for publication for gain. The appellant operated a pornography business by obtaining video tapes and duplicating them. Six of the seized tapes portrayed children being sexually exploited. His sentence of 18 months' imprisonment on each count concurrent was reduced on appeal to 12 months.   **13–170**

In *R v. Pursey* [1996] 2 Cr.App.R.(S) 32, the sentence of 12 months' imprisonment was upheld against the appellant who had pleaded guilty to distributing indecent photographs and sending obscene articles by post. The appellant had claimed that he derived pleasure from the torture of little children and encouraged others to do the same. The court found that the recorder could easily have imposed a longer sentence and must have had regard to mitigation in imposing the sentence he did.

(b) Indecent photographs

13–171 An indecent photograph includes an indecent film, a copy of an indecent photograph or film, and an indecent photograph comprised in a film (s.7(2)). Photographs (including those comprised in a film) shall, if they show children and are indecent, be treated as indecent photographs of children and so as respects pseudo-photographs (s.7(3) as amended by s.84(3)(a) of the CJPOA 1994).

References to a photograph include: (a) the negative as well as the positive version; and (b) data stored on a computer disc or by other electronic means which is capable of conversion into a photograph (s.7(4) as substituted by s.84(3)(b) of the CJPOA 1994). *R v. Fellows*; *R v. Arnold, The Times,* October 3, 1996, which was decided on the pre-CJPOA 1994 legislation, held that images held in digital form on a computer connected to the Internet were copies of photographs for the purpose of the Protection of Children Act 1978, thus it seems making the substitution of section 7(4) unnecessary!

A film includes any form of video-recording (s.7(5)).

13–172 A pseudo-photograph is defined as an image, whether made by computer-graphics or otherwise howsoever, which appears to be a photograph (s.7(7) as inserted by s.84(3)(c) of the CJPOA 1994). If the impression conveyed by a pseudo-photograph is that the person shown is a child, the pseudo-photograph shall be treated for all purposes of the Act as showing a child and so shall a pseudo-photograph where the predominant impression conveyed is that the person shown is a child notwithstanding that some of the physical characteristics shown are those of an adult (s.7(8) as inserted by s.84(3)(c) of the CJPOA 1994). References to an indecent pseudo-photograph include: a copy of an indecent pseudo-photograph; and data stored on a computer disc or by other electronic means which is capable of conversion into a pseudo-photograph (s.7(9) as inserted by s.84(3)(c) of the CJPOA 1994).

(c) Child

13–173 A "child" is, subject to the provisions of section 7(8), a person under the age of 16 (s.7(6) as inserted by s.84(3)(c) of the CJPOA 1994).

The age of the child is a material consideration for the court in determining whether the photograph of the child was in fact indecent (*R v. Owen* [1988] 1 W.L.R. 134) since the word "indecent" qualifies the words "photograph of a child". A person is taken to have been a child at any material time if it appears from the evidence as a whole that he was then under the age of 16 (s.2(3)). The motives of the photographer and the circumstances in which the photograph was taken are irrelevant to the question of whether the photograph is indecent (*R v. Graham-Kerr* [1988] 1 W.L.R. 1098).

(d) Evidential requirements

A successful conviction for taking an indecent photograph is reliant on **13–174** proving that the defendant took the photograph deliberately and intentionally, and here, the motives of the photographer and the circumstances in which the photograph was taken may well be relevant. The jury need to consider: whether the defendant acted deliberately and intentionally in taking the photograph; and whether, applying the test in *R v. Stamford* 56 Cr.App.R. 398, of applying the recognised standards of propriety, the photograph is indecent.

A person is to be regarded as distributing an indecent photograph or **13–175** pseudo-photograph if he parts with possession of it to, or exposes or offers it for acquisition by, another person (s.1(2) as amended by s.84(2)(c) of the CJPOA 1994). It was held in *R v. Fellows; R v. Arnold* (above) that images held in digital form on a computer connected to the Internet were distributed or shown by being made available for access by other computer users.

(e) Statutory defence

Where a person is charged with either distributing or showing or possessing **13–176** with a view to distribution or show, section 1(4) provides the defendant with the defence that: (a) he had a legitimate reason for distributing or showing the photographs or pseudo-photographs or (as the case may be) having them in his possession; or (b) that he had not himself seen the photographs or pseudo-photographs and did not know, nor had any cause to suspect, them to be indecent.

(f) Bodies corporate

Where a body corporate is guilty of an offence under the Act and it is proved **13–177** that the offence occurred with the consent or connivance of, or was attributable to any neglect on the part of, any director, manager, secretary or other officer of the body, or any person who was purporting to act in any such capacity he, as well as the body corporate, shall be deemed to be guilty of that offence and shall be liable to be proceeded against and punished accordingly (s.3(1)). Where the affairs of a body corporate are managed by its members, subsection (1) shall apply in relation to the acts and defaults of a member in connection with his functions of management as if he were a director of the body corporate (s.3(2)).

(g) Police powers

The power of the police to enter, search and seize is given by section 4 of the **13–178** Act:

"(1) The following applies where a justice of the peace is satisfied by information on oath, laid by or on behalf of the Director of Public Prosecutions or by a constable, that there is reasonable ground for suspecting that, in any premises in the petty sessions area for which he acts, there is an indecent photograph of a child."

It is worth noting that the Criminal Justice and Public Order Act 1994 has not inserted in either sections 4 or 5 "or pseudo-photograph" which, it is submitted, is more likely to be an oversight than intentional since it departs from the spirit of the 1994 Act given the other amendments and insertions. The section further states:

"(2) The justice may issue a warrant under his hand authorising any constable to enter (if need be by force) and search the premises, and to seize and remove any articles which he believes (with reasonable cause) to be or include indecent photographs of children.

13–179 (3) Articles seized under the authority of the warrant, and not returned to the occupier of the premises, shall be brought before a justice of the peace acting for the same petty sessions area as the justice who issued the warrant.

(4) This section and section 5 below apply in relation to any stall or vehicle, as they apply in relation to premises, with the necessary modiications of references to premises and the substitution of references to use for references to occupation."

(h) Forfeiture

13–180 The justice to whom articles are brought under section 4(3) may issue a summons to the occupier of the premises to attend and show cause why they should not be forfeited (s.5(1)). In addition to the person summoned, any other person who is the owner of the articles, or the maker or through whose hands they have passed shall be entitled to appear before the court to show cause why they should not be forfeited (s.5(3)). Providing that service of the summons is proved, the court shall order forfeiture of the articles whether or not the person summoned appears, if it is satisfied that the articles are in fact indecent photographs of children (s.5(2)). Forfeiture may also be ordered in respect of articles seized under section 4 following a conviction under section 1(1) of the 1978 Act or section 160 of the Criminal Justice Act 1988 (s.5(6)), but the order shall not take effect until the expiration of the ordinary time within which an appeal may be instituted or until the appeal is finally decided or abandoned (s.5(7)).

III. The Criminal Justice Act 1988

13–181 The Criminal Justice Act 1988 differs from the Protection of Children Act 1978 in so far as the 1988 Act requires no more than simple possession of an indecent photograph of a child for an offence to be committed.

13–182 Section 160(1) (as amended by s.84(4) of the CJPOA 1994) states:

"It is an offence for a person to have any indecent photograph or pseudo-photograph of a child in his possession."

(i) Sentencing guidelines

The offence is summary only punishable by up to six months' imprisonment   **13–183**
and/or a fine not exceeding level 5 on the standard scale, as defined in section
75 of the Criminal Justice Act 1982, ((s.160(3) as amended by s.86(1) of the
CJOPA 1994).

(ii) Statutory defences

Section 160 states: **13–184**

"(2) Where a person is charged with an offence under subsection 1 above,
      it shall be a defence for him to prove:
      (a) that he had a legitimate reason for having the photograph or
           pseudo-photograph in his possession; or
      (b) that he had not himself seen the photograph or pseudo-
           photograph and did not know, nor had any cause to suspect, it
           to be indecent; or
      (c) that the photograph or pseudo-photograph was sent to him
           without prior request made by him or on his behalf and that he
           did not keep it for an unreasonable time."

Sections 1(3), 2(3), 3 and 7 of the Protection of Children Act 1978 apply to   **13–185**
the 1988 Act: see paragraphs 3:168, 3:171, 3:172, 3:173, 3:177 and
above.

Possession of photographs before September 29, 1988, and pseudo-
photographs before February 3, 1995 is not an offence (s.160(5) as amended
by s.84(4)(c) CJPOA 1994).

IV. THE INTERNET

(See also Appendix 10.)

Since the advent of the information super-highway known as the Internet,   **13–186**
pornography, especially paedophile, has become readily available and can
easily be downloaded from the screen onto a user's disc. Policing the Internet
insofar as controlling the subject matter entered onto it is concerned, is
virtually impossible, but, subject to the statutory defences the recipient of the
information can be prosecuted.

The Protection of Children Act 1978 and the Criminal Justice Act 1988
especially since the amendments and substitutions made to them by the
Criminal Justice and Public Order Act 1994, the Obscene Publications Acts
1959 and 1964 and the Telecommunications Act 1988 provide offences
which can be used to deal with persons who are found receiving, downloading, storing or transmitting obscene material, photographs of children or
engaging in obscene or indecent conversations on the Internet.

K. UNSOLICITED GOODS

The rationale behind the Unsolicited Goods and Services Act 1971 is to   **13–187**
prevent people sending, and people unexpectedly receiving material which
contains pictorial or written descriptions of human sexual techniques.

Unsolicited Goods and Services Act 1971, s. 4 states:

"(1) A person shall be guilty of an offence if he sends or causes to be sent to another person any book, magazine or leaflet (or advertising material for any publication) which he knows or ought reasonably to know is unsolicited and which describes or illustrates human sexual techniques."

This section applies to such advertising material even though it does not of itself contain a description or illustration of human sexual techniques: *DPP v. Beate Uhse* (U.K.) Ltd [1974] Q.B. 158.

"Unsolicited" means, in relation to goods sent to any person, that they are sent without any prior request made by him or on his behalf (s. 6).

(i) Sentencing guidelines

13–188 The offence is summary only and carries a fine not exceeding level 5 on the standard scale (s. 4(2)). Proceedings may only be instituted by or with the consent of the Director of Public Prosecutions (s. 4(3)).

(ii) Bodies corporate

13–189 Where the offence has been committed by a body corporate and it is proved to have been committed with the consent or connivance of, or to be attributable to any neglect on the part of, any director, manager, secretary, or other similar officer of the body corporate, or of any person who was purporting to act in any such capacity, he as well as the body corporate shall be guilty of that offence and shall be liable to be proceeded against and punished accordingly (s. 5(1)). Where the affairs of a body corporate are managed by its members, s. 5(1) shall apply in relation to the acts or defaults of a member in connection with his functions of management as if he were a director of the body corporate (s. 5(2)).

L. PROHIBITION ON SENDING CERTAIN ARTICLES BY POST

13–190 The Post Office Act is designed to prevent material whether solicited or not, which is obscene or indecent from being sent through the post.
The Post Office Act 1953, s. 11(1) states:

"A person shall not send or attempt to send or procure to be sent a postal packet which:
(a) is not printed
(b) encloses any indecent or obscene print, painting, photograph, lithograph, engraving, cinematography film, book, card or written communication, or any indecent or obscene article whether similar to the above or not; or
(c) has on the packet, or on the cover thereof, any words, marks or designs which are grossly offensive or of an indecent or obscene character."

Sentencing guidelines

A person acting in contravention of section 11 shall be liable on summary   **13–191**
conviction to a fine not exceeding the statutory maximum or on indictment
to term not exceeding twelve months' imprisonment (s.11(2)).

I. Editors Of Newspapers

If owing to publication of advertisements in a newspaper informing persons   **13–192**
where they may obtain obscene prints etc., such obscene matter is forwarded
to the purchaser through the post, the editor of the newspaper may be
convicted of an offence under section 11 (*R v. De Marny* [1907] 1 K.B. 388).
By virtue of section 68 of the Act any person who solicits or endeavours to
procure any other person to commit an offence (punishable on indictment
under this Act) shall be guilty of an offence and be liable to imprisonment for
a term not exceeding two years.

II. Definitions

"Postal packet" means a letter, postcard, reply postcard, newspaper, printed   **13–193**
packet, sample packet, or parcel, and every packet or article transmissible by
post, and includes a telegram (Post Office Act 1953, s. 87).

"Indecent or obscene" is an alternative (*R v. Anderson* [1971] 3 All E.R.
1152) and a distinction can be drawn between what is indecent and what is
obscene.

In *R v. Stanley* [1965] 1 All E.R. 1035, the appellant was charged *inter alia*   **13–194**
with sending a postal packet contrary to section 11(1)(b) of the Post Office
Act 1953 and conspiring with others to contravene the same section. In the
summing-up, the jury were told that "indecent" simply meant something
that offended the ordinary modesty of the average man and that "obscene"
really meant something that tended to deprave and corrupt. The jury
convicted, having found that the films and brochure, the subject matter of the
charge, were indecent but not obscene. On appeal against conviction, it was
held dismissing the appeal, that the words "indecent or obscene" conveyed
one idea, namely that of offending against the recognised standards of
propriety and that "indecent" was at the lower end of the scale and
"obscene" was at the upper end of the scale, with the consequence that
although an indecent article was not necessarily obscene, an obscene article
must almost certainly be indecent.

In *R v. Anderson* (above), the court on appeal held that for the purposes of   **13–195**
section 11 of the Post Office Act 1953, the word "obscene" in its context as
an alternative to "indecent" had its ordinary meaning which included things
which were shocking or lewd.

As far as the 1953 Act is concerned, obscene does not have the same   **13–196**
meaning as that found in section 1 of the Obscene Publications Act 1959. A
single objective standard is to be applied and will not vary according to the
character of the addressee: *Kosmos Publications Ltd v. DPP* [1975]
Crim.L.R. 345 . Evidence is not admissible on the issue of whether or not the

article is obscene or indecent since it is a matter entirely for the jury or magistrate (*R v. Stamford* [1972] 2 All E.R. 427).

III. INTERCEPTION OF POSTAL PACKETS

13-197   Section 11(4) states:

"The detention by the authority of any postal packet on the grounds of a contravention of section 11 shall not exempt the sender thereof from any proceedings which might have been taken if the packet had been delivered in due course by post."

Chapter 14
Advertisements and the Promotion of Sex

A. ADVERTISEMENTS

I. THE VENEREAL DISEASES ACT 1917

The Venereal Diseases Act 1917 prevents the treatment of venereal diseases **14–01** otherwise than by a duly qualified person and places restrictions upon advertisements.

Section 1 states:

"(1) In any area in which this section is in operation, a person shall not, unless he is a duly qualified medical practitioner, for reward either direct or indirect, treat any person for venereal disease or prescribe any remedy therefor, or give any advice in connection with the treatment thereof, whether the advice is given to the person to be treated or to any other person.

(2) This section shall operate in any area to which it is applied by order of the Minister of Health, or in Scotland and Ireland, the Local Government Board for Scotland and Ireland respectively: provided that no order shall be made in respect of any area until a scheme for the gratuitous treatment of persons in the area suffering from venereal disease has been approved by the Minister of Health or, in Scotland and Ireland the Local Government Board for Scotland and Ireland respectively, and is already in operation."

The Act is now applicable to the whole of England and Wales. The powers **14–02** and duties of the Local Government Board are now exercised by the Minister of Health (Ministry of Health Act 1919, s.3). The Scheme referred to in subsection (2) was made under the Public Health (Venereal Diseases) Regulations 1916. The Act only prohibits treatment or advice given for reward.

Section 4 defines venereal diseases as: syphilis, gonorrhoea or soft chancre. Advice on AIDS and other sexually transmitted conditions are not illegal (subject to the Health and Medicines Act 1988 below).

14–03   Section 2 states:

"(1) A person shall not by any advertisement or any public notice or announcement treat or offer to treat any person for venereal disease, or prescribe or offer to prescribe any remedy therefor, or offer to give or give any advice in connection with the treatment thereof.

(2) Provided that nothing in this section shall apply to any advertisement, notification, or announcement, made or published by any local or public authority or made or published with the sanction of the Minister of Health, or in Scotland and Ireland the Local Government Board for Scotland and Ireland respectively, or to any publication sent only to duly qualified medical practitioners or to wholesale or retail chemists for the purposes of their business."

(i) Sentencing guidelines

14–04   The offences are triable either way. On summary conviction, they carry a fine or imprisonment not exceeding six months; on conviction on indictment, a term not exceeding two years.

(ii) The first case

14–05   The first case brought under the Act was *R v. Shadforth*; *R v. Wilson* (1919) 63 S. J. 799. S was a chemist who advertised in newspapers and a pamphlet a product which "dealt with neurasthenia, debility, tuberculosis and syphilis, which are all (the advertisement claimed) attributable to impure blood". There was however no suggestion made at the trial that the remedy was not an admirable one, or that it was a quack remedy. This was held to be an advertisement within the Act. W was S's servant. A purchaser asked him: "Is it (the remedy) any good for syphilis?" to which he replied in the affirmative. This was held to be the giving of advice.

14–06   Books advising on the recognition of the symptoms of venereal disease and recommending the patient to seek medical attention will, it is submitted, not be an offence. However, books dealing with alternative medicines, and herbal remedies may offend against the Act.

II. THE HEALTH AND MEDICINES ACT 1988

HIV testing kits and services

14–07   The Health and Medicines Act 1988, s. 23 states:

"(1) The Secretary of State may provide by regulations that a person:
(a) who sells or supplies to another an HIV testing kit or any component part of such a kit;

(b) who provides another with HIV testing services; or

(c) who advertises such kits or component parts or such services, shall be guilty of an offence.

(2) The power to make regulations conferred by this section shall be exercisable by statutory instrument, and a statutory instrument made by virtue of this section shall be subject to annulment in pursuance of a resolution of either House of Parliament.

(3) The power may be exercised:

(a) either in relation to all cases to which the power extends, or in relation to all those cases subject to specified exceptions, or in relation to any specified cases or classes of case; and

(b) so as to make, as respects the cases in relation to which it is exercised:

(i) the full provision to which the power extends or any less provision (whether by way of exception or otherwise);

(ii) the same provision for all cases in relation to which the power is exercised, or different provision for different cases or different classes of case, or different provision as respects the same case or class of case for different purposes;

(iii) any such provision either unconditionally, or subject to any specified condition,

and includes power to make such incidental or supplemental provision as the Secretary of State considers appropriate.

(4) If any person contravenes regulations under this section, he shall be liable: **14–08**

(a) on summary conviction to a fine not exceeding the statutory maximum; and

(b) on conviction on indictment to fine or to imprisonment for a term not more than two years, or to both.

(5) Where an offence under this section which is committed by a body corporate is proved to have been committed with the consent or connivance of, or to be attributable to any neglect on the part of, any director, manager, secretary or other similar officer of the body corporate, or any person who was purporting to act in any such capacity, he as well as the body corporate shall be guilty of that offence and shall be liable to be proceeded against and punished accordingly.

(6) In this section: **14–09**

'HIV' means Immunodeficiency Virus of any type;

'HIV testing kit' means a diagnostic kit the purpose of which is to detect the presence of HIV or HIV antibodies; and

'HIV testing services' means diagnostic services the purpose of which is to detect the presence of HIV or HIV antibodies in identifiable individuals."

The Secretary of State has provided the HIV Testing Kits and Services Regulations 1992 (S.I. 1992 No. 460).

B. INDECENT DISPLAYS

14–10   The purpose of the Indecent Displays (Control) Act 1981 is to prevent
members of the public and especially children being confronted unexpectedly
by displays of obscenity.
  Section 1 states:

> "(1) If any indecent matter is publicly displayed the person making the
> display and any person causing or permitting the display to be made
> shall be guilty of an offence."

Sentencing guidelines

14–11   An offence contrary to section 1(1) is punishable on summary conviction to
a fine not exceeding the statutory maximum, or a fine and/or a maximum
two years' imprisonment on indictment (s.4).

I. BODIES CORPORATE

14–12   Section 3 states:

> "(1) Where a body corporate is guilty of an offence under this Act and it
> is proved that the offence occurred with the consent or connivance of,
> or was attributable to any neglect on the part of, any director,
> manager, secretary or other officer of the body, or any person who
> was purporting to act in any such capacity he, as well as the body
> corporate, shall be deemed to be guilty of that offence and shall be
> liable to be proceeded against and punished accordingly.
> (2) Where the affairs of a body corporate are managed by its members,
> subsection (1) shall apply in relation to the acts and defaults of a
> member in connection with his functions of management as if he were
> a director of the body corporate."

II. PUBLIC DISPLAY

14–13   Section 1 states:

> "(2) Any matter which is displayed in or so as to be visible from any public
> place shall, for the purposes of section 1, be deemed to be publicly
> displayed."

III. PUBLIC PLACE

14–14   Section 1 states, further:

> "(3) In sub-section (2) above, 'public place' in relation to the display of
> any matter, means any place to which the public have or are per-
> mitted to have access (whether on payment or otherwise) while that
> matter is displayed except:

    (a) a place to which the public are permitted to have access only on payment which is or includes payment for that display; or

    (b) a shop or any part of a shop to which the public can only gain access by passing beyond an adequate warning notice; these exclusions applying only where persons under 18 years are not permitted to enter while the display in question is continuing."

IV. WARNING NOTICE

The warning notice is not adequate unless it contains the following words   **14–15** and no others:

"WARNING:

persons passing beyond this notice will find material on display which they may consider indecent No admittance to persons under 18 years of age."

The word "WARNING" must appear as a heading. No pictures or other   **14–16** matter shall appear on the notice and, the notice must be so situated that no one could reasonably gain access to the shop or part of the shop in question without being aware of the notice and it must be easily legible by any person gaining such access: section 1(6).

V. DEFINITIONS

"Matter" includes anything capable of being displayed, except that it does   **14–17** not include an actual human body or any part thereof: section 1(5).

"Indecent" means something that offends against the recognised standards of propriety and was at the lower end of the scale from obscene which required depravity and corruption. Consequently, while an obscene article must almost certainly be indecent, an indecent article was not necessarily obscene (*R v. Stanley* [1965] 1 All E.R. 1035: decided under the Post Office Act 1953). In determining for the purpose of section 1 whether any displayed matter is indecent, there shall be disregarded any part of that matter which is not exposed to view; and account may be taken of the effect of juxtaposing one thing with another: section 1(5).

VI. EXCLUSIONS

There are certain exclusions to section 1 of the Act given in section 1(4),   **14–18** namely:

"any matter:

    (a) included by any person in a television broadcasting service or other television programme service (within the meaning of Part 1 of the Broadcasting Act 1990);

    (b) included in the display of an art gallery or museum and visible only from within the gallery or museum; or

    (c) displayed by or with the authority of, and visible only from within a building occupied by, the Crown or any local authority; or

    (d) included in a performance of a play (within the meaning of the Theatres Act 1968); or

    (e) included in a film exhibition as defined in the Cinemas Act 1985:

        (i) given in a place which as regards that exhibition is required to be licensed under section 1 of that Act or by virtue only of section 5, 7 or 8 of that Act is not required to be so licensed; or

       (ii) which is an exhibition to which section 6 of that Act applies given by an exempted organisation as defined in subsection (6) of that section."

14-19   See paragraph 13.45 for the definition of television programme service in the Broadcasting Act 1990; paragraph 13.12 for the definition of film exhibition in the Cinemas Act 1985; and paragraph 13.94 for the definition of a play given in the Theatres Act 1968.

VII. POLICE POWERS

14-20   Section 2(2) gives a constable a power to seize any article which he has reasonable grounds for believing to be or to contain indecent matter and to have been used in the commission of an offence under the Act.

14-21   Under section 2(3), a justice of the peace may issue a warrant authorising any constable to enter premises specified in the information (if need be by force) to seize any article which the constable has reasonable grounds for believing to be or to contain indecent matter and to have been used in the commission of an offence under the Act. The information must be on oath and the justice must be satisfied that there are reasonable grounds for suspecting that an offence under the Act has been or is being committed. The issue and execution of the warrant must conform to the Police and Criminal Evidence Act 1984, ss.15 and 16.

C. VIDEO RECORDINGS ACT 1984

14-22   With the advent of video cassette recorders and the ability of the general public to rent or otherwise obtain video recordings, it became apparent that regulation was needed in respect of their supply and content. The result was the Video Recordings Act 1984 which established a system for the classification by the British Board of Film Classification of video recordings supplied to the public and created a number of offences relating to the supply, or possession for supply of video recordings which have either not been classified or have a false indication as to their classification.

    In *Wingrove v. United Kingdom, The Times*, December 5, 1996, the

European Court of Human Rights found on a majority vote that the refusal of the BBFC to grant W a certificate for his video work was justified as being necessary in a democratic society within the meaning of Article 10.2 of the European Convention on Human Rights and there had been no violation of his freedom of expression.

I. DEFINITIONS

Section 1(2) (as amended by para. 22 of Sched. 9 to the Criminal Justice   **14–23**
and Public Order Act 1994) states:

"a 'video work' means any series of visual images (with or without sound):
  (a)   produced electronically by the use of information contained on any disc, magnetic tape, or any other device capable of storing data electronically, and
  (b)   shown as a moving picture."

If a relatively brief series of visual images produced when a disk is run on a computer is long enough to show continuity of movement, it is "shown as a moving picture" (*Meechie v. Multi-Media Marketing (Canterbury) Ltd* May 4, 1995, Q.B.D.).
Section 1(3) states: **14–24**

"A 'video recording' means any disc, magnetic tape or any other device capable of storing data electronically containing information by the use of which the whole or a part of a video work may be produced."

It contains a video work if it contains information by the use of which the whole or a part of the work may be produced, but where a video work includes any extract from another video work, that extract is not to be regarded as a part of that other work (s.22(2)).
Section 1(4) states: **14–25**

" 'supply' means supply in any manner, whether or not for reward, and therefore, includes supply by way of sale, letting on hire, exchange or loan; and references to a supply are to be interpreted accordingly."

II. EXEMPTED WORKS

Certain works are exempted in accordance with section 2 of the Act, namely   **14–26**
a work which if taken as a whole: is designed to inform, educate or instruct; is concerned with sport, religion or music; or is a video game (s.2(1)). A "video work" appearing at the successful completion of a computer game, the game not being a "moving picture", is not of itself "taken as a whole ... a video game" and therefore cannot be "an exempted work" (*Meechie v. Multi-Media Marketing (Canterbury) Ltd* (above)).
This exemption does not include however, a work which, to any sig-   **14–27**
nificant extent depicts: (a) human sexual activity or acts of force or restraint

associated with such activity; (b) mutilation or torture of, or other acts of gross violence towards, humans or animals; (c) human genital organs or human urinary or excretory functions; (d) techniques likely to be useful in the commission of offences; or is likely to any significant extent to stimulate or encourage anything falling within (a) or, in the case of anything falling within (b), is likely to any extent to do so (s.2(2) as amended by s.89(3) of the CJPOA 1994). "Human sexual activity" can fall short of masturbation and a "video work" can be said to be designed to stimulate or encourage such activity even though it could not be regarded as hard core pornography or as offensive (*Kent County Council v. Multi-Media Marketing (Canterbury) Ltd and another*, The Times, May 9, 1995).

14-28   Nor is a video work exempted if, to any significant extent, it depicts criminal activity which is likely to any significant extent to stimulate or encourage the commission of offences (s.2(3) as inserted by s.89(4) of the Criminal Justice and Public Order Act 1994).

III. Exempted Supplies

14-29   Section 3 states:

"(1) The provisions of this section apply to determine whether or not a supply of a video recording is an exempted supply for the purposes of this Act.

(2) The supply of a video recording by any person is an exempted supply if it is neither:

   (a) a supply for reward, nor
   (b) a supply in the course or furtherance of a business."

"Business", except in section 3(4), includes any activity carried on by a club (s.22(1)).

Subsection (3) states:

Where on any premises facilities are provided in the course or furtherance of a business for supplying video recordings, the supply by any person of a video recording on those premises is to be treated for the purposes of subsection (2) as a supply in the course or furtherance of a business."

"Premises" includes any vehicle, vessel or stall (s.22(1)).

14-30   (4) states:

"Where a person (in this subsection referred to as the 'original supplier') supplies a video recording to a person who, in the course of a business, makes video works or supplies video recordings the supply is an exempted supply:

   (a) if it is not made with a view to any further supply of that recording, or
   (b) if it is so made, but is not made with a view to the eventual supply of that recording to the public or is made with a view to the eventual supply of that recording to the original supplier.

For the purposes of this subsection, any supply is a supply to the public unless it is:

(i) a supply to a person who, in the course of a business, makes video works or supplies video recordings,

(ii) an exempted supply by virtue of subsection (2) or subsections (5) to (10), or

(iii) a supply outside the United Kingdom.

(5) Where a video work: **14-31**

   (a) is designed to provide a record of an event or occasion for those who took part in the event or occasion or are connected with those who did so,

   (b) does not, to any significant extent, depict anything falling within paragraph (a), (b) or (c) of section 2(2) of this Act, and

   (c) is not designed to any significant extent to stimulate or encourage anything falling within paragraph (a) of that subsection, or, in the case of anything falling within paragraph (b) of that subsection, is not designed to any extent to do so, the supply of a video recording containing only that work to a person who took part in the event or occasion or is connected with someone who did so is an exempted supply.

(6) The supply of a video recording for the purpose only of the exhibition **14-32** of any video work contained in the recording in premises other than a dwelling-house:

   (a) being premises mentioned in subsection (7) below, or

   (b) being an exhibition which in England and Wales or Scotland would be a film exhibition to which section 6 of the Cinemas Act 1985 applies (film exhibition to which public not admitted or are admitted without payment), is an exempted supply.

(7) The premises referred to in subsection (6) above are— **14-33**

   (a) premises in respect of which a licence under section 1 of the Cinemas Act 1985 is in force.

   (b) premises falling within section 7 of that Act (premises used only occasionally and exceptionally for film exhibitions), or

   (c) premises falling within section 8 of that Act (building or structure of a movable character) in respect of which such a licence as is mentioned in subsection (1)(a) of that section has been granted.

(8) The supply of a video recording with a view only to its use for or in **14-34** connection with a programme service (within the meaning of the Broadcasting Act 1990) is an exempted supply.

(9) The supply of a video recording for the purpose only of submitting a video work contained in the recording for the issue of a classification certificate or otherwise only for purposes of arrangements made by the designated authority is an exempted supply.

(10) The supply of a video recording with a view only to its use:

   (a) in training for or carrying on any medical or related occupation,

   (b) for the purpose of:

> > (i) services provided in pursuance of the National Health
> > Service Act 1977 or the National Health Service (Scotland)
> > Act 1978
> >
> > (c) in training persons employed in the course of services falling
> > within paragraph (b) above,
> >
> > is an exempted supply.
> >
> > (11) For the purposes of subsection (10) above, an occupation is a medical
> > or related occupation if, to carry on the occupation, a person is
> > required to be registered under the Professions Supplementary to
> > Medicine Act 1960, the Nurses, Midwives and Health Visitors Act
> > 1979 or the Medical Act 1983.

14-35   (12) The supply of a video recording otherwise than for reward, being a
> > supply made for the purpose only of supplying it to a person who
> > previously made an exempted supply of the recording, is also an
> > exempted supply."

IV. THE BRITISH BOARD OF FILM CLASSIFICATION (BBFC)

14-36   In accordance with section 4(1), the Secretary of State designated the British
Board of Film Classification as the authority responsible for making
arrangements:

> (a) for determining whether a video work is suitable for a classifica-
> tion certificate to be issued, having special regard to the likelihood
> of the video being viewed in the home;
>
> (b) for making such other determinations as are required for the issue
> of classification certificates and for issuing such certificates; and
>
> (c) for keeping a record of the determinations and the video record-
> ings

14-37   The Criminal Justice and Public Order Act 1994, s. 90 inserted section
4A(1) which came into force on November 3, 1994 which requires the
authority in making any determination, to have special regard (among other
relevant factors) to any harm that may be caused to potential viewers or,
through their behaviour, to society by the manner in which the work deals
with:

> (a) criminal behaviour;
> (b) illegal drugs;
> (c) violent behaviour or incidents;
> (d) horrific behaviour or incidents; or
> (e) human sexual activity.

14-38   While section 4A(2) defines "potential viewer" as any person (including a
child or young person) who is likely to view the video work in question if a
classification certificate or a certificate of a particular description were
issued, it offers no guidance on the number of people required to satisfy the
"potential viewers" criteria.

"Suitability" means suitability for the issue of a classification certificate or **14–39** suitability for the issue of a certificate of a particular description; "violent behaviour" includes any act inflicting or likely to result in the infliction of injury; and any behaviour or activity referred to in (a) to (e) above shall be taken to include behaviour or activity likely to stimulate or encourage it (s. 4A(2)).

Section 4B states that the Secretary of State may make provision, by **14–40** statutory instrument, enabling the designated authority to review any determination made before November 3, 1994 as to the suitability of a video work and its classification certificate and *inter alia*, cancel the existing certificate or issue a different classification certificate.

Classification certificates must, by virtue of section 7 of the Act, contain a **14–41** statement that the video work concerned is suitable for:

(a) general viewing and unrestricted supply (with or without any advice as to the desirability of parental guidance with regard to the viewing of the work by young children or as to the particular suitability of the work for viewing by children or young children); or

(b) viewing only by persons who have attained the age (not being more than eighteen years) specified in the certificate and that no video recording containing that work is to be supplied to any person who has not attained the age so specified; or

(c) the statement in (b) together with a statement that no video recording containing that work is to be supplied other than in a licensed sex shop.

V. REQUIREMENTS AS TO LABELLING

Section 8 of the Act gives the Secretary of State a discretionary power to **14–42** make regulations as to labelling of video works.

VI. OFFENCES

Sections 9 to 14 of the Act set out the offences: **14–43**

Section 9: supplying video recording of unclassified work

"(1) A person who supplies or offers to supply a video recording containing a video work in respect of which no classification certificate has been issued is guilty of an offence unless:
  (a) the supply is, or would if it took place be, an exempted supply, or
  (b) the video work is an exempted work.
(2) It is a defence to a charge of committing an offence under this section to prove that the accused believed on reasonable grounds—
  (a) that the video work concerned or, if the video recording con-

tained more than one work to which the charge relates, each of those works was either an exempted work or a work in respect of which a classification certificate had been issued, or
   (b)   that the supply was, or would if it took place be, an exempted supply by virtue of section 3(4) or (5) of this Act."

14–44   *Section 10: possession of video recording of unclassified work for the purposes of supply*

   "(1)   Where a video recording contains a video work in respect of which no classification certificate has been issued, a person who has the recording in his possession for the purposes of supplying it is guilty of an offence unless:
      (a)   he has it in his possession for the purpose only of a supply which, if it took place, would be an exempted supply, or
      (b)   the video work is an exempted work.
   (2)   It is a defence to a charge of committing an offence under this section to prove:
      (a)   that the accused believed on reasonable grounds that the video work concerned or, if the video recording contained more than one work to which the charge relates, each of those works was either an exempted work or a work in respect of which a classification certificate had been issued,
      (b)   that the accused had the video recording in his possession for the purposes only of a supply which he believed on reasonable grounds would, if it took place, be an exempted supply by virtue of section 3(4) or (5) of this Act, or
      (c)   that the accused did not intend to supply the video recording until a classification certificate had been issued in respect of the video work concerned."

14–45   *Section 11: supplying video recording of classified work in breach of classification*

   "(1)   Where a classification certificate issued in respect of a video work states that no video recording containing that work is to be supplied to any person who has not attained the age specified in the certificate, a person who supplies or offers to supply a video recording containing that work to a person who has not attained the age so specified is guilty of an offence unless the supply is, or would if it took place be, an exempted supply.
   (2)   It is a defence to a charge of committing an offence under this section to prove:
      (a)   that the accused neither knew nor had reasonable grounds to believe that the classification certificate contained the statement concerned,
      (b)   that the accused neither knew nor had reasonable grounds to believe that the person concerned had not attained that age, or
      (c)   that the accused believed on reasonable grounds that the supply

was, or would if it took place be, an exempted supply by virtue of section 3(4) or (5) of this Act."

Section 12: certain video recordings only to be supplied in licensed sex   **14–46**
shops

"(1) Where a classification certificate issued in respect of a video work states that no video recording containing that work is to be supplied other than in a licensed sex shop, a person who at any place other than in a sex shop for which a licence is in force under the relevant enactment:

    (a)   supplies a video recording containing the work, or

    (b)   offers to do so,

is guilty of an offence unless the supply is, or would if it took place be, an exempted supply.

(2)   It is a defence to a charge of committing an offence under subsection (1) above to prove:

    (a)   that the accused neither knew nor had reasonable grounds to believe that the classification certificate contained the statement concerned,

    (b)   that the accused believed on reasonable grounds that the place concerned was a sex shop for which a licence was in force under the relevant enactment, or

    (c)   that the accused believed on reasonable grounds that the supply was, or would if it took place be, an exempted supply by virtue of section 3(4) of this Act or subsection (6) below.

(3)   Where a classification certificate issued in respect of a video work states that no video recording containing that work is to be supplied other than in a licensed sex shop, a person who has a video recording containing the work in his possession for the purposes of supplying it at any place other than in such a sex shop is guilty of an offence, unless he has it in his possession for the purpose only of a supply which, if it took place, would be an exempted supply.

(4)   It is a defence to a charge of committing an offence under subsection (3) above to prove:

    (a)   that the accused neither knew nor had reasonable grounds to believe that the classification certificate contained the statement concerned,

    (b)   that the accused believed on reasonable grounds that the place concerned was a sex shop for which a licence was in force under the relevant enactment, or

    (c)   that the accused had the video recording in his possession for the purpose only of a supply which he believed on reasonable grounds would, if it took place, be an exempted supply by virtue of section 3(4) of this Act or subsection (6) below.

(5)   In this section 'relevant enactment' means Schedule 3 to the Local Government (Miscellaneous Provisions) Act 1982 or, in Scotland, Schedule 2 to the Civic Government (Scotland) Act 1982, and 'sex shop' has the same meaning as in the relevant enactment.

(6)   For the purposes of this section, where a classification certificate

issued in respect of a video work states that no video recording containing that work is to be supplied other than in a licensed sex shop, the supply of a video recording containing that work:

(a)   to a person who, in the course of a business, makes video works or supplies video recordings, and

(b)   with a view to its eventual supply in sex shops, being sex shops for which licences are in force under the relevant enactment,

is an exempted supply."

14–47   *Section 13: supply of video recording not complying with requirements as to labels, etc.*

"(1) A person who supplies or offers to supply a video recording or any spool, case or other thing on or in which the recording is kept which does not satisfy any requirement imposed by regulations under section 8 of this Act is guilty of an offence unless the supply is, or would if it took place be, an exempted supply.

(2)   It is a defence to a charge of committing an offence under this section to prove that the accused:

(a)   believed on reasonable grounds that the supply was, or would if it took place be, an exempted supply by virtue of section 3(4) or (5) of this Act, or

(b)   neither knew nor had reasonable grounds to believe that the recording, spool, case or other thing (as the case may be) did not satisfy the requirement concerned."

14–48   *Section 14: supply of video containing false indication as to classification*

"(1) A person who supplies or offers to supply a video recording containing a video work in respect of which no classification certificate has been issued is guilty of an offence if the video recording or any spool, case or other thing on or in which the recording is kept contains any indication that a classification certificate has been issued in respect of that work unless the supply is, or would if it took place be, an exempted supply.

(2)   It is a defence to a charge of committing an offence under subsection (1) above to prove:

(a)   that the accused believed on reasonable grounds.

(i)   that a classification certificate had been issued in respect of the video work concerned, or

(ii)   that the supply was, or would if it took place be, an exempted supply by virtue of section 3(4) or (5) of this Act, or

(b)   that the accused neither knew or had reasonable grounds to believe that the recording, spool, case or other thing (as the case may be) contained the indication concerned.

(3)   A person who supplied or offers to supply a video recording containing a video work in respect of which a classification certificate has been issued is guilty of an offence if the video recording or any spool,

case or other thing on or in which the recording is kept contains any indication that is false in a material particular of any statement falling within section 7(2) of this Act (including any advice falling within paragraph (a) of that subsection) contained in the certificate, unless the supply is, or would if it took place be, an exempted supply."

(See para. 14–41 for the requirements given in s. 7(2)).

"(4) It is a defence to a charge of committing an offence under subsection (3) above to prove:
(a) that the accused believed on reasonable grounds:
  (i) that the supply was, or would if it took place be, an exempted supply by virtue of section 3(4) or (5) of this Act, or
  (ii) that the certificate concerned contained that statement indicated, or
(b) that the accused neither knew nor had reasonable grounds to believe that the recording, spool, case or other thing (as the case may be) contained the indication concerned."

Sentencing guidelines

Offences contrary to sections 9 and 10 committed before February 3,1995 **14–49** are summary only and punishable with a fine not exceeding £20,000 (s. 15(1) of the 1984 Act); thereafter, they are punishable on conviction on indictment, to imprisonment for a term not exceeding two years or a fine or both; and on summary conviction, to imprisonment for a term not exceeding six months or a fine not exceeding £20,000 or both (ss. 9(3) and 10(3) as inserted by s. 88 of the CJPOA 1994).

The remaining offences, if committed before February 3,1995 are punishable on summary conviction to a fine not exceeding level 5 on the standard scale (as defined in Criminal Justice Act 1982, s.75 (s.15(3)); thereafter, offences contrary to sections 11, 12 and 14 are punishable by a term of imprisonment not exceeding six months and\or a fine not exceeding level 5 on the standard scale (ss. 11(3), 12(4A) and 14(5) as inserted by s. 88 of the CJPOA 1994).

(a) Forfeiture

Following conviction the court, if satisfied that the video recording (or any **14–50** spool, case or other thing on or in which the recording is kept (s.21(3)) produced to it relates to the offence, may order it to be forfeited (s.21(1)), but only if a person claiming to be the owner of it or otherwise interested in it has been given the opportunity to show cause why the order should not be made (s.21(2)).

A forfeiture order shall not take effect until time has elapsed within which an appeal may be instituted, or where it is instituted has been finally decided or abandoned and for this purpose, an application for a case to be stated or for leave to appeal shall be treated as the institution of an appeal and where a decision on appeal is subject to a further appeal, the appeal is not finally decided until the expiration of the ordinary time within which a further appeal may be instituted or, where a further appeal is duly instituted, until the further appeal is finally decided or abandoned (s.21(4)). An affidavit exhibiting a computer disc which was the subject of proceedings under the 1984 Act can be appended to a case stated to ensure that the original material before the justices would subsequently be viewed by the Divisional Court (*Kent County Council v. Multi-Media Marketing (Canterbury) Ltd and another*, above).

(b) Bodies corporate

14–51 Where an offence committed by a body corporate is proved to have been committed with the consent or connivance of, or to be attributable to any neglect on the part of, any director, manager, secretary or other similar officer of the corporation, or any person who was purporting to act in any such capacity, he as well as the body corporate shall be guilty of the offence and shall be liable to be proceeded against and punished accordingly (s.16(1)). Where the affairs of the corporation are managed by its members, section 16(1) shall apply in relation to the acts and defaults of a member in connection with his functions of management as if he were a director of the body corporate (s.16(2)).

VII. Functions Of The Weights And Measures Authority

14–52 The Criminal Justice Act 1988, s.162 inserted a section 16A into the 1984 Act which includes in the functions of a local weights and measures authority, the enforcement in their area of the 1984 Act (s.16A(1)).

14–53 This was further extended by the CJPOA 1994 which added section 16A(1A), enabling the functions of a local weights and measures authority to include the investigation and prosecution outside their area of offences under the 1984 Act which are suspected to be linked to their area as well as the investigation outside their area of offences suspected to have been committed within it.

The functions available to an authority under sub-section (1A) are only exercisable in relation to any circumstances suspected to have arisen within the area of another local weights and measures authority without the consent of that authority (s.16A(1B). Offences in another area are "linked" to the area of a local weights and measures authority if—(i) the supply or possession of video recordings within their area is likely to be or to have been the result of the supply or possession of those recordings in the other area; or (ii) the supply or possession of video recordings in the other area is likely to be or to have been the result of the supply or possession of those recordings in their area (s.16A(4A) "investigation" and enforcement by the authority, includes the exercise of the powers conferred by sections 27 (power to make test purchases); 28 (power to enter premises and inspect and seize goods and documents); 29 (obstruction of authorised officers); and 33 of the Trade

Descriptions Act 1968 (compensation for loss, etc., of goods seized under s.28) (ss.16A(2) and (4A)(b)).

By virtue of section 16A(5) any enactment which authorises the disclosure of information for the purpose of facilitating the enforcement of the Trades Descriptions Act 1968 shall apply as if the provisions of the Video Recordings Act 1984 were contained in that Act and as if the functions of any person in relation to the enforcement of the 1984 Act were functions under that Act. The insertion of a section 16(B) into the 1984 Act extends the jurisdiction of justices of the peace to issue summonses or warrants or to try offences which are committed or suspected of having been committed outside the area for which the justices act if it appears to the justices that the offence is linked to the supply or possession of video recordings within the area for which they act. **14–54**

VIII. JUSTICES' WARRANT

By virtue of section 17, a justice of the peace may issue a warrant authorising any constable to enter premises, using reasonable force if necessary, and search for and seize anything found which he has reasonable grounds to believe may be required to be used in evidence in any proceedings for an offence under this Act. The justice, before he issues the warrant, must be satisfied by information on oath that there are reasonable grounds for suspecting that an offence under the Act has been or is being committed on the premises and that evidence of that is on those premises. **14–55**

IX. POLICE POWERS

A constable may only arrest without warrant a person who he has reasonable grounds for suspecting has committed an offence under the Act and who refuses or fails on request to provide the constable with his name and address or gives a name and address which the constable reasonably suspects to be false (s.18(1)). **14–56**

X. EVIDENCE OF CLASSIFICATION, OR NOT, BY CERTIFICATE

Section 19 makes provision for evidence of the fact of classification (or lack of it) to be admissible by way of certificate, provided that a copy of the certificate has, not less than seven days before the hearing, been served on the person charged with the offence. Service must be either by: (a) delivering it to him or to his solicitor; or (b) addressing it to him and leaving it at his usual or last known place of abode or place of business or by addressing it to his solicitor and leaving it at his office; or (c) sending it in a registered letter or by the recorded delivery service addressed to him at his usual or last known place of abode or place of business or addressed to his solicitor at his office; or (d) in the case of a body corporate, by delivering it to the secretary or clerk **14–57** of the body at its registered or principal office or sending it in a registered letter or by the recorded delivery service addressed to the secretary or clerk of that body at that office.

14-58   The certificate must purport to be signed by a person authorised in that behalf by the Secretary of State and state that: (a) he has examined: (i) the record maintained in pursuance of arrangements made by the designated authority and (ii) a video work (or part of a video work) contained in a video recording identified by the certificate, and (b) that the record shows that on the date specified in the certificate, no classification (s.19(1)) or a classification (s.19(3)) was issued in respect of the video work concerned.

14-59   Where there is no classification, the certificate may also state that: (a) the video work concerned differs in such respects as may be specified from another video work examined by the person so authorised and identified by the certificate and (b) that the record shows that, on a date specified in the certificate, a classification certificate was issued in respect of that other video work and that shall be admissible as evidence of the fact that the video work concerned differs in those respects from the other video work (s.19(2)).

14-60   Where there is a classification, a copy of the classification certificate is to be included with the section 19 certificate (s.19(3)(b)), and any such document or video recording identified in a section 19 certificate shall be treated as if it had been produced as an exhibit and identified in court by the person signing the certificate (s. 19(4)).

D. ORDERS PROSCRIBING UNACCEPTABLE FOREIGN SATELLITE SERVICES

14-61   The development of broadcasting technology has meant that persons within the United Kingdom are able to receive programmes transmitted from countries outside the United Kingdom, where, the law on the publication or transmission of pornography may be more relaxed. Through the medium of the Broadcasting Act 1990 the Independent Television Commission of the Radio Authority has the power to proscribe foreign satellite services, thus preventing people in the United Kingdom from being able to watch these programmes.

It should be noted however that it was decided by the European Court of Justice in *Commission of the European Communities (supported by French Republic, intervener) v. United Kingdom, The Times*, September 30, 1996, that the United Kingdom has no power to regulate the television programmes of a broadcasting company established in another part of the European Union. A broadcaster is "established" where it has "the centre of its activities", *i.e.* "the place where decisions concerning programme policy are taken and the programmes to be broadcast are finally put together". The Court held that the United Kingdom had failed to fulfil its obligations under a Community directive by applying different regimes under section 43 of the Broadcasting Act 1990 to domestic and non-domestic satellite television services and exercising control over certain broadcasts transmitted by broadcasters falling under the jurisdiction of other member states.

I. ORDERS PROSCRIBING FOREIGN SATELLITE SERVICES

Section 177 states: 14–62

"(1) Subject to the following provisions of this section, the Secretary of State may make an order proscribing a foreign satellite service for the purposes of section 178.

(2) If the Independent Television Commission of the Radio Authority consider that the quality of any relevant foreign satellite service which is brought to their attention is unacceptable and that the service should be the subject of an order under this section, they shall notify to the Secretary of State details of the service and their reasons why they consider such an order should be made.

(3) The Independent Television Commission or (as the case may be) the Radio Authority shall not consider a foreign satellite service to be unacceptable for the purposes of subsection (2) unless they are satisfied that there is repeatedly contained in programmes included in the service matter which offends against good taste or decency or is likely to encourage or incite to crime or to lead to disorder or to be offensive to public feeling.

(4) Where the Secretary of State has been notified under subsection (2), he shall not make an order under this section unless he is satisfied that the making of the order:
  (a) is in the public interest; and
  (b) is compatible with any international obligations of the United Kingdom.

(5) An order under this section:
  (a) may make such provision for the purpose of identifying a particular foreign satellite service as the Secretary of State thinks fit; and
  (b) shall be subject to annulment in pursuance of a resolution of either House of Parliament."

II. OFFENCES ARISING FROM SECTION 177

Section 178 states: 14–63

"(1) This section applies to any foreign satellite service which is proscribed for the purposes of this section by virtue of an order under section 177; and references in this section to a proscribed service are references to any such service.

(2) Any person who in the United Kingdom does any of the acts specified in subsection (3) shall be guilty of an offence.

(3) Those acts are:
  (a) supplying any equipment or other goods for use in connection

        with the operation or day-to-day running of a proscribed service;

  (b) supplying, or offering to supply, programme material to be included in any programme transmitted in the provision of a proscribed service;

  (c) arranging for, or inviting, any other person to supply programme material to be so included;

  (d) advertising, by means of programmes transmitted in the provision of a proscribed service, goods supplied by him or services provided by him;

  (e) publishing the times or other details of any programmes which are to be transmitted in the provision of a proscribed service or (otherwise than by publishing such details) publishing an advertisement of matter calculated to promote a proscribed service (whether directly or indirectly);

  (f) supplying or offering to supply any decoding equipment which is designed or adapted to be used primarily for the purpose of enabling the reception of programmes transmitted in the provision of a proscribed service."

(a) Statutory defences

14–64   Section 178 states:

> "(4) In any proceedings against a person for an offence under this section, it is a defence for him to prove that he did not know, and had no reasonable cause to suspect, that the service in connection with which the act was done was a proscribed service."

(b) Sentencing guidelines

14–65   Section 178 further states:

> "(5) A person who is guilty of an offence under this section shall be liable:
>
>   (a) on summary conviction, to imprisonment for a term not exceeding six months or to a fine not exceeding the statutory maximum, or both;
>
>   (b) on conviction on indictment, to imprisonment for a term not exceeding two years or to a fine, or both."

(c) Evidential presumption

14–66   Subsection states:

> (6) "For the purposes of this section a person exposing decoding equipment for supply or having such equipment in his possession for supply shall be deemed to offer to supply it."

(d) Definitions

Section 177 states: 14–67

(6)   In this section and section 178:
"foreign satellite service" means a service which consists wholly or
mainly in the transmission by satellite from a place outside the United
Kingdom of television or sound programmes which are capable of
being received in the United Kingdom;
"relevant foreign satellite service" means:
(a)   in relation to the Independent Television Commission, a foreign
satellite service which consists wholly or mainly in the transmission of television programmes; and
(b)   in relation to the Radio Authority, a foreign satellite service
which consists wholly or mainly in the transmission of sound
programmes.
Section 178(8) In this section "programme material" includes:
(a)   a film (within the meaning of Part I of the Copyright, Designs
and Patents Act 1988);
(b)   any other recording; and
(c)   any advertisement or other advertising material.
Section 178, subs. (7) states:

"Section 46 of the Consumer Protection Act 1987 shall have effect for the
purpose of construing references in this section to the supply of any thing
as it has effect for the purpose of construing references in that Act to the
supply of any goods."

E. CONTROL OF SEX ESTABLISHMENTS

The law relating to the control by licence of sex establishments is to be found   14–68
in Schedule 3 of the Local Government (Miscellaneous Provisions) Act 1982.
By virtue of section 2 of that Act, it is within the discretion of a local
authority (*i.e.* the council of a district; the council of a London borough; and
the Common Council of the City of London) to pass a resolution that
Schedule 3 shall apply to their area. Section 12 of the Greater London
Council (General Powers) Act 1986 in addition to enabling London Borough
Councils to apply Schedule 3 to their areas, also enables them to resolve that
amendments apply, for example in relation to sex encounter establishments
(see also *McMonagle v. Westminster City Council*, [1990] 1 All E.R. 993,
and *Willowcell Ltd v. Westminster City Council The Times*, April 14,
1995).

The provisions of Schedule 3 are mandatory, but not exhaustive (*R v.*   14–69
Preston, Trafford and Watford Borough Councils, The Times, March 22,
1984 and *R. v. Chester City Council, ex p. Quietlynn Ltd, The Times*, April
19, 1984).

The local authority must publish a notice that they have passed the   14–70 resolution in the local newspaper for two consecutive weeks, the first publication being not later than 28 days before the day specified in the resolution for the coming into force of Schedule 3.

I. Definitions

14–71   Sex establishments are sex cinemas and sex shops (Sched. 3, para.2) and are defined in paragraphs 3 and 4: "sex cinema" means any premises, vehicle, vessel (including any ship, boat, raft or other apparatus constructed or adapted for floating on water (para.5(1)), or stall used to a significant degree for the exhibition of moving pictures, by whatever means produced, which: (a) are concerned primarily with the portrayal of, or primarily deal with or relate to, or are intended to stimulate or encourage sexual activity or acts of force or restraint which are associated with sexual activity; or (b) are concerned primarily with the portrayal of, or primarily deal with or relate to, genital organs or urinary or excretory functions, but does not include a dwelling-house to which the public is not admitted.

14–72   Premises are not to be treated as a sex cinema by reason only: (a) if they are licensed under section 1 of the Cinemas Act 1985, of their use for a purpose for which a licence under that section is required; or (b) of their use for an exhibition to which section 6 of that Act (certain non-commercial exhibitions) applies given by an exempted organisation within the meaning of section 6(6) of that Act.

14–73   "Sex shop" means any premises, vehicle, vessel or stall used for a business which consists to a significant degree of selling, hiring, exchanging, lending, displaying or demonstrating: (a) sex articles; or (b) other things intended for use in connection with, or for the purpose of stimulating or encouraging sexual activity or acts of force or restraint which are associated with sexual activity.

Premises are not to be treated as a sex shop by reason only of their use for the exhibition of moving pictures by whatever means produced.

14–74   "Significant" means "more than trifling" and in deciding whether an establishment is a "sex shop", the ratio between the sexual and other aspects of the business will always be material, so also will be the absolute quantity of sales, and the character of the remainder of the business. The court must decide which considerations are material to the individual case and what weight is to be attached to them: *Lambeth London Borough Council v. Grewal* [1986] Crim L.R. 260.

14–75   "Sex article" means: (a) anything made for use in connection with, or for the purpose of stimulating or encouraging sexual activity or acts of force or restraint which are associated with sexual activity; and (b) to any article containing or embodying matter to be read or looked at or anything intended to be used, either alone or as one of a set, for the reproduction or manufacture of any such article and, to any recording of vision or sound which (i) is concerned primarily with the portrayal of, or primarily deals with or relates to, or is intended to stimulate or encourage, sexual activity or acts of force or restraint which are associated with sexual activity; or (ii) is concerned primarily with the portrayal of, or primarily deals with or relates to, genital organs, or urinary or excretory functions.

II. REQUIREMENT OF LICENCE

By virtue of paragraph 6, where Schedule 3 is in force, a person may not use premises, etc., as a sex establishment except in accordance with the terms of a licence granted by the local authority. This does not apply to the sale, supply or demonstration of articles which primarily relate to or are manufactured for the purposes of birth control (para.6(2)). It is open to a person under paragraph 7 to apply to the local authority for them to waive the requirement of a licence and the local authority has power under paragraph 7(4) and (5) to so waive if it considers that to require a licence would be unreasonable or inappropriate and for such period as it thinks fit.   **14–76**

Licences, may be granted and renewed for periods of up to a year on such terms and conditions and subject to such restrictions as may be so specified (paras 8 and 9). They may also be transferred, if the local authority thinks fit to another person on the application of that other person (para.9(2)).   **14–77**

(a) Application for licence

The application must be in writing (para.10(1)) and contain the following: **14–78**

"(2) unless the applicant is a corporate or unincorporated body, the full name, age and permanent address of the applicant;

(3) where the applicant is a body corporate or unincorporated body, its full name, address of its principal registered office and the full names and private addresses of the directors or other persons responsible for its management;

(4) the full address of the premises to be used;

(5) if the application relates to a vehicle, vessel or stall, where it is to be used as a sex establishment; and

(6) such particulars as the local authority may reasonably require in addition to the above."

Applicants must give notice, published in a local newspaper within seven days of the application, of the application for either grant, renewal or transfer of a licence (para.10(8) and (9)) and send a copy of the application to the chief officer of police (para.10(14)). In addition, where the application is in respect of premises, notice of it shall be displayed for 21 days beginning with the date of application, on or near the premises and in a place where the notice can conveniently be read by the public (para.10(10)). Notices can be in such form as prescribed by the local authority but must give the address of the premises or the position of the vehicle, vessel or stall to be used as a sex establishment (para.10(11), (12) and (13)).   **14–79**

A person wishing to object to the application must do so in writing to the local authority, setting out the terms of his objection, not later than 28 days after the date of the application (para.10(15)) and the local authority must give notice in writing of the general terms of the objection to the applicant   **14–80** but without revealing the personal details of the person objecting without his consent (para.10(16) and (17)).

14–81   When the local authority considers the application, it shall have regard to any observations submitted to it by the chief officer of police and any objections received under subparagraph 15 (para.10(18)). It shall also give an opportunity of appearing before and of being heard by a committee or sub-committee of the authority: (a) before refusing to grant a licence, to the applicant; (b) before refusing to renew a licence, to the holder; and (c) before refusing to transfer a licence, to the holder and the person to whom he desires that it be transferred (para.10(19)). Where the authority refuses to grant, renew or transfer a licence, it shall, if required to do so by the applicant or holder of the licence, give him a statement in writing of the reasons for its decision within seven days of his requiring them to do so (para.10(20)).

14–82   Where, before the date of the expiry of a licence, an application has been made for its renewal, it shall be deemed to remain in force notwithstanding that the date has passed until the withdrawal of the application or its determination by the authority (para.11(1)). Where, before the date of expiry of a licence, an application has been made for its transfer, it shall be deemed to remain in force with any necessary modifications until the withdrawal of the application or its determination, notwithstanding that the date has passed or that the person to whom the licence is to be transferred if the application is granted is carrying on the business of the sex establishment (para.11(2)).

(b) Persons who cannot hold licences

14–83   Licences shall not be granted to: (a) a person under the age of 18; (b) a person who is disqualified for revocation of a licence—the disqualification may only be for one year (para.17(3)); (c) a person, other than a body corporate, who is not resident in the United Kingdom or was not so resident throughout the period of six months immediately preceding the date when the application was made; (d) a body corporate which is not incorporated in the United Kingdom; (e) a person who has, within a period of 12 months immediately preceding the date when the application was made, been refused the grant or renewal of a licence for the premises, vehicle, vessel or stall in respect of which the application is made, unless the refusal has been reversed on appeal (para.12(1)).

(c) Applications for transfer

14–84   An application for the transfer of a licence may be refused on the grounds that (a) the applicant is unsuitable to hold the licence by reason of having been convicted of an offence or any other reason, or (b) that if the licence were to be granted, renewed or transferred the business to which it relates would be managed by or carried on for the benefit of a person, other than the applicant, who would be refused the grant, renewal or transfer of such a licence if he made the application himself (para.12(2)(b) and (3)). An application for the grant or renewal of a licence may be refused on the grounds given above and also because (c) the number of sex establishments in the relevant locality at the time the application is made is equal to or exceeds the number which the authority consider appropriate for that locality (nil may be an appropriate number (para.12(4))) or (d) that the grant or renewal of the licence would be inappropriate, having regard: (i) to the character of the relevant locality; or (ii) to the use to which any premises in the vicinity are put; or (iii) to the layout, character or condition of the premises, vehicle, vessel or stall in respect of which the application is made (para.12(2)(a) and (3)). The licensing authority is entitled to refuse an existing licence on the grounds in (d), despite the fact that there has not been any change of circumstances, provided it gives due weight to the fact that the licence has previously been granted and gives rational reasons for its refusal: *R v. Birmingham City Council, ex p. Sheptonhurst Ltd* [1990] 1 All E.R. 87.

(d) Regulations

Paragraph 13 allows the authority to make regulations prescribing standard terms, conditions and restrictions on or subject to which licences are in general to be granted, renewed or transferred in respect of: opening and closing times; displays or advertisements on or in the establishments; the visibility of the interior to passers-by; and any change of a sex cinema to a sex shop or vice versa. These provisions may be different for sex cinemas and sex shops, and for different kinds of sex cinemas and sex shops. Where the authority has made such regulations then a licence is presumed be subject to those standard conditions unless, expressly excluded or varied (para.13(4)). In any legal proceedings, production of a certified copy of the regulations is prima facie evidence of them (para.13(6)).   **14–85**

(e) Display of licence

A copy of the licence and any regulations must be kept exhibited by the holder in a suitable place specified in the licence: non compliance being an offence under sub-paragraph 21(2) punishable on summary conviction with a fine not exceeding level 3 on the standard scale. A copy shall also be sent to the chief officer of police (para.14).   **14–86**

(f) Death of licence holder

Where the holder of a licence dies, the licence, unless previously revoked, shall remain in force for three months from the date of death and may be extended on the application of the deceased's personal representatives for a further three months if the authority are satisfied that the extension is necessary for the purpose of winding up the deceased's estate and no other circumstances make it undesirable (para.16).   **14–87**

(g) Revocation of licence

Licences may be revoked, by virtue of sub-paragraph 17(1), on any ground specified in sub-paragraph 12(1) or on either of the grounds in sub-paragraph 12(3)(a) and (b). The authority must give the holder of a licence   **14–88** an opportunity of appearing before and being heard by them before revocation and shall give the holder a written statement of the reasons for their decision within seven days of his requiring them to do so (para.17(2)).

(h) Variation of terms

14–89   Under paragraph 18, the holder of a licence may apply at any time to the authority for a variation in the terms, conditions or restrictions on or subject to which the licence is held and the authority may grant the application in full or vary it as they think fit (whether in accordance with the application or not) or refuse it.

III. Offences

14–90   Schedule 3 has five paragraphs creating offences, three of which (20, 21 and 23) are punishable on summary conviction to a fine not exceeding £20,000.

Paragraph 20 states:

"(1) A person who:
  (a) knowingly uses, or knowingly causes or permits the use of any premises, vehicle, vessel or stall contrary to paragraph 6;
  (b) being the holder of a licence, employs in the business of the sex establishment any person known to him to be disqualified from holding a licence;
  (c) being the holder of a licence without reasonable excuse knowingly contravenes or permits the contravention of, a term, condition or restriction specified in the licence;
  (d) being the servant or agent of the holder of a licence, without reasonable excuse knowingly contravenes or permits the contravention of, a term, condition or restriction specified in the licence,
  shall be guilty of an offence."

14–91   The prosecution must establish not only that the person knew that the premises were used as a sex establishment but also that he knew that they were being so used without a licence. Knowledge may be proved either by proving actual knowledge or by showing that the defendant had deliberately shut his eyes to the obvious or refrained from inquiry because he suspected the truth but did not want to have his suspicions confirmed: *Westminster City Council v. Croyalgrange Ltd* [1986] 2 All E.R. 353.

14–92   Where a person is prosecuted for not having a licence as required, the court cannot investigate and determine the validity of a licensing authority's refusal to grant a licence: *Quietlynn Ltd v. Plymouth City Council* [1988] Q.B. 114.

14–93   Paragraph 21 states:

"any person who, in connection with an application for the grant, renewal or transfer of a licence, makes a false statement which he knows to be false in any material respect or which he does not believe to be true, shall be guilty of an offence."

Paragraph 23 states: 14–94

"(1) A person who, being the holder of a licence for a sex establishment:
 (a) without reasonable excuse knowingly permits a person under 18 years of age to enter the establishment; or
 (b) employs a person known to him to be under 18 years of age in the business of the establishment,
       shall be guilty of an offence."

(a) Police powers

Paragraph 24 gives a constable a power of arrest without warrant where he   14–95
suspects that a person has committed an offence under paragraph 20 or 23 and having been required to give his name and address, refuses or fails to do so or gives a name and address which the constable reasonably suspects to be false.

A constable and an authorised officer of a local authority may at any   14–96
reasonable time, enter and inspect any (the local authority officer is limited by paragraph 25(3) to establishments in the local authority's area) sex establishment in respect of which a licence is in force, with a view to seeing whether: (i) the terms, conditions or restrictions on or subject to which the licence is held are complied with; (ii) any person employed in the business of the establishment is disqualified from holding a licence; (iii) any person under 18 years of age is on the establishment; and (iv) any person under 18 years is employed in the business of the establishment (para.25(1)).

Where a constable or an authorised officer of a local authority has the   14–97
authority of a magistrates' warrant (to be produced if required (para.25(5)), he may enter and inspect a sex establishment (the local authority officer being limited as above) if he has reason to suspect that an offence under paragraph 20, 21 or 23 has been, is being or is about to be committed (para.25(2) and (4)). Any person who without reasonable excuse refuses to permit a constable or an authorised officer of a local authority to exercise any such power shall be guilty of an offence and for every such refusal be liable on summary conviction to a fine not exceeding level 5 on the standard scale (as defined by Criminal Justice Act 1982, s.75) (para.25(6)).

(b) Bodies corporate

Where an offence committed by a body corporate is proved to have been   14–98
committed with the consent or connivance of, or to be attributable to any neglect on the part of, any director, manager, secretary or other similar officer of the body corporate, or any person who was purporting to act in any such capacity, he as well as the body corporate, shall be guilty of the offence (para. 25(1)). Where the affairs of a body corporate are managed by its members, the above shall apply to the acts and defaults of a member in

connection with his function of management as if he were a director of the body corporate (para.25(2)).

(c) Eligibility and procedure for appeals

14-99   Paragraph 27 sets out eligibility and procedure for appealing against a decision of the authority. Certain persons do not have a right to appeal, namely an applicant whose application for the grant or renewal of a licence is refused, or whose licence is revoked, on any ground specified in paragraph 12(1), unless he seeks to show that the ground did not apply to him (para.27(2)); or on either ground specified in paragraph 12(3)(c) or (d)(para.27(3)). Apart from the above exceptions, an applicant for the grant, renewal or transfer of a licence whose application is refused; and an applicant for the variation of the terms, conditions or restrictions on or subject to which any such licence is held whose application is refused; a holder of any such licence who is aggrieved by any term, condition or restriction on or subject to which the licence is held; or a holder of any such licence whose licence is revoked may at any time before the expiration of 21 days beginning with the relevant date appeal to the magistrates' court acting for the relevant area (para.27(1)).

"The relevant date" is the date on which the person in question is notified of the refusal of his application, the imposition of the term, condition or restriction by which he is aggrieved or the revocation of his licence: paragraph 27(4). "The relevant area" means: (a) in relation to premises, the petty sessions area in which they are situated; and (b) in relation to a vehicle, vessel or stall, the petty sessions area in which it is used or, as the case may be, desired to be used as a sex establishment (para.27(4)).

An appeal against the decision of the magistrates' court may be brought to the Crown Court, and the decision of the Crown Court is final (para.27(5) & (6)).

14-100   On an appeal, the magistrates' court or the Crown Court may make such order as it thinks fit (para.27(7)) and it is the duty of the appropriate authority to give effect to an order of either court but not until the time for bringing an appeal has expired or the appeal is determined or abandoned (para.27(9)) and during that time, the form of the licence remains unchanged (para.27(10),(11) and (12)).

(d) Existing premises and the section 2 resolution

14-101   Paragraphs 28 and 29 deal with the arrangements for existing premises before and after a section 2 resolution. Where a person was using any premises, etc., as a sex establishment immediately before the authority passed a section 2 resolution and had applied for a licence, he may continue to use the premises as a sex establishment until his application is determined (para.28(1)). Applications made should not be considered until the day on which the Schedule comes into force has passed and all applications should be considered before any one is granted (para.29(2) and (3)). In considering which of several applications should be granted, the authority shall give preference over other applicants to any applicant who satisfies them: (a) that he is using the premises, etc. to which the application relates as a sex establishment and that he, or his predecessor was using the premises, etc. as a sex establishment on December 22, 1981 (para.29(4)).

(e) Schedule 3 and other offences

Finally, nothing in Schedule 3 shall afford a defence to a charge in respect of   **14–102** any offence at common law or under an enactment other than this Schedule; or shall be taken into account in any way: (i) at a trial for such an offence; or (ii) in proceedings for forfeiture under section 3 of the Obscene Publications Act 1959 or section 5 of the Protection of Children Act 1978; or (iii) in proceeding for condemnation under Schedule 3 to the Customs and Excise Management Act 1979 of goods which section 42 of the Customs Consolidation Act 1876 prohibits to be imported or brought into the United Kingdom as being indecent or obscene; or shall in any way limit the other powers exercisable under any of these Acts (para.1).

Appendix 1

POLICE AND CRIMINAL EVIDENCE ACT 1984: CODES
OF PRACTICE
CODE D.5 (AS AMENDED)

5 IDENTIFICATION BY BODY SAMPLES AND IMPRESSIONS

(a) Action

Intimate samples

5.1 Intimate samples may be taken from a person in police detention only:

   (i)   if an officer of the rank of superintendent or above has reasonable grounds to believe that such an impression or sample will tend to confirm or disprove the suspect's involvement in a recordable offence and gives authorisation for a sample to be taken; and
   (ii) with the suspect's written consent.

5.1A Where two or more non-intimate samples have been taken from a person in the course of an investigation of an offence and the samples have proved unsuitable or insufficient for a particular form of analysis and that person is not in police detention, an intimate sample may be taken from him if a police officer of at least the rank of superintendent authorises it to be taken, and the person concerned gives his written consent. [*See Note 5B and Note 5E.*]

5.2 Before a person is asked to provide an intimate sample he must be warned that if he refuses without good cause, his refusal may harm his case if it comes to trial. [*See Note 5A*] If he is in police detention and not legally represented, he must also be reminded of his entitlement to have free legal advice (see para. 6.5 of Code C) and the reminder must be noted in the custody record. If paragraph 5.1A above applies and the person is attending a police station voluntarily, the officer shall explain the entitlement to free legal advice as provided for in accordance with paragraph 3.15 of Code C.

5.3 Except for samples of urine, intimate samples or dental impressions may be taken only by a registered medical or dental practitioner as appropriate.

Non-intimate samples

5.4 A non-intimate sample may be taken from a detained person only with his written consent or if paragraph 5.5 applies.

5.5 A non-intimate sample may be taken from a person without consent in accordance with the provisions of section 63 of the Police and Criminal Evidence Act 1984, as amended by section 55 of the Criminal Justice and Public Order Act 1994. The principal circumstances provided for are as follows:

(i)   if an officer of the rank of superintendent or above has reasonable grounds to believe that the sample will tend to confirm or disprove the person's involvement in a recordable offence and gives authorisation for a sample to be taken; or

(ii) where the person has been charged with a recordable offence or informed that he will be reported for such an offence; and he has not had a non-intimate sample taken from him in the course of the investigation or if he has had a sample taken from him, it has proved unsuitable or insufficient for the same form of analysis [See *Note 5B*]; or

(iii) if the person has been convicted of a recordable offence after the date on which this code comes into effect. Section 63A of the Police and Criminal Evidence Act 1984, as amended by section 56 of the Criminal Justice and Public Order Act 1994, describes the circumstances in which a constable may require a person convicted of a recordable offence to attend a police station in order that a non-intimate sample may be taken.

5.6 Where paragraph 5.5 applies, reasonable force may be used if necessary to take non-intimate samples.

(b) Destruction

5.7 [Not Used]

5.8 Except in accordance with paragraph 5.8A below, where a sample or impression has been taken in accordance with this section it must be destroyed as soon as practicable if:

(a)   the suspect is prosecuted for the offence concerned and cleared; or

(b)   he is not prosecuted (unless he admits the offence and is cautioned for it).

5.8 In accordance with section 64 of the Police and Criminal Evidence Act 1984 as amended by section 57 of the Criminal Justice and Public Order Act 1994 samples need not be destroyed if they were taken for the purpose of an investigation of an offence for which someone has been convicted, and from whom a sample was also taken.[*See Note 5F*]

(c) Documentation

5.9 A record must be made as soon as practicable of the reasons for taking a sample or impression and of its destruction. If force is used a record shall be made of the circumstances and those present. If written consent is given to the taking of a sample or impression, the fact must be recorded in writing.

5.10 A record must be made of the giving of a warning required by paragraph 5.2 above. A record shall be made of the fact that a person has been informed under the terms of paragraph 5.11A below that samples may be subject of a speculative search.

(d) General

5.11 The terms intimate and non-intimate samples are defined in section 65 of the Police and Criminal Evidence Act 1984, as amended by section 58 of the Criminal Justice and Public Order Act 1994, as follows:

(a) "intimate sample" means a dental impression or a sample of blood, semen or any other tissue fluid, urine, or pubic hair, or a swab taken from a person's body orifice other than the mouth;

(b) "non-intimate sample" means:

    (i) a sample of hair (other than pubic hair) which includes hair plucked with the root [See Note 5C];

    (ii) a sample taken from a nail or from under a nail;

    (iii) a swab taken from any part of a person's body including the mouth but not any other body orifice;

    (iv) saliva;

    (v) a footprint or similar impression of any part of a person's body other than a part of his hand.

5.11A A person from whom an intimate or non-intimate sample is to be taken shall be informed beforehand that any sample taken may be the subject of a speculative search. [See Note 5D]

5.11B The suspect must be informed, before an intimate or non-intimate sample is taken, of the grounds on which the relevant authority has been given, including where appropriate the nature of the suspected offence.

5.12 Where clothing needs to be removed in circumstances likely to cause embarrassment to the person, no person of the opposite sex who is not a medical practitioner or nurse shall be present, (unless in the case of a juvenile or a mentally disordered or mentally handicapped person, that person specifically requests the presence of an appropriate adult of the opposite sex who is readily available) nor shall anyone whose presence is unnecessary. However, in the case of a juvenile this is subject to the overriding proviso that such a removal of clothing may take place in the absence of the appropriate adult only if the person signifies in the presence of the appropriate adult that he prefers his absence and the appropriate adult agrees.

Notes For Guidance

5A In warning a person who is asked to provide an intimate sample in accordance with paragraph 5.2, the following form of words may be used:

"You do not have to [provide this sample] [allow this swab or impression to be taken], but I must warn you that if you refuse without good cause, your refusal may harm your case if it comes to trial."

5B An insufficient sample is one which is not sufficient either in quantity or quality for the purpose of enabling information to be provided for the purpose of a particular form of analysis such as DNA analysis. An unsuitable sample is one which, by its nature, is not suitable for a particular form of analysis.

5C Where hair samples are taken for the purpose of DNA analysis (rather than for other purposes such as making a visual match) the suspect should be permitted a reasonable choice as to what part of the body he wishes the hairs to be taken from. When hairs are plucked they should be plucked individually unless the suspect prefers otherwise and no more should be plucked than the person taking them reasonably considers necessary for a sufficient sample.

5D A speculative search means that a check may be made against other samples and information derived from other samples contained in records or held by or on behalf of the police or held in connection with or as a result of an investigation of an offence.

5E Nothing in paragraph 5.1A prevents intimate samples being taken for elimination purposes with the consent of the person concerned but the provisions of paragraph 1.11, relating to the role of the appropriate adult, should be applied.

5F The provisions for the retention of samples in 5.8A allow for all samples in a case to be available for any subsequent miscarriage of justice investigation. But such samples—and the information derived from them—may not be used in the investigation of any offence or in evidence against the person who would otherwise be entitled to their destruction.

Appendix 2

NON-INTIMATE SAMPLES: PROCEDURE

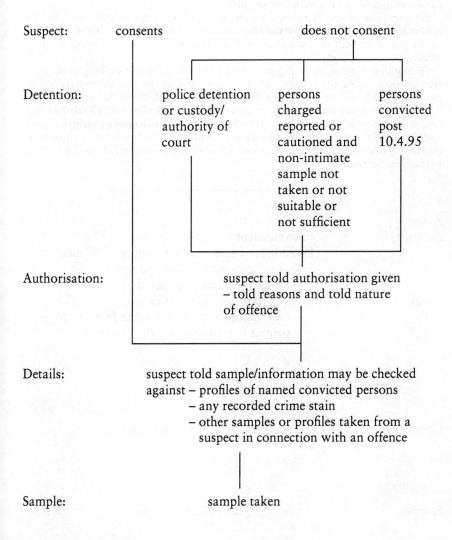

Suspect: consents   does not consent

Detention:

| police detention or custody/ authority of court | persons charged reported or cautioned and non-intimate sample not taken or not suitable or not sufficient | persons convicted post 10.4.95 |

Authorisation: suspect told authorisation given – told reasons and told nature of offence

Details: suspect told sample/information may be checked against – profiles of named convicted persons
– any recorded crime stain
– other samples or profiles taken from a suspect in connection with an offence

Sample: sample taken

Appendix 3

INTIMATE SAMPLES: PROCEDURE

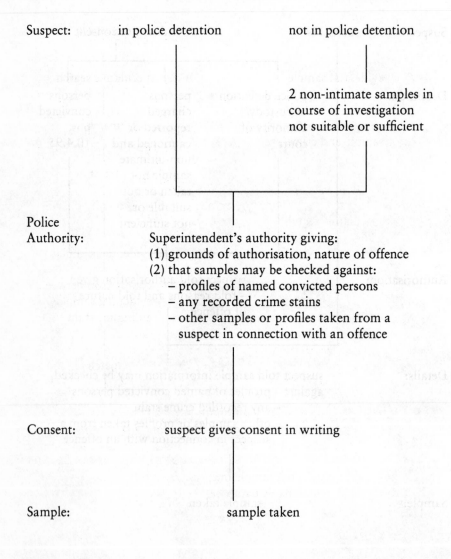

Suspect: in police detention   not in police detention

2 non-intimate samples in
course of investigation
not suitable or sufficient

Police
Authority: Superintendent's authority giving:
(1) grounds of authorisation, nature of offence
(2) that samples may be checked against:
    – profiles of named convicted persons
    – any recorded crime stains
    – other samples or profiles taken from a
      suspect in connection with an offence

Consent: suspect gives consent in writing

Sample: sample taken

Appendix 4

DNA INVESTIGATION

Suspect:

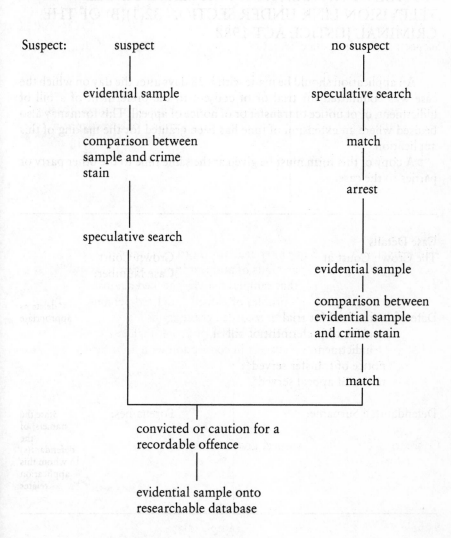

suspect

      evidential sample

      comparison between
      sample and crime
      stain

      speculative search

no suspect

      speculative search

      match

      arrest

      evidential sample

      comparison between
      evidential sample
      and crime stain

      match

convicted or caution for a
recordable offence

evidential sample onto
researchable database

Appendix 5

NOTICE OF APPLICATION FOR LEAVE TO USE TELEVISION LINK UNDER SECTION 32(1)(B) OF THE CRIMINAL JUSTICE ACT 1988

* An application should be made within 28 days after the day on which the case was committed for trial or of consent to the preferment of a bill of indictment, or of notice of transfer or of notice of appeal. This form may also be used where an extension of time has been granted for the making of this application.

* A copy of this form must be given at the same time to the other party or parties to the case.

Case Details

The Crown Court at   Crown Court
                                        Case Number:

                                                        *delete as
Date of: committal for trial*:   appropriate
          consent to preferment of bill of
              indictment*:
          notice of transfer served*:
          notice of appeal served*:

Defendant(s): Surname: Forenames: State the
                                                 name(s) of
                                                 the
                                                 defendant(s)
                                                 to whom this
                                                 application
                                                 relates

Application:

Name of Applicant:

Name of Applicant's Solicitor:

Address of Solicitor:

Reference:

Charges
Give brief details
of those charges
to which this
application applies

Name of Witness

Date of Birth:

If an application has been made to tender in evidence a video recording of testimony from the witness, state the date and (if known) result of that application:

Grounds for applying for evidence to
be given by television link:

Name of the person who is proposed to accompany the witness:

Occupation of this person:

Relation to the witness (if any):

Grounds for believing this person
should accompany the witness:

Signature of applicant
or
applicant's solicitor   Date
....

Appendix 6

NOTICE OF APPLICATION FOR LEAVE TO TENDER IN EVIDENCE A VIDEO RECORDING UNDER SECTION 32A OF THE CRIMINAL JUSTICE ACT 1988

* An application should be made within 28 days after the day on which the case was committed for trial, or of consent to the preferment of a bill of indictment or of notice of transfer, or of notice of appeal. If made after the expiry of this period, this notice can be used but should be accompanied by a statement giving good reasons why the application was not made within it.

* A copy of this form and any video recording(s) to which it relates must be sent at the same time to the other party or parties to the case. Where a defendant is unrepresented, a copy of the video recording should not be sent, but must be made available for viewing by him.

Case Details

The Crown Court at   Crown Court
                                     Case Number:

                                                    *delete
Date of: committal for trial*:   inappropriate
         consent to preferment of bill of
            indictment*:
         notice of transfer served*:
         notice of appeal served*:

Defendant(s): Surname: Forenames:

Application:

Name of Applicant:

Name of Applicant's Solicitor:

Address of Solicitor:

Reference:

Charges

Give details
of
those charges
to which this
application
applies

Location of mastertape

State name
and
address of
keeper
of mastertape

Details of copy

State when
and
by whom
each copy
accompanying
this notice
was made

[**Note:** A copy of any video recordings of other parts of the
interview with the witness which it is *not* proposed to tender in
evidence must be provided to the court and the other parties.
The details of each such recording must be given as above. Use
separate sheets where necessary.]

Grounds for application

I confirm that

    (a)   I believe the witness is willing and able to attend the trial for
cross-examination;

(b) The details given in the statement of the circumstances in which the video recording was made above are correct;

(c) Copies of the video recording(s) to which this application relates have been disclosed to the other parties and their agreement to them being tendered has been sought;

(d) A copy of this notice and the video recording(s) to which it relates have been served on each party to the proceedings.

Signature of applicant
or
applicant's Solicitor: Date:

....

Witness

Name:

Date of Birth:

Video recording(s)
Statement as to circumstances in which video recording made

These details need be completed on to the extent that the information is not contained in the video recording itself

Date(s) of video recording(s):

Time(s) of video recording(s):

State times at which recording began and finished including any interruptions

Location and normal function of premises where video recording made:

Give address and description of premises where recording made

---

Details of those present while recording made

Include name, age and occupation of anyone present, time for which present, relationship (if any) to witness and defendant

---

Equipment used

Include number, and type of camera (fixed or mobile), number and location of microphones, video format and whether single or multiple recording facilities used

---

Appendix 7

FORM 1: NOTICE OF TRANSFER OF CASE TO THE CROWN COURT

THE QUEEN

v.

[name/s of accused]

To the Clerk to the Justices, [address]

1. I am a Crown Prosecutor acting on behalf of the Director of Public Prosecutions.

2. [name of accused] {has} {have} been charged with the offence/s specified in the Schedule of Charges attached to this notice, being offence/s to which Section 32(2) of the Criminal Justice Act 1988 applies.

3. The Magistrates' Court has not begun to enquire into the case as examining justices.

4. I certify that in my opinion:

(a) the evidence of the offence/s charged is sufficient for [name of accused] to be committed for trial;

(b) a child who is alleged—

(i) to be a person against whom the offence/s {was} {were} committed

(ii) to have witnessed the commission of the offence/s will be called as a witness at the trial

and

(c) for the purpose of avoiding any prejudice to the welfare of the child, the case should be taken over and proceeded with without delay by the Crown Court.

5. Accordingly, the functions of the Magistrates' Court cease in relation to

the case, except as provided by paragraphs 2 and 3 of Schedule 6 to the Criminal Justice Act 1991 and by Section 20(4) of the Legal Aid Act 1988.

6. The proposed place of trial is the Crown Court sitting at [location].

7. (i) [name of accused] was on the   day of   199   remanded in custody to appear at [name] Magistrates' Court on the day of   199 . Notice has been given to him requesting him to indicate whether he consents to the Court exercising its powers under paragraph 2 of Schedule 6 to the Criminal Justice Act 1991 without being brought before the Court.

    OR

(ii) [name of accused] was on the   day of   199   remanded on bail to appear at [name] Magistrates' Court on the   199 . [Notice has been given to him that this requirement has now ceased but it that is his duty to appear before the Crown Court sitting at [location], or such other place as shall be notified to him, on a date to be notified to him]. (Notice has been given to him that this requirement continues).

8. I propose to invite the Magistrates' court to make an order under Section 1 of the Criminal Procedure (Attendance of Witnesses) Act 1965 in respect of each of the witnesses listed in the Schedule of Proposed Witnesses attached to this notice.

Dated this   day of   199 .

Branch Crown Prosecutor

NOTE
Where this Notice relates to more than one person, paragraph 7 must be completed in respect of each person to whom it relates.

CASE REFERENCE NO:

FORM 1

THE QUEEN

v.

[accused]

SCHEDULE OF CHARGES

Statement of offence:

Particulars of offence:

2

FORM 1

CASE REFERENCE NO:

FORM 1 *cont.*

SCHEDULE OF PROPOSED WITNESSES

Name   Address   Witness order requested

CASE REFERENCE NO:

FORM 1

SCHEDULE OF EXHIBITS

357

Appendix 8

FORM 2: NOTICE TO PERSON TO WHOM A NOTICE
OF TRANSFER RELATES

THE QUEEN

v

[name of accused]

To [name of accused]
of [address]

1. Under Section 53 of the Criminal Justice Act 1991 I have given to [name] Magistrates' Court a notice of transfer in relation to the charges specified in the notice, a copy of which is attached. Accordingly, the case is transferred to the Crown Court. The proposed place of trial is the Crown Court sitting at [location]

2. The Crown Court may give directions altering the place of trial. If you are dissatisfied with the proposed place of trial stated in the notice of transfer, or the place of trial as substituted by a direction of the Crown Court you may apply the Crown Court to vary the place of trial.

3. (i) On the   day of   199   [name] Magistrates' Court remanded you in custody to appear on the   day of   199   . (The Court later granted you bail subject to certain conditions which you failed to meet, and accordingly you have remained in custody to appear on that day.) Under paragraph 2(1) of Schedule 6 to the Criminal Justice Act 1991, the Magistrates' Court has power

    (a) to order that you shall be safely kept in custody until delivered in due course of law, or

    (b) to release you on bail in accordance with the Bail Act 1976 that is to say, by directing you to appear before the Crown Court for trial

The Magistrates' Court may exercise those powers without your being brought before the court if:

(a) you have given your written consent and

(b) the court is satisfied that, when you gave your consent, you knew that the notice of transfer had been issued.

You may give your consent by signing the attached form of consent and passing it to the prison governor for him to send it to the Magistrates' Court by the   day of   199   (the date of your next appearance).

OR

3. (ii) On the   day of   199   [name] Magistrates' Court remanded you on bail to appear on the   day of   199   . That requirement has ceased and in accordance with paragraph 2(6) of Schedule 6 to the Criminal Justice Act 1991 it is your duty to appear before the Crown Court sitting at [location] or at such other place as may be notified to you, on a date to be notified to you.

OR

3. (iii) On the   day of   199   [name] Magistrates' Court remanded you on bail to appear on the   day of   199   . You are required so to appear notwithstanding the giving of notice of transfer.

4. The bill of indictment against you may include, either in substitution for or in addition to any court charging an offence specified in the notice of transfer, any counts founded on material that accompanies the copy of that notice given to you, being counts which may lawfully be joined in the same indictment.

5. I enclose a list of witnesses:

(a) indicating those whom the Crown proposes to call to give oral evidence at your trial (and in whose case the Magistrates' Court will be invited to make a witness order under section 1(1) of the Criminal Procedure (Attendance of Witnesses) Act 1965; and

(b) indicating those whose attendance at your trial the Crown considers unnecessary on the ground that their evidence is unlikely to be required or unlikely to be disputed (and in whose case the Magistrates' Court will be invited to make a conditional witness order under section 1(2) of that Act) together with in each case copies of the statements or other documents outlining the evidence of those witnesses or any video recording/s which it is proposed to tender in evidence.

6. I also enclose a list of the exhibits in your case together with copies of those exhibits which are in documentary form.

7. At any time before you are arraigned at the Crown Court you may apply orally or in writing to the Crown Court for the charge/any of the charges to be dismissed on the ground that the evidence which has been disclosed is not sufficient for a jury properly to convict you of it. If you wish to apply for the

charge/any of the charges to be dismissed, you should make a written application not later than 14 days after the day on which the notice of transfer was given or give written notice within the same period of your intention to do so orally, in accordance with the requirements of the Criminal Justice Act 1991 (Dismissal of Transferred Charges) Rules 1992. These periods may be extended on application to the Crown Court.

Dated this   day of   199   .

Branch Crown Prosecutor.

FORM OF WORDS FOR INCLUSION IN FORM 2 IN THE SCHEDULE TO THE CRIMINAL JUSTICE ACT 1991 (NOTICE OF TRANSFER) REGULATIONS 1992

The video recording/s specified in the Schedule hereto and forming part of the evidence on which the prosecution relies has/have previously been supplied in the current proceedings on the occasion/s and to the party/ies specified in the same schedule and is/are therefore deemed to accompany the Notice.

SCHEDULE

Name of Witness	Detail of Video Recording Exhibit Reference Number	Party Served and Date

Appendix 9

AGES OF CONSENT

Marriage with consent unless a widow(er)	16
Marriage without consent	18
Vaginal intercourse—girl's age*	16
Vaginal intercourse—boy's age*	14
Other heterosexual conduct*	16
Anal intercourse (either heterosexual or homosexual)	18
Other homosexual conduct between men	18
Other homosexual conduct between women	16
Children in indecent photographs	16
Youth can be committed to the Crown Court for indecent assault as a grave crime	16

*It is not an offence for a woman to have intercourse with a boy under 16 provided that she does not touch him in a way which will constitute an indecent assault (*Faulkner v. Talbot* [1981] 1 Crim.L.R. 705, *R. v. Mason* [1968] 53 Cr.App.R. 12). It would be an offence contrary to the Indecency with Children Act 1960 if the child was under 14.

TIME LIMITS

a. Sexual Offences Act 1956, Sched. 2, para. 10—a prosecution for unlawful sexual intercourse with a girl under 16 contrary to section 6 must be commenced within 12 months of the offence.

b. Sexual Offences Act 1987, s.7—a prosecution for gross indecency between men, and buggery where no assault has taken place and the partner is 16 or over must be commenced within 12 months of the offence.

c. Telecommunications Act 1984, s.43—improper use of the public telecommunications system. By section 103, proceedings for any offence under this Act which is punishable on summary conviction may be commenced at any time within 12 months next after the commission of the offence.

Appendix 10

COMPUTERS AND SEX

Computers no longer work in isolation from each other. Since the 1960's there has grown a network which connects millions of computers around the world. Referred to as the Internet this network is now used by over 40 million people worldwide to transfer information between them by receiving information from other computors, sending information to other computers and to route information from an emitting computer to another specific receiving computer.

The Internet can be used to receive information in a number of different ways:

1. Usenet Newsgroups
2. The World Wide Web (WWW or W3)
3. File Transfer protocol (FTP)
4. Bulletin Board System (BBS)
5. Chat systems
6. E-Mail
7. CD-ROMS which many computers are capable of playing

To access the Internet, the computers most use will need to be connected via a local telephone connection to an Internet Service Provider (ISP) who provide the link into the Internet.

The Internet originated in the 1960s from American military needs and was designed by the Rand Corporation to be a destruction proof communications system. The resultant method called the Internet Protocol (IP) makes it virtually impossible to stop a message. The Internet today is therefore as a direct result, virtually impossible to police. In the United States of America the Communications Decency Act 1996 has not been implemented through fears that it is unenforceable.

The Internet is now one of the world's most valuable assets, potentially more useful than the world's interconnected postal system. Inevitably some use the system, as they do the postal system, to exchange obscene material but such transfers form a very small part of the total usage. It is vital that if controls are introduced they do not hamper the legitimate free transfer of information across the world.

There has been concern expressed that some people use the Internet to pass on illegal material such as pornography. Particularly concerning, is child pornography. The proportion of illegal material on the Internet is believed to be relatively small but even the most extreme material is available. The vast majority of net users find such material deeply offensive (reflecting society generally) and will report to the ISP or the police such material. Self-regulation is seen as the appropriate control. Specific legislation is unnecessary and undesirable. Communications carried by the net are subject to national legislation governing obscenity, in much the same way as any other communications.

The link into the Internet is, for most people via the ISP. There is an Internet Service Providers Association (ISPA) which with the London Internet Exchange (LINX) and the Safety Net Foundation proposed recommended and adopted a proposal for addressing the question of illegal material on the Internet, facilitated by the DTI, called the "R3 Safety Net". The full text of this document can be locate on the Internet at

http: dtiinfo1.dti.gov.uk/safety-net/r3.htm

The proposals are based upon Rating, Reporting and Responsibility.

The rating will be undertaken by the Safety—Net Foundation and will provide a rating, or indicator of the legality for the normal content of each Usenet News group. It will indicate if the group normally contains illegal material and will indicate the nature of that illegality (*e.g.* child pornography, copyright infringement).

The reporting consists of a Foundation's complaints line for members of the public to make complaints about the contents of material. Complaints may be made by telephone, mail, e-mail or fax. The complaints may then be passed on to the appropriate body, the ISP or perhaps the police.

The responsibility is provided by the ISP who will remove child pornography and seek to trace the origin of such material especially with regard to WWW pages and Usenet News groups. The proposal indicates that establishing such a reasonable, practical and proportionate approach can provide the ISP with a defence against charges of knowingly permitting services to be used for the distribution of illegal material. It points out however that ISP's in the United Kingdom can only address the problem where the source of the material is from their United Kingdom subscribers.

Nonetheless it is understood that during 1996 the police provided the ISP's with details of between 120 and 160 newsgroup sites used by paedophiles to transmit pornographic material and that these sites were closed.

Material travels faster on the Internet than the working speed of most computers. When a page or picture on the web is viewed, as opposed to being deliberately downloaded and saved, it is still retained in a part of the computer's hard disk called a "cache". The same procedure often applies to information being viewed from a CD-ROM. The software program controlling this interface will typically allow the material in the cache to be accessed, deleted or renewed. The programme may also allow the user to decide how long material remains in the cache before it is classified as stale and deleted. If the web is an information superhighway the cache or temporary internet file may be considered as an information parking lot. Graphics may be retained within it without the computer user making a conscious decision to save it.

An international W3 Consortium (W3C) has implemented PICS (Platform for Internet Content Selection) which has developed standards to assist parents' ability to block undesirable material. It provides the technical specifications for a Web page or other Net service and a Web browser which is PICS-compliant can block or allow access according to present criteria. PICS ratings cover nudity, sexual activity, bad language and violence. PICs can be found at: http://www.w3.org/pub/WWW/PICS/ or two e-mail addresses:

PICS-info @ w3.org and PICS- ask @ w3.org

The W3C maintains a list of compatible software but does not endorse any particular software. PICS can be used to restrict any material described with a URL. It cannot therefore be applied to e-mail.

Four levels of ratings for violence, language, nudity and sex have been created and maintained by the Recreational Software Advisory Council (RSAC) who can be located at http://www.rsac.org with details of the ratings themselves being at:

htttp://www.rsac.org/ratings01.htm1

I. USENET NEWSGROUPS

This is a system for the distribution of information through the Internet using a series of "newsgroups" sometimes also referred to as "bulletin-boards" (but not to be confused with the "Bulletin-board system" or BBS which is different). Newsgroups cover a large and diverse number of topics from the innocent to the most extreme illegal, allowing people of similar interests the chance to interact online. The newsgroups are downloaded and then viewed after which they can be stored or deleted.

Newsgroups probably present a more serious problem than the other facilities. They are said to have a long tradition of freedom of speech of which some may take full advantage. Some ISP's terminate newsgroup content after short periods of time because of the quantity of content.

Some refuse to carry binary newsgroups, *i.e.* those which are not limited to text but include pictures, videos, sound, etc.

The nature of the content of some newsgroups is evident from their structures or hierarchies. Those commencing "alt.sex" and "alt.binaries.pictures.erotica." sometimes contain very explicit text and photographs respectively. Those ending in ".d" are discussion groups. Some titles however are less explicit and it may be possible to download some undesired contents unknowingly.

II. THE WORLD WIDE WEB (WWW OR W3)

This consists of a global system containing hundreds of thousands of pages of information to be transferred. Each page has its own unique address and to find particular topics special computer software (*i.e.* a programme) called a "browser" is required to "browse" or view the pages of the Web going from one page to another.

A "search engine" is an automatic search facility which will locate the Web items of specified interest and obtain the best links to it. By entering key words it will automatically search Home Page information throughout the Web, classify them and answer requests for material.

A "Home Page" is a location on WWW where businesses, organisations and individuals can announce their existence using text, pictures, sounds and video. The address of the home page is called an Unique Resource Locator (URL). All information on the Web is transferred by Hyper Text Transfer Protocol and all Web sites URL's commence with http:// and most with http://www (hyper text transfer protocol, world wide web).

A "site" is a location where information or software can be found.

Information (and pictures) can be downloaded from the WWW page to the computer and stored (either on the computer hard disk or onto an external "floppy" disk).

Access to some sites can only be obtained after proof of age (*e.g.* by requesting the viewer joins an adult verification scheme) which is often connected with the production of a credit card. Most are American, the largest at the moment in Adult Check which is required by about 800 sites.

III. FILE TRANSFER PROTOCOL

This is an efficient method of "downloading" or transferring files from Internet libraries directly to a computer. It enables the client computer to copy files and programmes from the net.

IV. BULLETIN BOARD SYSTEMS

A BBS is a programme which allows a computer to answer the telephone automatically when another computer calls it. The programme allows the calling computer to copy files to it (upload) and copy files from it (download).

These are usually commercial sites which provide services (often of a sexual nature—photographs, live links, etc.) via a telephone computer connection via the modem (modulator/demodulator, the computer/telephone line link). They usually charge by increased telephone charges (similar to the 0891– numbers) or by subscription.

V. CHAT SYSTEMS

An Internet Chat or IRC type system allows instant direct communication via computer links. The system is more analogous to the Citizens Band radio than conversations by telephone. Modem developments now allow the inclusion of pictures and for video conferencing. This latter capability has allowed the Net to be used for nude live video teleconferencing.

VI. E-Mail

E-mail is electronic mail used to send and receive messages, documents and even software programmes directly form and to computers as an alternative to using the post.

E-mail may well arrive uninvited. Junk e-mail is as much a fact of net life as ordinary junk mail is in the real world, and some of it may be anonymous and obscene.

VII. CD-ROMS

Most new computers now are multi-media in that they contain radio and musical MIDI (Musical Instrument Digital Interface) systems. These play audio CD's (compact discs) and will have a sound card, speakers or headphones.

Similar to audio CD's are CD-ROM's (Compact Disc read only memory) which can contain large amounts of information, provide games to play on the computer or contain large numbers (*e.g.* 4,000) photographs and video clips. They play directly on the computer and are not related to the Internet in any way.

VIII. Pictures

Pictures on computers are of course recorded digitally and need to be converted by the computer back into a viewable picture format. There are a number of different systems for recording and viewing pictures which are not all compatible.

Gif (Graphics Interchange Format) is an image format for small pictures containing 256 colours.

JPEG (Joint Photographic Expert Group) is an alternative to gif with a higher compression using 16.7 million colours. The average human eye and most computers are incapable of distinguishing that number of separate colours and gif is more than adequate for pictures on the internet.

JPEG tends to be more granular because of the compression method and is used for small pictures.

The system screens out elements of the picture that it determines the human eye cannot perceive. This is known as "lossy" compression.

MPEG (Motion Picture Experts Group) is a compression format for video which allows good quality picture sequences to be stored on disk, MPEG 11 is a more advanced system.

Pictures have to be coded to pass through the net and then unencoded by the client computer by a undecoder.

Because pictures on computer are recorded digitally they can be manipulated and altered using software programmes. Many pictures are transferred onto the Internet which have been altered. Some have the faces of famous people superimposed on other pictures (usually naked) bodies. These are known as "fakes" or in some circles as "Frankensteins". It is also possible to take a photograph of a naked mature person, replace the face and make other alterations to the size of the breasts, pubic hair and other details to make the image appear that of a naked child or young person. Such psuedo-images are addressed by the English legal system.

IX. PRIVATE RESTRICTIONS

Many parents (and employers) are concerned to restrict their childrens' (and employees') access to sexual material on the Internet. One way to exercise this control is to initiate a package on the computer which restricts access to such material.

There are two main systems available:

Filtering the programme blocks all material which appears on the programme's "black list"—a database that lists banned URL and contains a list of banned words. If the system encounters a banned word it can record, and/ or block the access.

There are now some minor difficulties. Blocking the word "sex" will prevent access to research on "Geography of Essex" whilst a block on the word "fuck" can be got round by a distributor spelling the word "fuc:k".

Rating the programme only allows access to rated areas of the Net. It examines a page's HTML (hypertext makeup language) seeking to find a rating tag. If it is tagged, access can be granted or denied. Two systems of rating exist: one is SafeSurf developed by a group of parents (http://www.safe surf.com/index.html); and the other is an extension of the Recreational Software Advisory Council (RSAC) (http://www.rsac.org). Most programme packages use a combination of both rating systems (see above). More information on child safety can be found at

http://www.isa.net/isa/pubs/index.html

A third method is of course for parents not to allow children unlimited and unsupervised use of the family computer.

Appendix 11

GLOSSARY OF TERMS

"69"—mutual oral sex—*see* soixante-neuf

A

AIDS: (acquired immunodeficiency syndrome)—A fatal disease which prevents the proper functioning of the body's immune system caused by the human immunodeficiency virus—HIV. People with AIDS are unable to resist or fight off opportunist diseases (*e.g.* pneumonia or cancer), serious viral and bacterial infections. HIV is spread by any activity which results in direct bloodstream contact with an infected partner's body fluid (*e.g.* blood or semen). It is also passed to infants during pregnancy or by breast-feeding. It is easily spread by the use of shared infected needles by drug abusers. Because of the large mucosal surface area within the vagina and the quantity of semen ejaculated during intercourse AIDS spreads much more easily to women from men. Although small quantities of HIV are found in tears and saliva, no cases of its spread via either of these are recorded. AIDS is *not* spread by usual social contact such as hugging or shaking hands, through breathing near infected people or living or eating in the same household. People infected with HIV may not show any symptoms for many years, and may first show AIDS-related complex (ARC). This is characterized by chronic swollen lymph glands, weight loss, fatigue, thrush, vaginitis, sweating fever and diarrhoea. ARC is the first stage in the degeneration into full blown AIDS. There is, at this time, no cure for AIDS. Anyone who has had unprotected sex since 1980 is a potential HIV risk.

Albert—*see* Prince Albert.

Algolagnia—Greek—algos—pain, lagneia—lust. Now usually referred to as sado-masochism

Anilingus—oral—anal sex

ARC: *see* AIDS

Autoerotisism—self masturbation

B

Beaver—an American expression for the female pubis area or genitals. The word contains an implied reference to pubic hair.

BD—short for "bondage and discipline".

Bell-end—vulgar expression for glans.

Blow-job—oral sex

Boner—erection

Box—slang term for vagina

Brass—a prostitute

Brown sugar—(1)A young black woman; (2) excrement

Bugger—an unnatural act including anal sex and bestiality but excluding oral sex

Butch/femme—lesbian term used in the 1950's indicating butch—a male identified lesbian and femme—a female identified lesbian. The terms went out of use in 1970s but have now been revived in the 1990s.

C

C.S.A.—child sexual abuse.

Cat house—brothel, prostitute haunt.

Chancroid—a venereal disease exhibiting small septic sores around the sex organs with swelling in the groin.

Chicken—a young person (slang)

Clipper—a prostitute who takes a clients money and fails to provide the agreed service.

Clysteromania—sexual pleasure obtained from giving or receiving enemas.

Coprophilia—sexual intercourse involving excrement.

Cottage—a public toilet used by homosexuals as a meeting place.

Crunchy or extra crunchy—typically identifies the granola type of dyke lesbian often seen by other lesbians as being too politically correct. An American expression.

Cunnilingus—oral sex on a woman.

Cunny—shortened form of "cunt".

Cunt—female genitals.

Cypripareunia—sexual intercourse with a prostitute.

D

Dildo—an artificial penis used for masturbation (less common—dildoe)

Dirt-box—slang expression for rectum.

DP—double penetration—indicates that a picture on the Internet is of a woman having intercourse with two men.

Dyke—a lesbian with dominant or masculine tendencies.

F

Facetiae—euphenism used by libraries and publishers for pornography.

Fanny—(1) vagina; (2) behind. (US).

Fellatio—oral sex on a male.

Femme—*see* butch/femme.

Fetish (-ism)—an unbalanced sexual preoccupation with a particular body part, feature, item of clothing or type of material.

Fisting—sexual arousal involving the insertion of the whole fist to the forearm into the vagina or anus.

Flagellomania—erotic pleasure from whipping or being whipped.

Flashing—indecent exposure.

Frig—masturbate.

Frotteur (-ism)—a male who obtains sexual satisfaction by rubbing up against a woman—often her buttocks.

371

Fuck—slang expression for sexual intercourse. It is not an acronym for felonious unlawful carnal knowledge as it is often claimed but appears to be at least Tudor—Lyndesay Satyre (1535): "Bishops may fuck their fill and be unmarried".

G

Gam—gamahuche or gamaruche—oral sex.

Gay—homosexual—a term intended to show a happy and positive attitude to homosexuality.

Gerbilling—U.S. a peculiar practice developed by homosexuals on the West Coast of America which involves the placing of a live gerbil (sometimes enclosed in a condom) into the anal orifice. The practice in the United Kingdom would undoubtedly offend the legislation intended to prevent unnecessary cruelty to animals. (Protection of Animals Act 1911)

Glans—the head or tip of the penis.

G.L.B.—short for "gay, lesbian, bisexual" on the Internet.

Golden rain—urine.

Gonads—seed producing sexual organs, *i.e.* testicles and ovaries.

Gonorrhoea—the most common form of venereal disease in Britain. It can be spread by vaginal, anal or oral intercourse. It has poor survival outside the body and is unlikely to be spread other than sexually. However, anal infection in a woman does not indicate anal intercourse as it can spread along the perineum. In addition it can be spread by contact with an infected towel.

Goose—either anal sex or to pinch someone's bottom.

H

Hard-on—an erection.

Hepatitis B—an infection which may be passed sexually—very highly infective.

HIV—*see* AIDS.

Hooker—American term for a prostitute.

I

Inter-crural intercourse—intercourse simulated or accidentally achieved by rubbing the penis between the partner's legs. Sometimes mis-spelt: intra-crural.

J

Jail bait—an attractive girl under the age of consent.

Jerk-off—masturbate.

Jugs—slang expression for breasts.

K

Keister—U.S. slang. Lit: A bag for tools or satchel, also "the area upon which one sits", the buttocks.

K-Y Jelly—trade name of a water soluble lubricant used to facilitate sexual intercourse.

L

Lagnenomania—sadism in males.

Liquid gold—amil nitrate. A drug used as a muscle relaxant to aid intercourse including anal intercourse.

M

Machlaenomania—masochism in females.

Magpie—a code word used by some paedophiles to identify each other. Believed to derive from MAGazine of the Paedophilia Information Exchange.

Masochism—sexual arousal from submission to pain or humiliation.

Mastophallation—sexual activity by using the penis between a woman's breasts. A service increasingly offered by prostitutes since the advent of AIDS. A form of safe sex.

Masturbation—stimulation of the genitals to achieve pleasure.

Meapareunia—sexual act enjoyed by one partner only.

Meatus—a hole or entrance to an organ such as is found in the tip of the penis.

Menage-a-trois—literally "a household of three", a situation where one married partner has a lover living with them with the consent of the other partner. Now used for any sexual activity involving three people.

Minge—slang, female pudendum—the expression dates from the turn of the century.

Mooning—indecent exposure of the buttocks.

MOTAS—Internet acronym for "member of the appropriate sex".

MOTOS—Internet acronym for "member of the opposite sex".

MOTSS—Internet acronym for "member of the same sex".

Muff-diving—oral sex on a woman.

N

Necrophilia—intercourse with a dead body.

O

Onanism—self-masturbation.

P

Paederasty (pederasty)—anal sex with a young boy.

Paedophilia—love of young children.

Pander—a pimp.

Peeping Tom—*see* voyeurism.

Pimp—one who obtains clients for a prostitute.

Plate—(verb) oral sex.

Ponce—(1) one who lives off the earnings of a prostitute; (2) a homosexual.

Prince Albert—male genital piercing. It is said that Prince Albert had a penile ring designed to hold back his foreskin. The term is used for all male genital piercing but is often used to describe a metal bar totally transfixing the scrotum.

Proxenetism—pimping by other women.

Pudendum—external genitals especially of a woman. Literally means: "the parts one should be ashamed of."

Pussy or Puss—the female vulva. "To eat pussy"—to perform cunnilingus.

Q

Quail—a young child, a girl under the age of consent (used by paedophiles).

Queer—Homosexual (usually applied to male homosexuals). The term was originally intended as an insult but has recently become acceptable to some homosexuals.

R

R.A.D.—reflex anal dilation—a possible sign of anal abuse.

Rent-boy—male prostitute, a catamite.

Retifism—foot fetish.

Rim—anus

Rim service—anal sex.

Rubber—U.S. slang—condom.

S

Sadism—sexual arousal from inflicting pain or humiliation or by domination.

Saphism—love or sex between women.

Semen—male fluid ejaculations consisting of fluid from the seminal vesicle, prostate gland and sperm. Sperm constitutes only about 1 per cent of the total.

Shag—slang expression for sexual intercourse. The word is sometimes found offensive by feminists who believe it implies an act of violence towards a passive woman.

Shunamitism—older men sleeping with young girls in the belief that the closeness of young bodies can rejuvenate.

S&M—sado-masochism.

Smegma—a cheesy deposit accumulating under the male foreskin.

375

Smuff dippers—prostitutes.

Snatch—female pudendum, dates back to the turn of the century.

Snuff movie—a pornographic film in which an actual murder is recorded.

Sodomy—anal sex on a male.

Soixante-neuf—mutual oral sex from the supposed similarity of the bodies to 69.

Spanish fly—*canthariden*. A drug wrongly believed to be an aphrodisiac. It is made from crushed beetles found in Southern Europe. It is an irritant and is potentially a lethal poison.

Sperm—male reproductive cell

Split beaver—vagina, a stripper, a female teaser.

Spunk—vulgar term for sperm.

Syphilis—a serious venereal disease which can be fatal in its final or third stage. In man it is more commonly spread homosexually.

T

Tart—is not always an insult as the word has two meanings:
i) Rhyming slang for "sweetheart"—a term of endearment; ii) A prostitute or a woman of cheap and easy virtue, or one who dresses like such a woman.

Three-legged beaver—homosexual.

Tochus—(Tochus, Tokus)—U.S. = backside, buttocks, anus from Yiddish tokhesi: Hebrew tohat—beneath.

Transvestite—a person who derives pleasure from wearing clothes of the opposite sex. Almost all transvestites are heterosexual men although some homosexuals do cross dress.

Toss-off—to masterbate.

Toss-pot—although an insult, this expression is not obscene. It means a heavy drinker or a drunkard.

Tribaclism—sexual activity between two women involving rubbing the genitals together.

Trick—intercourse provided by a prostitute.

376

Tush—U.S. slang. The buttocks, derived from tochus q.v.

Twat (less commonly, Twot)—U.K: vagina, also a term of common abuse. U.S: sometimes means buttocks.

V

Vibrator—a dildo with an electric motor causing it to vibrate. Usually, but not always driven by batteries. Can be used—to massage various body areas particularly the genitals.

Voyeurism or peeping Tomism—pleasure derived from watching other people undress or having sex. Usually done in secret. It is rare, but not unknown for them to go further and harm the victim.

W

Wank—masturbation.

Wanker—insult, one given to self-abuse.

Welsh-style—anal intercourse.

Z

Zoophilia—bestiality.

INDEX

All references are to paragraph numbers.

ABDUCTION, 4–67—4–83
average sentence, 4–83
consent, 4–75
knowledge of age, 4–77
motive, 4–76
offences, 4–67—4–70
possession, and, 4–80
'to take', 4–71—4–74

ADVERTISEMENTS, 14–01—14–09
Health and Medicines Act 1988,
14–07—14–09
HIV testing kits and services,
14–07—14–09
Venereal Diseases Act 1917,
14–01—14–06
Ages of consent, App. 9

AIDING AND ABETTING,
rape, 4–12, 4–13

AIDS,
transmission of, 5–31, 5–32

ANAL EXAMINATION, 1–19—1–30
indications, 1–28—1–30
injuries, 1–25—1–27

ANAL INTERCOURSE. *See* SODOMY

ARMED SERVICES,
homosexual activities, 8–46, 8–47

ASSAULT,
indecent. *See* INDECENT ASSAULT
Sado-masochistic, 5–06—5–15

ATTEMPTED RAPE, 4–14, 4–16

BAIL, 3–47—3–49
absolute prohibition, 3–48, 3–49

BAWDY-HOUSES, 12–122

BESTIALITY, 8–03—8–09
meaning, 8–04—8–08
sentencing guidelines, 8–09
Woman forced to submit to, 8–08

BIND OVERS, 7–34—7–45
breach of the peace, 7–36—7–45
common law, 7–38
history, 7–34—7–37

BREACH OF THE PEACE,
bind overs, 7–36—7–45

BRITISH BOARD OF FILM
CLASSIFICATION,
14–36—14–41

BROTHERS, 12–87—12–117
acting or assisting in management,
12–100, 12–101, 12–102
allowing persons under 16 to be
in, 9–37
assisting in management, 12–93
definition, 12–91—12–98
detention of woman in, 4–89,
4–90
homosexual, 12–89
keeping, 12–99
letting premises, 12–103—12–105
wilful, 12–105
managing, 12–99
massage parlours, 12–91—12–93
occupation, 12–95, 12–96
occupation, 12–114
permitting use, 12–106—12–114
charging practice, 12–110
lessee, 12–111
sentencing guidelines, 12–109

BUGGERY, 8–01—8–28
definition, 8–02
mitigating factors, 8–28
sentencing guidelines, 8–25–8–28

BUGGERY OF A WOMAN, 8–24—8–28

BURGLARY WITH INTENT TO RAPE,
4–58—4–61

CHILD WITNESS PACK, 1–10

CHILDREN, 9–01–9–57

378

RAPE OFFENCE, 4–02—4–17

RECKLESSNESS,
rape, and, 4–44—4–47

SADO-MASOCHISTIC ASSAULT,
5–06—5–15
consent, and, 5–07—5–15
religious flagellation, 5–13
tattooing, 5–11, 5–12

SAMPLES, 1–36—1–56
consent, 1–37
evidential, 1–51
intimate, 1–45—1–50
non–intimate, 1–41—1–43
protection of witnesses, and,
2–90—2–95

SEARCH, POWER OF,
woman detained for immoral
purposes, 4–91

SENTENCING,
serious sexual offences,
3–60—3–78
balancing exercise, 3–69, 3–70
correct approach, 3–68—3–75
discretionary life prisoners,
3–76—3–78
medical reports, 3–71
protection of the public,
3–60—3–64
release under supervision,
3–73—3–75
sexual offences, 3–65—3–67
specimen counts, 3–57

SENTENCING ON SPECIMEN COUNTS,
3–57

SERIES OF OFFENCES, 3–50—3–52
child abuse cases, 3–52
corroboration, and, 3–51
severance, 3–52

SERIOUS SEXUAL OFFENCES,
sentencing,
protection of the public,
3–60—3–64

SEX ARTICLE,
meaning, 14–75

SEX ESTABLISHMENTS,
14–68—14–102
application for licence,
14–78—14–82

SEX ESTABLISHMENTS—cont.
applications for transfer of
licences, 14–84
bodies corporate, 14–98
control, 14–68—14–101
death of licence holder, 14–87
definitions, 14–71—14–75
display of licence, 14–86
eligibility, 14–99, 14–100
licence, requirement of, 14–76,
14–77
offences, 14–90—14–94, 14–101
persons who cannot hold licences,
14–83
police powers, 14–95—14–97
procedure for appeals, 14–99,
14–100
regulations, 14–85
revocation of licence, 14–88
section 2 resolution, 14–101
variation of terms, 14–89

SERIOUS ASSAULTS, 5–01—5–33

SEX OFFENDERS,
notification requirements. See
NOTIFICATION
REQUIREMENTS FOR SEX
OFFENDERS

SEX SHOP,
meaning, 14–73

SEX WITH CHILD UNDER AGE OF
CONSENT, 9–01—9–19
alternative verdicts, 9–19
consent, 9–03, 9–04
rape, 9–03
unlawful sexual intercourse,
9–04
girls under 13, 9–05—9–08
girls under 16, 9–09—9–17
consent, 9–14—9–17
sentencing guidelines,
9–11—9–13
limitations to prosecutions, 9–18

SEXUAL ASPHYXIATION, 5–23, 5–24

SEXUAL EXPERIENCE,
meaning, 2–166

SEXUAL INTERCOURSE, 4–05—4–13
consent, 4–07
ejaculation, 4–06
penetration, 4–05
unlawful, 4–09

SEXUAL OFFENCE,
meaning, 3–65

INDEX

WITNESSES—*cont.*
protected material,
    2–191—2–213. *See also*
    PROTECTED MATERIAL
protection, 2–42—2–51
    complainants in cases other
        than rape, 2–60—2–88
    contempt of court, 2–42, 2–43
    protection from cross-
        examination, 2–149
        children, 2–149—2–155
        sexual matters, 2–157—2–191
    screens, 2–90—2–95
    television links, 2–96—2–98,
        2–99—2–112
    video evidence, 2–113—2–125
        exclusion of part, 2–135

WITNESSES—*cont.*
video evidence—*cont.*
    jury requests, 2–143—2–148
    playing equipment, 2–137
    preliminary investigation of
        competence,
        2–139—2–142
    R. v. Day, 2–138—2–142
    replay, 2–143—1–148
    requirements, 2–126—2–132
    young children, 2–48, 2–49

WOMAN DETAINED FOR IMMORAL
    PURPOSES,
    powers to search for, 4–91

YOUNG SEX OFFENDERS,
    notification requirements, 3–215

388